SACRIFICE AND REBIRTH

AUSTRIAN AND HABSBURG STUDIES
General Editor: Gary B. Cohen, Center for Austrian Studies, University of Minnesota

Volume 1
Austrian Women in the Nineteenth and Twentieth Centuries: Cross-Disciplinary Perspectives
Edited by David F. Good, Margarete Grandner and Mary Jo Maynes

Volume 2
From World War to Waldheim: Culture and Politics in Austria and the United States
Edited by David F. Good and Ruth Wodak

Volume 3
Rethinking Vienna 1900
Edited by Steven Beller

Volume 4
The Great Tradition and Its Legacy: The Evolution of Dramatic and Musical Theater in Austria and Central Europe
Edited by Michael Cherlin, Halina Filipowicz and Richard L. Rudolph

Volume 5
Creating the Other: Ethnic Conflict and Nationalism in Habsburg Central Europe
Edited by Nancy M. Wingfield

Volume 6
Constructing Nationalities in East Central Europe
Edited by Pieter M. Judson and Marsha L. Rozenblit

Volume 7
The Environment and Sustainable Development in the New Central Europe
Edited by Zbigniew Bochniarz and Gary B. Cohen

Volume 8
Crime, Jews and News: Vienna 1890–1914
Edited by Daniel Mark Vyleta

Volume 9
The Limits of Loyalty: Imperial Symbolism, Popular Allegiances, and State Patriotism in the Late Habsburg Monarchy
Edited by Laurence Cole and Daniel L. Unowsky

Volume 10
Embodiments of Power: Building Baroque Cities in Europe
Edited by Gary B. Cohen and Franz A. J. Szabo

Volume 11
Diversity and Dissent: Negotiating Religious Difference in Central Europe, 1500–1800
Edited by Howard Louthan, Gary B. Cohen and Franz A. J. Szabo

Volume 12
"Vienna is Different": Jewish Writers in Austria from the Fin de Siècle to the Present
Hillary Hope Herzog

Volume 13
Sexual Knowledge: Feeling, Fact, and Social Reform in Vienna, 1900–1934
Britta McEwen

Volume 14
Journeys into Madness: Mapping Mental Illness in the Austro-Hungarian Empire
Edited by Gemma Blackshaw and Sabine Wieber

Volume 15
Territorial Revisionism and the Allies of Germany in the Second World War: Goals, Expectations, Practices
Edited by Marina Cattaruzza, Stefan Dryoff and Dieter Langewiesche

Volume 16
The Viennese Café and Fin-de-siècle Culture
Edited by Charlotte Ashby, Tag Gronberg and Simon Shaw-Miller

Volume 17
Understanding Multiculturalism and the Habsburg Central European Experience
Edited by Johannes Feichtinger and Gary B. Cohen

Volume 18
Sacrifice and Rebirth: The Legacy of the Last Habsburg War
Edited by Mark Cornwall and John Paul Newman

SACRIFICE AND REBIRTH
The Legacy of the Last Habsburg War

Edited by

*Mark Cornwall
and
John Paul Newman*

Published by

Berghahn Books

www.berghahnbooks.com

© 2016, 2018 Mark Cornwall and John Paul Newman
First paperback edition published in 2018

All rights reserved. Except for the quotation of short passages
for the purposes of criticism and review, no part of this book
may be reproduced in any form or by any means, electronic or
mechanical, including photocopying, recording, or any information
storage and retrieval system now known or to be invented,
without written permission of the publisher.

Library of Congress Cataloging-in-Publication Data

Sacrifice and rebirth: the legacy of the last Habsburg war / edited by Mark Cornwall and John Paul Newman.—First edition.
    pages cm. -- (Austrian and Habsburg studies ; volume 18)
Includes bibliographical references and index.
    ISBN 978-1-78238-848-7 (hbk. : alk. paper) -- ISBN 978-1-78533-835-9 (pbk. : alk. paper) -- ISBN 978-1-78238-849-4 (ebook)
1. War memorials—Europe, Eastern—History—20th century. 2. War memorials—Europe, Central—History—20th century. 3. Collective memory—Europe, Eastern—History—20th century. 4. Collective memory—Europe, Central—History—20th century. 5. World War, 1914-1918—Social aspects—Europe, Eastern. 6. World War, 1914–1918—Social aspects—Europe, Central. 7. World War, 1914–1918—Influence. 8. Habsburg, House of—History—20th century. 9. Europe, Eastern—History—1918–1945. 10. Europe, Central—History—20th century. I. Cornwall, Mark. II. Newman, John Paul, 1978–
D680.E852S23 2015
940.4'609437—dc23

                                                                    2015007890

British Library Cataloguing in Publication Data
A catalogue record for this book is available from the British Library

ISBN 978-1-78238-848-7 (hardback)
ISBN 978-1-78533-835-9 (paperback)
ISBN 978-1-78238-849-4 (ebook)

Contents

List of Illustrations ... vii

Acknowledgments ... ix

Introduction. A Conflicted and Divided Habsburg Memory ... 1
  Mark Cornwall

Part I. Sacrifice and the Vanquished

Chapter 1. Competing Interpretations of Sacrifice in the Postwar Austrian Republic ... 15
  Catherine Edgecombe and Maureen Healy

Chapter 2. "War in Peace": Remobilization and "National Rebirth" in Austria and Hungary ... 35
  Robert Gerwarth

Chapter 3. Apocalypse and the Quest for a Sudeten German Männerbund in Czechoslovakia ... 53
  Mark Cornwall

Chapter 4. The Divided War Remembrance of Transylvanian Magyars ... 75
  Franz Sz. Horváth

Part II. Sacrifice and the Discourse of Victory

Chapter 5. Framing the Hero: Photographic Narratives of War in the Interwar Kingdom of Serbs, Croats, and Slovenes ... 97
  Melissa Bokovoy

Chapter 6. National Sacrifice and Regeneration: Commemorations of the Battle of Zborov in Multinational Czechoslovakia ... 129
  Nancy M. Wingfield

| Chapter 7. | "In the Spirit of Brotherhood, United We Remain!": Czechoslovak Legionaries and the Militarist State
Katya Kocourek | 151 |
| Chapter 8. | Saving Greater Romania: The Romanian Legionary Movement and the "New Man"
Rebecca Haynes | 174 |

Part III. Sacrifice in Silence

Chapter 9.	Silent Liquidation? Croatian Veterans and the Margins of War Memory in Interwar Yugoslavia *John Paul Newman*	197
Chapter 10.	The Sacrificed Slovenian Memory of the Great War *Petra Svoljšak*	216
Chapter 11.	The Dead and the Living: War Veterans and Memorial Culture in Interwar Polish Galicia *Christoph Mick*	233
Chapter 12.	Divided Land, Diverging Narratives: Memory Cultures of the Great War in the Successor Regions of Tyrol *Laurence Cole*	258

| Select Bibliography | 287 |
| Index | 291 |

Illustrations

Map 1. Ex-Habsburg Europe in the Interwar Period	x
Figure 1.1. An Austrian radical comment on the Great War, 1924.	29
Figure 3.1. The Männerbund of the Sudeten German youth leadership school, 1936.	68
Figure 3.2. The Frýdlant war memorial, now in Frýdlant cemetery, Czech Republic.	70
Figure 5.1. Rista Marjanović, "Regulars."	99
Figure 5.2. Rista Marjanović, "In Albania."	100
Figure 5.3. Sampson Černov, "Eagle Eye on patrol at a forward position."	101
Figure 5.4. Rista Marjanović, "Burying the dead."	101
Figure 5.5. Rista Marjanović, "Lost Child."	109
Figure 5.6. Rista Marjanović, "Through Kosovo: Death and abandonment in the snow."	110
Figure 5.7. Sampson Černov, "In Albania."	113
Figure 5.8. Sampson Černov, "Hurry up! The children are cold."	113
Figure 5.9. Sampson Černov, "A veteran warrior."	114
Figure 5.10. "The wounded and their evacuation."	115
Figure 5.11. "Scenes from Serbian village life."	116
Figure 5.12. Sampson Černov, "Type of Serbian soldier advancing."	117
Figure 5.13. Rista Marjanović, "King Petar crossing the bridge at Ljum-Kula."	118

Figure 6.1. "To your health, Father Masaryk!", 1926. 130
Figure 6.2. Still from Czech film *Zborov*, 1938. 144
Figure 6.3. Still from Czech film *Zborov*, 1938. 144

Acknowledgments

This volume stems from the research project, "Memorialization and Regeneration: The Male Wartime Generation in the Successor States," which was based at the University of Southampton (UK) and funded by the Arts and Humanities Research Council. We would like to thank all those who have helped shape our ideas about war memory in interwar East-Central Europe. Special thanks to John Horne, Keith Jeffery, Péter Apor, Julia Eichenberg, Eva Fisli, Neil Gregor, Silviu Hariton, Karen Petrone, Robert Pynsent, Martyn Rady, Valentin Săndulescu, Nikolai Vukov, Jay Winter, and Martin Zückert.

Mark Cornwall
John Paul Newman
September 2015

Map 1. Ex-Habsburg Europe in the Interwar Period

Introduction

A CONFLICTED AND DIVIDED HABSBURG MEMORY

Mark Cornwall

In one famous novel of the 1920s, a young Austrian officer returns to Vienna from a Russian prisoner-of-war camp at the end of the war and meets an old work colleague. Their perspectives differ due to their age and experience. For the officer, the four-year struggle is by no means over—he aims to return to Russia to settle old scores—while his civilian colleague is about to retire to the tranquil Austrian province of Vorarlberg. The civilian exclaims however: "Tragic, really tragic. All those youngsters gone, and for what, I ask you?"[1]

The Habsburg monarchy—Austria-Hungary as it was usually known from 1867 to 1918—had been completely destroyed by World War I. Over the previous century it had faced disaster several times. During the French revolutionary wars, Napoleon had forced the empire that stretched across East-Central Europe into a humiliating peace (1809) and carved off sizeable chunks of territory in the north and south. In 1848 the internal threat to the Habsburgs was stronger as the regime struggled and finally managed to suppress revolution and secession. The Great War of 1914–1918 was then the final test of the monarchy's ability to justify its existence on the European stage, both as a Great Power and as a legitimate empire in the eyes of its eleven main nationality groupings. In July 1914 the Habsburg elite had known the risks they took in pushing for war against Serbia, but felt that by not scotching that "nest of vipers" they would demonstrate irretrievable weakness at home and abroad. It would be, Field Marshal Conrad von Hötzendorf predicted, "a hopeless struggle, but even so we must engage, for such an ancient monarchy and such a glorious army cannot perish ingloriously."[2]

It proved indeed to be a suicidal decision. Despite some intermittent successes that spurred on its military leadership, Austria-Hungary failed to win a decisive victory on any of its three fronts (Eastern, Balkan, and Italian). The war steadily eroded confidence in the imperial regime and from 1916, with a mounting food crisis and war weariness, a major transfer of allegiance took place to local leaders—often nationalist—who seemed to offer citizens a more secure future. By the end of hostilities, eight million men had been enlisted to fight for the Habsburg empire and about a million of those (13 percent) had died for it, roughly on a par with British deaths, but half the number of Russian casualties. Two million Austro-Hungarian soldiers (25 percent) had been wounded in some way, while over one and a half million (21 percent) had been taken prisoner.[3] In October 1918, as military defeat became a certainty, regional governments in Prague, Zagreb, Cracow, and Budapest moved to seize power on behalf of their various nationalities and the Habsburg monarchy speedily broke apart.[4]

The result, as confirmed in the peace treaties of 1919–20, was that out of Austria-Hungary's ashes arose six "successor states." Two—Austria and Hungary—were now treated as defeated countries, responsible for provoking the war and its traumatic impact; they suffered huge losses of their "national" territory as well as economic reparations and other restrictions to their sovereignty. Four successor states, however, posed as victor states in the New Europe—Czechoslovakia, Yugoslavia, Romania, and Poland—and secured a privileged place at the Paris peace conference. Ostensibly they had gained their national independence, or at least expanded their national territory, thanks to the monarchy's destruction. The official discourse in these states was likely to be triumphant when interpreting what had been lost and what had been gained from the apocalypse.

This basic division in interwar Europe—an official dialectic between the victors and the vanquished—is the starting point in this volume of essays. But our aim is to problematize that divide when exploring the legacy of the Habsburgs' final war. Despite the mass death and physical destruction that marked 1914–18 across East-Central Europe, there has been surprisingly little research on how World War I was interpreted by contemporaries in the different successor states of Austria-Hungary. In most historiographies, the year 1918 forms a watershed with few attempts to connect the experience of Habsburg wartime sacrifice with the transition, especially the transition undergone by military veterans, to life in the post-Habsburg world. Isolated studies do exist that span the watershed moment: for instance, on the memories of the Habsburg elite;[5] on the fate of Habsburg officers;[6] on constructing a Czechoslovak army out of the Austro-Hungarian forces;[7] on German war memorials in Transylvania and Czechoslovakia;[8] or on the economic dimension to total war and its after effects.[9] Most research has tended to focus on one successor state or one national grouping, as a case study in relative isolation from other experiences in the region. Although understandable in that it mirrors the splintering of "Habsburg historiography" after 1918, this tends to privilege the postwar geopolitical framework and automatically obscures the similar or comparative legacies that emerged from the old Habsburg unit.

This book, *Sacrifice and Rebirth*, while divided geographically, seeks to offer a comparative dimension to how the Great War was remembered and interpreted across the space formerly united under the Habsburg monarchy. Part I focuses on those states or regions where the Great War was usually discussed using a language of "defeat" and where it was difficult to find any meaning for the mass sacrifice. At a minimum it was felt that the dead should be honored by the living, but various discourses soon suggested that the wartime survivors were continuing to make sacrifices in a communal struggle that was not yet over. In the chaotic first Austrian Republic, as Catherine Edgecombe and Maureen Healy reveal, there were immediately conflicting perspectives on the sacrifice and how best to commemorate it. These divisions were often between Austrian regions or localities, but they were also informed by sharp political and ideological stances in the interwar Republic, where some prioritized sacrifice for an Austrian or a German fatherland, while others viewed the past and the future through a socialist or even Habsburg ("legitimist") prism. This produced a lack of any inclusive memorialization across Austria, something notable within all the successor states. In turn it suggested a hierarchy of sacrifice. Battle-weary men almost always overshadowed women, while Jews and other "outsiders" were often disparaged in a competition to dictate exclusive interpretations of the Austrian experience and legitimize particular postwar agendas.

While this reaction mirrored the interwar struggle in the Austrian rump state to forge a new national identity, postwar Hungary witnessed a militantly nationalist public discourse precisely because of its new ethnically-demarcated borders. It was easier, after the disastrous Treaty of Trianon assigned 75 percent of territory to neighboring states, to tie Hungarian wartime sacrifice closely to Greater Hungary's decimation by the victors. The struggle in Hungary for some postwar "regeneration" was enveloped by Magyar nationalists into a crusade to reverse Trianon. Moreover, as Franz Horváth's chapter shows, in the Hungarian case the postwar Habsburg legacy had unique features since Magyar communities, separated by new state borders, were subordinated in Romania and Czechoslovakia to alternative and dominant narratives of the war (only the division of Tyrolean Germans between Austria and Italy is really comparable: see Laurence Cole's analysis). Horváth's case study focuses on the Transylvanian Magyars whose military veterans could now only organize and commemorate in exile— in "Hungary proper." In Transylvanian Romania meanwhile, any Magyar memorialization was very subdued or silenced by the Romanian authorities. It was a contrast not only to the native Saxon Germans who posed less of a threat to Bucharest,[10] but also to a certain tolerance of special commemorations among the Magyar communities in (Czecho-) Slovakia.

Most German-Austrian and Magyar communities typically adopted annual commemorative rituals to express their grief and their obligation to the dead. Yet a minority of junior veterans reacted proactively to the "culture of defeat" (often challenging the very concept) with militant behavior. Two essays in Part I introduce us to this theme: how the struggle and comradeship of the wartime trenches could be transferred into new idealistic crusades across the successor states. The priority in these was not on words or political engagement but on action. In 1918–19, many soldiers returning home found a chaotic domestic scene at odds with the values they had fought for. How they reacted depended greatly on the stability of the new state frameworks. Although some militant work could start immediately, it often had to be a long-term objective. Robert Gerwarth's chapter highlights paramilitary violence in the year after the armistice, especially in Hungary where a mixture of aggrieved veterans and young men who had missed out on fighting produced "explosive subcultures of ultra-militant masculinity." The aim of their protest, apart from the thrill of action, was to reassert order in the nation, combating internal traitors while mindful of a wider European struggle against international threats (Bolshevism and Jewry).[11] It was the unstable phenomenon of Bolshevik Hungary in 1919 that allowed some veterans to remobilize almost immediately behind a new banner; and although their public militancy then subsided, it would resurface in the Fascist Europe of the 1930s to support Hungary's agenda of reversing Trianon.

A longer-term struggle took place among those nationalist veterans who found themselves among the German minority of Czechoslovakia. Their Sudeten German crusade too would reach fruition in the 1930s but, as Chapter 3 reveals, its origins owed as much to the prewar Czech-German nationalist clash in Bohemia as to the militancy injected by the wartime trenches. Above all, Sudeten nationalist veterans after 1918 tended to make sense of their sacrifice by transforming what had previously been a Habsburg/German-Austrian fight into a specifically anti-Czech mission to break out of their new state "straitjacket." Rather than showing much nostalgia for the Habsburgs, they now aspired to their own Sudeten national rebirth on a par with what their Czech antagonist had achieved in 1918. However, because postwar Czechoslovakia lacked Hungary's instability (notwithstanding the relative chaos in Slovakia in 1919), Sudeten German militancy had to be carefully and privately channeled. It became a long-term vision, with some veterans seeking to perpetuate the virtues of trench comradeship through a *Männerbund*, a new national regime based on chivalric male bonding. This mission also relied on recruiting the postwar male generation. Just as youth was vital for national regeneration after the wartime catastrophe, young males who had missed the war were attracted to an energetic, idealistic adventure. Thus as in Hungary, some Sudeten German veterans and young men continued the wartime sacrifice in a refocused form. If Magyar militancy fed off the Trianon calamity, the Sudeten mission consistently drew its purpose and inspiration from the overwhelming (Czech) narrative of the Czechoslovak state.

In Part II we turn from defeated communities to "victor states" that in the interwar period asserted a hegemonic national narrative of the Great War. Yugoslavia and Czechoslovakia were the key manufactured states to emerge from the Habsburg ruins. There began what Rogers Brubaker has termed "nationalizing nationalism," the new state authorities seeking to consolidate victory by forging together one nation out of a multi-national conglomerate.[12] The war was officially interpreted as the final rebirth or liberation after centuries of oppression, the culmination of a long struggle for national unification. This meant imposing upon the population an exclusive narrative of heroic and worthwhile sacrifice. Key events were selected for the nation to remember (the 1915 Serbian anabasis across Albania, the 1917 Czech victory at Zborov), and usually it was the myth of foreign resistance alongside the victorious western Allies that was prioritized. Less attention was paid to voices from the home front where—whether in wartime Bohemia, Polish Galicia, or occupied Serbia—a messier picture existed of opportunism and simple accommodation in the face of Austro-Hungarian rule. For Czechs and Serbs certainly, the recent battles could be portrayed as deliverance from an oppressive Habsburg yoke. But usually this was magnified into a more dramatic crusade, constructed first in a European-wide framework with the small nation playing a disproportionate role, and second within a grand, national narrative that stretched back into medieval times.

Melissa Bokovoy's chapter analyzes the Serbian hegemonic discourse within the new Kingdom of Serbs, Croats, and Slovenes (Yugoslavia). While other historians have recently shown how this blended into a Yugoslav memorial culture,[13] Bokovoy explains how the Serbian authorities subtly massaged the photographic narrative in order to foreground Serbian heroic exploits and military masculinity. They emphasized Serbia's overwhelming contribution to the creation of Yugoslavia, setting out as in the other successor states a hierarchy of sacrifice. They also framed the struggle as one of linear, primordial progression: reaching back to Serbia's martyrdom at the hands of the Turk in the fourteenth century and reaching forward to help new generations learn their duty to perpetuate the Serbian national mission. In this way, as in the defeated states, the struggle was not over but was being refocused.

Nancy Wingfield explains the similar dominant (Czech) narrative within interwar Czechoslovakia. The legendary 1917 battle of Zborov on the Eastern front was commandeered as supposedly representative of the Czech military experience, reverentially commemorated, and immortalized in Czech literary, theater, and memorial culture (including the Czechoslovak "Unknown Soldier" in Prague). By encouraging this, the Czech authorities deliberately privileged the heroic exploits of the Czechoslovak Legion, those ex-Habsburg soldiers who had deserted or been taken prisoner mainly on the Eastern front, and had then fought on the Allied side as a resistance force. In contrast, the Zborov myth marginalized those thousands of Czech soldiers who had continued to fight, loyally or obediently, in the Austro-Hungarian ranks. The Czechoslovak hegemonic war discourse was exclusive in other ways too. While it often chafed against Slovak aspirations within the new state framework, the exclusive mythology had little room for Sudeten German or Magyar interpretations of the recent sacrifice either. These groups were rarely incorporated into the Czechoslovak commemorative culture, in war memorials for instance.[14] Instead, they had to seek meaning for the mass carnage in a parallel war discourse that could challenge the very legitimacy of the new state.

Yet even within the dominant narratives of the "victor states" there was also much vigorous and violent dispute. Specifically, it emerged because the phenomenon of discontented veterans or would-be soldiers was by no means confined to the "defeated nations" of the Habsburg monarchy. Indeed, it was ubiquitous that a minority of returning soldiers wished in peacetime society to assert the military ethos of discipline and order they had experienced at the front. They were joined by a younger male generation who hankered after a war experience, who felt alienated by the fast return to bourgeois politics instead of the chance of continued militant action to "regenerate" the nation. Katya Kocourek's chapter highlights the ideological split that soon developed among Czechoslovak legionary veterans. The crux lay in how the controversial legionary legacy was to be interpreted in Czechoslovakia. One legionary branch exited from the war with a social agenda close to that of the country's founding fathers. Another smaller group pursued a "state-forming legionary tradition" nearer to the militant, anti-Bolshevik crusade that had characterized the Legion's anabasis across Siberia. For veterans like Rudolf Medek, if legionary martyrdom was not to be in vain, their heroic, disciplined, and patriotic spirit had to be inculcated into all Czechoslovak citizens in order to maintain the new state against hostile outsiders. As Kocourek reveals, such a project had some success, not least with publicity in commemorative rituals and writings, through attaching itself to sympathetic elements of the Czechoslovak military establishment.

This militant legionary mentality also had distinct parallels in interwar Romania. Although this successor state, like Poland, was not characterized by a specific "Habsburg" inheritance, its main territorial expansion after the war was at the empire's expense (Transylvania), and its violent political culture was partly defined by a struggle to defend and nurture Greater Romania in a hostile Europe. The hegemonic, often anti-Magyar, war narrative was clear in Transylvania and in Romanian memorial culture more widely.[15] But as Rebecca Haynes shows, this official interpretation of Romania's "rebirth" was inadequate for some young Romanians who had missed the war and yearned for a militant mission. Like disgruntled youths or veterans in Hungary or Czechoslovakia, the new Romanian Legion saw its role as one of correctly honoring the veterans' wartime sacrifice with its own sacred and selfless crusade, challenging the corrupt and unrepresentative world of Romanian politics.[16] What marked the Romanian crusade as distinct across the successor states was its young leadership, drawn largely from a postwar generation. It also had a powerful mystical dimension to its rebirth, rooted in homegrown Christian Orthodoxy, which set it apart from the "spiritual nationalism" of Croatian or Sudeten German interwar Fascism. Lastly, it proved to be a particularly disruptive force in Romanian society by the 1930s, a militant cuckoo permitted to survive in the national nest. In other "victor states" in contrast, such militancy within the dominant nation was either safely subsumed into a militarized state culture (*Sanacja* Poland), or it was checked and stayed within respectable bounds until an international crisis hit the state (Czechoslovakia).

The New Europe confirmed in Paris in 1919–20 shattered any coherent Habsburg war memory, and quickly redefined the war experience to appear as one of victors against vanquished. Yet as we have seen, this simple dialectic always belied complex realities even in the victor states, for individuals at the grassroots rarely fitted themselves neatly into the newly constructed patriotic narratives. Part III takes us further into those regions where there could be no clear or hegemonic discourse about the Great War sacrifice. The former Habsburg allegiance could become embarrassing for some national communities (Slovenes, Croats, or Poles) who now found themselves in triumphant Yugoslavia or Poland. This was the culture of "hidden defeat," which also included the Italians of Trentino. Moreover, in the case of Poland, the abrupt unification of three separate wartime histories made it extremely difficult for the Polish state to narrate any coherent story of the Great War. The effect in many communities was a very muted discourse, whether in literature or in commemoration of the dead. At the same time, the ubiquitous phenomenon of the postwar veteran— often distressed or disabled—ensured that the experience of 1914–18 lived on, only gradually displaced by new state concerns or new sacrifices expected from postwar generations.

The Croatian case stands as a good example of local communities finding war memory distinctly problematic. Here, perhaps not surprising in view of Croatia's reputation as "Habsburg loyalist," there were some postwar echoes of Habsburg allegiance of a kind otherwise most noticeable in interwar Austria. And the prevalent reaction in Croatia seems to have been low-key, with a paucity of memorial culture compared to Romanians, Czechs, Germans, or Serbians (who admittedly had many more local sites of bloodshed). However, where the Croatian voice could be heard in all its diversity was through veterans' organizations. As John Paul Newman indicates, Croatian veterans were by no means unusual across the successor states in finding their new state neglectful. Where their treatment stood out was in the state's tendency to actively discriminate against Croat and Slovene soldiers who had fought for Austria-Hungary while giving economic privileges to the minority who had been recruited as "Yugoslav volunteers" in the Serbian forces. The division was comparable to the privileging of interwar Czech legionaries over "Habsburg Czechs" but was more pronounced in view of Serbian-Croatian tensions within Yugoslavia. There was also room in Croatia, home to many frustrated political aspirations, for militant responses from a mixture of postwar male youth and veterans. Some of these were even more assertive about pursuing an idealistic Yugoslav state mission. Others—like Sudeten veterans in Czechoslovakia—now shifted their former (Austrian) allegiance in a radical direction, focusing on militant Croatian nationalism in order to overturn the new hybrid state. Only in the 1940s, in the Ustasha Fascist state, could a new Croatian narrative of the war be fully reasserted.[17]

Petra Svoljšak's chapter on the Slovenian "memory hole" usefully complements this Yugoslav picture. She too highlights the absence of any coherent Slovene war narrative, partly in the face of Serbian-Yugoslav hegemony but also thanks to the conflicted loyalties of many Slovenes during and after the war.[18] The result was a muddled semi-official discourse, a tendency to ignore Slovene military performance in the Habsburg ranks, while at the same time lauding the experience of those who had either contributed to the "Yugoslav victory" (the Serbian narrative) or had suffered in Russian captivity. Other voices however could be heard wishing simply to remember the dead. Slovene war veterans, in contrast to their Croatian counterparts, seemed more confident about building war memorials and establishing a commemorative culture that had hints of the Czech legionary phenomenon in Prague. Svoljšak also hints at how the distinctive Slovene language facilitated, through poetry, a special expression of the Slovenian tragedy. Yet the primary focus of Slovenian bloodshed, the Italian front, still remained largely untouchable. This was not just because of its embarrassing confluence with the Habsburg war, but because it proved impossible to mourn Slovene sacrifice properly in regions annexed after the war by the Italian state. Caught between Italian, Serbian, and Habsburg versions of the war, Slovenian war memory was therefore vague, distorted, or (in Italy) completely obliterated.

Our final case studies reinforce in a graphic way how, with the European map suddenly redrawn, memories of the Habsburg war could be deliberately sidelined even in those regions where the most blood had been spilled on behalf of the monarchy. Austrian Galicia had been one of the major battlegrounds within the empire's borders and had even witnessed the wartime creation of cemeteries dedicated to Austro-Hungarian heroes. Yet with the end of hostilities, and Galicia's full annexation by a new Polish state, this memorial space was largely forgotten, the Polish or Ukrainian wartime graves almost as neglected as those of imperial Austrian or Russian soldiers. The reason, as Christoph Mick's chapter shows, was that Poland—even more so than Yugoslavia—found it impossible to create a clear commemorative discourse out of a war where Poles had fought against each other. Since the fight for Polish rebirth outlasted the Great War by two years, it was possible as in Hungary to transpose the focus of national sacrifice onto the postwar struggle and tie it to the new regime's legitimacy. Most official commemorative rituals in interwar Poland, including veneration of an Unknown Soldier (always a litmus test of the main discourse), could then concentrate on a clear Polish message and simply ignore the Habsburg war. This facilitated a hegemonic narrative as in the other "victor states," one into which Jewish memories had to be subsumed, yet one which chafed badly against the sacrifice of Ukrainian soldiers from eastern Galicia. In Poland the fate of many veterans mirrored their shabby treatment in the other successor states but, in the hierarchy that developed, it was Poles who had fought too soon (during 1914–18) who were usually at the bottom of the ladder. Most maligned were Ukrainian veterans of all persuasions who had no Polish credentials or had actively contested Polish "rebirth." They might share a vision, akin to some Magyar, German-Austrian, or Sudeten veterans, of an eventual rebirth of their own that would topple the "artificial" postwar order.

Where Poland's unity served to entangle war memories in one new state, the peacetime division of Austrian Tyrol between Italy and Austria created a splintered memory culture that mirrored in a fascinating microcosm most of the characteristics from across the other ex-Habsburg territories. Like Galicia, the former war theater of Tyrol was now a region where it was problematic to assert publicly the local sacrifice and suffering of 1914–18, since most Austrian commemoration was obscured under Italian hegemony. As Laurence Cole reveals, although local conciliatory voices surfaced to challenge the official militant narratives, it was the latter that tended to prevail on both sides of the new Austro-Italian frontier. With its territorial amputation, the defeated Austrian Tyrol resembled irredentist Hungary in fixing 1920 as a new date to commemorate sacrifice and injustice. But the official regional discourse also parroted the kind of primordial myths buried deep in Czech or Serbian society, namely that this was just one phase in a cycle of Tyrolean martyrdom where any disunity would soon be reversed. In contrast in "victorious" Italy, especially after the 1922 Fascist takeover, German-Italian Tyrolean commemoration was muted. German South Tyrol resembled Ukrainian Galicia (or even Magyar Transylvania) in that a community's memorial culture was overwritten. Italy's heroic wartime narrative dominated here visually, as ossuaries were constructed to mark out the landscape and former Habsburg subjects were even reburied as "Italians." For ex-Habsburg Italians of the Trentino, the nationalization of memory was even more complex. Set against the "hidden defeat" experienced by many Italian families, it was the Italian legionary or irredentist struggle that was privileged as a vital element of the "national rebirth." Thus Trentino too had parallels with Transylvania, where the sacrifice of (ex-Habsburg) Romanians seems to have been commemorated modestly in the face of a triumphant discourse of liberation.

Across all the interwar successor states, whether victors or vanquished, there reverberated official slogans of "sacrifice" and "regeneration." The latter implied an ongoing national mission that was being asserted or upheld in order to justify the former. Yet when the war of 1914–18 was publicly interpreted in this way, many voices remained silent or were obscured by hegemonic narratives. Most notable perhaps—a real elephant in the room—was the way that sacrifice on behalf of the Habsburg monarchy or its emperor-king was obliquely obscured; here a comparison with Soviet Russia's supposed amnesia over the Great War of the Romanov empire is a valid one.[19] Fighting the last Habsburg war was certainly recalled and explained in interwar memoirs of the Habsburg military and political elite, or in the official Austro-Hungarian military history emanating after 1930 from the Vienna war archives. But with the death of the last emperor (1922), the eclipse of old Habsburg officials, and little evidence that the monarchy could be restored in the New Europe, it was contemporary national discourses and works that overwrote the Habsburg narrative while often fencing combatively against it. This was facilitated by the fact that across the former Austro-Hungarian empire there had always been a balance between Habsburg and national/regional loyalties, and the former were now simply declared moribund.

Perhaps too easily, the historian may follow those voices from the successor states that shouted loudest. Many quiescent and often non-national viewpoints—for example, those of Croat peasant soldiers, of old Habsburg officials, of women who recalled sacrifice on the home front—need to be resurrected, even if their footprints in the sources are faint and obscured by bolder tracks. The essays in this volume also suggest further rich opportunities for transnational comparison. Thus we will reassert in the historiography a "Habsburg mental space" that many contemporaries retained even when their old territorial empire had disappeared from the European map.

Mark Cornwall is Professor of Modern European History at the University of Southampton, specializing in the late Habsburg monarchy and its successor states. His major publications include *The Undermining of Austria-Hungary: The Battle for Hearts and Minds* (2000); *The Devil's Wall: The Nationalist Youth Mission of Heinz Rutha* (2012); and a chapter on Austro-Hungarian wartime morale and censorship in volume XI/I of *Die Habsburgermonarchie: Der Erste Weltkrieg* (2016). He is currently writing a book about treason and loyalty in the last decades of Austria-Hungary.

Notes

1. Leo Perutz, *Little Apple* (London, 1991), 54. First published in 1928 as *Wohin Rollst Du, Äpfelchen.*
2. Gina Gräfen Conrad von Hötzendorf, *Mein Leben mit Conrad von Hötzendorf: Sein geistiges Vermächtnis* (Leipzig, 1935), 114.
3. Edmund Glaise von Horstenau and Rudolf Kisling, eds., *Österreich-Ungarns letzter Krieg 1914–1918*, 7 vols. (Vienna, 1930–1938), vol. 7, *Das Kriegsjahr 1918* (Vienna, 1938), 831, and Beilage 37, "Die Verluste der kriegführenden Heere im Weltkriege." In addition, 478,000 officers and men died as prisoners of war, while another 437,000 were taken prisoner by the Italian army at the end of the war.
4. For the various perspectives as the war ended, see Mark Cornwall, "Austria-Hungary," in *At the Eleventh Hour: Reflections, Hopes and Anxieties at the Closing of the Great War, 1918*, ed. Hugh Cecil and Peter Liddle (London, 1998), 285–300.
5. Gergely Romsics, *Myth and Remembrance: The Dissolution of the Habsburg Empire in the Memoir Literature of the Austro-Hungarian Political Elite* (New York, 2006).
6. István Deák, *Beyond Nationalism: A Social and Political History of the Habsburg Officer Corps 1848–1918* (Oxford, 1990), 205–12 and Appendix I.
7. Martin Zückert, *Zwischen Nationsidee und staatlicher Realität: Die tschechoslowakische Armee und ihre Nationalitätenpolitik 1918–1938* (Munich, 2006).
8. Bernhard Böttcher, *Gefallen für Volk und Heimat: Kriegerdenkmäler deutscher Minderheiten in Ostmitteleuropa während der Zwischenkriegszeit* (Cologne, Weimar, and Vienna, 2009). See also Martin Zückert, "Getrennte Erinnerung. Gefallendenkmäler und Weltkriegsdeutung in den böhmischen Ländern," in *Das Gedächtnis der Orte. Sinnstiftung und Erinnerung*, ed. Elisabeth Fendl (Freiburg, 2006), 285–305.
9. Eduard März, *Austrian Banking and Financial Policy: Creditanstalt at a Turning Point 1913–1923* (New York, 1984).
10. See Böttcher, *Gefallen für Volk und Heimat*, 265–391.
11. For further examples, but mostly from outside the "Habsburg arena" in 1918–23, see Robert Gerwarth and John Horne, eds., *War in Peace: Paramilitary Violence in Europe after the Great War* (Oxford, 2012). See also Robert Gerwarth and John Horne, "Vectors of Violence: Paramilitarism in Europe after the Great War, 1917–1923," *The Journal of Modern History* 83 (2011): 489–512.
12. Rogers Brubaker, *Nationalism Reframed: Nationhood and the National Question in the New Europe* (New York, 1996).
13. See, for example, Aleksandar Ignjatović, "From Constructed Memory to Imagined National Tradition: The Tomb of the Unknown Yugoslav Soldier (1934–38)," *The Slavonic and East European Review* 88/4 (2010): 624–51.
14. An unusually inclusive German-Czech memorial however was that erected in Liberec (Reichenberg) in 1928. The dramatic figure of a traumatized man is the cover picture of this book.
15. See Franz Horváth's chapter in this volume, and also Maria Bucur, *Heroes and Victims: Remembering War in Twentieth Century Romania* (Bloomington and Indianapolis, 2009).
16. See the classic study by Henry Roberts, *Rumania: Political Problems of an Agrarian State* (New Haven, 1951).
17. Comparable, as Franz Horváth shows, to the revitalized Magyar narrative in Transylvania, and also to the suppression of any Czech legionary narrative in the Nazi Protectorate of Bohemia and Moravia.

18. See Pavlina Bobič, *War and Faith: The Catholic Church in Slovenia 1914–1918* (Leiden, 2012); Mark Cornwall, "The Great War and the Yugoslav Grassroots: Popular Mobilization in the Habsburg Monarchy," in *New Perspectives on Yugoslavia: Key Issues and Controversies* ed. Dejan Djokić and James Ker-Lindsay (London and New York, 2011), 27–45.
19. See the revisionist work of Karen Petrone, *The Great War in Russian Memory* (Bloomington and Indianapolis, 2011).

Part I

SACRIFICE AND THE VANQUISHED

Chapter 1

COMPETING INTERPRETATIONS OF SACRIFICE IN THE POSTWAR AUSTRIAN REPUBLIC

Catherine Edgecombe and Maureen Healy

In September 1934, a war memorial was unveiled in Vienna. Christened the "Heldendenkmal", the heroes' memorial, it was built into the existing Burgtor, a structure completed in 1824 under the patronage of Franz I. The Burgtor trumpeted on one side the Habsburg motto in Latin, "Justice, the foundation of rule," and on the other side, an inscription added in 1916, "Laurel, for soldiers worthy of the laurel."[1] Presiding over the ceremony was Chancellor Kurt von Schuschnigg, leader of the authoritarian Fatherland Front, a movement founded in 1933 to unite "loyal Austrians" under one banner. The monument's planners had envisioned "not an unknown soldier following the western model" but something specifically Austrian.[2] The unveiling was coordinated with a three-day "Comrades' Convention" for which tens of thousands of veterans came to Vienna from the provinces, subsidized by discounted train tickets and sightseeing packages. The socialists had been defeated in a brief civil war seven months earlier, and Schuschnigg noted with apparent relief that "finally" the Austrian capital could boast "a worthy commemoration" of the Great War.[3]

As will become clear, however, Schuschnigg's "finally" did not mean "at last"; rather, his emphasis lay on "worthy." During the First Austrian Republic, a dizzying number of smaller war-related memorials had been erected, and several more unrealized projects existed on paper. The Heldendenkmal ceremony was just one of many moments when citizens in interwar Austria tried publicly to ascribe meaning to the experiences of the Great War. In the planning of these memorials and in the inscriptions they bore, we find a cacophony of claims, disclaimers, accusations, and denials about sacrifice: who had sacrificed during the war? What had they sacrificed? And for what higher cause? *Opfer,* an ambiguous term meaning both "sacrifice" and "victim," had lent itself to flexible interpretation during the war.[4] It is genuinely difficult to identify individuals in interwar Austria who did not conceive of themselves as war victims, as having sacrificed in some way, or to find electoral constituencies that did not include victimhood as a part of their collective raison d'être.

For understanding the discourse of sacrifice after 1918, in which victimhood and loss loomed large, the following definition is a useful starting point. Sacrifice is *the destruction of something valued or desired for the sake of something having a higher or more pressing claim*. It is *the loss entailed by devotion to some other interest*.[5] During the First Republic no compelling, universally accepted narrative emerged on the "higher cause" for which these sacrifices had been made. Elsewhere, as essays in this volume demonstrate, Czech legionaries and South Slav volunteers could claim the cause of victory. But in Austria no group could make such a straightforward claim.[6] Instead, Austrians interpreted wartime sacrifice in five discernible ways: for the fatherland, for God, for the Emperor, for the Republic, and for the spirit of comradeship. Paradoxically, despite extensive public commemoration of one or another of these variants of sacrifice, many felt that the returning soldiers were not receiving adequate gratitude for their wartime deeds. Further, a process of *erasing* and *forgetting* accompanied the ostensible *remembering* of the war conflict. The wartime sacrifices of certain groups, notably Jews and women, were muted or missing in most public commemorations. With so many conflicting claims in circulation, the Austro-Fascist government that came to power in 1934 aimed to bring "order" to the messy story of Austrian sacrifice. It attempted at the Heldendenkmal ceremonies to clean up apocryphal versions of who had sacrificed what for whom. That multiple stories (and omissions) are evident in the great memorial itself attests to the impossibility of weaving from particular and competing claims a universal narrative of Austrian wartime sacrifice.

Commemorative Flurry

Historian Ernst Hanisch writes of "the heroicizing of the fallen soldiers: the dead returned in the monuments and ceremonies for heroes. In every village all over the country war memorials were erected in the early 1920s."[7] By 1929, in the Neunkirchen region of Lower Austria, memorials had been constructed in the vast majority of communities. They were built by returning soldiers' or veterans' organizations, by parochial authorities, or by local committees representing these groups. As "symbolic foci of bereavement," such memorials offered the local community tangible sites at which to gather, remember, and commemorate the war and, in some cases, view the names of the fallen of that locality.[8] The memorials took the form of columns, crosses, or plaques on church walls. They were ordered from stonemasons or architects and unveiled by local dignitaries at small-scale, quiet ceremonies. However, while such memorials served important functions within local communities, not all of this commemorative activity was welcome. The federal memorial office (Bundesdenkmalamt), an imperial office given powers in the Republic in December 1918 and formally recognized by law in 1923, had not standardized the aesthetics of local memorials. Letters to the Bundesdenkmalamt and articles in the press raised concerns that many of these memorials lacked the artistic merit and the quality of construction to properly convey messages about the war to future generations.[9]

The shortcomings of local memorials perceived by some commentators were undoubtedly linked to the practical problems faced by those seeking to construct memorials. The sapper regimental memorial in Krems is one such memorial. Construction began during the war, but the bronze needed for its completion was requisitioned at the end of hostilities so the memorial was not finished. In 1920, the Sapper Memorial Association was founded to complete it and, at a ceremony to raise funds and awareness that year, the still unfinished memorial was unveiled by the town authorities.[10] After various modifications and renewed fundraising efforts, the temporary plaques were replaced by permanent bronze ones.[11] In 1930, after undergoing further improvements, the completed memorial was unveiled. By then many compromises in design and construction materials had been made.[12] This long process was a feature of much memorial construction in interwar Austria. Finished memorials were often the result of protracted negotiations between changing committee members and interested groups. Building was limited by financial resources and fundraising attempts were undermined by inflation.

Memorials were constructed not only by veterans' organizations and local communities but also by academic institutions, employers, and other civilian groups. A typical example of this was a 1930 memorial that was unveiled at the seventieth anniversary of the founding of the Higher Federal Academy for Winegrowing, Fruit Growing, and Horticulture for the fallen soldiers of that institution. This memorial was funded by a professional association and it commemorated the fallen along with their prewar colleagues rather than their co-combatants.[13] Similarly, in 1923 the Austrian Bicycle Riders' Association held the first annual "Heroes' Bike Races" to commemorate fallen members of the Bike Sport Association.[14] Fallen Austrian soldiers were commemorated as residents of a town, village, region, or state; as members of a regiment; as former colleagues or members of a profession; as students; or as members of leisure associations.

Although many memorials were rooted in local communities or organizations, some commemorative activity aspired to grander scale. Plans were made to construct a memorial on the Grossglöckner, the highest point in Austria. The Austrian Minister of Defense Carl Vaugoin argued that the question of accessibility was not important in this case. The primary aim of the memorial was "to put a sign of thanks for the sacrifices of soldiers as close to the heavens as possible," an aim, he argued, that would have been undermined by building the memorial anywhere else.[15] A member of the socialist Volkswehr proposed that the most appropriate memorial would not be in bronze and stone at all. He wrote, "[t]he most beautiful, ideal monument that could be erected for the victims of the World War is the League of Nations."[16] One of the most controversial memorials, unveiled in 1925 in the Viennese central cemetery and funded by the Social Democrat municipal government, depicted a woman in mourning and bore the title *Schmerzensmutter* or grieving mother. The leading Social Democrat newspaper, the *Arbeiter-Zeitung*, argued that the new memorial was a monument to sadness and reconciliation, rather than a traditional war memorial.[17] As we shall see, many in Austria did not count a female figure in stone as a legitimate tribute to wartime sacrifice, and did not consider it a war memorial at all.

A perceived lack of a "worthy" monument of national scale in the capital city sparked initiatives that eventually culminated in the Heldendenkmal celebrations of 1934. Groups from outside Vienna petitioned for its creation. In 1933, the Amstetten branch of the Comradeship Association of Former Warriors sent a petition to the Defense Ministry calling for the introduction of a specific "Austrian" day of national mourning on 30 August and the construction of an Austrian War memorial in Vienna.[18]

Thus, as this brief review suggests, no single memorial was universally accepted as *the* Austrian memorial. The range of activities and proposals illustrates the extent of attempts to commemorate and come to terms with the experience of the Great War. But they also present us with a paradox. Why, in spite of the commemorative flurry described above, did some Austrians still feel that wartime sacrifice was not being properly acknowledged? Why, at the unveiling of the Heldendenkmal, did speakers from the Fatherland Front claim that it had heretofore been "impossible" during the Republic to erect a suitable monument in the capital to honor wartime sacrifice?[19] Building monuments *per se* had not been impossible; rather, reaching consensus on the underlying meaning of sacrifice had. Austrians were divided along partisan lines over questions about who had sacrificed during the war, for what higher purpose, whose sacrifices warranted remembering, and whose would be erased. The answers were complex, sometimes contradictory, and sometimes overlapping, especially in light of the defeat of the Habsburg armies, the end of the dynasty, the dismemberment of the empire, and the lack of faith in the new state. German nationalists, Catholics, and socialists in Austria interpreted sacrifice in starkly different terms. So too did some men and women.

"With God, for Emperor, and Fatherland"... and Republic and Comrades

The list of possible higher purposes for which the war had been fought grew after 1918. Of course, the war was begun and waged by the imperial Habsburg state. How Austrians remembered wartime sacrifice would be intimately tied to the ways they remembered three hundred years of Habsburg rule. For soldiers fighting for Austria-Hungary, the war's higher purpose, in theory at least, was the multinational empire. Commemorative activity began during the war, and the official meaning of the sacrifice of the fallen and those still fighting was clear. They were fighting "With God, for Emperor, and Fatherland" for the ultimate victory of the Habsburg armies, although naturally this view was not shared by all combatants. Once the empire collapsed, the republican government in Austria faced a situation similar to that in Weimar Germany: a sacrifice vacuum. In Germany, more than in Austria, postwar commemorators could more plausibly substitute nation or fatherland as the *something*, the *pressing claim* for which lives had been destroyed. With the nation-ness of German-Austria in obvious dispute, Austrians came up with the five variants on the *something* for which they had sacrificed. "Fatherland" was the first of them.

Despite the dismemberment of the empire, the idea of "dying for the fatherland" retained currency, especially among German nationalists. They trumpeted the heavy "*Blutopfer* [blood sacrifice] that the German people ha[d] just made to the fatherland."[20] Such appeals to honor those who had fallen for their fatherland were widespread in the immediate postwar period. In a letter lamenting the state of military cemeteries in Innsbruck, the Innsbruck military authorities stated: "The frequently used words 'Heroes Graves' awaken in all the image of a grave that is lovingly built and cared for in grateful thanks to the dead who made the ultimate sacrifice for their fatherland.... The state of the final resting places of brave, honest soldiers, who did their duty loyally and honestly until their final breaths, is deeply shameful."[21] Here, those appealing for funds for the graveyard stressed that the fallen had fought and died for their fatherland, which now owed them a worthy resting place.

Yet fatherland was a multivalent term, and commemorators appealed to different variations of it. For some commemorating groups, the fatherland for which the soldiers had sacrificed was a Greater German fatherland. In 1930 plans emerged for a "Heroes Organ for the German People" at the Geroldseck Fortress in Kufstein. This was a memorial for all fallen German people.[22] In the brochure published for its unveiling in 1931 the pipe organ was described as "the first and only joint war memorial in the German Lands." The organ concerts raised money for war invalids in Germany and Austria.[23] This memorial was not for the Austrian soldiers of the Habsburg army as soldiers of that army but rather for all German soldiers. Similar sentiments were expressed at the unveiling of the Siegfriedskopf memorial at the University of Vienna in 1923.[24] All discussion of the war at the ceremony referred to the battles of the German people, and no mention was made of the Habsburg army in which the German-Austrian soldiers actually fought.[25] German nationalist ideas were also present in attempts to introduce a German *Volkstrauertag* (National Day of Mourning) in Austria. The Black Cross organization that looked after war graves argued that the German and Austrian peoples shared a common destiny, so their fallen heroes should be commemorated together. The day was not officially introduced but was celebrated in some circles and provinces.

However the Greater German interpretation was not the only instance in which "dying for the Fatherland" was used. Even during the imperial period many Austrians had identified very closely with their province, and some of those who fought in the war did so in defense of this smaller, regional *Heimat*. In the postwar period, when few had faith in the small Republic and division was rife, sacrifice for a regional *Heimat* was conflated with dying for the Fatherland. In Carinthia many commemoration ceremonies took place on 10 October, the anniversary of the Carinthian plebiscite. This was a specifically Carinthian day and the commemoration on the same day of those who had died in the war and in postwar fighting gave this event a uniquely Carinthian character. At a reburial ceremony for fallen Carinthian soldiers exhumed in Italy and returned home in 1924, a representative of the defense ministry honored returning souls: "On your journey to your eternal resting place, the first homage is paid to you in Carinthia. Carinthia, this wonderful Land, with its glorious people and its heroic sons, whose love of their *Heimat* and the people of their *Heimat* was worth more to them than their lives."[26] This regional emphasis allowed some continuity between wartime and postwar interpretations of sacrifice.

"God and religion" combined to form the second important lens through which Austrians interpreted their experiences of war and loss. All Souls' Day, a Catholic day of remembrance of the dead, became the most important date for mourning the wartime dead. By 1921 it was clear that All Souls' Day had been semiofficially adopted as the occasion for mourning the fallen. For example, the Black Cross organization in Upper Austria passed a motion in September officially adopting All Souls' Day (2 November) as a *Landestrauer- und Opfertag* (Day of Mourning and Victimhood).[27] Although the Black Cross was a charitable organization it was funded partly by government subsidy and its All Souls' Day commemoration ceremonies were attended by leading figures from the government and military. During the 1920s, commemoration ceremonies for the fallen on All Souls' Day became more formal. By 1923 the Defense Ministry felt it necessary to issue official guidelines for the participation of the military.[28] A pattern was established that continued through the years. The main military commemoration ceremony took place at the Central Cemetery in Vienna and began with a Mass followed by a laying of wreaths on the graves of the fallen soldiers.²⁹ Similar events took place at the war graves sections of cemeteries in other major cities. Veterans' associations were encouraged to attend these ceremonies although the participation of paramilitary organizations in uniform was illegal under the provisions of the Treaty of St Germain and therefore strongly discouraged.³⁰ The official ceremonies took place on a day of religious significance and had a religious form. Unsurprisingly, not all viewed the prominence of religion in commemoration positively. *Der freie Soldat*, a Social Democrat soldiers' publication, complained of the coercion of soldiers of the Republic into religious commemoration ceremonies.³¹

The official military All Souls' Day commemoration ceremony was by no means the only ceremony held at the Central Cemetery in Vienna. On the day before All Souls', the Viennese branch of the Association of War Invalids, Widows, and Orphans held a commemoration and wreath-laying ceremony at the war graves section of the cemetery. On the morning before the start of the official military commemoration, a ceremony was also held by the Iron Corps, a group of right wing veterans' associations including the Front Fighters Association and the Alpine Association of War Participants. In addition to these three organized ceremonies, many thousands of ordinary Viennese people would visit the cemetery to lay flowers on the graves of fallen soldiers, as well as those of other family members laid to rest in the cemetery.³² It is clear that there was a great range of activities on this day, from organized, politicized events to individual pilgrimages. The link between these organized and personal commemorative activities was All Souls' Day. The vast majority of other commemoration ceremonies and memorial unveiling ceremonies also contained Catholic elements, often a Mass or the consecration of a memorial by a priest.

Religion played a similarly important role in physical memorials to the fallen. Many memorials either took the form of a cross or incorporated a cross within the design. For example, the memorial at Traiskirchen, unveiled in September 1920 by the local Comradeship Association with funds raised from the community, was in the form of an obelisk, topped by a stone wreath and a cross.³³ The use of a cross on the memorial reminded mourners of their belief in eternal salvation but also established a link between the suffering of soldiers and the suffering of Christ on the cross.³⁴ Sometimes this link was made more explicit. In Gutenstein in August 1925 a memorial plaque with the inscription, "To those sons of our community who did not return from the war, 1914–1918," was unveiled. The plaque was surrounded by the names of the fallen of Gutenstein and showed an image of a soldier on horseback passing before Christ on the cross.³⁵

One small group of Catholics—monarchists hoping for a Habsburg revival—kept alive the wartime discourse of sacrifice for the Emperor and the supranational *Staatsidee*. The Party of Black-Gold Legitimists read their suffering through the exiled emperor and his family. When former Emperor Karl died on the island of Madeira in 1922, the legitimists cried "murder!" They urged Austrians to show themselves worthy of the emperor's sacrifice: "You are in debt to your Emperor who perished on your behalf." Karl was depicted as a Christ-like figure who had died for the love of a people whom the legitimists now called on to rise against the Republic. "If you have honor, then show at last that you are men, Austrians worthy of the love that his majesty the Emperor has bestowed upon you."[36] Despite such impassioned appeals, the hailing of sacrifice for the emperor and Habsburg dynasty faded dramatically in the postwar period.

Indeed, in the early 1920s monarchist (or "legitimist") sentiment existed only in small sections of the population and was subject to ridicule from the political left. Emperor Karl's botched attempts to retake the Hungarian throne in 1921 cast the monarchist movement in an amateurish light. The Kaiserliche Volkspartei, founded on a platform of Habsburg restoration, received fewer than fifteen hundred votes in the national elections of 1923. At the Salzburg All Souls' Day commemorations a year later, the Republican Schutzbund (the Social Democrat paramilitary organization) laid wreaths on soldiers' graves with the inscription, "To the bloody victims of the wicked Habsburgs."[37] Although this is an extreme example, it reveals that fighting and dying for the emperor had little commemorative traction in the early years of the Republic.

But monarchism saw a resurgence in the late 1920s and 1930s in response to growing Nazism in Austria.[38] Veneration of Habsburg traditions was a way for some Austrians to express their reservations about (or resistance to) German nationalism. This broader shift in Austrian politics was in turn reflected in commemorative practices. One example of a newly invigorated focus on the Habsburg legacy was the renovation of the Elisabeth Chapel on Hochschneeberg. This chapel, the highest church in Lower Austria, had been built in 1901 in memory of the assassinated Empress Elisabeth, but fell into disrepair after the war. In 1927 a committee was formed to renovate the chapel and adapt it as a memorial site for the fallen. Still known as the "Elisabeth Kirchlein", it was partially completed and unveiled in 1931, thereby asserting a link of war commemoration to the Habsburg dynasty.[39] The year 1930 was also the centenary of Emperor Franz Joseph's birth. The occasion was duly marked by a commemoration ceremony in Vienna, attended by a range of veterans' organizations. Here the Viennese author Hans Sassmann argued that

> in the long term no people can live without its history. The more abrupt the separation from the past, the stronger revive the memories of the eternal values, maintained for a thousand years, for which their ancestors fought and suffered. A people that has no history has no future. Austria is separated from its 600-year-history by twelve years of senseless attempts to place a people with no historical basis in a new space.[40]

In this ceremony the war was set in a context of the Habsburg dynasty. After a brief interruption in the early years of the Republic, fighting and dying for the Emperor once again had an explanatory role.

The camp most vocally opposed to the prospect of Habsburg rehabilitation—even in memory—were the socialists. They scoffed at the idea that the Emperor and his family had suffered or been sacrificed after the war. Julius Deutsch, socialist leader of the postwar Volkswehr, countered rather that the "poor, ill, invalid soldiers" who were now being housed at Habsburg palaces seized by the Republic were the true embodiment of sacrifice.[41] For supporters of the Republic, wartime sacrifice had engendered a new social order. In 1919, Dr. Neumann, fellow member of the Volkswehr, explained that "the victims of the war unknowingly became the laborers of liberation. [W]ith their blood they laid the ground for a social order bringing happiness for all people, for socialism."[42] While leftists were loath to look for a silver lining in the catastrophe of war, some did offer the Republic itself as that for which men had (unknowingly) died. In this reading, it was the new, democratic and republican Austria that gave meaning to the soldiers' sacrifices.

Social Democrats were also quick to counter readings of the war that sought to glorify the conflict. In 1921 Field Marshal Conrad von Hötzendorf celebrated his fiftieth anniversary as an officer. Generaloberst Viktor Dankl delivered a speech, claiming that although in the present climate there was little understanding of the heroic battles of the Habsburg armies, the soldiers who had served under him were deeply indebted to Conrad, as he had allowed the army to maintain its honor.[43] Social Democrats reacted to this event with outrage. In the *Volkszeitung* an article mocked the military establishment by suggesting that the defeat had all been a dream: "Because if it was not a dream or a delusion, how would the field marshals, general staff chiefs and army commanders have the audacity to celebrate as though they were enjoying the spoils of victory after the defeat, the shame and the annihilation."[44] The idea that many of the higher commanders of the Habsburg armies failed to acknowledge defeat was often reiterated in the left wing press. Following an Italian remembrance ceremony in Mauthausen (Upper Austria), the *Linzer Tagblatt* newspaper complained that in Austria "the ruling classes want to preserve the memory of the black and gold glory at their reunions, those glorious victories that eventually led to a decisive defeat, while the rest of the world is filled with a longing for peace."[45] For Social Democrats the birth of the new Republic could to some extent compensate for the wartime sacrifice; but they viewed with disdain attempts to hark back to the triumphs of the Habsburg empire.

The fifth and final lens through which Austrians interpreted the meaning of sacrifice was "comradeship." In many commemoration ceremonies and particularly at soldiers' reunions the idea of bonds of comradeship, forged in wartime and maintained into peace, was a crucial positive legacy of the war. Much power was ascribed to comradeship. In wartime "all the differences which normally separate people, as well as classes and castes, fell away. The real mark of these times was comradeship and true fraternity for life and beyond the grave."[46] The idea that comradeship was a positive and inclusive legacy of the war was echoed widely throughout the period. Yet this idea was also complex. Comradeship could be a more divisive than unifying force in society. Excluded from this discourse on comradeship were men who did not fight due to their age, health, or service at home. Afterwards, noncombatants' perceived failure to sacrifice led some to call for special punitive taxes against them that would provide for the care of invalids who had.[47] Some veterans on the far right envisioned a postwar society in which power would belong "only to the front-soldiers."[48] Likewise, the male nature of the perceived bonds of comradeship excluded all memory of female participation in the war. The bonds of comradeship also did not help heal divisions between officers and soldiers or between the general staff and frontline troops in the postwar period. For example, on their return to Austria, the officers' new status was brought home to them in the starkest terms. Some were attacked, and the wearing of their uniforms, once a source of pride, was now regarded as a provocation.[49] Many comradeship organizations excluded Jewish veterans from their ranks. At a 1921 meeting of the Anti-Semitic League in Vienna, speakers from the Front Fighters Association explained that "the German people were robbed of the fruits of their bravely fought four-year war by betrayal. This betrayal had its roots in the Jewish spirit, which corroded the powers of the German people. The Entente victory was only due to the negative effects of the Jewish spirit."[50] Excluded from the nationalists' brand of "comradeship," Jewish veterans often held separate commemoration ceremonies.[51]

Similarly, when it came to commemorating the fallen of the conflict, disabled veterans tended to participate in separate events. A typical example of this was the All Souls' Day commemoration ceremony in Styria in 1924. On 1 November widows, orphans, and invalids held a simple ceremony, during which the mayor of Graz reminded the participants that the fallen served as a constant warning to work on behalf of war victims and towards reconciliation. On the following day, veterans' associations with able-bodied participants held a ceremony that was far more militaristic in tone.[52] Invalids held a similar status to widows and orphans as victims of the conflict, whereas the able-bodied veterans tended to celebrate wartime heroism and sacrifice. Likewise, groups with nontypical wartime experiences, such as prisoners of war, often felt excluded from these bonds of comradeship. According to an article prompted by a commemoration ceremony in 1926 in the journal of the main POW organization, the failure to recognize their experiences made their wartime suffering harder to bear:

> Alongside the infinitely sad truth [of captivity] is the unique experience that our nameless martyrs have been forgotten by their own homeland, where an understanding, correct engagement and appropriate relationship to prisoners of war is still missing. People do not know, or do not want to know, how men were taken prisoner

or what captivity, the tragic fate of soldiers, the most difficult experience of suffering, sacrifice, soul searching and silent heroism, meant.[53]

The same publication, *Der Plenny* (the newspaper of the Association of Former Prisoners of War), argued that despite their attempts to improve the situation, their relationship with the majority of veterans remained distant.[54]

In Austria, the experience of captivity also had an additional negative connotation because of the activities of a small number of high-profile deserters who had switched sides after capture. The idea that the "stain of cowardice" was stopping recognition of POW's sacrifices was raised in 1926 by one of the representatives of the organization at the unveiling of a memorial painting. The German Nationalist politician Ertl Leistung admitted that "for the Germans of Austria the words prisoner of war have a particular connotation, because it is true that in the old army a certain number of traitors did cross over to the enemy."[55] Yet despite these divisions, many veterans agreed that those who had died had sacrificed themselves for their comrades. The bonds between the surviving soldiers were seen as a productive, positive legacy of the war and offered meaning to the experiences of the fallen comrades.

The Great Ingratitude

If comradeship was a powerful bond, it was also a divisive one pitting "us" against "them": *they* were the noncombatants who failed to remember and honor the sacrifice *we* made. Before the first postwar plaque could be posted or village shrine erected, a particular complaint had set in among returning men: the Austrians' *anticipated* failure to remember. The war had been over less than two months when a chorus of veterans charged that the forgetting had begun. A poster advertising a 1919 socialist-dominated memorial service for dead comrades warned, "[t]he fatherland has forgotten its warriors and their sacrifices!"[56] Such charges came more frequently from rightist circles than leftist, and from officers more than common soldiers.[57] Generalmajor Carl Jaschke, president of the committee to build the 1934 Heldendenkmal recalled this "great ingratitude": "Upon return the brave received no thanks. Robbed of their army, mocked and vilified, often by precisely those for whom they had suffered and bled, the men were greeted with ingratitude."[58]

If, as Jaschke claimed, combatants were the ones forgotten, who was doing the forgetting? Under the new republican government's burgeoning welfare system some women were eligible to receive unemployment benefits, and this fed the growing sentiment that women were taking advantage of men's losses rather than honoring their sacrifices. The unemployed woman living a life of luxury on welfare, benefiting while real victims suffered, was a stock figure in stories about postwar ingratitude.[59]

Curiously, amid the chorus of accusations about forgetting the dead and maimed, some of the most concrete acts of remembrance were undertaken by women. Organized into groups such as the Women's Aid Committee for the Liberation of Prisoners of War and the Free Association of Mothers and Wives of Prisoners of War in Russia, Siberia, and Turkestan, these groups worked together with the Austrian State Commission for POWs to keep in the public consciousness the plight of Austrian men still in captivity. Around two million Habsburg soldiers were in POW camps by the end of the war, and the State Commission estimated that in 1919 there were still three hundred thousand POWs in Siberia alone.[60] In 1920, as "women of Austria" addressing "all citizens," female POW advocates proclaimed that "six years ago our men were torn from our arms," and had continued to suffer (and die) in captivity. The ongoing sacrifice of these men hurt not only their individual families but all of Austria.[61] While thousands of women attended rallies, advocacy for POWs became one of the main areas of interest among the handful of women elected to the National Assembly early in the First Republic. The board of the Women's Aid Committee included female parliamentarians from different political parties.[62] The organization embarked on fundraising drives, noting that "the repatriation of a single prisoner costs forty thousand crowns."[63] To this end, the women urged others to donate generously during the so-called *Opfertage* of the postwar period.

This discourse of women donating continued the wartime promotion of women's labor as *Liebesdienst*.[64] Now giving of money (or "love" more generally) was cast as a primary postwar duty as well. Promoters of "a great *Liebeswerk*" explained that the state alone could not heal the scars of war: "Everyone among us will contribute her mite, conscious of the responsibility" to those who had suffered and sacrificed. An article about the *Opfertage* in June 1919 emphasized this donation by women: organizers urged women to "give [the victims] everything you can spare so that never once they can say that they made their heavy sacrifice to the fatherland in vain."[65] The term used here, *umsonst* (in vain), imposed a very heavy burden on women. An unspoken fear of this *umsonst*, that the war had indeed been in vain, permeated postwar Austrian politics. In her everyday life, through acts of generosity, kindness, empathy, and selflessness, the individual woman was assigned to give meaning to wartime sacrifice (not her own, of course) and transform the Great War into a war worthy of being waged.

Remembering and Forgetting at the Heldendenkmal

When Austro-Fascists "finally" celebrated what they considered *the* monument honoring Austrian sacrifice, the 1934 Heldendenkmal, they were attempting to clean up and bring order to the multitude of competing claims made about sacrifice during the Republic. In claiming that Vienna lacked a war memorial they overlooked two existing monuments in their midst. The first was the aforementioned woman in stone, the *Kriegerdenkmal der Gemeinde Wien* at the Central Cemetery. Why did this striking monument of a grieving woman—Christian, but not recognizably Austrian—not count as a proper war memorial in the speeches of 1934? Why, too, did a 1929 memorial, also in the Central Cemetery, for Jewish soldiers who had died, not register in the minds of those who lamented (incorrectly) that Vienna lacked a memorial?[66] In right-wing remembrance, female and Jewish sacrifices were forgotten, or erased outright, but for different reasons. If we recall the generic definition of sacrifice—the *destruction or surrender of something valued for the sake of something having a higher claim*—women were erased on the first count and Jews on the second. The female figure of 1925 had clearly suffered, but she was still alive. She had not sacrificed her life, but had only "given" a son, husband, or father; her sacrifice was of the second order. (This story of women's lesser sacrifice had roots long predating the Great War). Bearing the inscription *Den Gefallenen des Weltkrieges der Stadt Wien* she was also a relic of the despised socialist government of Red Vienna. In the ferociously anti-semitic nationalist and Christian Socialist politics of the First Republic, Jewish sacrifice similarly did not count because Jews belonged neither to the German nation nor to Catholic Austria. They were no longer among the "soldiers worthy of the laurel," who had been honored in 1916 on the Burgtor.

With the wartime sacrifices of these particular groups discounted, the planners of the Heldendenkmal faced other decisions concerning the *what* and the *who* of the memorial. The speeches given on 9 September 1934 indicate that the monument became a hodgepodge of remembrance, created by committee. Which state or higher cause would be honored in the memorial? A report from the summer of 1934 suggests some semantic confusion. On the one hand, those planning for September's Comrades' Convention and the unveiling of the monument felt that "[b]y avoiding the words Austria-Hungary, imperial, Habsburg [and] black and gold, the present-day constitutional system will be accommodated. Through emphasis on Austria, the patriotic sentiments of Austrians are placed in the foreground."[67] But would it be possible simply to substitute "Austria" for "Habsburg" in a memorial for World War I? In one of the side rooms built on to the Burgtor, twenty-four types of Habsburg soldiers had been depicted in stone, including men of the imperial army as well as the separate Austrian and Hungarian defense forces; there were references there to Habsburg glories over the centuries, "from the Balkans to Spain, from Italy to Denmark."[68] Moreover, was the monument specifically commemorating the sacrifice of 1914–18? Ernst Rüdiger Fürst von Starhemberg, leader of the Fatherland Front after the assassination of Chancellor Dollfuß, certainly focused his remarks on the heroes of the recent war. Federal President Miklas however claimed that the monument was not intended to honor the sacrifice of the Great War specifically, but rather the "glorious rule of the former monarchy."[69] We see that consensus on sacrifice was elusive even when the prominent leftist interpretations were left out.

Whichever past the monument was supposed to commemorate, there were various interpretations of what the monument meant for the present. According to Minister of Defense Wilhelm Zehner, the monument would offer relief to grieving women, for it could, metaphorically speaking, bring back the dead to Austrian soil. "The many Austrian mothers and wives whose love, thoughts, memories, and longings had been tethered to distant graves in foreign lands" would now have a mourning site in the *Heimaterde*.[70] The same speaker also prophesied a cathartic effect on the population at large: the monument would "liberate the fatherland from a burning debt of thanks."[71] Debt was a recurring theme in the discourse of remembering; here the monument in stone could alleviate the burden of thanks, the heaviness of gratitude that Austrians had shouldered for a decade. Finally, the monument offered relief of a more practical nature. Supporters touted the monument as a work site. Employing around 250 laborers, the monument "served not only the glory of the old army but also helped to relieve the unemployment of the present generation."[72]

The Heldendenkmal and other memorial sites did not question the assumption that the war had been worthwhile, that it had been *for* something and not pointless. But as demonstrated in this chapter, the "something" was in dispute: contenders included the fatherland, God, the Emperor and Habsburg dynasty, the new republican socialist social order, and the legacy of wartime comradeship. Rare was the party or organization willing to question this underlying assumption, to suggest that the war had brought immense suffering but to no noble end. If, as George Mosse has argued, postwar remembrance took on the features of a cult, to claim that soldiers' sacrifices had been in vain was blasphemous.[73] But let us conclude with two exceptions that venture in this direction.

The first comes from a journalist at the liberal daily *Neue Freie Presse* newspaper. The 1919 All Souls' Day commemoration ceremony prompted the following reflections:

> Seven million dead.... The catastrophe that has affected us all is like an irrecoverable sea of suffering, before which even the deepest of human feeling must fail. Many freely admit to envying those who rest under the fields. Many, who are disgusted by this beggar's existence, will think enviously of those who have departed and no longer know how it is when worries fill your heart and the disturbances of tomorrow cloud today. Because they are not the fallen. We are.[74]

"Many" might have felt this, but few said it publicly. It is unusual to find (in print) the suggestion that the living were worse off than the dead. Even if a sentiment expressed in private, this idea was by and large absent from the public interwar Austrian discourse of sacrifice.

Figure 1.1. An Austrian radical comment on the Great War, 1924.

A second iteration of it appeared in a women's newspaper. In July 1924, *Die Unzufriedene*, a small-circulation publication billing itself as "an independent weekly for all women," ran a special issue to mark the tenth anniversary of the beginning of the war.[75] The lead illustration drew on themes similar to those in the monument of the mourning woman in Vienna's Central Cemetery, but here the objects of women's grief are more specific. They are mourning "murdered men," "starving infants," and the "starving elderly." Two things make this a highly unusual postwar comment on sacrifice. First are the seemingly interchangeable wreaths, for while many are scattered on the ground, others are waiting to be laid. Solemn wreath-laying ceremonies were a staple of postwar commemoration, but in this picture one could keep laying wreaths indefinitely and still not discover the meaning of the war. Second is the caption attributed to Confucius beneath the drawing: "The glory of a thousand battles blows past. What remains of heroism? A decaying mound of weeds red as fire." While Austrians across the political spectrum had offered competing interpretations of who sacrificed in the war and for what higher purpose, the most radical proposal—one made only rarely in public and perhaps bordering on the unspeakable—was that the war had been fought for nothing at all.

Catherine Edgecombe secured a first class degree in History and German from the University of Southampton and completed her PhD there in 2008. Its title was *"With God and Fatherland": The Commemoration of the Great War in the First Austrian Republic, 1918–1934*.

Maureen Healy is Associate Professor of History at Lewis & Clark College in Portland, Oregon. She was an IFK-Fulbright Senior Fellow in 2011–12, and has held fellowships at the National Humanities Center, Research Triangle Park, NC, and the Woodrow Wilson Center in Washington, DC. In 2005 her book, *Vienna and the Fall of the Habsburg Empire: Total War and Everyday Life in World War I*, won the Herbert Baxter Adams Prize from the American Historical Association. Her current research project is entitled *Beyond the Siege: Cultural Traffic between Austrians and Turks, 1878 to the Present*. She is the Book Review Editor of the *Austrian History Yearbook*.

Notes

1. http://peter-diem.at/Monumente/burgtor.htm (accessed 17 August 2007). On memorials and Austrian identity, see Stefan Riesenfellner, ed., *Steinernes Bewusstsein: Die öffentliche Repräsentation staatlicher und nationaler Identität Österreichs in seinen Denkmälern*, vol. 1 (Vienna, 1998).
2. Austrian State Archives (Österreichisches Staatsarchiv: hereafter ÖstA), Archiv der Republik (AdR), Bundesministerium für Landesverteidigung (BMfLV), Heldendenkmal, karton 302, *Gedenkschrift anläßlich der Weihe des österreichischen Heldendenkmales am 9. September 1934* (hereafter *Gedenkschrift*), 49.
3. *Gedenkschrift*, 4.
4. For wartime uses of the term *Opfer*, see Maureen Healy, *Vienna and the Fall of the Habsburg Empire: Total War and Everyday Life in World War I* (Cambridge, 2004), chapter 1; also Greg Eghigian and Matthew Paul Berg, eds., *Sacrifice and National Belonging in Twentieth-Century Germany* (College Station, TX, 2002).
5. Oxford English Dictionary (http://dictionary.oed.com, accessed 16 August 2007).
6. Nancy M. Wingfield, *Flag Wars and Stone Saints: How the Bohemian Lands became Czech* (Cambridge, MA, 2007), 16; Ivo Banac, "South Slav Prisoners of War in Revolutionary Russia," in *Essays on World War I: Origins and Prisoners of War*, ed. Samuel R. Williamson and Peter Pastor (New York, 1983), 120.
7. Ernst Hanisch, "Die Rückkehr des Kriegers: Männlichkeitsbilder und Remilitarisierung im Österreich der Zwischenkriegszeit," *Transit/Europäische Revue* 16 (Winter 1998/99): 114.
8. Stefan Goebel, "Re-membered and Re-mobilized: The 'Sleeping Dead' in Interwar Germany and Britain," *Journal of Contemporary History* 39/4 (2004): 487. Goebel distinguishes

between the "grief school" and the "functionalist school" in the historiography of war commemoration.
9. See Bundesdenkmalamt (BDA), Vienna, Kriegerdenkmäler, Fasz 1: 1912–15, Landeskonservatorenamt Salzburg to Staatsdenkmalamt, 12 February 1915. Such calls persisted into peacetime. In 1919, following concerns raised by local residents, a representative of the Federal Memorial Office went to Axams in Tyrol to examine plans for an "ugly and inappropriate" memorial and persuaded the local authorities to opt for one "more fitting for the village." See BDA, Kriegerdenkmäler, Fasz 3: 1918–29, Landesdenkmalamt Innsbruck to Deutschösterreichische Staatsdenkmalamt, 3 July 1919.
10. Fundraising difficulties were exacerbated by a disagreement between the town authorities, who wanted the memorial to be dedicated to the fallen of the town, and the Sapper Association, who felt this would undermine the true meaning of a "memorial built by Sappers for Sappers." It was unveiled by the town authorities against the wishes of the Sapper Association in 1920. ÖStA, AdR, Bundesministerium für Heereswesen (BMfHW), Abteilung 8, karton 695, (34—2/9), Zl. 2341, Sapperdenkmalverein to BMfHW, undated [1920].
11. ÖStA, AdR, BMfHW, Kanzleistelle A, karton 2466, (2—1/5) Zl. 30476, Rudolf Ambrozy, Sapperdenkmalverein to Bundeskanzler Seipel, 10 November 1928. The long and fragmented construction process meant that only three years after the memorial was finally unveiled, repairs were required.
12. ÖStA, AdR, BMfHW, Abteilung 6, karton 3629, (45—4/3), Zl. 47248, Stadtgemeinde Krems an der Donau to BMfHW, October 1933.
13. ÖStA, AdR, BMfHW, Kanzleistelle A, karton 2922, (54—3/1), Zl. 47818, Höhere Bundeslehranstalt und Bundesversuchsstation für Wein, Obst und Gartenbau in Klosterneuburg to BMfHW, 15 October 1930.
14. ÖStA, AdR, BMfHW, Abteilung 5, karton 1637, (27—2/3), Zl. 3481, Österreichischer Radfahrerbund to BMfHW, 31 August 1923.
15. His solution to the problem of inaccessibility was to place a marker referring to the Grossglöckner monument on every other war memorial in Austria: ÖStA, AdR, BMfHW, Kanzleistelle A, karton 1977, (54—3/1), Zl. 7675, Bundesminister für Heerewesen to 6th Brigadekommando, 12 February 1925.
16. ÖStA, AdR, Bundeskanzleramt (BKA) Inneres 15/3, karton 2435, #547/19, Polizei-Direktion Wien report to Staatsamt des Inneres, 5 January 1919.
17. "Das Kriegerdenkmal der Gemeinde Wien im Zentralfriedhof," *Arbeiter-Zeitung*, 29 October 1925.
18. ÖStA, AdR, BMfHW, Kanzleistelle A, karton 3629, (45—4/3) Zl. 3972, Gruppenverband der Kameradschaftsverein ehemaliger Krieger (Heimkehrervereinigungen) für den politischen Bezirk Amstetten, 18 February 1933.
19. *Gedenkschrift*, 43.
20. ÖStA, AdR, BKA Inneres 15/3, karton 2435, #1565/19, Polizei-Direktion Wien report to Staatsamt des Inneres, 12 January 1919.
21. ÖStA, AdR, BMfHW, Abteilung 8, karton 695, (34—1/24) Zl. 6331, Heeresverwaltungsstelle Innsbruck to StAfHW, 9 August 1920.
22. ÖStA, AdR, BMfHW, Kanzleistelle A, karton 2922, (54—3/1), Zl. 54278, Werbeausschuss für das Heldendenkmal des Deutschen Volkes auf Geroldseck to Tiroler Landesregierung, 21 November 1930.
23. ÖStA, AdR, BMfHW, Kanzleistelle A, karton 3147, (54—3/1), Zl. 56513, brochure, Heldenorgel auf Geroldseck, 1931.
24. Ulrike Davy and Thomas Vasek, *Der "Siegfried-Kopf": Eine Auseinandersetzung um ein Denkmal in der Universität Wien* (Vienna, 1991).

25. "'Mit Gott für Freiheit, Ehre und Vaterland': Totenfeier und Enthüllung des Heldendenkmals an der Wiener Universität," *Reichspost*, 10 November 1923. Subsequent ceremonies at the memorial also stressed the German character of the conflict. ÖStA, AdR, BMfHW, Kanzleistelle A, karton 1990, (75—1/3) Zl. 5478, pamphlet, Deutschvölkische Studentenbewegung, 1925.
26. "Stadt Villach, Heldenfeier," *Kärntner Tagespost*, 1 June 1924.
27. ÖStA, AdR, BMfHW, Abteilung 1, karton 923, (31—6/5) Zl. 1852, Linzer Schwarzes Kreuz to BMfHW, 21 October 1921.
28. ÖStA, AdR, BMfHW, Abteilung 5, karton 1930, (75—1/2) Zl. 4321, information from BMfHW to Brigades 1—6.
29. ÖStA, AdR, BMfHW, Kanzleistelle A, karton 1778, (75—1/3), Zl. 36262, BMfHW notice, 4 October 1924.
30. ÖStA, AdR, BMfHW, Kanzleistelle A, karton 1778, (75—1/3), Zl. 36262, Ortskommando Salzburg to BMfHW, 3 November 1924.
31. "Gekaufte Religiosität," *Der freie Soldat*, 1 April 1930.
32. "An die Stätten der Toten," *Tagespost*, 3 November 1924.
33. BDA, Kriegerdenkmäler, Fasz 5: Bezirk Baden, 1930—Traiskirchen. Further examples of memorials in the form of crosses in the district of Baden were from Oeynhausen (1921), Lindabrunn (1922), and Thenneberg (1922).
34. Joachim Giller, Hubert Mader, and Christina Seidl, *"Wo sind sie geblieben?" Kriegerdenkmäler und Gefallenehrung in Österreich* (Vienna, 1992), 102.
35. BDA, Kriegerdenkmäler, Fasz 6: Bezirk Wiener Neustadt, 1930—Gutenstein.
36. Archive of the Federal Police Authority, Vienna (Archiv der Bundespolizeidirektion), Schober Archiv, 47/1922, "Österreicher!" brochure.
37. ÖStA, AdR, BMfHW, Kanzleistelle A, karton 1778, (75—1/1), Zl. 61605, Ortskommando Wiener Neustadt to BMfHW, 4 November 1924.
38. Blair R. Holmes, "The Austrian Monarchists, 1918–1938: Legitimism versus Nazism," in *Conquering the Past: Austrian Nazism Yesterday and Today*, ed. F. Parkinson (Detroit, 1989), 91–109.
39. ÖStA, AdR, BMfHW, Kanzleistelle A, karton 2692, (18—7) Zl. 40399, Verein zur Erhaltung der Gedächtniskirche auf dem Hochschneeberg to BMfHW, undated.
40. ÖStA, AdR, BMfHW, Kanzleistelle A, karton 2922, (50—3/1) Zl. 50725, Vorbereitender Ausschuss der Kaiser-Franz-Josef-Gedächtnisfeier to BMfHW, 15 December 1930.
41. Julius Deutsch, *Schwarzgelbe Verschwörer* (Vienna, 1925), 4. See also "Die Totenfeier des Republikanischen Schutzbundes: Für die Opfer des Weltkrieges," *Arbeiter-Zeitung*, 1 November 1925.
42. ÖStA, AdR, BKA Inneres 15/3 karton 2435 #547/19, Polizei-Direktion Wien report to Staatsamt des Inneres, 5 January 1919.
43. "Eine Ehrung des Feldmarshalls Conrad: Anlässlich seines 50jährigen Offiziersjubiläums," *Innsbrucker Nachrichten*, 5 August 1921.
44. "Die 'Verdienste' Hötzendorfs", *Volkszeitung*, 9 August 1921.
45. "Das Friedensfest in Mauthausen," *Linzer soz. demo. Tagblatt*, 31 May 1924.
46. "Zu Ehren der gefallenen Helden," *Grazer Volksblatt*, 3 November 1924.
47. See Maureen Healy, "Civilizing the Soldier in Postwar Austria," in *Gender and War in Twentieth-Century Eastern Europe*, ed. Nancy M. Wingfield and Maria Bucur (Bloomington, 2006).
48. Robert Weishut, *Vademecum für Heimkehrer* (Alt-Aussee, 1919), 11.
49. Wolfgang Doppelbauer, *Zum Elend noch die Schande: Das altösterreichische Offizierskorps am Beginn der Republik* (Vienna, 1988), 17–18.
50. ÖStA, AdR, BMfHW, Abteilung 1, karton 922, (14—7), Zahl 568, Police report on Antisemitenbund meeting, 14 March 1921.

51. On Jewish veterans in the First Republic and formation of the Bund jüdischer Frontsoldaten Österreichs, see Michael Berger, *Eisernes Kreuz—Doppeladler—Davidstern: Juden in deutschen und österreichisch-ungarischen Armeen. Der Militärdienst jüdischer Soldaten durch zwei Jahrhunderte* (Berlin, 2010), 151–68; Erwin A. Schmidl, "Jews in the Austro-Hungarian Armed Forces, 1867–1918," in *Studies in Contemporary Jewry* vol. 3 (Oxford, 1987), 141–42. For comparative historiography on Jewish veterans' commemorations in Germany, see Tim Grady, "Fighting a Lost Battle: The *Reichsbund jüdischer Frontsoldaten* and the Rise of National Socialism," *German History* 28 (2010): 1–20.
52. ÖStA, AdR, BMfHW, Kanzleistelle A, karton 1778, (75—1/1) Zl. 61605, newspaper cuttings.
53. "Totengedenk- und Denkmalentüllungsfeier der B. e. ö. K. Dem Andenken der Siebenhunderttausend," *Der Plenny*, December 1926.
54. "I. Ehrentag österreichischer Krieger. Allgemeines Wiedersehensfest in Krems," *Der Plenny*, May 1928.
55. "Totengedenk- und Denkmalenthüllungsfeier der B. e. ö. K. Dem Andenken der Siebenhunderttausend," *Der Plenny*, December 1926.
56. AdR, BKA, Inneres 15/3, karton 2435, #1076–19, flyer for "Dank- und Gedächnisfeier für die gefallenen Krieger."
57. Historian Christa Hämmerle has argued that officers' experiences have been universalized and those of common soldiers neglected by historians, due in part to the fact that officer memoirs were more likely to be published. See "'Vor vierzig Monaten waren wir Soldaten, vor einem halben Jahr noch Männer …' Zum historischen Kontext einer 'Krise der Männlichkeit' in Österreich," *L'Homme: Zeitschrift für feministische Geschichtswissenschaft* 19/2 (2008): 64.
58. *Gedenkschrift*, 43.
59. For women's economic and political changes after 1918, see Gabriella Hauch, *Vom Frauenstandpunkt aus: Frauen im Parlament 1919–1933* (Vienna, 1995); on the reactions of some men to these changes, see Elisabeth Malleier's extraordinary article, "Der 'Bund für Männerrechte.' Die Bewegung der 'Männerrechtler' im Wien der Zwischenkriegszeit," *Wiener Geschichtsblätter* 58 (2003): 208–33.
60. Figures from Edmund Glaise von Horstenau et al., eds., *Österreich-Ungarns letzter Krieg*, 7 vols (Vienna, 1930–38), VII: 41–42; and *Mitteilungen der Staatskommission für Kriegsgef.- u. Zivilinterniertenangelegenheiten*, 29 September 1919, 4.
61. *Mitteilungen der Staatskommission für Kriegsgef.- u. Zivilinterniertenangelegenheiten* 2, no. 8–9, 20 March 1920, 1.
62. Gabriella Hauch, "Rights at Last? The First Generation of Female Members of Parliament in Austria," *Contemporary Austrian Studies* 6 (1998): 56–81.
63. *Mitteilungen der Staatskommission* 2, nr 8–9, 20 March 1920, 1.
64. Christa Hämmerle, "'Zur Liebesarbeit sind wir hier, Soldatenstrümpfe stricken wir…' Zu Formen weiblicher Kriegsfürsorge im Ersten Weltkrieg." PhD diss., Vienna 1996.
65. *Mitteilungen der Staatskommission* 1, nr. 3, 28 June 1919, 2.
66. Martin Senekowitsch, *Ein ungewöhnliches Kriegerdenkmal: Das jüdische Heldendenkmal am Wiener Zentralfriedhof* (Vienna, 1994).
67. ÖStA, AdR, BMfLV, Heldendenkmal karton 305, "In Deinem Lager ist Österreich: Fünf Jahrhunderte Geschichte unter Österreichs Kriegsfahnen."
68. ÖStA, AdR, BMfLV, Heldendenkmal karton 304, Wehrmann im Eisen, "Zum Führer durch das österreichische Heldendenkmal."
69. Bundespräsident Miklas in *Gedenkschrift*.
70. *Gedenkschrift*, 7.
71. Ibid., 6.

72. Ibid., 79.
73. "The cult of the fallen soldier became a centerpiece of the religion of nationalism after the war, having its greatest political impact in nations like Germany which had lost the war and had been brought to the edge of chaos by the transition from war to peace": George Mosse, *Fallen Soldiers: Reshaping the Memory of the World Wars* (Oxford, 1990), 7.
74. "Dem Andenken der Gefallenen: Ein Jahr nach dem Waffenstillstand," *Neue Freie Presse,* 1 November 1919.
75. *Die Unzufriedene* 2, nr. 30, 26 July 1924, 1.

Chapter 2

"WAR IN PEACE"
Remobilization and "National Rebirth" in Austria and Hungary

Robert Gerwarth

On 25 May 1919, the conservative Austrian daily, *Innsbrucker Nachrichten*, observed that the end of the Great War had not made Europe a more peaceful place. Under the headline "War in Peace," the paper pointed to the extraordinarily high levels of ethnic and revolutionary violence that had erupted in various parts of Europe since November 1918. The *Innsbrucker Nachrichten* did even have to look as far as Russia to prove its point. The former Habsburg empire, too, was affected by mounting ethnic tensions and revolutionary violence, and it was only a matter of time, the paper maintained, before it would escalate into a civil war in Central Europe.[1]

Paramilitary violence in the successor states was generally most marked in the ethnically diverse borderlands of the shattered Habsburg empire. Irregular Austrian, Hungarian, Ukrainian, and Slovenian militias, "nationalized" through imperial implosion and newly imposed border changes, fought against both internal and external enemies for territorial control, material gain, or ideological fulfillment. In these contested borderlands, military conflict continued unabated, often taking a more unconventional (and sometimes even more brutal) form than during the Great War because the activists were no longer "restrained" by traditional military discipline. It is this wave of postwar paramilitary violence in post-imperial Austria and Hungary, its origins, manifestations, and legacies, which this chapter seeks to explore. More specifically, the purpose is to analyze the ways in which German-Austrian and Magyar veterans and members of the "war youth generation" made the painful transition from war to peace, and how their search for a postwar project to justify their wartime sacrifices found its expression in their attempt to "cleanse the nation" of social elements perceived to be obstacles to a "national rebirth." The chapter will investigate nationalist perceptions of defeat and revolution in the post-1918 rump states of Austria and Hungary and explain how these perceptions and memories served as a source of remobilization in the emergence of right-wing paramilitary groups in both successor states.

Empirically, the investigation will focus on those demobilized officers, officer cadets, and nationalist students who formed the backbone of right-wing paramilitary organizations in both countries. Such an investigation can build upon a surprisingly rich body of largely neglected primary sources, including memoirs, diaries, and letters written by former activists, in which the experiences of the immediate postwar period are narrated from a personal perspective.[2] For this study, samples were taken from the autobiographical accounts and unpublished private papers of more than a dozen Austrian and Hungarian activists who played key roles in the remobilization of the male wartime generation in German-Austria and Hungary. Handled with care, the memoirs, letters, and diaries of those who lived through these turbulent months provide illuminating insights into the deep sense of cultural anxiety, chaos, and personal trauma that shaped the activists' mindsets.

The Great War and the Phenomenon of Postwar Brutalization

The transitional period of 1918–19, characterized by the traumatic experiences of defeat, revolution, and territorial disintegration, had highly divergent effects on the male wartime generation of German-Austria and Hungary. What Benjamin Ziemann has called the "transfiguration" of wartime experiences into peacetime society could take different forms: from conscious abstinence in the world of politics to pacifist activism or indeed a violent refusal to accept the new realities in postwar Central Europe's cultures of defeat. While the vast majority of the roughly seven million Habsburg veterans who had survived the Great War returned to peaceful civilian lives in November 1918, tens of thousands of ex-servicemen did not. They constituted a small, but very active, minority of veterans committed to solving the problems of post-imperial nation-building through the use of violence. But even for those who joined Austrian or Hungarian paramilitary groups after November 1918, the experiences of the postwar period were highly divergent, not least because the levels of actual violence in Austria and Hungary differed remarkably: while approximately 1,500 people died in Hungary in 1919–20, the vast majority of the 859 political murders in interwar Austria occurred in the early 1930s, not in the immediate postwar period.[3]

In order to explain the relative salience of the Austrian right in the years immediately after 1918, two factors need to be taken into consideration.[4] First, the apparently limited activism (in comparison to the situation in Hungary and further east) of the Austrian right owed much to the existence of a strong militarized left, most notably the Volkswehr and the socialist party guard, the Schutzbund.[5] In Tyrol, for example, 12,000 Heimwehr men, two-thirds of them armed, faced roughly 7,500 Schutzbund members in 1922.[6] Both sides kept each other in check and their self-limitation was, in many ways, a strategy for survival since victory in a potential civil war was anything but a foregone conclusion.[7] Hence, throughout the 1920s, both sides largely confined themselves to symbolically charged gestures of military strength such as the largely non-violent Heimwehr and Schutzbund marches through "enemy territory."[8]

Second, and this is frequently ignored in historical analyses of interwar Austria, many of the most violent activists of the right spent much of the period from 1918 to 1921 *outside* Austria. Austrian members of the infamous Freikorps Oberland, for example, including the future Heimwehr leader, Ernst Rüdiger Starhemberg, helped to crush the Munich Council Republic in 1919. During the third Polish Uprising of 1921, to give another example, student volunteers from Innsbruck University joined the Upper Silesian Selbstschutz in its struggle against Polish insurgents.[9] In Hungary, on the other hand, the concrete experience of the Béla Kun dictatorship and the Romanian invasion created a climate in which the desire for violent vengeance seemed much more pressing and feasible, particularly after the victory of Admiral Horthy's counterrevolution.

Despite the important quantitative difference in the levels of postwar violence, paramilitary subcultures in both successor states shared important characteristics. In both Austria and Hungary, the leading figures involved in setting up and running paramilitary organizations of the right were former junior officers such as Hanns Albin Rauter, Ernst Rüdiger Starhemberg, Eduard Baar von Baarenfels, István Hejjas, Pál Prónay, and Gyula Osztenburg, who had been educated and trained in the military academies of the late Habsburg empire.[10] In Hungary, it was not only Gyula Gömbös's powerful veterans' organization MOVE (Magyar Országos Véderő Egylet: Hungarian National Defense Union) or the Union of Awakening Hungarians, but also the much bigger Hungarian National Army that was dominated by former combat officers. Of the 6,568 volunteers who followed Horthy's initial recruitment call of 5 June 1919 for the formation of the counterrevolutionary National Army, almost 3000 were former army and cavalry officers and an additional 800 men were officers from the semi-military border guards, the Gendarmerie. Many of them came from rural backgrounds and notably from border regions where notions of embattled ethnicity were much more tangible than they were in larger cities such as Budapest or Szeged. The large influx of refugees from Transylvania, however, contributed to the further radicalization of the atmosphere in a capital already militarized by the experiences of revolution and temporary foreign occupation.[11]

The vast majority of paramilitary activists in both successor states came from middle- or upper-class backgrounds.[12] Born between the late 1880s and the early 1900s, the activists reached maturity in the turbulent years before or during the Great War which remained the crucial experience of their adolescent lives. As Starhemberg, the future Heimwehr leader who had volunteered for military service in 1916, emphasized in his memoirs, he had been a soldier "with all my body and soul. For me it was the fulfillment of all my dreams and the self-evident purpose of my upbringing!"[13]

The often glorified experience of combat was inextricably linked with notions of the home front's "betrayal," culminating in the central European revolutions of autumn 1918.[14] In explaining their refusal to demobilize and their determination to continue their soldierly existence after November 1918, paramilitary activists in Austria and Hungary frequently invoked the horrors of returning from the front in 1918 to an entirely hostile world of upheaval, triggered by the temporary collapse of military hierarchies and public order.

Hanns Albin Rauter, who returned to Graz at the end of the war, characterized his first contact with the "red mob" as an "eye-opener": "When I finally arrived in Graz, I found that the Communists had taken the streets." Confronted by a group of Communist soldiers, "I pulled my gun and I was arrested. This was how the *Heimat* welcomed me." Being arrested by soldiers of lower rank reinforced Rauter's perception of having returned to a "world turned upside down," a revolutionary environment where hitherto unquestionable norms and values, social hierarchies, institutions, and authorities had suddenly become obsolete.[15]

Experiences in Budapest were not dissimilar. Upon arrival in Hungary from the front in the winter of 1918, the Hussar officer Miklós Kozma was one of many veterans "welcomed" by disorderly crowds shouting abuse at the returning troops as well as by ordinary soldiers physically attacking their officers.[16] The broader central European context of revolutionary turmoil echoed such impressions. The future Austrian Vice-Chancellor and Heimwehr activist, Eduard Baar von Baarenfels, for example, reported back to Austria from revolutionary Munich how he had witnessed jewelry shops being plundered and officers disarmed and insulted.[17] Again and again, it was the "unruly crowd" that featured prominently in these narratives of humiliation. In Kozma's narrative, revolutionary activists always appeared as an effeminate "dirty crowd" often led by "Red Amazons," a crowd "that has not washed in weeks and has not changed their clothes in months; the smell of clothes and shoes rotting on their bodies is unbearable."[18]

What Baarenfels, Rauter, Kozma, and many others described was a nightmare that had haunted Europe's conservative establishment since the French Revolution, a nightmare that had apparently become reality: the triumph of a faceless revolutionary crowd over the forces of law and order. The image they invoked was partly influenced by a vulgarized understanding of Gustave Le Bon's *Psychologie des foules* (1895), whose ideas were widely discussed in rightwing circles across Europe from the turn of the century. Le Bon's juxtaposition of the "barbarian" masses and the "civilized" individual was also reflected in the ways in which many Austrian and Hungarian ex-officers described the humiliating experiences of being stripped of their military decorations by agitated crowds or lower-ranking soldiers.[19] Confronted with public unrest and personal insults, Starhemberg's "bitter anger" over defeat and revolution turned into "a burning desire to return to my soldier's existence as soon as possible, to stand up for the humiliated Fatherland...." Only then, "the shame of a gloomy present" could be forgotten.[20]

Equally important for the remobilization of Austrian and Hungarian veterans was the experience of territorial disintegration. In the Treaty of St Germain, the German-Austrian rump state was forced to cede South Tyrol to Italy, Southern Styria to the Kingdom of Serbs, Croats and Slovenes, Feldsberg and Böhmzell to Czechoslovakia, while also being denied the *Anschluss* with the German Reich, a ruling rightfully interpreted by politicians of the moderate left and right alike as a flagrant violation of the Wilsonian principle of national self-determination. Hungary was hit even harder: it lost two-thirds of its prewar territory and one-third of its population according to the provisions of the Treaty of Trianon.[21]

Until the summer of 1919, and in some cases even later than that, veterans in all successor states, except Czechoslovakia, tried to create new territorial realities through (para-) military action, "realities" which they believed the peacemakers in Paris could not ignore. From November 1918, for example, Austrian volunteers were militarily engaged with Yugoslav troops in Carinthia.[22] As a "victory in defeat," the violent clashes between Yugoslav troops and Austrian volunteers in Carinthia soon played a crucial role in paramilitary memory culture because they testified to the activists' unbroken spirit of defiance against both external enemies and the "weak" central government. "Carinthia" was also synonymous with the Austrian paramilitaries' alleged military superiority over the Slav enemy. A popular poem of 2 May 1919, the day of the "liberation" of the Carinthian village of Völkermarkt, celebrated the Carinthian freedom from the Slav yoke by emphasizing that "the freedom fighters triumphed over treason ... You, Slav, should remember the important lesson that Carinthian fists are hard as iron."[23]

The interconnected experiences of defeat, revolution, and territorial disintegration also contributed to the mobilization and radicalization of the "war youth generation", those adolescent boys who had been too young to serve in the war and who were to gain their first combat experiences on the postwar battlefields of the Burgenland, Styria, Carinthia, or indeed in Upper Silesia, where hundreds of Tyrolese student volunteers fought alongside German Freikorps troops. For many of these young officer cadets and nationalist students, who had grown up on tales of heroic bloodshed but had missed out on their first-hand experience of the "storms of steel," the militias appear to have offered a welcome opportunity to live their fantasies of a romanticized warrior existence. As Starhemberg correctly observed, many members of the war youth generation tried to compensate for their lack of combat experience through "rough militarist behavior", which was "nurtured as a virtue in large parts of postwar youth" and which deeply affected the general tone and atmosphere within paramilitary organizations after 1918.[24]

These younger paramilitaries, who under different circumstances would probably have lived "normal" peaceful existences, were probably motivated by both a violent rejection of an unexpected defeat and revolutionary unrest, and a strong desire to prove themselves in battle. Austrian and Hungarian officer cadets, in particular, who had been mentally and physically prepared for a heroic death on the battlefield, felt a deep sense of betrayal when the war ended abruptly in 1918. Once they had joined paramilitary units dominated by former shock-troop officers, they were keen to prove their worthiness within a community of often highly decorated warriors and "war heroes," a community that offered them the opportunity to act upon their adolescent power fantasies and to live up to the idealized image of militarized masculinity promoted in wartime propaganda.[25]

However, abstract ideological goals and romanticized fantasies about "warriordom" were not the only reasons for joining a paramilitary formation. In addition, and this applied primarily to Hungary, large numbers of landless laborers were attracted by the prospect of theft, plunder, rape, extortion, or simply by the opportunity to settle scores with neighbors of different ethnicity without fear of state reprisals. With respect to Austria (and Germany), local paramilitary groups were often formed because of the fears of disbanded and impoverished soldiers, not with a clearly defined counterrevolutionary aim.[26]

Together, the veterans and members of the war youth generation formed explosive subcultures of ultra-militant masculinity in which violence was not merely perceived as a politically necessary act of self-defense in order to suppress the communist revolts of Central Europe, but also as a positive value in itself, as a morally correct expression of youthful virility that distinguished the activists from the "indifferent" majority of bourgeois society unwilling to rise in the face of revolution and defeat. In marked contrast to the upheaval that surrounded them, the militias offered clearly defined hierarchies and a familiar sense of belonging and purpose. The paramilitary groups were fortresses of soldierly camaraderie and "order" in what the activists perceived to be a hostile world of democratic egalitarianism and communist internationalism. These groups were held together with this spirit of defiance, coupled with the desire to be part of a postwar project that would imbue meaning to an otherwise pointless experience of mass death during war, devalued by defeat. They perceived themselves to be the nucleus of a "new society" of warriors, representing both the eternal values of the nation and new authoritarian concepts for a state in which that nation could thrive.[27]

The paramilitaries' inclination to use violence against their enemies was further exacerbated by the fear of world revolution and news (some true, some exaggerated or imagined) about communist atrocities both inside and outside their respective national communities.[28] Although the actual number of casualties inflicted during the "Red Terror" of 1919 was relatively low, accounts of mass murder, rape, corpse mutilations, and prisoner castrations by revolutionary "savages" in Russia and Central Europe featured very prominently in paramilitaries' autobiographies where they served the purpose of legitimizing the use of violence against dehumanized internal and external enemies accused of pursuing a policy of total annihilation.

Even in Austria, where only five representatives of the state executive were killed by communist insurgents through the course of the revolution, there was an acute fear of being slaughtered by the Reds.[29] As the high school teacher Karl Hellering wrote in the journal *Grobian*: "Before waiting until some Jewish-paid menial crushes my skull with a club or sticks a knife between my ribs, I will rather shoot as long as I have bullets."[30] Since the number of deaths inflicted by revolutionaries in Austria was remarkably low, such paranoid fantasies were largely the result of external events. Local newspapers in Austria frequently offered detailed reports about violent developments in Italy, Finland, Russia, Ukraine, Hungary, and Bavaria which profoundly affected the way in which counterrevolutionary activists in Austria perceived their own situation.[31] The revolutions in Munich and Budapest in particular featured prominently in the minds of Austrian paramilitary activists (if only as a scenario they desperately wanted to avoid) and many of the atrocities attributed to the revolutionary left were a direct reflection of the horror stories about the "Red Terror" that raged in Austria's border-states. In addition, some Heimwehr activists felt inspired by the example of Hungarian or German militias who fought in the borderlands or against communist insurgents, defying the pacifist majority in their countries. "Full of envy," Starhemberg recalled, "we fantasized about participating in the struggles of our German comrades who overthrew the Council Republic after Eisner's assassination, or the actions of the Hungarian volunteer army which restored Hungary's honor under Horthy's leadership."[32]

In Hungary, where the Red Terror of 1919 claimed the lives of between four and five hundred victims, violent fantasies of retribution were based on much more tangible first-hand experiences. The atrocities committed by the "Lenin Boys" under the leadership of József Cserny in particular spurred the imagination of nationalist activists. After the fall of the Béla Kun regime, the time had come to avenge these crimes. The former Hungarian officer, Miklós Kozma, wrote in early August 1919:

We shall see to it … that the flame of nationalism leaps high … We shall also punish. Those who for months have committed heinous crimes must receive their punishment. It is predictable … that the compromisers and those with weak stomachs will moan and groan when we line up a few red rogues and terrorists against the wall. The false slogans of humanism and other "isms" have helped to drive the country into ruin before. This second time they will wail in vain.[33]

Victims of Postwar Retribution

Wherever a temporary power vacuum allowed the militia men to act upon these fantasies of violent retribution, they did. Prominent intellectual critics of the Hungarian White Terror such as the journalist Béla Bacsó and the editor of the Socialist Democratic daily *Népszava*, Béla Somogyi, were abducted and murdered by members of the Prónay battalion.[34] A further seventy-five thousand individuals were imprisoned, and a hundred thousand went into exile, many of them to Soviet Russia where Stalin eventually killed those who had escaped Horthy's death squads. Given that many leaders of the Hungarian revolution, including Béla Kun, managed to escape before they could be arrested, others had to pay for their "treason."[35]

Socialists, Jews, and trade unionists, when caught, were dragged into the barracks and beaten unconscious. "On these occasions," the infamous Hungarian militia leader and temporary head of Horthy's bodyguard, Pál Prónay, recalled, "I ordered an additional fifty strokes with the rod for these fanatic human animals, whose heads were drunk with the twisted ideology of Marx."[36] For Prónay and many others, the dehumanized ("human animal") and denationalized (Bolshevik) enemy could be tortured and killed without remorse because these acts were legitimized and necessitated by the holiness of their cause: the salvation of the nation that was threatened by a socialist abyss and territorial amputation. Against the background of war and revolution, the activists were convinced that they lived in an age of unfettered violence, in which the internal enemy, who had broken the rules of "civilized" military conduct, could only be stopped through the use of the same kind of extreme violence that their opponents were—rightly or wrongly—believed to have employed during the brief "Red Terror" in Bavaria and Hungary.

The postwar project of "cleansing" the nation of its internal enemies was viewed as a necessary precondition for a national rebirth, a form of violent regeneration that would justify the sacrifices of the war despite defeat and revolution. In some ways, this abstract hope for national rebirth out of the ruins of empire was the only thing that held together the highly heterogeneous paramilitary groups in Austria and in Hungary. The paramilitary upsurge of the months after November 1918 looked more like an attack on the new political establishments and the territorial amputations imposed by the Western Allies than a coordinated attempt to create any particular form of authoritarian new order. Despite their common opposition to revolution and the common hope for national revival, the activists involved in right-wing paramilitary action did not necessarily share the same ideological aims and ambitions. Quite the opposite: paramilitary activists of the political right in Austria and Hungary were in fact deeply divided by their divergent visions of the future form of the state. There were strong "legitimist" forces, particularly in the Hungarian community in Vienna, from where two attempts were made to restore the last Habsburg emperor Karl to the throne of St Stephen, and at the same time there were also proto-Fascist activists who despised the monarchy nearly as much as they loathed communism. Some royalist paramilitaries in Austria, too, demanded a restoration of the Habsburg monarchy (though not necessarily under the old Emperor) and found themselves in direct confrontation with those in favor of a syndicalist form of independent Austrian government. Others, notably those organized in the Austro-Bavarian "Oberland League," a radical minority of about a thousand men, favored unification with the German Reich.[37] For the *großdeutsch* right in Austria, defeat and imperial dissolution thus offered another postwar project whose fulfillment would justify the wartime sacrifices: the creation of a Greater German Reich. General Alfred Krauss, for example, who in 1914 had interpreted the Great War itself as a unique opportunity to "renegotiate" the power structure of the Habsburg empire in favor of its German citizens, saw the collapse of the multi-ethnic Habsburg monarchy as an opportunity for the ethnic "unmixing of peoples."[38] "Great is the time in which we live," Krauss noted in 1920 in a somewhat deluded essay, for *großdeutsch* "unification can no longer be hindered."[39]

Furthermore, as the Oberland League phrased it in its pamphlet *The Policy of German Resistance*, national rebirth was only possible through a thoroughly critical engagement with the ideas of 1789, the ideas of the ages of the enlightenment and humanism. "The ideas of 1789 are manifest in modern individualism, bourgeois views on the word and economy, parliamentarianism, and modern democracy.... We members of the Oberland League will continue on our path, marked out by the blood of the German martyrs who have died for the future Reich, and we will continue, then as now, to be the shock troops of the German resistance movement."[40] Waldemar Pabst, the Heimwehr's chief military organizer, articulated similarly abstract ideas when he called for "the replacement of the old trinity of the French Revolution [*liberté, egalité, fraternité*], ... with a new trinity: authority, order, and justice."[41]

Both pamphlets demonstrated quite clearly that the paramilitary world of post-Habsburg Central Europe was a world of action, not ideas. Against whom these actions should be directed was consequently one of the most widely discussed themes in paramilitary circles. For Alfred Krauss, former commander-in-chief of the Habsburg empire's Eastern Armies, the "enemies of the German people" included "the French, the English, the Czechs, the Italians"—a clear indication of the continuity of wartime propaganda after 1918. More dangerous than the nationalist enemies of other countries, however, were the internationalist enemies: "the Red International," the "Black International" (political Catholicism), and, "above all," the "Jewish people that aims to dominate the Germans." All other enemies, Krauss was certain, stood in the paid service of the Jews.[42]

Unsurprisingly, given such widespread sentiments, the Jews, although a small minority of no more than 5 percent of the Austrian and Hungarian populations, suffered most from right-wing paramilitary violence after the Great War. As Jakob Krausz, a Jewish refugee from the Hungarian White Terror, observed in 1922:

> Anti-semitism did not lose its intensity during the war. Quite the opposite: it unfolded in a more beastly way. This war has only made the anti-semites more brutal.... The trenches were flooded with anti-semitic pamphlets, particularly those of the Central Powers. The more their situation deteriorated, the more intense and blood-thirsty the anti-semitic propaganda became. The postwar pogroms in Hungary, Poland, and Ukraine, as well as the anti-semitic campaigns in Germany and Austria were prepared in the trenches.[43]

As Krausz correctly observed, one of the main reasons for the violent anti-semitism in Central Europe after 1918 was that the Jews became the projection screen for everything the paramilitary right despised. Paradoxically, they could simultaneously be portrayed as the embodiment of a pan-Slavic revolutionary menace from "the East" that threatened the traditional order of Christian Central Europe, as "red agents" of Moscow, and as representatives of an obscure "Golden International" and Western democratization.

In Hungary, in contrast to German-Austria, anti-semitic violence was tolerated by the state authorities and at times applauded by the nationalist press.[44] A report on anti-semitic violence published by Vienna's Jewish community in 1922 reported that "more than 3,000 Jews were murdered in Transdanubia," the broad region of Hungary west of the Danube.[45] Although these figures are probably exaggerated, there can be no doubt that the White Terror specifically targeted Jews in substantial numbers. A typical case of anti-semitic violence in Hungary was reported to the police by Ignaz Bing from Bőhőnye in 1919: "During the night before 1 October, a group of sixty White Guards came to our community and ordered that every Jewish man should appear immediately on the market square. The Jewish men, seventeen altogether, who were entirely innocent of Communist activity, followed the order." When they had assembled, "they were beaten and tortured and—without any interrogation—they [the soldiers] started hanging them." This was an act of violence that served the dual purpose of eliminating the "source of Bolshevism" and providing a public demonstration of what would happen to an enemy who fell into their hands.[46]

In Austria, anti-semitism was similarly widespread though it never even remotely assumed a similar violent character prior to 1938. Before 1914, anti-semitism in Austria had been common currency among right-wing politicians who bitterly complained about the high numbers of Jews from Galicia and the Bukovina who had migrated to Vienna. When in 1918 Galicia fell to Poland and the Bukovina to Romania, the number of Jewish migrants further increased, accelerated by large-scale pogroms in Galicia and Ukraine. In 1918, 125,000 Jews lived in Vienna, although German-Austrian nationalists maintained that the number was as high as 450,000.[47] The postwar influx of "Eastern Jews" fanned anti-semitic feelings in Vienna that—since the days of Karl Lueger and Georg von Schönerer—were never far from the surface and had been reinforced by the popular wartime stereotype of the "Jewish profiteer."[48] After 1918, right-wing veterans maintained that "the Jew" had become the "slaveholder" of a defenseless German people, determined "to exploit our peril in order to make good business ... and to squeeze out our last drop of blood."[49] The identification of "the Jewish people" as the "wire-pullers" behind revolution and imperial collapse was generally linked to the hope that "the German giant will rise again one day" and that then, "the day of reckoning must come for all the treason, hypocrisy, and barbarism, for all their crimes against the German people and against humanity."[50]

As in Hungary, anti-semites in Austria usually appealed to Christian principles and linked the notion of Jewish responsibility for the military collapse to older Christian stereotypes of "Jewish treason."[51] Consequently, Christian Social politicians such as the Tyrolese Heimwehr leader, Richard Steidle, suggested that "only a thorough reckoning with the spirit of Jewry and its helpers can save the German Alpine lands."[52] Anti-semitism after 1918 was further exacerbated by the widespread perception that a "Jewish conspiracy" was at the heart of the revolutions of 1918–19. The fact that the intellectual leader of the Red Guards, Leo Rothziegel, and prominent members of the Social Democratic Party such as Victor Adler and Otto Bauer were Jewish was constantly referred to.

In Hungary, too, the revolution and the "Red Terror" of the immediate postwar period were, in the eyes of conservative officers, inextricably linked with Jews, most importantly with the revolutionary leader, Béla Kun, and his chief military advisor, Tibor Szamuely.[53] Immediately after the fall of the Kun regime in early August 1919, the lawyer Oszkár Szőllősy published a widely circulated newspaper article on "The Criminals of the Dictatorship of the Proletariat," in which he identified Jewish "red, blood-stained knights of hate" as the main perpetrators of the Red Terror and the driving force behind Communism.[54] In Hungary (as in Austria), Jews were also held directly responsible for the military defeat of the Central Powers. According to Gyula Gömbös, Hungary's later prime minister, defeat was a direct consequence of the fact that the Jewish proportion of Habsburg empire's population was substantially higher (1:56) than in the Entente countries (1:227).[55]

To proclaim publicly one's anti-semitism and to pride oneself on having used merciless violence against Jewish civilians subsequently became a common mark of distinction among the paramilitary activists of Central Europe. In Hungary, where paramilitary atrocities against Jews were usually carried out with the tacit acquiescence of the authorities, the situation was particularly extreme. Pál Prónay, for example, collected the chopped-off ears of his Jewish victims as lucky charms.[56] At a dinner party conversation, one of Prónay's officers, György Geszay, proudly remarked that he had an excellent appetite that evening as he had spent the afternoon roasting a Jew alive in a train locomotive.[57]

In Austria, the situation was far less extreme. However, the language of violence used by Austrian paramilitaries certainly foreshadowed the infinitely more dramatic wave of anti-Jewish violence of the late 1930s and 1940s. Whether Hanns Albin Rauter expressed his aim to "get rid of the Jews as soon as possible" as a student leader in Graz, or Starhemberg attacked the "Jewish war profiteers" as "parasites," the rhetoric of violent anti-semitism constituted a tradition on which radical nationalists would build in subsequent decades.[58]

Crude notions of violently "unmixing" the ethnic complexity of the Habsburg lands, coupled with militant anti-Bolshevism and radicalized anti-semitism created fateful legacies for both successor states. The Hungarian White Terror revealed much of the later chauvinist and racist mood in the country, notably through its sudden and sanguinary animus against the Jews. It was revived with added fury (and on a broader popular basis) in the 1930s, exacerbated by the frustrations caused by the Great Depression. In Austria, too, anti-semitism and anti-Slav sentiments would resurface with renewed intensity after the brief moment of political stabilization in the mid-1920s gave way to economic depression and political turmoil. For many Austrian and Hungarian Fascists of the 1930s, the experiences of 1918–19 provided a decisive catalyst for political radicalization and a catalogue of political agendas whose implementation was merely postponed during the years of relative stability after 1923. Some of the most prominent paramilitary activists of the immediate postwar period would resurface in the central European dictatorships of the right. In Hungary, Ferenc Szálasi and many other Arrow Cross members of the 1940s, including the infamous militia leader Pál Prónay, repeatedly pointed to the period between November 1918 and the signing of Trianon as the moment of their political awakening. In Austria, too, personal continuities between the immediate postwar period and the late 1930s are easy to identify. Robert Ritter von Greim, leader of the Tyrolean branch of the Oberland League after 1922, became Hermann Göring's successor as commander of the German Luftwaffe in 1945; Hanns Albin Rauter, who had contributed decisively to the radicalization of the *großdeutsch* wing of the Styrian Heimwehr, became Higher SS and Police Chief in the Nazi-occupied Netherlands, while his compatriot and friend, Ernst Kaltenbrunner, succeeded Reinhard Heydrich as head of the Nazis' Reich Security Main Office. For all of these men, the Fascist dictatorships provided the opportunity to settle old scores and "solve" some of the issues which the inglorious defeat of 1918 had raised.

Yet, the relationship between post-1918 paramilitarism and Nazism was more complicated than is often suggested. Many of the most prominent paramilitaries of the immediate postwar period—including Horthy and Starhemberg—were dedicated anti-Bolsheviks and committed anti-semites in 1918, but their conservatism and regional loyalties made them suspicious in the eyes of the Nazis. Starhemberg, who had entertained close personal relations with Hitler until 1923 (and participated in the unsuccessful Munich putsch of 1923), began to oppose the Austrian Nazi movement throughout the 1930s, rejected his own postwar anti-semitism as "nonsense," insisted on Austrian independence in 1938, and even served in the British and Free French forces during World War II.[59] Starhemberg was not the only prominent former paramilitary leader whose vision for a national Austrian "rebirth" was incompatible with that of Nazism. Captain Karl Burian, founder and head after 1918 of the monarchist combat organization Ostara, paid for his continued royalist beliefs in the 1930s with his arrest by the Gestapo and execution in 1944.[60] Not entirely dissimilar to the situation in Germany, where the direct personal continuities between the Freikorps and the Third Reich ended with the Night of the Long Knives (1934), some Austrian paramilitary veterans came to realize that Nazism was not always compatible with the ideas for which they had fought in 1918.

National Redemption Through Violent Exclusion

Post-imperial Austria and Hungary witnessed the emergence of a sizeable paramilitary subculture, one that was shaped by the successive traumatizing experiences of war, defeat, revolution, and territorial disintegration. Those members of the male wartime generation active in this subculture fed on a doctrine of hyper-nationalism and shared a determination to use violence in order to suppress a (real or imagined) revolutionary threat and to avenge their perceived humiliations at the hands of external and internal enemies.

If the war laid the foundation for the creation of a violent subculture of demobilized officers, defeat and revolution significantly contributed to the radicalization and enlargement of this paramilitary milieu. Former officers brutalized by the war and infuriated by the outcome joined forces with, and transmitted their "values" to, members of a younger generation, who compensated for their lack of combat experience by often surpassing the war veterans in terms of radicalism, activism, and brutality. Together the veterans and members of the war youth generation formed an ultra-militant masculine subculture that differed from the "community of the trenches" in its social makeup, its "liberation" from the constraints of military discipline, and its self-imposed postwar mission of destroying both the external and internal enemy in order to pave the way for national rebirth.

Everywhere in the region, anti-Bolshevism, anti-semitism, and anti-Slavism—often amalgamated into a single enemy image of "Jewish-Slav Bolshevism"—operated as touchstones for paramilitary movements. Unlike during the Great War, violence was primarily directed against civilians and more specifically against those perceived to be "community aliens" who had to be "removed" in one way or another before a new utopian society could emerge from the debris caused by defeat and revolution. The desire to "cleanse" their new nation-states from these broadly defined enemies went hand-in-hand with common dislike of their now overblown "Red" capitals, Vienna and Budapest, and a fundamental distrust of the democratic, capitalist West whose promises of national self-determination clashed violently with postwar realities in Austria and Hungary. If, however, paramilitaries in the successor states shared similar fantasies of violence, they differed in their ability to realize these fantasies. Whereas in post-revolutionary Hungary, fantasies turned into reality on a large scale, Austrian paramilitaries at home either had to "confine" themselves to small-scale fighting in the Austrian borderlands with Yugoslav troops or they had to join forces with German Freikorps in Munich or Upper Silesia where violent action against similar enemy groups was possible.

Although a small minority everywhere in the former Habsburg monarchy, paramilitary activists managed to overcome their marginality among the majority of Austrian and Hungarian veterans by creating parallel universes of tightly knit veteran communities with few ties to mainstream society and by linking their postwar fate to similar paramilitary groups in other defeated states of Central Europe who shared their determination to challenge the moral and political authority of the postwar European order.

These international ties with other revisionist forces in Central Europe were one of the lasting legacies of the immediate transitional period from war to "peace." Perhaps more importantly, those members of the male wartime generation in Austria and Hungary that continued their military careers well into the postwar period, created a language (and practices) of violent exclusion of all those they perceived as obstacles to a future national rebirth, which could justify the sacrifices made during the war. It was this legacy of national redemption through violent exclusion which proved to be of fatal significance for the successor states in subsequent decades.

Robert Gerwarth is Professor of Modern History at UCD and Director of the Dublin Centre for War Studies. He has held research fellowships or visiting professorships at Harvard, the Institute for Advanced Study in Princeton, and Sciences Po Paris. In 2013–14 he was a Humboldt Senior Research Fellow at the Herder Institute and a Fernand Braudel Fellow at the EUI. He has published widely on the history of violence in the twentieth century, including the co-edited volumes *War in Peace: Paramilitary Violence in Europe after the Great War* (2012, with John Horne) and *Empires at War, 1911–23* (2014, with Erez Manela).

Notes

I am most grateful for the financial support I received to work on this project from the Irish Research Council for the Humanities and Social Sciences, the Harry Frank Guggenheim Foundation and the European Research Council. I also thank Dr Ursula Falch for her helpful research assistance, and the Starhemberg family for granting me unrestricted access to the private papers of Ernst Rüdiger Starhemberg in the Upper Austrian Provincial Archive, Linz (Oberösterreichisches Landesarchiv: hereafter OÖLA).

1. *Innsbrucker Nachrichten*, 25 May 1919.
2. On this genre of "ego-documents," see Michael Epkenhans et al., eds., *Militärische Erinnerungskultur: Soldaten im Spiegel von Biographien, Memoiren und Selbstzeugnissen* (Paderborn, 2006).
3. On the "transfigurations" in postwar Germany, see Benjamin Ziemann, *War Experiences in Rural Germany 1914–1923* (Oxford and New York, 2007), 214ff. The exact number of deaths inflicted by postwar paramilitary violence is still disputed. For Hungary, a member of the 1918 Károlyi government, Oszkár Jászi, estimated that the counterrevolution claimed the lives of at least four thousand victims, but this figure has recently been revised down to fifteen hundred. See Oszkár Jászi, *Revolution and Counter-Revolution in Hungary* (London, 1924), 120; Béla Bodo, "Paramilitary Violence in Hungary after the First World War," *East European Quarterly* 38 (2004): 167. For Austria, Gerhard Botz has established the relatively low figure of 859 victims of political violence during the First Austrian Republic (12 November 1918 to 11 February 1934), but this figure does not account for the murders committed by the numerous Austrian volunteers who fought in German Freikorps. See Gerhard Botz, *Gewalt in der Politik: Attentate, Zusammenstöße, Putschversuche, Unruhen in Österreich 1918 bis 1938*, 2nd ed. (Munich, 1983), 237.
4. On the salience of the Austrian revolution, see John W. Boyer, "Silent War and Bitter Peace: The Revolution of 1918 in Austria," *Austrian History Yearbook* 34 (2003): 1–56.
5. On this, with particular reference to the Tyrol, see Richard Schober, "Die paramilitärischen Verbände in Tirol 1918–1927," in *Tirol und der Anschluß: Voraussetzungen, Entwicklungen, Rahmenbedingungen 1918-1938*, ed. Thomas Albrich et al. (Innsbruck, 1988), 113–41.
6. Verena Lösch, "Die Geschichte der Tiroler Heimatwehr von ihren Anfängen bis zum Korneuburger Eid (1920–1930),"PhD diss., Innsbruck 1986, 162.
7. Gerhard Botz, "Handlungsspielräume der Sozialdemokratie während der 'Österreichischen Revolution'," in *Festschrift Mélanges Felix Kreissler*, ed. Rudolf Altmüller et al. (Vienna, 1985), 16.
8. See Österreichisches Staatsarchiv, Vienna (hereafter ÖStA), Kriegsarchiv, B 60/5e, Krauss papers: Alfred Krauss, "Revolution 1918?" 1.

9. Michael Gehler, "Studentischer Wehrverband im Grenzlandkampf: Exemplarische Studie zum 'Sturmzug Tirol' in Oberschlesien 1921," *Oberschlesisches Jahrbuch* 5 (1989): 33–63; Michael Gehler, *Studenten und Politik: Der Kampf um die Vorherrschaft an der Universität Innsbruck 1918–1938* (Innsbruck, 1990); Sabine Falch, "Zwischen Heimatwehr und Nationalsozialismus: Der 'Bund Oberland' in Tirol," in *Geschichte und Region* 6 (1997): 51–86; Hans Steinacher, *Oberschlesien* (Berlin, 1927).
10. See, for example, the very detailed autobiographical account of this education: ÖStA, B 844/74, Heydendorff papers: Ernst Heydendorff, "Kriegsschule 1912–1914."
11. Béla Kelemen, *Adatok a szegedi ellenforradalom és a szegedi kormány történetéhez* (Szeged, 1923), 495–96.
12. For Hungary: Kelemen, *Adatok*, 495–96. For Austria, Walter Wiltschegg, *Die Heimwehr: Eine unwiderstehliche Volksbewegung?* (Munich, 1985), 274–80.
13. OÖLA, Starhemberg papers: Ernst Rüdiger Starhemberg, "Aufzeichnungen des Fürsten Ernst Rüdiger Starhemberg im Winter 1938/39 in Saint Gervais in Frankreich," 16.
14. On the deterioration of the relationship between the home front and the military front in the later stages of the war, see Richard G. Plaschka, et al., eds., *Innere Front: Militärassistenz, Widerstand und Umsturz in der Donaumonarchie 1918*, 2 vols. (Munich, 1974); Mark Cornwall, *The Undermining of Austria-Hungary: The Battle for Hearts and Minds* (New York, 2000); Manfred Rauchensteiner, *Der Erste Weltkrieg und das Ende der Habsburgermonarchie* (Vienna, Cologne, and Weimar, 2013). That the revolution was brought about by men who had not served at the front was a common accusation made by right-wing veterans. See, for example, Starhemberg, "Aufzeichnungen," 21
15. Netherlands Institute for War, Holocaust and Genocide Studies, Amsterdam (hereafter NIOD): Rauter papers, Doc I 1380, H, 2.
16. Miklós Kozma, *Makensens Ungarische Husaren: Tagebuch eines Frontoffiziers, 1914–1918* (Berlin and Vienna, 1933), 459.
17. ÖStA, B 120/1: Eduard Baar von Baarenfels, "Erinnerungen (1947)," 10–13. See also Anita Korp, "Der Aufstieg vom Soldaten zum Vizekanzler im Dienste der Heimwehr: Eduard Baar von Baarenfels," MA thesis, Vienna 1998.
18. Kozma, *Ungarische Husaren*, 461. On the "Red Amazons," see also the article in *Innsbrucker Nachrichten*, 23 March 1919, 2.
19. Starhemberg, "Aufzeichnungen," 16–17. See also Emil Fey, *Schwertbrüder des Deutschen Ordens* (Vienna, 1937), 218–20.
20. Starhemberg, "Aufzeichnungen," 20–22.
21. For a general account of the effects of St Germain and Trianon, see Robert Evans, "The Successor States," in *Twisted Paths: Europe 1914–45*, ed. Robert Gerwarth (Oxford, 2007), 210–36.
22. On Carinthia, see *Darstellungen aus den Nachkriegskämpfen deutscher Truppen und Freikorps*, vols. 7 and 8 (Berlin, 1941–42); and the autobiographical account by Jaromir Diakow, in: ÖStA, B727, Diakow papers. See also Walter Blasi, *Erlebte österreichische Geschichte am Beispiel des Jaromir Diakow*, unpublished MA thesis, Vienna, 1995.
23. On Carinthia and a reprint of the poem, see the anonymous text "Der Sturm auf Völkermarkt am 2. Mai 1919," in ÖStA, Kriegsarchiv, B 694, Knaus papers, 31.
24. Starhemberg, "Aufzeichnungen," 26.
25. Robert Gerwarth, "The Central European Counter-Revolution: Paramilitary Violence in Germany, Austria and Hungary after the Great War," *Past & Present* 200 (2008): 175–209.
26. Béla Bodó, "Militia Violence and State Power in Hungary, 1919–1922," *Hungarian Studies Review* 33 (2006): 121–67, particularly 131–32; Ziemann, *War Experiences*, 227ff.
27. Jürgen Reulecke, *"Ich möchte einer werden so wie die …": Männerbünde im 20. Jahrhundert* (Frankfurt am Main, 2001), 89ff.

28. See for example: "Revolution überall," *Innsbrucker Nachrichten*, 12 November 1918, 2; "Bestialische Ermordung von Geiseln" [by Bavarian Communists], *Innsbrucker Nachrichten*, 3 May 1919, 2.
29. Botz, *Gewalt,* 229–30.
30. Hellering, as quoted in: Botz, *Gewalt,* 91.
31. See, for example, the following articles in the *Innsbrucker Nachrichten*: "Der Krieg im Frieden," 25 May 1919; "Gegen den Bolschewismus," 17 November 1918; "Die Sowjetherrschaft in Ungarn," 26 March 1919; "Die Verhältnisse in Bayern," 10 April 1919; and "Bayern als Räterepublik," 8 April 1919.
32. Starhemberg, "Aufzeichnungen," 23. In a transnational context, see Gerwarth, "Central European Counter-Revolution," 175–209. See also Bruno Thoss, *Der Ludendorff-Kreis: München als Zentrum der mitteleuropäischen Gegenrevolution zwischen Revolution und Hitler-Putsch* (Munich, 1978); Lajos Kerekes, "Die 'weiße' Allianz: Bayerisch-österreichisch-ungarische Projekte gegen die Regierung Renner im Jahre 1920," *Österreichische Osthefte* 7 (1965): 353–66; Ludger Rape, *Die österreichischen Heimwehren und die bayerische Rechte 1920–1923* (Vienna, 1977); Horst G. Nusser, *Konservative Wehrverbände in Bayern, Preussen und Österreich* (Munich, 1973).
33. Miklós Kozma, *Az összeomlás 1918–1919* (Budapest, 1935), 380. On Kozma's war experience, see Kozma, *Tagebuch eines Frontoffiziers 1914–1918.*
34. On the assassination of Somogyi and Bacsó, see Ernő Gergely and Pál Schönwald, *A Somogyi-Bacsó-Gyilkosság* (Budapest, 1978).
35. Rudolf Tökés, *Béla Kun and the Hungarian Soviet Republic: The Origins and Role of the Communist Party of Hungary in the Revolutions of 1918–1919* (New York and Stanford, 1967), 159. See also Gyorgy Borsanyi, *The Life of a Communist Revolutionary: Béla Kun* (New York, 1993).
36. Pál Prónay, *A határban a halál kaszál: fejezetek Prónay Pál feljegyzéseiből,* ed. Ágnes Szabó and Ervin Pamlényi (Budapest, 1963), 90. See also Bela Bodo, *Pál Prónay: Paramilitary Violence and Anti-Semitism in Hungary* (Pittsburgh, 2011).
37. See Hans Jürgen Kuron, "Freikorps und Bund Oberland," PhD diss., Munich 1960, 134; Falch, "Bund Oberland," 51; Lösch, "Die Geschichte der Tiroler Heimatwehr," 162.
38. ÖStA, B 60, Krauss papers: Alfred Krauss, "Schaffen wir ein neues, starkes Österreich!" (1914).
39. Alfred Krauss, *Unser Deutschtum!* (Salzburg, 1920), 8–9.
40. ÖStA, B 1477: "Die Politik des deutschen Widerstands" (1931).
41. Bundesarchiv (Berlin), Pabst papers, NY4035/6, 37–39. On Pabst, see also Doris Kachulle, *Waldemar Pabst und die Gegenrevolution* (Berlin, 2007).
42. Krauss, *Unser Deutschtum!,* 7–13.
43. Jakob Krausz, ed., *Martyrium: ein jüdisches Jahrbuch* (Vienna, 1922), 17. See also Frank M. Schuster, *Zwischen allen Fronten: Osteuropäische Juden während des Ersten Weltkriegs (1914–1919)* (Cologne, 2004).
44. On Hungarian anti-semitism after 1918, see Robert M. Bigler, "Heil Hitler and Heil Horthy! The Nature of Hungarian Racist Nationalism and its Impact on German-Hungarian Relations 1919–1945," *East European Quarterly* 8 (1974): 251–72; Béla Bodo, "'White Terror,' Newspapers and the Evolution of Hungarian Anti-Semitism after World War I," *Yad Vashem Studies* 34 (2006); Nathaniel Katzburg, *Hungary and the Jews: Policy and Legislation, 1920–1943* (Ramat Gan, 1981); and Rolf Fischer, *Entwicklungsstufen des Antisemitismus in Ungarn, 1867–1939: Die Zerstörung der magyarisch-jüdischen Symbiose* (Munich, 1998).
45. Josef Halmi, "Akten über die Pogrome in Ungarn," in Krausz, *Martyrium,* 59. See also Oskar Jászi, *Magyariens Schuld: Ungarns Sühne* (Munich, 1923), 168–79; Josef Pogány, *Der Weiße*

Terror in Ungarn (Vienna, 1920); British Joint Labour Delegation to Hungary, *The White Terror in Hungary: Report of the British Joint Labour Delegation to Hungary* (London, 1920); and The National Archives (TNA), London: FO 371/3558/206720: "The Jews in Hungary: Correspondence with His Majesty's Government, presented to the Jewish Board of Deputies and the Council of the Anglo-Jewish Association," October 1920.
46. Halmi, "Pogrome," 64.
47. See Bruce F. Pauley, "Politischer Antisemitismus im Wien der Zwischenkriegszeit," in *Eine zerstörte Kultur: Jüdisches Leben und Antisemitismus in Wien seit dem 19. Jahrhundert*, ed. Gerhard Botz et al. (Buchloe, 1990), 221–23.
48. On the history of anti-semitism before 1914 see Peter Pulzer, *The Rise of Political Anti-Semitism in Germany and Austria*, 2nd revised edition (Cambridge, MA, 1988); and John W. Boyer, "Karl Lueger and the Viennese Jews," *Yearbook of the Leo Baeck Institute*, xxvi (1981), 125–44. On the image of the "Jewish profiteer" in wartime Vienna, see Maureen Healy, *Vienna and the Fall of the Habsburg Empire: Total War and Everyday Life in World War I* (Cambridge, 2004). On anti-semitism in Austrian universities, see Michael Gehler, *Studenten und Politik: Der Kampf um die Vorherrschaft an der Universität Innsbruck 1919–1938* (Innsbruck, 1990), 93–98.
49. Krauss, *Unser Deutschtum!*, 20.
50. Ibid., 16–17.
51. See, for example, the article series on "The Racial-Political Causes of the Collapse," *Neue Tiroler Stimmen*, 9, 10, and 30 December 1918 and 2 January 1919, as quoted in F.L. Carsten, *Revolution in Central Europe, 1918–1919* (London, 1972), 261. See also *Innsbrucker Nachrichten*, 8 April 1919. On the broader context, see Paul Rena, "Der christlichsoziale Antisemitismus in Wien 1848–1938," PhD diss., Vienna 1991; and Christine Sagoschen, "Judenbilder im Wandel der Zeit: die Entwicklung des katholischen Antisemitismus am Beispiel jüdischer Stereotypen unter besonderer Berücksichtigung der Entwicklung in der ersten Republik," PhD diss., Vienna 1998.
52. *Tagespost* (Graz), 27 May 1919.
53. On the continued importance of such views in the Hungarian Army, see Thomas Lorman, "The Right-Radical Ideology in the Hungarian Army, 1921–23," *Central Europe* 3 (2005): 67–81, esp. 76.
54. Oszkár Szőllősy, "The Criminals of the Dictatorship of the Proletariat," as printed in Cecile Tormay, *An Outlaw's Diary*, 2 vols. (London, 1923), 2: 226.
55. Thomas Sakmyster, "Gyula Gömbös and the Hungarian Jews, 1918–1936," *Hungarian Studies Review* 8 (2006): 161.
56. Bodo, "Paramilitary Violence," 134.
57. Bundesarchiv (Koblenz), Bauer papers, NL 22/69: memoirs of Max Bauer's secretary, 33
58. NIOD, Rauter papers, Doc I 1380 Pr 6-12-97, 46–47; OÖLA, Starhemberg papers: Starhemberg, "Meine Stellungnahme zur Judenfrage."
59. In the 1930s, Starhemberg rejected the myth of a Jewish world conspiracy as "nonsense" and "scientific" racism as a propagandistic "lie." See ibid.
60. See the Gestapo file on Burian, in ÖStA, B 1394, Burian papers.

Chapter 3

APOCALYPSE AND THE QUEST FOR A SUDETEN GERMAN MÄNNERBUND IN CZECHOSLOVAKIA

Mark Cornwall

In Germany before 1914, a key theme pursued by the enigmatic poet Stefan George was that a violent catastrophe had to occur in order to produce the necessary national renaissance. In his most elaborate work, *The Seventh Ring* (1907), he coldly portrayed the dawning of a new world after mass slaughter where leadership in society would be assumed by an elite of young male heroes.[1] In postwar Czechoslovakia in the wake of just such a slaughter, George's apocalyptic vision gained a fervent following in some nationalist circles among the so-called Sudeten German minority. In Sudeten German literature of the 1920s, a consistent idea was the dream of some "national rebirth"—either focused on the Sudeten Germans or as part of a broader German revival. The poetry of one southern Bohemian writer, Hans Watzlik, was typical. He urged his fellow men to cultivate their native soil assiduously, for "out of fire, ruins, torment and blood / our people must blossom in a new miracle / rising into spring and eternity."[2]

This Sudeten German national mission was to be completed in the future, in contrast to that of the Czechs who in 1918 had supposedly regained independence for their age-old nation after centuries of servitude. For many Sudeten nationalists the mission was a way of making sense of four years of otherwise meaningless sacrifice—perhaps a hundred and twenty thousand deaths—and of coping with their invidious subordinate position in a Czechoslovak national state. They set out fresh and positive goals: first to build up and unite a Sudeten

German *Volk*, then to challenge the Czech "dominance" introduced suddenly into Central Europe.

From the start, many national agitators, eager to cultivate a specifically Sudeten German *Heimat*, envisaged "male youth" as playing a crucial role in the new crusade. Youth after all represented regeneration, like a fountain spurting up in a lake as one youth leader described them.[3] The postwar generation would replace those young men from the German Bohemian lands who, though lost in the conflict, were still deemed immortal since their "national sacrifice" would continue in a revitalized form. In the post-apocalyptic world, a mass of youth groups quickly sprang up across the German regions of Czechoslovakia. They catered to adolescents who had missed out on the war experience, but were also stimulated by "youthful" adult mentors who had been traumatized by the war and sought new meaningful ventures in peacetime.

Most of the key Sudeten youth leaders of the 1920s had specific views on what needed to be learned and passed on from the wartime experience. They could all agree on the need for some generic "*Heimat* renewal," but a key matter of dispute became how far to focus on a cultural or political agenda. While some saw education as an end in itself, or at least a national development with a "slow burn," others were impatient to channel youth in a more immediate, politicized direction in order to solve the contemporary national crisis. It was particularly the Turner gymnastics movement (the Deutsche Turnverband) that took the lead in this regard in Czechoslovakia. By the late 1920s the movement was developing a quasi-military framework with precepts of leadership, discipline, and obedience to the fore, in order to create an elite male league or Männerbund. Early in the 1930s, it was calling upon all adolescents to enter its organization. The Turner movement pushed itself forward as the leading educational body for the *Volk*, the place where Sudeten young men would undergo a systematic and disciplined training in order to become the vanguard of the nation.

This vibrant postwar pedagogic youth mission, with its concomitant quest to shape a Sudeten Männerbund, has been marginalized in the historiography of interwar Czechoslovakia, largely confined to the memoirs of youth leaders and receiving little attention from historians, either German or Czech.[4] Yet it was crucial to the formation of the new interwar Sudeten German identity, and it does much to explain the real dynamism of Sudeten German nationalism in the 1930s, especially its ability to challenge the Czechoslovak national state through a fresh generation. As a youth case study—one of "regeneration from defeat" or life out of death—it deserves comparison with youth campaigns elsewhere in East-Central Europe, particularly in terms of the generational experience.[5]

It also serves as an important regional study of the Männerbund. This phenomenon has received some attention from historians in a specific German Reich context but, as Jürgen Reulecke has noted, there is much scope for investigating it further afield geographically.[6] There were some German men from the

Bohemian Lands who, on returning from the front, sought out new opportunities for male-bonding and comradeship in their local communities. To paraphrase one historian, some returnees—albeit a minority—"transfigured their war memories" into militant public activities in peacetime.[7] In Czechoslovakia in the 1920s they would be a small but restless element. And they lived alongside that majority of veterans who wished simply to forget the trenches and return to civilian normality, or, at most, occasionally to meet up with former comrades for social or commemorative occasions.[8]

The Männerbund Tradition in the Bohemian Lands

Let us first probe the concept of the Männerbund. The way that it gradually invaded the discourse of Sudeten German nationalists in the postwar decade can best be illustrated through the perspective of one leading exponent, the later head of the Turnverband, Konrad Henlein. As a war veteran, respected in his local community near Reichenberg (Liberec), he threw himself into the regional Turner movement of north Bohemia after 1919 and sought to reverse alleged emasculation and lack of discipline in the ranks. In 1925, one of his first articles in the *Turnzeitung* pressed Turners to "dress in a manly way":

> Our age bears all the signs of decadence and decline. Maleness [*Mannestum*] and a sense of heroism have been rare among us Germans: a weaker, slacker, more effeminate trait is dominant, something emasculating which will never be constructive for our people!

While effeminate men could dress foppishly with decorated shoes, puffed-out trousers (covering flabby, weak-kneed legs) and pretty, colorful ankles, the Turner costume should be completely different:

> We want to dress in a smart, tasteful, and noble fashion, eschewing all slovenliness. But what we wear should be close-fitting, neat and manly, displaying the same spirit that lives in us! We Turners want to be complete men! And our dress should be worthy of German men![9]

A few years later, when he had moved up the Turner hierarchy, Henlein was publicly using the word "Männerbund" to describe an organization with a radical agenda for governing Sudeten German society. Indeed, by 1930 he portrayed his Sudeten Turnverband as part of a widespread common-sense phenomenon sweeping across central Europe. In his words, "disciplined Männerbünde rule the present: Fascism, the Hitler movement, the Heimwehr, etc."[10]

This privileging of a particular hegemonic masculinity by many Sudeten German nationalists was shaped by their trench trauma. At the front, they had passed through their formative lifetime experience, living and suffering in an overwhelmingly male world that had divorced and alienated them from the norms of civilian society. But the outcome meshed too with theories nurtured in the wartime youth movement in the (German) Bohemian Lands. Thus the postwar Sudeten German Männerbund was to be honed from complex and diverse sources; and it would steadily change shape as it found new hosts to accommodate it.

The original Männerbund concept stemmed from Germany, ascribed usually to the ethnographer Heinrich Schurtz and his seminal work of 1902, *Altersklassen und Männerbünde*. On the basis of anthropological observation, Schurtz had concluded that while women were motivated solely by the family, for men there was a "social urge" that went far beyond it. The key foundations for public life and the state were the "sympathetic unions" made between young men and, even when they had married, men tended to indulge in a *männerbundisch* lifestyle that set them comfortably apart from the female.[11]

This basic notion was taken up and "sexualized" a few years later by Hans Blüher, the first historian of the Wandervogel, the key youth movement of Germany.[12] In his prewar writing, Blüher had caused a furor by describing the Wandervogel as an "erotic phenomenon": a model body of male friendships that, particularly between older and younger lads, had a conscious "erotic tone." Although this could produce physical homosexual desire and expression, Blüher, like the classical Greek philosophers Plato and Socrates, estimated that it was the spiritual-pedagogic dimension of each relationship that was the finest form of "Eros." However, homosexuality, or "inversion" as Blüher preferred to term it, was especially embodied in those heroic leaders (*Männerhelden*)—youth leaders like Wilhelm Jansen—who moved only in male society and attracted youths as disciples "like a piece of crystal in brine."[13] These were the formative creative figures in the Wandervogel who, through their erotic magnetism, were educating and nurturing youth in a charged homoerotic environment, producing the spark that gave the movement its real dynamism.

From 1915, Blüher took this theory of male heroes a stage further, beyond the Wandervogel, claiming the Männerbund to be the "most intensive organ for the spiritualization of the *Volk*."[14] Explicitly on a par with Stefan George who preached about heroic "Christ-like" figures surrounded by obedient disciples, Blüher in his next major work set out the creative masculine forces at the root of human states and societies throughout history. He described on the one hand the female world of the family, propagated through male-female Eros, while on the other hand, rivaling the family and far superior, there was the world of the Männerbund, a male society under creative heroes who by sublimating and steering their sexual urges (male-male Eros) were alone able to produce "stateforming impulses." The "*Männer*" states they created were therefore based on homoerotic bonds while the female-based family was always secondary. These states, moreover, were bound to be hierarchical, aristocratic and absolute, the exact opposite of liberal democracy, which by moving towards equality for all citizens was deemed a female concept.[15]

Blüher's vague theories were initially constructed from what he observed in the Wandervogel and late imperial German society. In turn, they quickly stimulated enormous discussion in wartime youth groups across Central Europe, helping to shape many adolescents' views that male-bonding was a priority and had a really serious purpose.[16] This was as true for the Wandervogel movement in the Bohemian Lands and Austria as for the larger phenomenon in Germany. It was entirely understandable why Blüher's construction should have a particular resonance in Bohemia-Moravia. First, it spoke to male-bonding among German adolescent nationalists who wanted to play a creative role in the Great War; and second, toward the end of hostilities, it suggested that the Wandervogel might be transformed into a Männerbund and placed at the service of the postwar German community in order to challenge the Czechoslovak experiment.

In Bohemia, the Wandervogel had officially been founded in 1911 by a number of secondary school teachers who were enthused by the reform pedagogy of the early twentieth century and wished to streamline their pupils into a healthy nationalist lifestyle. As in Germany, the mission was Janus-like, looking back to an idealistic past and forward toward a regenerative future. It rejected the urban, liberal, bourgeois existence of the ruling generation, seeking instead to restore a "traditional national community" by training a youthful male elite who would proceed to permeate bourgeois society with their values. In prewar Bohemia-Moravia where a radical Czech-nationalist discourse had existed since 1900, the youth mission had a specific regenerative agenda to the benefit of Germans and to the detriment of the Czech "invader." Although mentioned obliquely, the future goal was defined against the Czech majority population, seeking to bolster the supposedly primordial cultural values of German Bohemia at Czech expense. For key Wandervogel mentors like Karl Metzner, a mathematics teacher in Leitmeritz (Litoměřice), it was about physically toughening boys, encouraging firm comradeship but also discipline and obedience as a prototype army. Thus already in 1913, Metzner could pronounce with a flourish that while a supreme commander-in-chief was based in Vienna with his general staff, "in Bohemia there sits a high-ranking general, commanding all Bohemian Wandervogel battalions, which on his signal can be mobilized."[17]

In the all-male Wandervogel environment there was therefore much potential for those who were intrigued by Männerbund theory. The various branches, usually of middle-class secondary school boys were encouraged by adult mentors to cultivate an elitist mentality: they sought "true national values" by regular hiking in the Bohemian countryside (away from artificial urban culture), and distinguished themselves as wholly different from the Czechs who were their neighbors. The elitism encouraged careful selection of members and it had both racial and, through male bonding, potentially homoerotic implications.

The war years when men were pushed together in a new enforced "camaraderie" increasingly raised the ideal of a Männerbund to new heights.[18] Many German youth leaders from Bohemia and Moravia departed enthusiastically for the front. As one elder explained, "from this young generation a new nation will arise … For our descendants it will be better in the future when this purifying stream has rushed through society."[19] The Wandervogel mission of renewal was shifted in a less romantic and more practical direction, and hundreds proceeded to pay the ultimate sacrifice. They died for the mixture of fluid allegiances that made up German national identity in the late Habsburg Bohemian Lands: for "German Bohemia," for "Austria" (and the Habsburgs), or occasionally for a greater German cause that included the German Reich.

Meanwhile, on the home front, many of those either unable or too young to enlist carved out their own national mission in order to play their part. The departure of so many young men inevitably allowed female groups to become more prominent. Girls had entered the Bohemian Wandervogel before 1914, their inclusion provoking some unease about their actual contribution and how much they should be allowed to mix with boys. Early in the war, some female leaders argued for their own patriotic role. As Anni Grund, whose brother had been killed at the front, asserted:

> We too want to keep and cherish [Wandervogel] ideals, so that our "wander-brothers," who are now out bravely defending our fatherland, see on their return home that we have not been idle.[20]

Nevertheless, some male youth leaders, while respecting female-only rural expeditions, would draw the lesson that strict gender roles should be enforced and a special male vision prioritized for the future. Either these were men engulfed by the Männerbund phenomenon in the trenches, or, in many cases, they were those left behind on the home front who yearned for a martial adventure, the chance to stand shoulder to shoulder with fellow Wandervögel in battle. Male bonding was therefore defined not just against an unsatisfactory feminine alternative but against a militarized and dynamic ideal of masculinity.

If during the war a "creative Männerbund" seemed most obviously expressed at the front, it was also being stirred among youths in the hinterland, all the more so because front and hinterland were constantly interacting. For many nationalist youth leaders who would carry into peacetime some form of Männerbund theory, the Wandervogel struggle had dramatically expanded into the wartime trenches, but martial experience was in turn steadily absorbed into the German-Czech struggle in Bohemia. While some Wandervogel soldiers proceeded to bond together in the war zone and organize Wandervogel groups there, when on leave they were fêted by hinterland compatriots eager to learn about military adventure. The youth leader Otto Kletzl exemplified this new type of Wandervogel who flew between front and hinterland, fighting on the Italian front and periodically recounting his exploits to adolescents in his native group in Böhmisch Leipa (Česká Lípa). Finally in 1918, having lost two brothers in the war, he assumed leadership of the Bohemian Wandervogel and began to ponder the postwar nationalist mission.

From the intense front-hinterland interaction, nationalist youth circles at home naturally began to discuss the kind of role that Wandervogel military veterans might play in the future. Many elders, who had either outgrown the youth movement or matured quickly in the trenches, envisaged a postwar enterprise where visionary veterans would take the lead in defending the national community. As hostilities progressed, enlisted Wandervögel had gained special attention. In August 1916, the Austrian federal Wandervogel organization appointed a "military officer" (Ignaz Göth) who in 1917 began to issue a soldiers' journal as a mouthpiece for veterans. It was a development wholly in tandem with others who were taking stock of the wartime experience and contemplating the postwar world: for example, in 1917 an association of German war invalids for the Bohemian Lands was formally created in Reichenberg.[21]

Aside from this social dimension however, the future veteran environment—a step toward some kind of domestic Männerbund—was especially encapsulated in the notion of a *Landsgemeinde* or Bohemian "territorial community." It was first suggested by Wandervogel elders in late 1916 when the Habsburg war effort seemed more precarious, when Czech politicians seemed more openly "disloyal" and there were increasing rumors circulating about Czech military desertions at the front. It envisaged gathering a host of war veterans together as a council to lead the future national community. Since one of their primary tasks would be pedagogic, to help reinforce a German community adjacent to the Czech, it was university students (veterans) clustered together in academic societies or *Freischaren* who would be some of the key "action men." In the words of one Wandervogel leader in late 1917, "with action men we will finally come together for many days' discussion in order to establish new directions and goals."[22]

Yet it was only in the last year of the war that the German youth "veterans" really considered the Czech threat to their national regenerative goal and focused on saving German Bohemia.[23] By this time both Czech and German political camps in Austria were setting out "national courses" that largely excluded or ignored each other. In terms of a fresh direction for the youth movement, as well as the fate of senior youth leaders, a crucial staging post was the last wartime Austrian Wandervogel gathering held in August 1918 in Krummau (Český Krumlov) in southern Bohemia. It revealed much about how the war years had affected the youth leaders differently. For many elders, Karl Metzner and Johannes Stauda for instance, it was time to move on from the youth enterprise and leave it in the hands of "autonomous youth," the new generation. Alarmed at the imminent collapse of the Habsburg empire, Metzner now set out more precisely a postwar regenerative mission for German Bohemia, to be led by Wandervogel veterans who would launch a chivalrous crusade to educate the German grassroots. He termed the new entity the Duchy of Bohemia (*Herzogtum Böhmen*), a name that conjured up a utopian Bohemian past dominated by a German aristocracy.[24]

A Chivalrous Youth Crusade

These plans were being formulated when the sudden collapse of Austria-Hungary in October 1918 presented a shocking fait accompli. As one female youth leader exclaimed, "What will become of our *Deutschböhmerland*, of our German Bohemian people? A depressing feeling, a dark presentiment holds us all spellbound. Our people are in danger!"[25] It was amidst the chaos of late 1918, as frontline soldiers returned to find the Czech authorities annexing their "national territory," that the *Herzogtum* project was pushed forward. While Otto Kletzl tried to organize a soldier-student community in Prague—a possible microcosm for the *Herzogtum* as one youth leader suggested—Karl Metzner sent out a circular to galvanize returning German-Bohemian soldiers.[26] The upshot of the campaign was a meeting of thirty veteran youth leaders at the castle of Schreckenstein (Střekov) at Aussig (Ústí nad Labem). Although it is not known how much those present knew of Hans Blüher's recent work, or even if they envisaged themselves as a Männerbund, they had many characteristics of such a body. They saw themselves as aristocratic males standing aside from the mainstream chaos around them. Together they had risen in the national youth movement partly through their charisma and leadership qualities; they had bonded through the years in pursuit of a romantic ideal; and most had played their part in a wider military struggle at the front.

As Nicholas Sombart has suggested, the very concept of a Männerbund had chivalrous origins.[27] It conjured up the image of a sworn band of crusaders battling against the infidel or protecting the Holy Grail like the knights in Richard Wagner's *Parsifal*. Typically, those gathering at Schreckenstein (the inspiration itself for Wagner's *Tannhäuser*) assembled in the Knight's Hall of the castle ruins, perched on the top of a cliff with a panoramic view of the river Elbe and "national territory" spread out beneath them. There they took an oath to the Duchy of Bohemia and the renewal of the German spirit in the Bohemian Lands. This was, to use Blüher's language, a "state-forming impulse" by men who defined themselves as heroes. And the means towards the elusive objective (the Duchy) was to be a new organization, headed by Metzner, called the "Bohemian Lands Movement" (BLB: Böhmerlandbewegung).[28]

The BLB proved to be the first example, loosely conceived, of a Männerbund in action. But, unlike elsewhere in post-Habsburg lands to the south, this did not have any paramilitary or violent pretensions, as it was realistic about the Czech-dominated state environment it encountered. Thus, having taken the

Schreckenstein oath, the soldiers and youth veterans proceeded to establish a network of *Heimat* initiatives across what they would soon call the "Sudetenland"—the German-speaking regions of the new state. One BLB leader later described the movement as a "secret band of blood brothers," working quietly towards the common goal of regenerating the homeland. Through an intangible spiritual union across German space, the aim was to galvanize a national community and prepare for a new type of state adjacent to the Czech entity. Certainly, over the next six years—until 1925 when the BLB voluntarily dissolved in response to Czech vigilance—its *Heimat* creed penetrated widely. Its message was propagated through newsletters, books, and journals (like *Böhmerland*) issued by Johannes Stauda; its members gathered annually in training camps to debate the needs of the Sudeten homeland. In short, the BLB, despite its amorphous nature was a key cultural medium for spreading a regenerative, *völkisch* creed. Male veterans from the trenches and wartime youth movement were at the forefront of planting seeds for a fresh nationalist growth. In the 1920s they furthered the notion of a specific "Sudeten German" identity across what were in fact loose and often disconnected German-speaking communities.[29]

While the adult pioneers of the BLB might self-identify as a prototype Männerbund, most felt that the next generation of postwar male youth was the crucial tool for Sudeten national renewal. In the words of the Schreckenstein oath, "the selfless, active cooperation of maturing youth will help regenerate public life."[30] Some older veterans like Metzner and Stauda were content to steer the BLB in a cultural-pedagogic direction, focusing on *Heimat* education for adolescents or even (in Metzner's case) setting up their own school to train model pupils.[31] But others, like Heinz Rutha or Walter Hergl, after the Schreckenstein oath quickly viewed the BLB as too cultural and insufficiently masculine (full of "effeminate youth" according to Hergl).[32] Their perspective was more militant and political, impatient to shape some kind of vibrant Männerbund out of Sudeten young men. Behind this commitment was, first, a desire to continue in adulthood their own leadership of youth, building on their Wandervogel and short frontline experiences (both Rutha and Hergl had served briefly on the Italian front). Second, they believed that something of the character-forming trench spirit needed to be injected into the next generation as a spur for confronting and overcoming "Czech aggression." Both aspects therefore might be personally cathartic for men who felt traumatized by the war and sought a meaningful role for themselves in the postwar Sudeten German community.

Later, the Sudeten German historian Josef Pfitzner would dramatically summarize this postwar confluence of national activists as follows: "One symbol sustaining our reconstruction after 1918 was the inexhaustible force of youth, while the second was front-experience and the spirit of comradeship." The symbiosis was perfectly personified in one youth leader, Heinz Rutha, whom Pfitzner acknowledged to be a pioneer seeking to instill in the burgeoning postwar youth groups a "fully controlled manliness."³³ Rutha's unusual youth-leadership background (as head of the Bohemian Wandervogel in 1916–17), and his late service at the front in 1918, made him balk at the idea of simply returning to civilian life. As he explained:

> We young soldiers recognized on our return from the front and from the collapse that no front could be victorious without the most profound national unity in the rear! … Pioneers of a new nation could be created only from those frontline men who had not become self-satisfied veterans or mercenaries, but whose own self-discipline served as a model for the masculine discipline of the whole nation and all young men…. Here it was a question of firmly organizing a new education out of the simple laws of masculinity. First out of that, a new political will could grow. But not just from the frontline soldiers! It also required the glow of young men [*Jungmannschaft*], and that both of them—youths and soldiers—should have the deepest understanding of history and of our people's strengths and weaknesses, in order to learn lessons and behave accordingly in the future.³⁴

In this vision Rutha was not alone. There were many other young "Sudeten" soldiers who in peacetime continued to dwell on male-bonding and strict discipline as a way of solving the national apocalypse. One was the former soldier Konrad Henlein who had fought on the Italian front and, on returning from captivity, envisaged creating a strong German Männerbund out of the regional Turners.³⁵ Yet it was Rutha who, while significantly influencing Henlein's direction, was a real pioneer among the nationalist veterans; he practically conceived a Männerbund as the dynamo for a future Sudeten German state. Already at Schreckenstein he had introduced a fresh ingredient into the *Herzogtum* mission, envisaging the existing Wandervogel as its key building block and stressing that the revitalized youth movement should be guided by charismatic "leader-personalities." The origins of this hybrid term are obscure, but probably owed as much to Blüher as to Rutha's own perception of deficient Habsburg military leadership in the trenches.³⁶ His conclusion was that while forging a national community in the Bohemian Lands was the priority, the crusade must be led by heroic individuals who would spontaneously emerge through their own dynamic character traits.

From May 1919 and continuing for three years, Rutha issued his own youth-leadership journal, "Pages from a Fresh Life" (*Blätter vom frischen Leben*), elaborating this vision for Sudeten renewal through the Wandervogel. When he found it impossible to impose his notion of leader-personalities on the rest of the movement (including a strict segregation of the sexes), he turned to building up his own male group of charismatic disciples as a model. Increasingly independent, with a special uniform and tight discipline, the "Rutha youth circle" by 1926 had left the Wandervogel for good and sought a new home. Its militant model meanwhile began to be copied by other Sudeten German youth groups such as the Pfadfinder (Scouts) and the Catholic Staffelstein (the latter training young men to promote both "faith and nation" as their spiritual mission).[37]

In these youth bodies a common discourse was about training the best young men to serve and strengthen the threatened (Sudeten) *Heimat*. But a few youth leaders certainly also subscribed, albeit inadvertently, to Blüher's extra theory that homoerotic bonding was crucial for these "creative heroes." Indeed, for some who had such feelings, like Oskar Just or Heinz Rutha, the Männerbund ideal helped them make sense of their homosexual inclinations while providing a certain security and sense of integrity for their mission with the postwar generation. The case of Rutha stands out not just as the best documented but because in the 1920s he constructed his own model for a Sudeten Männerbund that would rely on a charismatic, homoerotic leadership and undergo methodical training before reaching full adulthood. Although he publicly rejected Blüher in the early 1920s as "unchaste and cynical," it seems clear that he slowly appropriated much of Blüher's Männerbund theory to shape his own philosophy.[38]

Reinforcing this creed of an erotically-charged Männerbund were writings both classical and contemporary—including Plato and Stefan George. From the former, Rutha—again in the spirit of Blüher—felt he had discovered an (ancient) society where the spiritual relationship between an older man and a male youth was lauded as the purest form of Eros. Stefan George meanwhile exemplified a charismatic individual who himself had selected a cohort of disciples and who prophesied a chivalrous Männerbund guiding the German people out of disaster. By the late 1920s Rutha would write privately that he was propelled forward in his postwar nationalist mission by the "world-force of Eros"; the essence of that mission was "awakening youth" whose spirit, he noted, "must be directed towards the great ideas of the *masculine* universe."[39]

It should be stressed that the concept of a Sudeten German Männerbund in the postwar decade was always elitist and selective, and deliberately at variance with the political framework of the new Czechoslovak state. The vibrancy of a Männerbund stemmed on the one hand from continuity with the male-based struggle in the trenches. On the other hand, those taking the lead always saw themselves as a select minority who knew best and had been called upon to staunch the flood swirling around the national community. That flood was of course defined racially as against the primary Czech antagonist. (In contrast to Austria, Hungary, or indeed Germany, Jews featured minimally: anti-semitism was never a prominent trait of interwar Sudeten German nationalism). But it also meant a distinct approach to postwar politics. In the words of Walter Hergl, the veterans felt "revolted and sickened" by traditional party politics that, in their eyes, only encouraged national disunity and had led the regional Germans to their present sorry predicament.[40] Therefore, a new type of radical politics was necessary tangential to the traditional. It must eschew the parliamentary liberalism that Czechoslovakia was continuing to normalize and with which, disappointedly, many Sudeten German politicians were still prepared to engage. It would rest upon principles of hegemonic masculinity, a national leadership imposing its will on the burgeoning nation and in turn garnering grassroots support because of its self-evident sacrifice on behalf of the whole.

Comrades as Political "Action Men"

If the short-lived BLB had attributes of a Männerbund, as a male elite seeking to galvanize the *Heimat* along the road towards national cohesion, a second experiment in the late 1920s was much more coherent in envisaging a future Sudeten German state. By 1926 there was greater confidence among Sudeten "negativists"—those who rejected cooperation with the Czechoslovak state—and just at a time when German "activist" politicians were entering the Czechoslovak coalition government and suggesting to the world that ethnic relations were improving. By 1926, for some "negativists," both the vehicle and the long-term goal of a Männerbund enterprise directed against Czech hegemony were taking shape. For many youth leaders who interacted with male cohorts (including Turners) the term Männerbund probably had only a vague meaning, but other veterans like Rutha or Hergl saw it as a concrete and serious enterprise. As we have seen, by 1922 Rutha had taken the risk of launching his own "youth circle" in north Bohemia, describing it publicly as "a new more manly youth education than previously."[41] This "Jungenschaft," although small (perhaps a hundred adolescents), would naturally grow to adulthood, turning into a "Jungmannschaft," and by 1925 such a body was emerging. When a dozen members of Rutha's Jungenschaft entered Prague's German university, they set up a new student society there named the Pedagogical Community. Since all were elders of Rutha's circle, they could be envisaged by him as his personal Männerbund, men who having already inspired youth, having closely bonded with each other, were now ready to go out and forge a Sudeten German nation out of their comradeship.

It required however a new philosophy to raise this mission beyond the utopian and to suggest a practical framework for the future Sudeten German state and society. The theory that seemed to mesh best with the Männerbund vision was that of Othmar Spann, a Viennese sociologist who had personally experienced pre-1914 Czech-German tensions (in Brno), and who honored the German nation as being the most creative. According to Spann, society in Central Europe had to be reorganized hierarchically along the lines of premodern estates or corporations, where all would supposedly work in harmony under the firm guidance of a select political leadership. On this model, the region should be split into various states according to the various German tribes, but in turn the German nation would easily interact as one large spiritual community across Central Europe.

It is easy to see why this vision—despite its own inherent idealism—might resonate with many Sudeten German nationalists in the 1920s. It had echoes not only of a romantic "German-dominated" Holy Roman Empire, but also of the loose Austrian imperial connections they had known in their youth. But above all, it offered a radical way forward for Sudeten Germans to break out of the Czechoslovak national vice, asserting their own statehood in the Bohemian Lands while communing spiritually with the German national diaspora to the north and south. Another factor that made Spann's model enticing was its hierarchical structure. It offered a place for a male elite, a Männerbund of leader-personalities, either in state leadership or as managers of the various socio-economic estates that would constitute each state.[42]

Spann's theory was effectively brought to Sudeten German attention by Walter Heinrich, one of his most devoted disciples who hailed from north Bohemia and who by 1920 had befriended Rutha. At Christmas 1925, Rutha, Heinrich, and Hergl founded in Reichenberg a Study Group for Social Sciences (Arbeitskreis für Gesellschaftswissenschaften) devoted to exploring the practical application of Spannism in Czechoslovakia. It was the successor of the BLB in taking forward the concept of an embryonic Sudeten state dominated by a male elite who would agitate in German communities. As Hergl wrote later, the Study Group expressly "esteemed masculine thinking and experience, in other words [it privileged] the political Männerbund." It envisaged a network of both specialized leaders and charismatic individuals who could energetically draw together different male organizations into a united and uniform whole: a Männerbund writ large across Sudeten German society.[43]

In practical terms this Study Group, or "Comrades Union" (KB: Kameradschaftsbund) as it became known, soon consisted of dozens of young men who had been recruited through connections of friendship, particularly originating in the homosocial Sudeten youth movements. Rutha's growing Pedagogical Community acted as just one springboard. At most the KB only numbered three hundred, with an inner core of about fifty enthusiasts who were loosely attached. They met up occasionally for lectures as well as an annual conference to discuss Spannism and the tasks facing a Sudeten German Männerbund.[44] Contemporaries and some historians have tended to dwell on the secretive, almost Masonic nature of the KB, since it did not register as an official society until 1930. In fact, its aims were not particularly mysterious, and its "secrecy" simply reflected the lack of attention that the Czech authorities paid to nonparty political German activity in the 1920s.

The lectures delivered at the KB's 1928 conference illustrate well how this Männerbund saw itself and its goals. At a chateau near Teplitz in north-western Bohemia, Kurt Hildebrandt, a pupil of Stefan George, explained that great individuals were always highly valued for it was the heroes who created states; but at the same time individuals must be ready to sacrifice themselves on behalf of the national community. Heinz Rutha then set out the priorities of the Männerbund for the KB audience. On the one hand, those present needed to continue inspiring male adolescents and training the next generation to understand their sacred national purpose. On the other, the KB elite, the key bearers of creative action, must go forth into the Sudeten communities, planting themselves in diverse organizations as "germ cells." As "resolute minorities" they would take the lead in all corners of the nation, and be ready to assemble as a leaders' council to run the future state.[45]

If these ideas owed much to the earlier BLB, the KB's novelty lay in its Spannist philosophy and its clear political agenda: in short, it was to be a political (Sudeten) Männerbund at work, not just stimulating a national consciousness to match the Czech adversary but consciously seeking to build a new state edifice within Czechoslovakia. And if the operation still seemed rather amorphous, it was certainly becoming more tangible. For amid the organizations that might host "germ cells," the KB leaders by 1928 explicitly viewed the Turner movement as the ideal organism wherein a male body (*Männerschaft*) could be trained. Over the next four years this idea took shape.

Its attractiveness was self-evident, based not only on the Turnverband's long tradition and status in the Bohemian Lands but also on its dynamic potential. The Turnverband was the leading grassroots *völkisch* movement across German-speaking communities. In the 1920s it had about a hundred and fifty thousand members in a thousand local groups.[46] While its *völkisch* nationalist outlook usually made it alert to rejecting those of "non-German blood," it was otherwise socially inclusive (above-party), but with an overwhelmingly male membership. From the late nineteenth century it had become a social gymnastics organization present in every town and village, but underneath there had always lingered something of its inherent militant purpose. Its origins lay in Germany in the Napoleonic age as a grassroots defense against French invaders.

On this stable and historic basis therefore the KB leaders by 1928 saw much to their advantage. They were especially drawn to the Turnverband because out of the Great War some veterans emerged who also wanted to reenergize the movement and return it to first principles as a body of men serving the nation. The most notable innovator was Konrad Henlein, who by 1926 was active in western Bohemia with a program of reform, transforming the gymnastics movement there into a disciplined army of volunteers, hierarchically organized, physically tough through competitive exercise, but at the same time holistically educated with a Sudeten *völkisch* mentality.[47] One of his models was the Czech Sokol (national gymnastics movement), which he personally observed performing with militant precision at its 1926 festival in Prague. For anxious Sudeten nationalists, the Czech nation always seemed more united and focused, and the Czechoslovak Legion—seemingly confident and privileged in the 1920s—may also have influenced Sudeten Männerbund thinking.[48]

However, Henlein's primary stimulus came from the Sudeten wartime sacrifice and out of that grew his determination to inject into his Turnverband a "spirit of masculinity, unity, military discipline and subordination." While trying to harness a front-line spirit via those war veterans who were still receptive, he understood well from Rutha that systematic youth training was crucial if the Männerbund was to sustain and regenerate itself (especially as many veterans undoubtedly did not wish to be remobilized).[49] Henlein's own credentials were never in doubt: he was an early KB adherent and, despite his relative lack of charisma, he seemed to many to be a "leader-personality" through his sheer ordinariness and diligence. Indeed, when in 1931 he became head of the whole Turnverband, the course was set fully to inculcate KB principles into the movement. In June 1932 he called upon all Sudeten youth bodies to fuse into the revitalized Turnverband for systematic training on behalf of the nation. Adult Turners meanwhile had for some years been subject to the new regime, for the Turnverband under Henlein's reforms had begun to embody all strands of the Sudeten Männerbund idea: a disciplined body of men charged with a creative state-forming mission at odds with the existing Czechoslovak state. As Henlein stressed as early as May 1928: "Individual leader-personalities and the followers bound to them by loyalty—it is they who make world history."[50]

In the 1930s, the concept of a strident Männerbund was wholly integrated into the Sudeten German nationalist discourse—whether in the Turnverband or in the Sudeten German Home Front created by Henlein in late 1933 as a political organism outside party frameworks. In elevating the creative power of the Sudeten man, the discourse inevitably set up the Czech nation as its main adversary, and it also suggested a distinct role for the Sudeten woman in the nationalist crusade. This was not quite the misogynistic viewpoint expressed by Blüher in the war years (even if to most Henleinists any notion of a comparable "Frauenbund" was absurd). Rather, the woman was now allotted her own creative place in the Sudeten national experiment. As Henlein observed, "while in the man something of the warrior is always visible, the woman always embodies some form of motherliness."[51] Her regenerative responsibility, her sacrifice for the *Volk*, was to create and nurture the Sudeten German child and family, while at the same time supporting her husband whose energy must be preserved for his higher national work (*Volkstumsarbeit*). This did not exclude women from *völkisch* training, either physical or mental, but it meant that their education—for example in the Turner movement—would follow a curriculum enhancing their qualities as a healthy wife who must rear healthy children.[52]

Meanwhile, the dominant position of men in steering the Sudeten German nationalist movement (Henlein's Sudeten German Party after 1935) perhaps made the public evocation of a Männerbund less important. Where the concept endured best was in the Turnverband. Between 1934 and 1938 a systematic program was implemented to train male adolescents for their national adult responsibilities. Following Henlein's call, most youth groups apart from the socialists amalgamated or recognized the Turnverband's pedagogic primacy. And for those enthusiasts like Heinz Rutha who still saw shaping a Männerbund as the foremost objective, another piece of the puzzle was introduced in 1935. This was the construction of a youth leadership school at Wartenberg in northern Bohemia by an elite cadre of unemployed adult Turners. The product was to be two-fold in terms of producing Männerbund specimens. Not only were the muscular builders in this "work camp" given a thorough physical and *völkisch* education on the spot, but the final building (never completed) was also intended to house charismatic youth leaders who would train the next generation before themselves entering society as creative heroes.[53] Wartenberg was part of a phenomenon of "work camps" that mushroomed across mid-1930s Europe and proved popular in many of the successor states, as Rebecca Haynes shows in her discussion of Romania.

Figure 3.1.
The Männerbund of the Sudeten German youth leadership school, 1936 (Courtesy Státní okresní archiv Liberec).

Elsewhere, in various rituals of the Henlein movement before World War II, the Sudeten public was periodically reminded of how the past wartime sacrifice was always directly informing the present. The contemporary Männerbund, in fashioning a Sudeten German rebirth from the ashes of the Habsburg empire, was portrayed as communing with the fallen, honoring their memory, and transmitting their values reliably to the next male generation. In August 1937 in western Bohemia this was a sentiment dramatically expressed by Konrad Henlein when he unveiled a huge fresco titled "Resurrection of the Heroes" in the Eger (Cheb) memorial hall. There he intoned before a huge audience of Sudeten German veterans:

> We the living dedicate this monument to the dead, who were our comrades. Anyone who speaks of that time must always face the eternal countenance of our dead heroes. For their sacrifice was inherited by the living, their death was an exhortation to the future. Their life could not have been for nothing. We were called up as sons of an era when the idea of community was alien. But through struggle and hardship we experienced an inner transformation that promised a new youth for our people. The comradeship of the front became the germ cell for the nation's wonderful new community. In the trenches, in the offensive or on night patrol, we became new men. Through the luck or misfortune of individuals we experienced for the first time our people's fate. And that fate bound together the living and the dead. The comrade who fell yesterday bequeathed to me a double obligation to fight; and the greater the army of the fallen, the tougher was our common purpose … [Thus] it was the spirit of the trench struggle which was the creative force producing our new community of youth.[54]

Mediating Past and Future Sacrifice

The number of real zealots promoting a Männerbund theory was always a minority in the German border regions of interwar Czechoslovakia. This was true not just across the swathes of the population who became committed Sudeten German nationalists within a Czechoslovak national state, but also among military veterans from various periods of the four-year conflict. At the German grassroots, nationalist activists were naturally heterogeneous in how they envisaged future progress. While many preferred to work pedagogically in schools or cultural societies, some were even prepared to engage with local party politics in the new (Czech) political environment. As for the men returning from the front, in 1918–19 they had generally been shocked at the chaotic state of the *Heimat* they encountered. The new Czechoslovak regime's efficiency in suppressing the abortive German governments thrown up in late 1918 and the lack of weaponry or any coherence among returning German regiments (many of whose veterans remained in enemy captivity until 1920) prevented a militant violent response of the kind witnessed in unstable Hungary.

Figure 3.2. The Frýdlant war memorial, now in Frýdlant cemetery, Czech Republic (Author's photograph).

But it also seems clear that many former combatants were averse to being remobilized for a new struggle anyway, wishing to reintegrate into civilian normality. Some, as war invalids, would champion their own social status and gain succor from invalid comradeship in the face of a hostile state.[55] Others, in line with strict Czechoslovak limitations on what was permitted to German veteran societies, confined themselves to social or commemorative reunions. Some regimental associations were behind the erection of war memorials, but often it was the older generation who had lost sons who took the lead. By the late 1920s a mass of monuments had sprung up across the border landscape.[56]

Yet out of the war there had also emerged an enticing Männerbund ideal that, though initially diffuse and inconsequential, grew by the 1930s to be an integral element in the Sudeten German nationalist discourse. Its theory had been honed before 1914 and had seeped into the Bohemian youth movement. The comradeship and intensity of the wartime trenches gave it resonance. But it was the traumatic postwar environment that allowed it to flourish—as a charismatic male cohort with "state-forming impulses." This elite defined itself first in terms of recent heroic sacrifice, lauding the continuation into peacetime of a hegemonic masculinity and a struggle at odds with domesticity and family life. Second, it found in the Czech nation a worthy adversary. Both racially and in their liberal political system, the Czechs appeared anathema to any Sudeten Männerbund, yet they offered a model of national rebirth that Sudeten Germans could envy and emulate. As in other successor states, some veterans felt they were witness to continued sacrifice, which was then mythologized into a new national narrative. For example, the notorious Czech "massacre" of German civilians in March 1919 served this purpose, extending bloodshed into peacetime.[57]

In the 1920s the concept of a Männerbund, adapted to the specific Sudeten German environment, gained ground with new adherents. This reflected increasing German nationalist confidence in Czechoslovakia and the degree to which the liberal state permitted the existence of "cultural" organizations that could advance national cohesion in the Sudetenland. But it was also a case of generational shifts. While youth leaders and younger veterans (the 1890s generation) were the initial Männerbund zealots, by the late 1920s, as they expected, a fresh cohort was emerging: adolescents who, having missed out on the war adventure, could be enticed via the youth movements towards an idealistic national crusade. They would be the bedrock of the Sudeten mission in the 1930s.

Indeed, the Sudeten German Männerbund's force lay in appealing across several male generations and appearing both traditional and revolutionary in its nebulous vision for the region. While it posed as the embodiment of past wartime sacrifice, it also asserted its leadership in the contemporary and future national crusade. Through fresh sacrifice the Czech "stranglehold" would be broken, finally giving birth to that Sudeten German organism, which, it was argued, should have been allowed to rise from the ashes of the Habsburg monarchy.

Mark Cornwall is Professor of Modern European History at the University of Southampton, specializing in the late Habsburg monarchy and its successor states. His major publications include *The Undermining of Austria-Hungary: The Battle for Hearts and Minds* (2000); *The Devil's Wall: The Nationalist Youth Mission of Heinz Rutha* (2012); and a chapter on Austro-Hungarian wartime morale and censorship in volume XI/I of *Die Habsburgermonarchie: Der Erste Weltkrieg* (2016). He is currently writing a book about treason and loyalty in the last decades of Austria-Hungary.

Notes

1. Robert E. Norton, *Secret Germany: Stefan George and his Circle* (Ithaca and London, 2002), 359–69.
2. Rudolf Wolkan, *Geschichte der deutschen Literatur in Böhmen und in den Sudetenländern* (Augsburg, 1925), 129–31.
3. Heinz Rutha, in *Blätter vom frischen Leben* 1, no. 2, 15 May 1919, 13.
4. See, for example, Johannes Stauda, *Der Wandervogel in Böhmen 1911–1920*, 2 vols. (Reutlingen, 1975–78); Hans Schmid-Egger and Ernst Nitter, *Staffelstein: Jugendbewegung und katholische Erneuerung bei den Sudetendeutschen zwischen den Großen Kriegen* (Munich, 1983); Peter Becher, ed., *Deutsche Jugend in Böhmen 1918–1938* (Munich, 1993). Exceptions are also Andreas Luh, *Der deutsche Turnverband in der esrten Tschechoslowakischen Republik* (Munich, 1988); Daniel Langhans, *Der Reichsbund der deutschen katholischen Jugend in der Tschechoslowakei 1918–1938* (Bonn, 1990); and Tomáš Kasper, *Výchova či politika? Úskali německého pedagogického hnutí v Československu v letech 1918–1933* (Prague, 2007). A new overall analysis is Mark Cornwall, *The Devil's Wall: The Nationalist Youth Mission of Heinz Rutha* (Cambridge, MA, 2012).
5. See, for instance, Deborah S. Cornelius, *In Search of the Nation: The New Generation of Hungarian Youth in Czechoslovakia 1925–1934* (New York, 1998). Her case study shows that a sense of national mission for Hungarian youth in Slovakia developed only after the war (first through the Scouts).
6. Jürgen Reulecke, *"Ich möchte einer werden so wie die..." Männerbünde im 20. Jahrhundert* (Frankfurt and New York, 2001), 71. For Germany, the most recent discussion is by Claudia Bruns, *Politik des Eros: Der Männerbund in Wissenschaft, Politik und Jugendkultur (1880–1934)* (Cologne, 2008), but she only briefly studies the interwar period. Previous works include Gisela Vögler and Karin Welck, eds., *Männerbande, Männerbünde: Zur Rolle des Mannes in Kulturvergleich*, 2 vols. (Cologne, 1990); Bernd Widdig, *Männerbünde und Massen: Zur Krise männlicher Identität in der Literatur der Moderne* (Opladen, 1992); and Helmut Blazek, *Männerbünde: Eine Geschichte von Faszination und Macht* (Berlin, 1999).
7. Benjamin Ziemann, *War Experiences in Rural Germany, 1914–1923* (Oxford, 2007), 212, 248.
8. For the German veteran associations, see Martin Zückert, "Memory of War and National State Integration: Czech and German Veterans in Czechoslovakia after 1918," *Central Europe* 4:2 (2006):114–16. One major veterans association had seventy thousand members in 1930.
9. Gaudietwart Henlein, "Turner, kleidet euch männlich," *Turnzeitung des Deutschen Turnverbandes* (hereafter *TZ*), 1 January 1925, 84.
10. Konrad Henlein, "Der Neuaufbau unserer Führung," *TZ*, 1 December 1930, 362.

11. Bruns, *Politik des Eros*, 79–106; Reulecke, *"Ich möchte einer werden,"* 38–39. See also Nicolaus Sombart, "Männerbund und politische Kultur in Deutschland," in *Typisch deutsch: die Jugendbewegung. Beiträge zu einer Phänomengeschichte*, ed. Joachim H. Knoll and Julius H. Schoeps (Opladen, 1988), 162–69.
12. For good context and a thorough analysis of Blüher's ideas, see Bruns, *Politik des Eros*, 267ff.
13. Hans Blüher, *Die deutsche Wandervogelbewegung als erotische Phänomenon: Ein Beitrag zur Erkenntnis der sexuellen Inversion* (Berlin-Tempelhof, 1914), 35.
14. Reulecke, *"Ich möchte einer werden,"* 78.
15. Julius Schoeps, "Sexualität, Erotik und Männerbund," in *Typisch deutsch*, 141–46; and Hans Blüher, *Die Rolle der Erotik in der männlichen Gesellschaft* vol. 1 (Jena, 1917), 7, 225. For a good summary Claudia Bruns, "Der homosexuelle Staatsfreund: Von der Konstruktion des erotischen Männerbunds bei Hans Blüher," in *Homosexualität und Politik in Deutschland 1900–1945*, ed. Susanne zur Nieden (Frankfurt and New York, 2005), 100–17. Also Bruns, *Politik des Eros*, 410–37.
16. See Ulfried Geuter, *Homosexualität in der deutschen Jugendbewegung: Jungenfreundschaft und Sexualität im Diskurs von Jugendbewegung, Psychoanalyse und Jugenpsychologie am Beginn des 20. Jahrhunderts* (Frankfurt am Main, 1994), 94–103.
17. *Burschen heraus! Fahrtenblatt der Deutschböhmen*, June 1913, 11–13.
18. George Mosse, *Nationalism and Sexuality: Middle-Class Morality and Sexual Norms in Modern Europe* (Madison, 1985), 128.
19. Rudolf Feldberger, "Wandervögel," *Burschen heraus!*, July 1914, 156.
20. Anni Grund, "Vom Leipschen Wandervogel," *Burschen heraus!*, July 1915, 142.
21. Natali Stegmann, "Deutsche Kriegsgeschädigte in der Tschechoslowakei 1918–1938," *Bohemia: Zeitschrift für Geschichte und Kultur der böhmischen Länder*, 48/2 (2008): 452.
22. Stauda, *Der Wandervogel*, I, 60–62; II, 112–13.
23. Ibid., II, 122. By this time it seems to have been common knowledge that the German human sacrifice had been far greater than the Czech, something publicized in the dubious statistical analysis of Wilhelm Winkler. See the critique in Ivan Šedivý, *Češi, české země a velká válka 1914–1918* (Prague, 2001), 148–49.
24. Cornwall, *The Devil's Wall*, 97.
25. Stauda, *Wandervogel*, II, 143. For broader context on the immediate aftermath of the war, see Hans Haas, "Konflikt při uplatňování nároků na právo sebeurčení: od habsburského státu k Československu—Němci v českých zemích v letech 1918 až 1919," in *První světová válka a vztahy mezi Čechy, Slováky a Němci*, ed. Hans Mommsen, Dušan Kováč and Jiří Malíř (Brno, 2000), 113–77; and J.W. Bruegel, *Tschechen und Deutsche 1918–1938* (Munich, 1967), 48–60.
26. Stauda, *Wandervogel*, I, 73–74; II, 144–47.
27. Nicolaus Sombart, "Männerbund und politische Kultur in Deutschland," in *Typisch deutsch*, 164–66. For Blüher's contemporary theory of the Männerbund as a new "spiritual aristocracy" which would arouse the *Volk*'s productive energies, see Bruns, *Politik des Eros*, 424–25.
28. Johannes Stauda, "Das Böhmerland," *Sudetenland* 4 (1975): 280; Josef Fischer, Václav Patzak, Vincenc Perth, *Jejich boj: co chce a čemu slouží Sudetendeutsche Partei* (Prague, 1937), 73–74; Josef Pfitzner, *Sudetendeutsche Einheitsbewegung: Werden und Erfüllung*, 2nd edition (Carlsbad and Leipzig, 1937), 35–37.
29. Stauda, "Das Böhmerland," 281–83.
30. Ibid., 280.
31. On Metzner's postwar career as a reform-pedagogue, see Kasper, *Výchova či politika?*, 209–25.
32. See Hergl's retrospective view from 1936 of the BLB (a "mad undertaking") in his huge manuscript, *Die deutsche-tschechische Frage im Rahmen der gesamtdeutschen Politik*, 128 (in Politischen Archiv des Auswärtigen Amt, Berlin: R103654).

33. Pfitzner, *Sudetendeutsche Einheitsbewegung*, 34, 69.
34. Heinz Rutha, "Sudetendeutschtum auf dem Wege zur Einigung," *Volk und Führung*, 2 (1935): 52–53.
35. Pfitzner, *Sudetendeutsche Einheitsbewegung*, 76.
36. See, for example, Blüher's prewar thinking in Bruns, *Politik des Eros*, 321–22. It is clear too that Rutha's concept of "leader-personalities" was shaped by the maxims of Georg Stammler (pseudonym for Ernst Krauss) that he knew well: see Georg Stammler, *Worte an eine Schar* (Heidelberg, 1914), 9, 33-4.
37. See Cornwall, *The Devil's Wall*, 111–22.
38. *Blätter vom frischen Leben* 3, no. 5, 1 July 1922, 82.
39. State District Archive, Litoměřice (Státní okresní archiv), Česká Lípa krajksý soud, trestní spisy, karton 242, Tk 665/37/147, Rutha to [Walter Heinrich], 22 October 1928. For detail on Rutha's Eros mission, see Cornwall, *The Devil's Wall*, 140–51.
40. Hergl, *Die deutsche-tschechische Frage im Rahmen der gesamtdeutschen Politik*, 125.
41. Quoted in Cornwall, *The Devil's Wall*, 120.
42. For studies of Spannist theory see Martin Schneller, *Zwischen Romantik und Faschismus: Der Beitrag Othmar Spanns zum Konservatismus der Weimarer Republik* (Stuttgart, 1970); Klaus-Jörg Siegfried, *Universalismus und Faschismus: Das Gesellschaftsbild Othar Spanns* (Vienna, 1974). There is as yet no thorough analysis of Spann's impact on the Bohemian Lands.
43. Hergl, *Die deutsche-tschechische Frage*, 130.
44. See Walter Becher, "Der Kameradschaftsbund: Eine Mittlergruppe zwischen Jungendbewegung und verantwortlicher Politik," in *Deutsche Jugend in Böhmen 1918–1938*, ed. Peter Becher (Munich, 1993), 13–18; Fischer, Patzak, and Perth, *Jejich boj*, 41–43; and for an introduction in English, John Haag, "'Knights of the Spirit': The Kameradschaftsbund," *Journal of Contemporary History* 8:3 (1973).
45. These lectures (by Rutha, Hildebrandt, and Walter Heinrich) were privately published as *Die erste Position* (1929). See particularly Rutha's contribution (writing as Richard Lenk): "Der sudetendeutsche Stammeskörper," 12–30.
46. Luh, *Deutsche Turnverband*, 90.
47. For the context and content of Henlein's reform agenda, ibid., 163–81.
48. See Rudolf Jahn, *Konrad Henlein: Leben und Werk des Turnführers* (Carlsbad, 1938), 73–74. How the Czechoslovak Legion was perceived by Sudeten German nationalists requires more research.
49. Jahn, *Konrad Henlein*, 67, 92 (Henlein quotation).
50. Cited in ibid., 95.
51. Ibid., 148. See 146–57 for an overall discussion.
52. Luh, *Deutsche Turnverband*, 334–35; Cornwall, *The Devil's Wall*, 166.
53. Ibid., 168–73.
54. *Rundschau*, 28 August 1937, 1. A war memorial was also dedicated in Carlsbad at this time in the presence of ten thousand war veterans. During World War II the special sacrifice of "Sudeten warriors" from the Great War continued to be emphasized: see Konrad Leppa, *Die Sudetendeutschen im Weltkriege 1914-18. Ein Heldenbuch* (Vienna, 1940).
55. See Stegmann, "Deutsche Kriegsgeschädigte," 452–56.
56. Zückert, "Memory of War," 115.
57. See Karl Braun, "Der 4. März 1919. Zur Herausbildung sudetendeutscher Identität," *Bohemia* 37 (1996): 353–80.

Chapter 4

THE DIVIDED WAR REMEMBRANCE OF TRANSYLVANIAN MAGYARS

Franz Sz. Horváth

In December 1927, a leading article titled "Ten Years on the Minority Road" appeared in the most important newspaper of the Transylvanian Magyar minority.[1] The occasion of the article, written by István Zágoni, a war veteran, journalist, and politician, was the tenth anniversary of the occupation of the city of Kolozsvár (Klausenburg, Cluj) by Romanian troops in 1918. This was seen as the last and main chapter of the Great War by most Transylvanian Magyars since, for them, remembering the war primarily meant thinking about how the war had ended. It is striking, when reading articles in Hungarian newspapers that in 1928 commemorated the tenth anniversary of the end of the Great War, that the dismemberment of the Habsburg monarchy, the union of Transylvania with Romania, and the fate of the minority in the Romanian Kingdom were the most important issues. For the Magyars of Transylvania therefore, public remembrance had almost nothing to do with suffering on the battlefields or the psychological consequences of warfare.

This chapter examines the key aspects of war remembrance among Transylvanian Magyars from 1918 to 1944. It begins with a description of how Magyars across Greater Hungary commemorated fallen soldiers and gave meaning to their sacrifice. This is relevant to the Transylvanian case study because, until the end of 1918, Transylvania was still an integral part of Greater Hungary and had already adopted similar practices of remembrance (similarities that persisted in the interwar period, when Transylvanian Magyars kept close contact with Budapest). The second section then analyzes war remembrance as articulated in the publications of a Veteran Union, based in Budapest but whose members were from Transylvania. The activities of Magyar veterans' associations were often suppressed in Romania, so this case study allows us to observe "uncensored" how Transylvanians commemorated the war.[2] The third section turns to forms of Magyar war memory in interwar Romania, as depicted through memorials, in literature, and in the attitude of the postwar generation. The activities of former Magyar soldiers in interwar Romanian politics are also assessed. Finally, this interwar memory is contrasted with the memory of World War I from 1940 to 1944, when northern Transylvania was once again part of Hungary. The chapter concludes by arguing in favor of differentiating Hungarian war remembrance on the basis of both time and space; in other words, that in the interwar period the Magyars living in Trianon Hungary, compared to those in Transylvania, had other opportunities to express remembrance. Still, even in Transylvania the forms of remembrance changed, differing between 1920 and 1940 and when the region belonged to Hungary again in the 1940s.

War Remembrance in Hungary

By the late nineteenth century, Magyar nationalists in Hungary were promoting an image of their nation that emphasized its eternal military prowess. In particular, they remembered the revolution of 1848, which had led to short-lived independence for Hungary, and in 1896 they celebrated the Millennium, the thousand-year anniversary of the Magyars' arrival in the Danubian basin. In this context, artists in Hungary developed several motifs that highlighted Hungarian military prowess such as the figure of a sitting lion, the neo-pagan motif of a Turul bird,[3] or battle scenes and depictions of weapons.[4] Scholars researching nationalism and nation-building processes have interpreted these and similar activities as a key component of constructivist efforts to promote a national consciousness in Hungary. New national holidays and supposedly "Hungarian" customs and memorials were introduced, affecting the patriotic feelings between the Magyar and non-Magyar populations.[5]

Soon after the outbreak of war, in November 1914, the Society of Applied Arts in Budapest launched an initiative for a memorial to commemorate fallen soldiers.[6] Although this proposal was unsuccessful, rejected due to the poor quality of the submitted plans, it was resubmitted the following year. The second bid stated that the monument should "immortalize Hungarian heroes [and their] greatest and bloodiest war."[7] According to Ferenc Herczeg, a leading author and intellectual of his time, a soldier's grave should express the fact that he was regarded by his country as part of the "nation's dead." In 1917, with the war in its third year, the Hungarian parliament finally passed a law that compelled all towns and villages to commemorate these soldiers.[8] It is due to this law, in force during the interwar period, that there now exist more than two thousand Great War monuments throughout Hungary (five hundred are sculptures).[9]

After the passing of this law, the erection of monuments became an official matter and subsequently a propaganda instrument for Hungarian politicians to use in the interwar period. In 1927, the Hungarian politician György Lukács made it clear what kind of sentiments and what ideology the officials were expected to portray in these monuments. They should, he said, create a sense of pride in the heroic sons who had sacrificed their lives for the fatherland, the artist expressing not only the Hungarian nation's belief in truth, but also its righteous and noble anger at the Treaty of Trianon, which Hungary had been forced to sign in 1920. Furthermore, the monuments needed to show Hungary's conviction that the status quo would be changed either through honorable hard work or through the "holy martyrdom and blood of new generations."[10] The monuments therefore had an explicitly militarist dimension and were assigned a pedagogic and political duty to influence future generations.

Since hundreds of monuments were erected in interwar Hungary, the majority of them had little artistic value except in villages where more authentic memorials were created by local amateurs. These local memorials however usually contained not an ideological or aggressive message, but rather some simple wording together with the names of those men from the village who had died in service.[11] According to Ildikó Nagy's categorization, the majority of monuments in Hungary can be divided into ten groups: the idealized soldier; the fighting soldier; the hero's death; the mourning soldier; equine sculptures; allegorical monuments (such as a lion symbolizing the strength of Hungary, or the nation in female form); monuments depicting Hungarian history; the Hungarian family (often fleeing from the homeland); memorials featuring the Turul bird; and those with a resonant symbol, such as a cross or the Holy Crown of Hungary.[12] Most of these motifs had already been used in other contexts before the war. Since a huge numbers of memorials were erected to great acclaim and publicity, we can assume that the cultural and political elites of Magyar minorities in the neighboring states were themselves very aware of the vibrant memorial culture of interwar Hungary.

A Transylvanian-Magyar Veteran Case Study

Between 1918 and 1924 over two hundred thousand Magyars emigrated from Transylvania to Hungary. The majority of these were members of the middle class: landowners, priests, teachers, members of the state bureaucracy, or career soldiers.[13] Because the rump Hungarian state had to reduce the size of its bureaucracy and army, many of these refugees suffered great economic hardship. In Hungary, they built a network of organizations whose aim was to keep alive the idea of their eventual return to Transylvania. Several veteran societies were part of these networks. Every year the former soldiers assembled, commemorated fallen comrades, and published newsletters and pamphlets.

One of their most prominent leaders was Károly Kratochvill (1869–1946), a retired field marshal, who was a head of the Veterans Union of the 4th Honvéd Infantry Regiment (HIR) and, after 1928, president of the so-called Association of the Székely Division. The Székely Division had been created at the end of the war by Kratochvill himself. In November 1918, after returning from the Italian front, he had been ordered to organize military resistance in Transylvania against the invading Romanian army. In the city of Kolozsvár a large number of Magyar soldiers had gathered, arriving in the city from the Italian, Eastern, and Balkan fronts. Most of them had made no plans for the future because much of their Transylvanian homeland was already occupied by the Romanian army; others were prepared to continue the war, but now against Romania.[14] It was therefore not difficult for Kratochvill to recruit soldiers to his cause, and after just two weeks fifteen thousand men had enrolled in his division. Between January and April 1919 the Székely Division was quite successful at repulsing attacks by the Romanian army, but it officially surrendered to Romania after Béla Kun's Communist regime came to power.[15] Many soldiers of the division who refused to surrender found their way to Szeged where they joined Admiral Horthy's counterrevolutionary army.[16] By 1920 most of the division had left Transylvania and resettled in Hungary. Kratochvill himself served until 1924 as a lieutenant-general in the Hungarian army before being forced to retire due to reductions in the Hungarian forces. In 1928, together with approximately fifty other officers, he established the Association of the Székely Division. Its aim was to keep the memory of the division alive, to prevent the complete return of veterans to civilian life, and to help in writing the history of the division and its military exploits.[17] The Association's other assignments included helping Székely-Magyar youth to secure a patriotic education, providing financial and moral support to widows, and promoting national awareness among the civilian population.[18] How successful the Association was in promoting these goals remains unknown.

About eight to ten thousand soldiers of Kratochvill's Székely Division had moved to Hungary. Yet by the end of the 1930s only six hundred of these men were members of the Association of the Székely Division (less than 10 percent of all veterans of the division living in Hungary).[19] The Association of the Székely Division was integrated into the Union of Transylvanian Men (Erdélyi Férfiak Egyesülete) and was involved in a network of Transylvanian refugee organizations, which edited books, held meetings, and had a striking influence on Hungarian public opinion.[20] Kratochvill himself, as president of the division and through the 4th HIR Veterans Union, was very active in promoting ideas about his men's heroism during the war, as well as the Székely Division's activity in 1919. He visited battlefield locations in Italy where the 4th HIR had fought, authored several book chapters and articles, and delivered speeches commemorating fallen comrades.[21] A number of recurring themes can be seen in these speeches and written works. Kratochvill often claimed that the war had been initiated by Serbia and Russia because they desired the dismemberment of Hungary. He also argued that Magyar soldiers had fought and died without ever being defeated on the battlefield. Instead, it was social turmoil in the hinterland that had produced the unfavorable outcome of the war, Mihály Károlyi's bourgeois government, and, eventually, Béla Kun's communist regime. The "catastrophic" peace treaty was regarded by Kratochvill as a consequence of these social and political developments, a sort of Hungarian "stab in the back" legend.[22] Károlyi's and Kun's political activities were, of course, ideal scapegoats for the loss of territories in the Trianon peace treaty.

In order to overcome the desperate situation in interwar Hungary, deprived of reputation and power, the Transylvanian veterans (like many of their brethren in the other successor states) cultivated a military attitude toward the education of the next generation and indeed toward all of Hungarian society. They believed that in order to strengthen national consciousness it was necessary to reflect on past glories, something essential for building a rejuvenated Magyar nation that would be capable of recovering its lost territories.

Later, in 1938, Kratochvill would point out that Hungary, unlike Germany, did not need a "Führer," for they already had such a leader in the person of the Regent Admiral Horthy.[23] This claim was made at a time when the Hungarian parliament was debating anti-Jewish legislation. Kratochvill's statement was therefore directed against right-wing radicals in Hungarian society who strove for stronger ties with Germany. The position of the Association of the Székely Division was very conservative and nationalist, but it appears that most members refrained from joining the radical right within Hungarian society. The evidence of Kratochvill's own speeches suggests that he, like other many Hungarian veterans or politicians with a Transylvanian background (for example István Bethlen), subscribed to traditional conservative values, not to those asserted by the radical right.

To sum up, it is clear that in the interwar period the Association concentrated on keeping the Transylvanian question on the political agenda. This was the aim of Kratochvill's speeches, of the published material, as well as the good contacts the Association established with high-ranking politicians. How far the Association succeeded in contacting and activating the veterans who remained in Transylvania requires more research, but letters found in Kratochvill's correspondence suggest that he made some efforts to influence the Magyar minority in Romania too.[24]

The War Remembrance of Magyar Communities in Transylvania

In Transylvania, remembering the war primarily meant remembering the "unification" of this territory with the Romanian Kingdom.[25] In Transylvania each ethnic group acquired its own way of recalling this event. On 1 December the Romanians celebrated the declaration of the union of Transylvania with Romania in the town of Alba Iulia. Regardless of the defeat of the Romanian army by Habsburg and German troops in 1916, Romania viewed Transylvania's acquisition as a result of Romanian victory on the battlefield (as opposed to an Allied decision at the Paris peace conference). Accordingly, several war memorials were erected in Transylvania depicting heroic Romanian soldiers. New research by Bernhard Böttcher has shown that in the interwar period Transylvanian Saxons (Germans) tried to develop some kind of dual loyalty both to their own regions in Transylvania—their *Heimat*—and to the Romanian state.[26] Inscriptions on Saxon war memorials mentioned both the sacrifice of fallen Saxon soldiers fighting for their *Heimat* and the promise that Saxons would be devoted to the new state even under post-1918 circumstances.

How did Transylvanian Magyars commemorate what they had experienced during the war on the front and at home? They could probably take little pride in their record in uniform, and mourning the way in which the war ended was inopportune because increasingly nationalist circles in Romania paid close attention to their attitudes and activities. A Hungarian folk song sung in public or flowers arranged in the colors of the Hungarian flag were reason enough for people to be put on trial for irredentism or even treason.[27] In this kind of atmosphere it was only in the Romanian parliament that Magyar politicians could occasionally admit that "while 1 December is a day of joy for the Romanian people, it is a day of mourning for the Hungarian nation, because it brought catastrophe to Hungary."[28] József Willer, the politician who made this remark, was able to speak freely on account of his parliamentary immunity. In the same speech he underlined why the Hungarian Party did not participate in the unification celebrations. It would be dishonest, he argued, for the Magyar minority to act as if that was a day of celebration; non-participation was not an act of disloyalty for the party had expressed its loyalty on several occasions, but nobody would think them sincere if they celebrated on 1 December. Under such circumstances, Transylvanian Magyars were unable to establish veteran associations of their own, nor could they raise monuments that conveyed a blatantly Magyar nationalist message. Romanian archives have scant documentation on Magyar veteran associations, and what documentation there is usually pertains to Romanian societies.[29] Unlike Magyar veterans, Romanians were allowed to commemorate their comrades, to erect memorial plaques, and hold festivals of remembrance (as they did on the tenth anniversary of unification in 1928).

Magyar commemoration was inevitably less prominent than its Romanian counterpart. Two examples will suffice to illustrate this point. In 1926, in the Hungarian village of Backamadaras (in Maros county, twelve kilometers from the town of Marosvásárhely) a memorial plaque appeared on one building commemorating "the memory of heroes who passed away or disappeared during the world war (1914–1918)."[30] The inscription on the plaque mentioned nothing aside from the war, the time period, and a list of those who had died or disappeared. No ideological or political message was present, and nothing was written about the motivation of soldiers to fight, nor the homeland they had fought for. The plaque also had no religious message, nor was the significance of the supreme sacrifice alluded to. The only village official inscribed was a teacher who had supported the plaque's unveiling; the names of the village priest and mayor were also absent. It is nevertheless notable that the inscription refers to the war as the "world war": the villagers of Backamadaras understood the magnitude of World War I and the impact it had had on their community in comparison to previous conflicts.

The second example comes from the village of Csíkmadaras (Csík county, today in Hargita county) where in the 1920s a stone memorial was erected in the village cemetery.[31] In its original form its inscription omitted the names of fallen or missing soldiers (these were added on separate stones during the 1990s). But like the plaque at Backamadaras, this memorial contained no political, religious, or mythical imagery, and it is the absence of such messages on Magyar monuments in interwar Transylvania that is so striking. It was a meaningful and telling silence in the face of official Romanian war remembrance. It seems clear that the Magyars living in Transylvania preferred no message at all, or even no monument, rather than one with an inscription that, perhaps acceptable to Romanian national sentiment, would be an inappropriate commemoration of the Magyar community's sacrifice. There is another explanation too for the absence of prominent Magyar memorials from the interwar period. Magyar communities may have balked at such commemoration after their traumatic experiences in the wake of unification. Some Romanian communities had acted forcefully to take control of the postwar public space, destroying Magyar statues or monuments, which seemed to them to symbolize the former Hungarian regime.[32]

Nevertheless, some Transylvanian Magyars moved to commemorate the war in other forms: through novels, military almanacs and journal articles, or in works of art. Two concerning Hungary's war are especially important. The novel *Siberian Garrison* by Rodion Markovits (born 1888) describes the author's experience from 1915 to 1921, first as a soldier on the Eastern front and then as a prisoner in Russia. The first edition of this novel was published in 1927 and was soon translated into a number of foreign languages (the English version was published in 1929).[33] The novel's subtitle could be translated as "Collective

Reportage" and indicates the novel's unusual provenance. In 1926, when Markovits asked readers of a Kolozsvár newspaper, *Keleti Újság*, to share with him their memories from the war, he received over a hundred letters in response. He decided to shape his novel according to what he read in his respondents' letters, hoping that the end result would read as an authentic and representative account of the typical Magyar soldier's wartime experience. Markovits' "microcosm of war" followed a very simple narrative.[34] His protagonist is a young lawyer (whose name is omitted as he is to be understood as representing all soldiers) who volunteers to fight at the outbreak of the war. Shortly thereafter he is captured by the Russians and sent with thousands of other prisoners (Magyars and non-Magyars) from one prison camp to another, eventually arriving in Siberia where he remains until 1920.

The novel's message was pacifist and anti-militarist. Markovits' lead character greets the news of the assassination of Archduke Franz Ferdinand and the outbreak of war with indifference, considering the affair a matter that could have been solved by the royal court without affecting his everyday life. Nevertheless he is swept up in the wave of war enthusiasm in August 1914 and in this respect his behavior matches that of the good soldier Švejk, the hero of Jaroslav Hašek's classic Czech novel. Once at the front, Markovits describes the experience as one of horror, endless pain, and senseless killing. There is no heroism or nationalist pathos in his description of the front, nor is there any kind of nationalist rivalry among the soldiers of the multinational army or any justification for the war. The conflict seems only to serve the interests of the upper classes, maintaining their control over those beneath them. The author emphasizes this point in an important part of the novel dealing with imprisonment. Markovits' protagonist is sent to a camp for officers where most of his fellow inmates remain proud of their rank even while in captivity. Although in the eyes of their Russian captors the prisoners are almost equal, the officers follow their own rules based on rank, and there is a very severe and self-imposed code of conduct and discipline in the camp, as if the soldiers are part of a regular peacetime army. Markovits does not hide his critical stance towards the officers' conduct. Not only does the protagonist show sympathy for the fate of non-officers, but he increasingly focuses on similarities between his homeland and Russia, as well as between the soldiers of the Habsburg and Russian armies:

> Of course, not every mountain could be called Mátra, but from a distance these mountains also looked blue, and the train stations all resembled the stations at home. There were exits here too, the tickets were collected upon leaving the platform, and the station masters always saluted the trains. Was the station-master's salute different from theirs? ... And if so, then what? That was no reason to shoot at each other.[35]

After a few years of imprisonment even the cause of the war's outbreak loses meaning, becoming almost ridiculous: "Of course, once upon a time we wanted revenge! Serbian infamy, where is revenge now? How far we are from it now! ... How can one be enthusiastic if one does not know what one is fighting for?"[36]

In its pacifist message and lack of sympathy for nationalism, Markovits' work was similar to a number of other novels and poems written by Transylvanian Magyars such as Aladár Kuncz, Benő Karácsony, or János Darvas.[37] In Hungarian literature, the war was typically commemorated by underlining its horror, rather than praising heroic death and sacrifice. Markovits' novel ends in 1920–21 when, after the Russian Civil War has ended, the novel's protagonist is allowed to return to his village. This fate was typical of many Magyars, caught in Russia and unable to return home for many years after the war. In this context, it is important to note that Magyars elsewhere across Greater Hungary identified the Treaty of Trianon of June 1920 as the real end of the war. "Trianon" gradually became a synonym for the catastrophic outcome of the war for Hungary, the focus of all Hungarian political and sociological thought.

Unspoken questions about how and why the catastrophe of Trianon was possible are at the center of Imre Mikes' book, *The Path of Transylvania from Greater Hungary to Greater Romania*.[38] Mikes was born in 1900 and he participated in the war as a sailor in the Austro-Hungarian navy. After the war he became a journalist in Transylvania, and published this work in 1931. The book is a mixture of fact and fiction. On the one hand, Mikes describes how Romania's leading politicians decided to become involved in the war simply to conquer Transylvania. On the other hand, the book is full of reported dialogues that the author could not have known at the time. It is also full of emotionally descriptive language: "tragic event," "sad," "dramatic."[39] It can be read as a young Magyar's attempt to analyze how and why the war contributed to the dismemberment of Hungary and how and why it lost territory to Romania.

Mikes' main concerns were the end of the war and its outcome; he was less interested in its outbreak, its conduct, or the suffering of civilians. For young Magyars like him, the war meant above all an end to Hungarian statehood: a caesura. And this was more important than any postwar continuity of Hungarian statehood in a diminished country. Mikes did seek an answer to the question, "what caused the outbreak of war?" but his answer was rather plaintive: the war was caused by chauvinism, jingoism, and nationalism.[40] He especially stressed the role of the Romanian irredentist movement and the disloyalty of Transylvanian Romanians before and during the Great War, whose position had been backed by Archduke Franz Ferdinand as an enemy of the Magyars. Step by step Mikes therefore constructed a sort of conspiracy theory in which the Archduke and the Romanians had joined forces in order to sabotage Hungarian statehood.[41] Uninterested in military history, Mikes then concentrated on high diplomacy and Romanian behavior. In a manner of thinking very typical of most of his Magyar contemporaries, he regarded the end of the war as a "double collapse," in other words, the "agony of the army" combined with the domestic collapse of the monarchy.⁴² Mikes also claimed that Romanian politicians acted "ingeniously" in 1918 when they achieved the union of Transylvania with Romania, but at the same time accused Romanians residing in Transylvania of starting a revolution against Hungary in 1918. In light of this cunning Romanian plot, the Magyar leadership was blameless for the war's denouement, for they had done their best to protect the nationalities at all times. Instead, it was the Romanians who were especially culpable. Mikes had found his scapegoat for the defeat and dismemberment of Hungary.

Comparison between the works of Markovits and Mikes reveals significant differences. Markovits concentrated on the war itself, describing its negative sides (horror, pain, death) and the social impact of hostilities. Mikes, in contrast, was concerned with the political disintegration of Hungary during the war and the role played by the nationalities in that disintegration. His study of war began at the end, as it were, although he did mention the phenomenon of mass death. As representative of the outlook of ordinary Transylvanian Magyars, both authors' approaches have some validity. Markovits was above all a writer motivated by humanist emotions, trying to express the feelings of a large number of former Magyar soldiers. Mikes was a journalist belonging to a younger generation, who attempted to rationalize and explain to his readers why Hungary was forced to relinquish Transylvania. They both (but especially Markovits) were very influential, and their works went through several editions and attracted public attention.

Mikes' book additionally raises the question of how the younger (postwar) generation in Transylvania thought about the war. Born at the turn of the century, Mikes was certainly not alone among a young Magyar elite preoccupied with the war and its memory. At the end of the 1920s the generation born between 1900 and 1910 became very active in Hungarian society.⁴³ Many of them went to Hungary for their studies, eventually returning to Transylvania, or in some cases attended university in Romania and became proficient in the Romanian language. At the time it was believed that the war had made a huge demographic impact on Transylvania's Magyar minority: either young men had been killed in the fighting or they had sought refuge in Hungary. If true, this would explain the lack of any influential youth movements in the region in the postwar decade.

Only at the end of the 1920s did change really occur, when the generation born at the turn of the century was graduating and trying to carve out a status and role within the Magyar minority community. As adolescents they had come to realize the difficulties faced by their parents' generation in the new Romanian state (language, cultural and economic problems, discrimination).⁴⁴ They started to ponder the causes of this new, reduced Magyar status, and several groups of the younger generation of different political orientations singled out the war as the major cause. Like Mikes, many were convinced that it was a watershed in history and society and, generally speaking, they distinguished between a prewar and postwar era in almost all spheres of life, whether in high politics, society and economics, in ideology, or in the arts and literature. They considered Hungary's wartime defeat and the catastrophe of Trianon as proof that the Hungarian elites of the previous generation and their methods had failed, discrediting the prewar ideologies. Therefore the new generation cried out for new ideologies and a radical new approach to politics.

In the postwar period, many educated young men in Transylvania identified prewar economics with a sort of wild capitalism that they held responsible for the economic problems of the Magyar minority.[45] Part of this generation sympathized with communism as a valid alternative to capitalism, but a corporatist system was also considered, and some Catholic groups were inspired by Christian Socialist thinking. In politics this youth generation—in common with its peers across the former territories of Austria-Hungary—tended to criticize the prewar system, branding it liberal and individualistic (in a negative sense).[46] According to their vision, while the lower classes must play a greater role, national cohesion now had to be a priority in order to reinvigorate the national community. In this connection some young Magyars felt a strong affinity toward village life, distancing themselves from towns and urban modernity. They developed an interest in peasant life and tried to ignore the world of politics by focusing on local problems. Behind this critical stance lay a certain social conscience. Feeling that neglect of the lower classes had been one of the greatest mistakes of prewar politicians, they knew that they themselves were the future leaders of the Magyar minority. They therefore wanted to learn from the previous errors and understand living conditions in the Transylvanian countryside.[47]

All this was closely connected to the impact of the war upon Transylvanian society, underlining how it was a watershed in the consciousness of the younger generation. Many desired something new, in politics, economics and society—a quest that led them naturally to embracing various utopias. While some turned to communism, some adopted *völkisch* principles and a right-radical ideology. While the communists preached a classless society (in contrast to prewar society), right-wing elements promoted a pure Magyar community without the influence of Jews and other "aliens".[48] Right-wing youth was particularly critical of what they saw as prewar Hungarian tolerance and assimilation. In fact, as these youths turned against the ruling classes and promoted a society formed exclusively of "true" Hungarians rather than social classes, their views overlapped with the communists. In 1939, at the beginning of World War II, members of the *völkisch* group (most of whom had not fought in the Great War) were enthusiastic about the forthcoming conflict, speaking of the opportunity for heroism, the death of humanism, and the birth of a new European political order.⁴⁹ This "new order" called for the shattering of the old and, of course, the members of the *völkisch* group were optimistic that Transylvania would soon return to Hungary.

The behavior of right-wing Magyar war veterans was sometimes contradictory and can be illustrated through three leading figures. In 1932, a scandal occurred in Magyar politics in Transylvania when, at a local meeting of the Magyar Party in Kolozsvár, a group of young men led by politician István Sulyok demanded a more nationalist position and a realization of the "right-wing spirit" within.⁵⁰ Though they were vague about what a right-wing spirit really meant, it is clear that Sulyok and his group represented a radical element among the Magyar minority. As a veteran of the Austro-Hungarian army, Sulyok was by the 1930s the most right-wing Magyar journalist and politician, with strong national-socialist and anti-Semitic convictions.⁵¹ He was also a colleague of Elemér Gyárfás, a veteran and former wartime comrade of Gyula Gömbös, the later Hungarian prime minister. In Transylvanian society, Gyárfás was known to support a militarist and autocratic approach, cultivating a *Führerkult* on the model of Gömbös and Mussolini.⁵² But politically he belonged to the conservative-Catholic circles of the Magyar Party and was a leading figure within that organization. In the Romanian parliament, he demonstrated also the impact of his wartime experience by making speeches in favor of Transylvanian invalids (who as veterans of the Habsburg forces typically received lower pensions than veterans of the Romanian army).⁵³ Another leading veteran was the party's vice-president, Elemér Jakabffy, who had been a member of the Hungarian parliament before 1914, served as an officer in the war (though not on the front line), and in the interwar period was very active in European minority politics.⁵⁴ Within the Magyar minority he supported a conservative-liberal line and was often at odds with the attitudes of Sulyok and Gyárfás.

The political views of these three war veterans demonstrate the ideological heterogeneity of the Magyar Party and the Magyar minority in Transylvania, and specifically the ideological diversity of Transylvanian war veterans. In terms of socio-economic background they all belonged to the so-called ruling classes of prewar Hungary. Gyárfás and Jakabffy belonged to the same generation, but there were big differences in their political attitudes. In interwar Transylvania they did not have the opportunity to organize themselves into a veterans' union or similar commemorative organizations as in Hungary. However, through their role in the Magyar Party, and as journalists, they were able to wield influence over the regional Magyar communities. The Party itself made efforts to integrate such personalities who held contradictory opinions, for it wanted to extend its influence over the various strata of Magyar society. And considering the results the Magyar Party achieved in interwar elections, it can be said that its strategy was very successful.⁵⁵

War Memory Returns to Northern Transylvania

In August 1940, the second Vienna Award returned the northern part of Transylvania to Hungary. This territory had a population of 2.5 million, 1.3 million of whom were ethnically Magyar.[56] In northern Transylvania festivities were held to greet Hungarian troops as they entered the towns, evidence of how well-received they were by the Magyar minority.[57] For most Magyars this event was perceived as their liberation from Romanian rule and reunification with the homeland. Many refugees now returned to Transylvania, but together with the new Hungarian rulers came new ideas, movements and parties, which had developed in interwar Hungary but were almost unknown in Transylvania.[58]

One such movement was the "State Flag Movement" (Országzászló mozgalom), initiated in 1923 in Budapest by Nándor Urmánczy, a Transylvanian-born aristocrat who in the wartime parliament had been a highly vocal defender of Magyar interests.[59] The movement's aim was to raise as many Hungarian flags as possible in order to commemorate Trianon and keep alive the memory of the Magyar diaspora. Soon after the Vienna Award, the movement spread into Transylvania with towns from "inner Hungary" and refugees donating flags to their former homeland. In Transylvania the flags were hoisted in lengthy ceremonies with the local population participating in traditional dress. Local and non-local politicians delivered speeches, with soldiers and veterans from Hungary often present; priests celebrated Mass, children recited patriotic poems, and choirs sang folk songs and the national anthem. These celebrations were not only opportunities to strengthen national consciousness and create a new national cohesion in wartime; they also gave communities a fresh chance to remember the first war and commemorate fallen soldiers. Thus it became quite common to combine flag ceremonies with the dedication of new war memorials and commemorative plaques.[60]

It is worth analyzing some of the monuments raised to the dead of the Great War in the 1940s. An interesting example is the memorial erected in June 1941 in the village of Rety. Here, the monument dedicated to the memory of the 24th HIR was built by the Honvéd Comrades Union from Hungary, aided by a major donation from Ferenc Pál, a veteran of the regiment.[61] The memorial exhibits the impressive figure of an unknown Magyar soldier prepared to defend his country. It was unveiled in the presence of the armed forces, who used the opportunity to demonstrate their strong wartime connections to the native population. Civilians present at the unveiling were dressed in traditional costume and displayed Hungarian flags representing the national symbols that had been banned under Romanian rule.

By taking a closer look at several other dedications we can see how each festivity enabled local Magyars to take up positions that had previously been forbidden.

Thus the memorial unveiled in August 1941 in Páva was donated by a rich family from the village and placed in front of the state school with the intention of inspiring the pupils with patriotism.[62] The memorial featured the Turul bird, the symbol of Hungarian revisionism that had been banned in interwar Transylvania.[63] In the middle of the monument the Transylvanian coat of arms could be seen beneath which was the inscription, "In Memory of Our Dead Heroes." On its lower part there was also a map of "Greater Hungary," that is, Hungary prior to Trianon. Referring to the map, the memorial was inscribed with the revisionist slogan, "It was like this, it will be like this" (*Így volt – így lesz*). Therefore, the memorial represented a combination of local traditions and symbols, such as the Transylvanian coat of arms, with adopted rituals and messages from Hungary like the revisionist slogan. Most war memorials erected in Northern Transylvania in the 1940s included such symbolism. In Kézdiszentkereszt, for example (Háromszék county, today Kovászna county), one could read "In memory of our return," combined with the Holy Crown of Hungary and the interwar "Hungarian Credo" (a sort of prayer for the return of the lost territories).[64] In Sepsiszentgyörgy (Háromszék county, today Kovászna county) the "Horthy-hand," another revisionist symbol, was placed atop the monument.[65] Often, the memorials made reference to the twenty-two years of Romanian rule, describing them as "occupation" and years of the greatest injustice.

Explaining Divided Memory

This chapter has suggested that Transylvanian Magyars had a divided memory of Austria-Hungary's last war. The Magyars who remained in Transylvania remembered the war differently from those who had left the region; the former also altered their remembering during the interwar period and World War II. This diversity is not so surprising when we consider the heterogeneity of the Transylvanian Magyars and the circumstances in which they found themselves, whether in Transylvania or in Hungary. The principle difference between the forms of remembrance was that Transylvanians in Hungary could imbibe the "official" war memory (and also contribute to it), while those who remained in Transylvania had to adopt a more subtle way of remembering the wartime sacrifice. Due to their minority status, their war memorials and plaques were devoid of any particular message related to national sentiment or patriotism, and gave no clear instruction to future generations.

Here also there was a marked difference between the behavior of the minority in Transylvania and its equivalent in Czechoslovakia. For example, Magyar inhabitants of Kamocsa village in Slovakia (formerly Komárom county, today Nyitra county), not only raised funds for a plaque to commemorate the fallen, but also organized a large celebration on the occasion of its unveiling in 1925, at which politicians and even a Protestant bishop made speeches. The bishop officiating was László Ravasz who had left Transylvania in 1918, and his speech serves as another Transylvanian Magyar interpretation of the war. Ravasz proclaimed the wartime sacrifice as an "award," asserting that "the death of a young hero in the bloom of his life is not a broken life but a full life, a finished life, because death is a more exalted mission than a full life could have been."[66] Essentially, Ravasz was suggesting that surviving veterans were less worthy than those who had fallen in the war; if the war dead had been granted a full life they would have been better compatriots. Ravasz duly identified wartime death as a "desirable endeavor" and a pedagogic "model." He then turned to the widows of Magyar soldiers and said: "You can go back to life as fighting and praying women—like heroic women—and educate your children." With these words he was targeting the next generation, which he felt needed to be educated in the spirit of their forefathers to become heroes ready to sacrifice themselves on the altar of the nation. This militant attitude was believed to be the best means of restoring old Hungary. And in this context it is unsurprising that the local priest, Kálmán Boross, also declared that "the true merit for mankind, for your fatherland, for your religion, is to burn yourself."[67] Boross meant the fire from weapons in wartime; war was a "saintly cause" and he regarded as martyrs those who died fighting. These findings suggest that the Magyars in Czechoslovakia benefited from more freedom of expression than their co-nationals in Transylvania. They were allowed to use religious and national vocabularies, something that was unthinkable in the Transylvanian case.

Transylvanian Magyars were more focused on coming to terms with their experiences through literature, in novels and poems. In this context, authors such as Rodion Markovits identified with the "ideology of Transylvanianism" that meant searching for ways to live peacefully with other ethnic groups.[68] In the 1930s, however, in the context of growing ideological pressures (coming from the Romanian government, but also influenced by Nazi ideas) more and more members of the younger generation refused to believe in the possibility of peaceful coexistence and accused their fathers' prewar generation of being too liberal. They regarded the war as a caesura and the manner of its ending as justification for rejecting any prewar ideology of liberalism and equality.

After the second Vienna Award, Transylvanian Magyars quickly adopted a memory of the war similar to that long developed by their co-nationals in interwar Hungary. It is worth noting that these Magyars were divided in their ideology and political attitudes: in the early 1940s many called for a discriminatory minority policy (against Romanians and Jews) that was at odds with the treatment they had demanded for their own minority in Romania before 1940.[69] During World War II, remembrance in Transylvania then assumed a special role. As we have seen, the purpose of Hungarian wartime memorials was not only to commemorate at last the dead soldiers of the Great War. Memorials in Transylvania also supported the national self-confidence of the Magyar communities, demonstrating that they were an inseparable part of the Hungarian nation. Erecting monuments and plaques, most of them inscribed with revisionist slogans, strengthened people's sense of reconnecting and belonging to Hungary. They thus represented a certain compensation for the preceding decades when Magyars had been denied the right to declare their Hungarian allegiance.

The often religious character of the rural festivities (the "Hungarian Credo" for instance), and the large crowds who participated in commemorations, now enabled many to express their grief about the fallen of World War I, while also contributing positively to the new national unity of the war years. Typically, remembrance of the earlier Great War sacrifice and struggle was closely integrated with Hungary's successful crusade during the interwar period to reestablish its former borders. Participation in World War II on the side of the Axis forces was intended finally to realize those aims (to recover the southern part of Transylvania as well as the north). This helps explain the use of an overwhelming number of revisionist symbols on Transylvanian memorials. Those built in the 1940s clearly demonstrated not just Transylvanian Magyar communities in mourning, but a war remembrance that was manipulated to reinforce Hungarian national consciousness.

Franz Sz. Horváth received his PhD in 2006 and is currently an independent scholar in Frankfurt. His research interests include: ethnic minorities in Eastern Europe, Jewish-Gentile relations and anti-semitism, and the Holocaust. His publications include *Zwischen Ablehnung und Anpassung: Die politischen Strategien der ungarischen Minderheitselite in Rumänien 1931–1940* (2007), and "Minorities into Majorities: Sudeten German and Transylvanian Hungarian Political Elites as Actors of Revisionism Before and During the Second World War," in *Territorial Revisionism and the Allies of Germany in the Second World War*, ed. Marina Cattaruzza, Stefan Dyroff, and Dieter Langewiesche (2012).

Notes

1. István Zágoni, "Tizedik esztendő a kisebbségi úton," *Keleti Újság*, 27 December 1927, 35.
2. On the situation of the Transylvanian Magyars in interwar Romania, see C.A. Macartney's judgement of 1937: "In 1914, Transylvania was ruled by and for the Magyars, without and largely against the Roumanians, with the Saxons occupying a sort of middle position. Today it is ruled by and for the Roumanians, against the Magyars, with the Germans still in the middle—culturally better off, socially and economically worse off. Where the Magyars formerly had the political power, the Roumanians have it today. Instead of the Magyars and a few German officials, and no Roumanian, there will soon be Roumanian, a few German, and no Magyars. Instead of a State-supported Magyar education, with struggling Roumanian and German schools, there is now State-supported Roumanian education, while the

Magyars (and the Germans again) have to struggle to keep their schools in existence. Where Magyar industry and agriculture got easy credits, Roumanians get them now; and so on and so on." C.A. Macartney, *Hungary and her Successors* (London, 1937), 348.
3. The Turul is the most important mythological bird of the origin myth of the Magyars. In Hungarian mythology it is a messenger of God sitting on top of the tree of life; the bird symbolizes God's power and will.
4. Miklós Szabó, "A magyar történeti mitológia az első világháborús emlékműveken," in *Monumentumok az első háborúból*, ed. Ákos Kovács (Budapest, 1990), 46–63.
5. Some recent publications are Árpád von Klimó, *Nation, Konfession, Geschichte: Zur nationalen Geschichtskultur Ungarns im europäischen Kontext (1860–1948)* (Munich, 2003); Ákos Kovács, *A kitalált hagyomány* (Pozsony, 2006).
6. Ildikó Nagy, "Első világháborús emlékművek: Esemény- és ideológiatörténet," in *Monumentumok*, ed. Kovács, 131.
7. Ibid., 133.
8. Ibid., 136.
9. Ibid., 125. Nagy's opinion is that less than a dozen of these monuments are of interest for art historians.
10. Ibid., 137.
11. Ibid, 131. Márta Kovalovszky, "Kegyeletszolgáltatás: Az első világháborús emlékművek történetéhez," in Kovács, *Monumentumok*, 100.
12. Nagy, "Első világháborús emlékművek," 126, 128.
13. Ernő Raffay, *Erdély 1918–1919-ben* (Budapest, 1987).
14. See the letter sent to Kratochvill by István Zágoni, a former officer of the Székely Division. Together with a huge number of sources related to the Division, Zágoni's letter can be consulted in Kratochvill's papers. These are in Veszprém County Archives, Hungary (Veszprém Megyei Levéltár: hereafter VeML), Kratochvill Károly irathagyatéka, XIV. 10., box nr. 11.
15. For the history of the Division's battles see László Fogarassy, "Adalékok a székely hadosztály és az erdélyi kérdés történetéhez (1918–1919)," in *Magyar történeti tanulmányok XIX*, ed. Géza Veress (Debrecen, 1986), 59–90; László Fogarassy, "Az ismeretlen székely hadosztály," in *A Debreceni Déri Múzeum évkönyve 1971*, ed. Imre Dankó (Debrecen, 1972), 225–52.
16. István I. Mócsy, *The Uprooted: Hungarian Refugees and their Impact on Hungarian Domestic Politics 1918–1921* (New York, 1983), 39 (on the Division's flight to Szeged); 91–94 (on the refugees' political attitude); 127 (the role played by Transylvanian refugees in the Prónay detachment).
17. VeML, XIV. 10., box 1, unit 3, pieces 83 and 86: Tárgysorozat az 1927. május hó 8. megtartandó Székely Hadosztály összejövetelére, and Tárgysorozat az 1928. május hó 5-én megtartandó Székely Hadosztály összejövetelre.
18. *A Székely Hadosztály Egyesület Alapszabályai* (Budapest, 1941), 2. §.
19. For more details see Ferenc Sz. Horváth, "Kratochvill Károly és a Székely Hadosztály Egyesület tevékenysége az észak-erdélyi zsidók védelmében (1943–1944)," *Századok* 142/1 (2008): 123–52.
20. Mócsy, *The Uprooted*, 91–94.
21. "Szent Kereszthegyi Kratochvill Károly: Az utolsó harcok az olasz hadszíntéren," in *A magyar gyalogság: A magyar gyalogos katona története*, ed. József Doromby and László Reé (Budapest, [1941]), 413–22; "Szent Kereszthegyi Kratochvill Károly: A székelyt a forradalom se győzte le," in *A magyar katona: Századunk legszebb magyar csatái*, ed. Endre Ajtay, 3rd edition (Budapest, 1944), 397–416; Károly Kratochvill, "Magyarország legelső ellenforradalmi, antibolsevista alakulata," *Hargitaváralja* 18 (15 September 1939): 544–46.
22. Ibid; and VeML, XIV. 10., box 1, unit 3, piece 59: M. kir. debreceni katonai körletparancsnokság. Tiszti parancs (Debrecen, 29 December 1921).

23. *25. számú Egyesületi Értesítő* (Budapest, 1938), 2.
24. See also István Zágoni's letter to Kratochvill, written in 1933: VeML, Kratochvill Károly irathagyatéka, XIV. 10., box nr. 11.
25. The term "unification," of course, already reflects the Romanian point of view. The contemporary Hungarian press in the interwar period only used descriptions such as "changing of rules," "the outcome of the war," etc.
26. Bernhard Böttcher, "'Treue zur Heimat und zu dem Staate, von dessen Grenzen unsere Heimat umschlossen ist'—Doppelte Loyalität bei den Siebenbürger Sachsen," in *Staat, Loyalität und Minderheiten in Ostmittel- und Südosteuropa 1918–1941*, ed. Peter Haslinger and Joachim von Puttkamer (Munich, 2007) 159–85; and Bernhard Böttcher, "German First World War Memorials in Transylvania," *Central Europe* 4/2 (2006): 123–30. See also Bernhard Böttcher, *Gefallenen für Volk und Heimat: Kriegerdenkmäler deutscher Minderheiten in Ostmitteleuropa während der Zwischenkriegszeit* (Vienna, 2009).
27. A number of examples can be found in the column "Itéletek" ("Sentences") of the Hungarian newspaper *Magyar Kisebbség*, edited by the politician Elemér Jakabffy between 1922 and 1941.
28. "Willer József képviselő nyilatkozata a december 1 megünneplése tárgyában a kamara 1932 december 2-iki ülésén," *Magyar Kisebbség* (hereafter MK), 11/24 (16 December 1932), 784.
29. See for example, National Archives of Bihor county (Arhivele Naționale Bihor), Oradea, Fond Nr. 75, Uniunea foștilor voluntari români din Bihor.
30. Sándor Pál-Antal, ed., *Backamadaras 600 éve (1392–1992)* (n.p.; n.d.), 60.
31. Sándor Pál-Antal et al., *Csíkmadaras: Egy felcsíki falu hét évszázada* (Marosvásárhely, 1996).
32. One example was in the town of Székelyudvarhely (Odorheiu) where the Romanian minority destroyed a Magyar monument and erected a statue of the wartime Romanian king Ferdinand in its place. For further examples, see Maria Bucur, *Heroes and Victims: Remembering War in Twentieth Century Romania* (Bloomington, IN, 2009).
33. Rodion Markovits, *Siberian Garrison*, trans. George Halász (London, 1929).
34. "Microcosm of war" was the title of Horace Liveright's *Time Magazine* review on 16 December 1929.
35. Markovits, *Siberian Garrison*, 177.
36. Ibid., 217.
37. I am referring here to Kunz's novel *Fekete kolostor* (Black Monastery), 1931 in Hungarian and 1934 in English; Karácsony's novel *A napos oldal* (The Sunny Side) of 1936, and the poem *Harctéri eset* (Occured on the Front) by János Darcasi, which appeared in the Transylvanian Magyar newspaper *Pásztortűz* in 1923, 52. For more details on Kuncz and Karácsony as well as on Hungarian literature in general see Lóránt Czigány, *The Oxford History of Hungarian Literature: From the Earliest Times to the Present* (Oxford, 1984).
38. Imre Mikes, *Erdély útja Nagymagyarországtól Nagyromániáig* (Sepsziszentgyörgy, 1996; originally Brassó, 1931).
39. Ibid., 26.
40. Ibid., 14.
41. Ibid., 64, 72.
42. Ibid., 105–7.
43. On the question of the Magyar minority generations, see Nándor Bárdi, "Generation Groups in the History of Hungarian Minority Elites," *Regio* English version (2005) 109–25.
44. For more details on the younger Magyar generations in Transylvania see Franz Sz. Horváth, *Zwischen Ablehnung und Anpassung: Politische Strategien der ungarischen Minderheitselite in Rumänien 1931–1940* (Munich, 2007), 106–29, 193–214.
45. Ibid., 125–26.
46. Ibid., 194–95.

47. Ibid., 115.
48. For more details, ibid., 196–99, 250–55.
49. Ibid., 332.
50. Ibid., 120–21.
51. For more details on Sulyok see ibid., 260–62, 268–70, 402.
52. For more details on Gyárfás see ibid., 223, 401.
53. "Gyárfás Elemér interpellációja az erdélyi hadirokkantak ügyében a népjóléti miniszterhez a szenátus 1929 április 13-iki ülésén," MK 8/10 (16 May 1929), 381–82.; "Gyárfás Elemér interpellációja az erdélyi hadirokkantak nyugdíjának egyenlősítése tárgyában a szenátus 1932 március 4-iki ülésén," MK 11/6 (16 March 1932), 190–91.
54. See Sabine Bamberger-Stemman, *Der Europäische Nationalitätenkongreß 1925 bis 1938: Nationale Minderheiten zwischen Lobbystentum und Großmachtinteressen* (Marburg, 2000).
55. For more details see Horváth, *Zwischen Ablehnung*, 141.
56. There are, of course, a lot of conflicting statistical data in the literature. See Keith Hitchins, *Rumania 1866–1947* (Oxford, 1994), 450, 486.
57. See Horváth, *Zwischen Ablehnung*, 359–68.
58. See the analysis of the contemporary ideological debates by Gábor Egry, *Az erdélyiség "színeváltozása": Kísérlet az Erdélyi Párt ideológiájának és identitáspolitikájának elemzésére 1940–1944* (Budapest, 2008).
59. See Mark Cornwall, *The Undermining of Austria-Hungary: The Battle for Hearts and Minds* (New York, 2000), 363.
60. Many examples can be found in Álmos József, *Országzászló-állítások Háromszéken* (Sepsiszentgyörgy, 2006).
61. Ibid., 91.
62. Ibid., 87–89.
63. On the relationship between erecting war memorials and irredentist symbols in interwar Hungary, see Miklós Zeidler, *A magyar irredenta kultusz a két világháború között* (Budapest, 2002), 17. The meaning of such symbolism in today's Hungary has been analyzed by Eric Beckett Weaver, *National Narcissism: The Intersection of the Nationalist Cult and Gender in Hungary* (Oxford, 2006).
64. The "Hungarian Credo" sounded: "I believe in one God / I believe in one Homeland / I believe in one divine eternal justice / I believe in the resurrection of Hungary. Amen."
65. József, *Országzászló-állítások*, 53, 99.
66. Kálmán Boross, *A világháború kamocsai áldozatainak emlékkönyve* (Komárom, 1925), 8.
67. Ibid., 7.
68. The "ideology of Transylvanianism" had several faces and directions (political, literary, etc.) in which Magyars, Romanians, and Saxons were involved. For more details see Zsolt K. Lengyel, *Auf der Suche nach dem Kompromiß: Ursprünge und Gestalten des frühen Transsilvanismus 1918–1928* (Munich, 1993).
69. For more details see Egry, *Az erdélyiség*.

Part II

SACRIFICE AND THE DISCOURSE OF VICTORY

Chapter 5

FRAMING THE HERO
Photographic Narratives of War in the Interwar
Kingdom of Serbs, Croats, and Slovenes

Melissa Bokovoy

In late 1920, the internationally known Serbian photojournalist, Rista Marjanović, wrote to the press bureau in the Ministry of Foreign Affairs of the Kingdom of Serbs, Croats, and Slovenes requesting money for the reproduction, storage, and publication of his photographs, sketches, articles, and documents that detailed "the horrible suffering of the Serbian people, during the long wars."[1] In this letter, Marjanović worried that those abroad as well as those within the new kingdom were beginning to forget—or choosing not to remember—the Serbian people's experiences during the Balkan Wars and World War I and that there was "the need to remember" their heroic efforts. He proposed "pictorial propaganda" as the means to remember. Drawing on his experience in the field of photojournalism, Marjanović argued that visual imagery could influence the "popular masses" in ways that "dry text" did not. He proposed not only creating a separate "place" for the collection and reproduction of such documents, but also advocated the immediate production of an "inexpensive album" of photographs. Marjanović saw them as powerful tools for shaping, categorizing, and solidifying memories of the war. He was neither an amateur nor was he alone in such efforts.

Almost twenty years later, in the spring of 1939, another of Serbia's wartime photographers, Dragoljub Pavlović, exhibited over seven hundred photographs from the Balkan Wars and the Great War in Belgrade. Jovan Obićan, in a review for *Vreme* wrote admiringly of war correspondents and photojournalists:

> We see them in the action, with cameras in hand, in the trenches, bravely moving forward with the assault … We see how, for the love of the sensational picture, they ignore common sense. In the moment when the soldier looks not to lose his head or seeks shelter, the war correspondent seizes that moment in the battle…. crouching, he braves thousands of dangers [for the picture].[2]

In the review of the exhibition and in the exhibition itself, there were no explicit references to the horrors of war, its cruel indignities, the suffering of those who died, or death as painful and grotesque. Instead this exhibition, and a numerous and diverse array of pictorial representations produced from 1914 to the late 1930s, portrayed the recent wars as conflicts in which the ideals of "manliness, the honor of self-sacrifice, and romantic, redemptive death" had been embraced by Serbs; it presented Serbs as honorably and courageously fighting and dying for the "liberation and unification" of the South Slavs.[3] Over the previous twenty years, the Serbian public had grown accustomed to seeing photographs displaying their best selves, a brave, selfless, heroic and self-sacrificing nation of citizen soldiers ready to do battle with the enemy in order to defend other south Slavic peoples.

During the interwar period, patriotic photographic albums, collages, essays, exhibitions, commemorative postcards and posters, calendars, almanacs, and photographic films circulated among the citizens of Yugoslavia. However, the center of publication and distribution of such commemorative material was in Serbia where the publishing houses produced the bulk of this "pictorial propaganda."[4] Relative to other types of commemorative sites or performances such as monuments, plaques, holidays and anniversary celebrations, photographs captioned in Cyrillic and depicting the Serbian war experience were the most accessible of all commemorative items.[5] These were some of the first such artifacts produced and available to the Serbian public and helped to create the narrative of Serbia at war.

This chapter will examine how "official Serbia," i.e., the Serbian High Command, the royal court, military organizations loyal to the Karadjordjević dynasty, and Serbian politicians and intellectuals, utilized photographs to shape how Serbian soldiers, their leaders, their defeats and their victories, were to be remembered among the citizens of Yugoslavia. These images told a distinctly Serbian story that became the hegemonic interwar narrative of the South Slavs' wartime experience. From the very beginning of the Kingdom's founding, official war commemoration and remembrance focused almost entirely upon Serbian sacrifice and heroism and excluded the other peoples of the Kingdom (notably Croats and Slovenes), their wartime suffering, their deaths, and their sacrifices.[6]

In the new kingdom, the official narrative emanating from military, royal, and political circles depicted the ideal citizen as male and possessing a masculinity based on valor, honor, sacrifice, and selflessness. This ideal man, in photographs, was represented as a soldier who willingly marched to war, preferably with comrades, fought valiantly, protected the virtue of the innocent and weak, and sacrificed himself for his fellow soldiers, family, village, and nation.

This type of individual became the interwar model for the average citizen as many men came to see their experience at war, either in the Serbian or Austro-Hungarian armies, as a proving ground for manliness.[7] Male combatants had become privy to a sacred world that in the course of the war became ever more distinct from the profane world of the rear guard of the civilians. Returning to their homes, some veterans looked upon civilian leadership as incapable of meeting the challenges facing their national communities. In the case of Serbia, the Karadjordjević dynasty, officers in the Serbian army, and Serbian politicians sought to legitimize their leadership in the new kingdom and its institutions, and embraced the martial masculinity memorialized in wartime pictures and stories.[8] Similar memorialization was taking place within political circles in Croatia. Some returning veterans to Croatia, many of whom had been POWs in Russia, became critical of the Croatian Peasant Party's leadership as well as Stjepan Radić's civic virtue and pacifism. During the 1920s these veterans

Figure 5.1. Rista Marjanović, "Regulars." Photo from the beginning of the First Balkan War, published in the *New York Herald* (Paris) under the caption: "Not Sending Army to Front; Entire Nation will Fight," *New York Herald* (Paris), 12 October 1912, A1. Repurposed for *L'Illustration*, 15 January 1916 and captioned, "Young Serbian recruits, called up at the moment of the Austro-German offensive, leaving their villages and singing, coming to take up arms against the invaders." This photograph is from Andra Popović, *Ratni Album, 1914–1918* (Belgrade, 1926). Photograph courtesy of the Military Museum (Vojni Muzej) Belgrade, Serbia.

called for a more revolutionary response to Belgrade's hegemony.[9] Thus, those who had struggled for national unification through different channels such as political negotiation, compromise, and political declarations, and trod a path of civic virtue could be portrayed as lesser citizens, not worthy of their community's foremost accolades, rewards, or political leadership. Interwar histories and remembrances of wartime experiences utilized gendered language, tropes, symbols, and images to promote a "myth of war experience:"[10] those who survived and sacrificed were the ones fit to transform their national communities in both Serbia and Croatia.

The adoption of martial masculinity in the service of "liberation and unification" as the highest of all male virtues in the new kingdom was greatly aided by the photographic albums and images circulating during and after hostilities. These portrayed ideal manhood in the form of hypervirile martial images of men—the gallant soldier, the vigilant protector, and the challenged paterfamilias.[11]

Even though Serbian women marched alongside their men, provided labor on the battlefield and behind the lines, and bore the brunt of the Austrian-Bulgarian occupations after November 1915, the women celebrated and publically remembered as heroic were those very few who became actual soldiers or those foreign female medical staff who had come to help Serbia. During and after the war, Serbian women were mostly portrayed as victims, martyrs, and mourners. Displayed and published photographs helped reinforce this image of women as grieving, huddled, and helpless (see figure 5.4).

Figure 5.2. Rista Marjanović, "In Albania." First appeared in *Balkanski rat*, March 1913. Photograph courtesy of the Military Museum (Vojni Muzej) Belgrade, Serbia.

Framing the Hero in Interwar Yugoslavia | 101

Figure 5.3. Sampson Černov, "Eagle Eye on patrol at a forward position." Photograph courtesy of the Military Museum (Vojni Muzej) Belgrade, Serbia.

Figure 5.4. Rista Marjanović, "Burying the dead." Reproduced during the war in Alexis Karageorgevitch, *For the Better Hour* (London, 1917). Photograph courtesy of the Military Museum (Vojni Muzej) Belgrade, Serbia.

In the case of Croats in interwar Yugoslavia, it was difficult to assert male privilege if their contributions as volunteers in the Serbian army and their service as soldiers of the monarchy were not recognized, their images not publicly displayed, or if their wartime sacrifice was only fleetingly acknowledged.[12] In the hierarchy of masculinity within the new kingdom, Serbian men could and would claim a position of first among equals. In addition, Serbian women's valor and heroism would rank higher than other South Slav men (even those who were Austro-Hungarian soldiers) and other South Slav women.[13]

In the successor states of Central and South-Eastern Europe after 1918, identifying, defining, and then celebrating "patriots" was neither obvious nor without substantial contestation and debate. Territorial conquests and annexations, declarations of independence, and international treaties created new states and citizenries whose wartime experiences were by no means the same. Prewar citizenship and imperial or state loyalties, prewar and wartime politics, ideological proclivities, and class, ethnic, and gender identities made the telling of a unified, homogenous wartime narrative impossible without the new elites being able, through different commemorative acts, to transform real experiences into mediated ones. It is within this mediated form that the actions and experiences of individuals are defined, celebrated, and solidified as patriotic and heroic, or sacrificial.

Yet how did the successor states transform the real into the mediated? Nancy Wingfield, Christoph Mick, and others in this volume document how the interwar national or political elites utilized the resources and instruments of state building to privilege and promote one or two dominant heroic narratives stemming from the Great War, which obscured or vanquished the experiences of others. Holidays, monuments, commemorative memorabilia, and memoir literature of the Great War focused the new citizenry of the successor states on those moments that involved a battle or action sequence that could be construed as sacrificing for and defending the nation. Often the very first medium to focus the public's attention on a specific event and the actions of their soldiers was the news story, sometimes accompanied by photographs. News stories and photographs operated as narratives that transformed the real to the mediated. However, Rista Marjanović knew that "dry text" might not be able to solidify memories of the war. Instead he was convinced that a more effective approach would be photographs grouped and displayed publicly in order to narrate Serbia's wartime experience and sacrifice.

Serbia's Wars of Liberation, 1912–1918: Framing Violence, Creating Heroes

Creating heroes often means framing the violence of war.[14] During and after the Balkan Wars, the Serbian government, its military High Command, and its domestic and foreign allies, had purposefully framed historical events in order to shape the collective memory of the conflict and all public discourse surrounding its commemoration. Framing the violence of war had begun in 1912 when the chief of Serbian Intelligence, Dragutin Dimitrijević-Apis, invited Marjanović to document the experiences of Serbian soldiers during the First and then the Second Balkan War. Marjanović, who took a leave of absence from his job as illustrations editor at the European edition of the *New York Herald* (Paris), was one of forty-five journalists from all parts of the world assembled in Belgrade to report on the mobilization and the subsequent war. Jaša Tomić, a Serbian journalist from the Habsburg empire, noted for the First Balkan War that the Serbian general staff only permitted journalists to travel with the army and not to strike out on their own.[15] Foreign correspondents, unless cleared by the General Staff, were not permitted in the forward positions during the duration of hostilities.[16]

When Austria-Hungary declared war on Serbia in late July 1914, the Serbian High Command ordered similar restrictions. In August 1914, the Chief of the Serbian General Staff, Field Marshal Radomir Putnik, issued the first military order governing photography and visual imagery of the battlefield. It stipulated that "in order to protect the most important moments of war for history in pictures," and "especially the trail of cruelties and barbarism which the enemy will leave behind them," photographs and sketches had to be produced by photographers and painters with academic training and experience and attached to the newly created photographic section of the army.[17] Eventually each regiment, division, and army had a photographer or artist accompanying them on the battlefield and all photographs were subject to military control and censors. No image was to be developed or distributed without permission from the Serbian General Staff.[18]

In the Great War, the Serbian government and military were very fortunate, for not only did they have a seasoned photojournalist in Marjanović but they adopted as their own Samson Černov, a Russian Jew with French citizenship, who had come to Serbia in 1912.[19] Černov was sent to the Balkans in 1912–13 by the Russian newspapers, *Novoe Vremya* and *Russkoe Slovo*, and was also a special correspondent for the French journal, *L'Illustration*, as was Marjanović. When war broke out again in Serbia in the summer of 1914, Černov returned as a correspondent for *L'Illustration* and *Novoe Vremya*. He quickly received permission to accompany the Second Army of Stepa Stepanović and was a favorite of the General Staff and the royal family for his stark yet contemplative wartime portraits. After the Serbian counteroffensive in December 1914, Černov was entrusted with the task of photographing the deaths of Serbian civilians along the front with Austria-Hungary, many of whom had been killed by Habsburg units.[20] In 1915, he accompanied the Second Army on its retreat through Albania to Corfu.[21] From Corfu and at the request of the Serbian High Command and government, he left for London where he gathered his photographs into the most ambitious photographic exhibition of any theater of the war to date, titled simply "Exhibition of Serbian War Pictures." It took place at the Royal Institute Galleries from June to August 1916 and then toured France and the United States until the end of the war.

This exhibition on foreign soil, as well as the creation of war albums in the postwar period, demonstrates a concerted effort by "official Serbia" to frame the violence of war. By exhibiting its photographs in Allied countries as well as setting up photographic displays for Serbian and Allied soldiers along the Salonika front in 1917 and 1918, official Serbia tried to mediate the visual encounter between viewer and image. Thereby it controlled the message and prevented an unmediated encounter where viewers might determine for themselves a photograph's meaning and subvert the emerging official narrative of the wars.

The London exhibition of June 1916 was one of the first arenas to articulate Serbian heroism. According to press reports, it consisted of 260 photographs and "illustrated the terrible suffering of Serbia during the last three years."[22] It is interesting that the Balkan Wars were accepted with such ease as part of Serbia's narrative of heroism and suffering. As this exhibition and others toured over the next two years, press reports added continuing knowledge about Serbia's war that resulted in a powerful and evocative story about the country's redemption and rebirth as a "liberator" of the South Slavs.[23] From this wartime propaganda a powerful mythical story with religious imagery emerged: the liberator king (Petar), the unifier king (Aleksandar), and the homeland (Serbia) had battled valiantly; endured unimaginable hardships and the pain of retreat, evacuation, and occupation; and then regrouped to drive the invaders out of the Balkans resulting in the liberation and unification of the South Slavs.[24]

This was a remarkable turnaround of opinion. Just before war erupted in July 1914, the Carnegie Endowment for International Peace had published its official investigation of the Balkan Wars, reinforcing and providing documentary proof, especially through photographs, of the violence that Serbs had visited upon Bulgarian and Macedonian communities.[25] Serbia's wartime display of photographs obscured and shrouded Serbian violence and thus represented a public relations success for Serbia.[26] Official Serbia clearly understood the significance of how violence was framed. It consciously and with great care presented the violence of war and the shame of defeat and retreat as tragedy, martyrdom, resurrection, and redemption.

The groundwork for the exhibition had been laid when a Serbian delegation from Corfu, led by Crown Prince Aleksandar, traveled to England in order to apprise the British of how they had abandoned Serbia. They brought with them "an extraordinary collection of relics and photographs from the Serbian battlefields," which was to be exhibited in order to demonstrate the efforts of the "gallant countrymen." Utilizing the British media, Aleksandar portrayed Serbia's war as a continuation of its centuries-long fight against the barbaric "other" for national liberation. He stated, "we have been fighting literally for our national existence for centuries. Our struggle with the invaders from the Orient is historic, but for the last years, with the Turks, Bulgarians, Albanians, and now with the Teutonic powers, we have been engaged in wars that I think would have exhausted a less spirited people."[27] Aleksandar and others interested in constructing narratives of the war fell back on "existing cultural templates."[28] In the case of Serbia, the template most readily available for enduring suffering was Serbia's medieval history that became the frame by which Serbia's wartime experiences were presented and narrated.

One influential Serbian publisher of the 1920s, Dušan Šijački, duly utilized these cultural templates of medieval Serbia and Serbia's age-old struggle against its neighbors in his two short-lived illustrated journals, *Vidovdan: An Illustrated History of the Serbian Wars, 1912–1918* and *Balkan War (1912–1913)*.[29] In *Vidovdan's* first issue in 1918, Šijački chose to represent Serbia's wars not as wars of national liberation for all South Slavs but as liberation for the Serbian people. The title not only betrayed the journal's vision but the cover carried a design that tied the wars of 1912–18 to the Battle of Kosovo by encircling the date 1389, the year of that battle, with the dates 1912 and 1918. The journal's editorial statement declared that its initial goal was "to protect from forgetting, to remember those wonderful heroes on whose graves rest our glory and from whose death will spring our life and our happiness."[30] To guard against this forgetting and to commemorate these heroes, the editors asked readers to relinquish their private mementos, photographs, and remembrances from the war. "We are asking for pictures and all pertinent information and statistics about fallen officers and [living] officers, especially those that can serve as an example to the next generation on how to love the Fatherland and defend freedom."[31]

Throughout the pages of his two magazines, Šijački laid out war photographs, etchings, and historical paintings, captioned occasionally with historical references, in order to give his reader the sense of a linear progression from past to present. In many cases he referenced Serbia's medieval kingdom and its expulsion from Kosovo, Macedonia, and other parts of its fourteenth-century state. He linked these distant historical episodes to Serbia's "return" to those areas in 1912–13 and then again in 1918. As one scholar of photography has noted about this strategy, "the viewer seemed to be confronted not by a subjective historical

representation of a geographically and nonlinear event, but by 'history itself'."³²
The images combined with captions and texts laid out in the magazine offered a kind of template for the construction of war experience in Serbian collective memory.

This type of template, the blending of past and present historical events, was not unique to the Serbian cultural and political nation. In a recent work, Allen Frantzen, a literary historian, traces the chivalric ideals emanating from wartime Great Britain and Germany back to their origins in the Middle Ages. He shows how a wide selection of literature and images from the medieval period was used by nineteenth- and twentieth-century writers, journalists, and painters, to shape the ideals of duty, sacrifice, and heroism, to rouse their citizens, and "teach them how to war."³³ He argues that nations at war portrayed the "bloody good of chivalry" in visual material such as posters, photographic postcards, and war memorials, in order to mobilize their male citizens. "The importance of these images was not for the professional military men who had a deeply ingrained understanding of continuities between medieval and modern military behavior that we think as chivalric." Instead these images were for the citizen-soldier and those connections had to be demonstrated in some way.³⁴ The photographs, sketches, and collages in Šijački's journals were perfect for this purpose.

At the end of the Second Balkan War in August 1913, a medium for demonstrating to Serbia's peasant soldiers that their chivalric behavior and sacrifice was on par with their leaders appeared—a memorial poster designed to place a picture of an individual soldier alongside Serbian royalty in order to commemorate the recent victories of the Serbian army over the Turks. Three small portraits of King Petar and his sons, Aleksandar and Djordje, dominated the top of the poster and in its center was a blank frame for a small portrait photograph. A similar poster was issued after 1918 with victories over the Austrians and Bulgarians celebrated as well. The publishers of these posters, a commercial press from Belgrade, took out quarter-page advertisements in Serbia's main papers and promoted their commemorative poster. The publishers declared that

> for each brave officer and soldier, this memorial poster is the most beautiful memento of the magnificent victories of the Serbian army ... The [collage of] pictures [on the poster] show all of the more important towns in the newly unified kingdom and the capital Belgrade, his royal highness with his sons, as well as military trophies. In the middle picture is an empty place reserved for a photograph of the courageous Serbian hero.³⁵

At the bottom of the advertisement, the publishers continued their sales pitch: "Each soldier, from the highest to the lowest rank, who participated in the wars of national liberation needs to purchase this poster and to frame it as an eternal reminder for future generations."³⁶ The poster was available in either black and white (at one dinar) or color (one dinar and twenty para).

The inclusion of an individual photograph on this poster illustrated "the transference of an object created for remembering one individual into a collective assemblage where he, or much less often she, becomes one among others."[37] The use of collage—combining photographs with other visual elements, such as sketches, postcards, and words—transformed the poster into a vehicle that overcame the narrative limits of an individual photograph. The placing of the photograph in the middle of this collage was an act that located the soldier, alive or dead, into a brotherhood of national heroes who had sacrificed and died for Serbia's expansion and later during the Great War for the liberation and unification of all South Slavs.

The publishers as well as Šijački were selling their commemorative materials in a country that had for the previous forty years inculcated its youth, through education and cultural activities, with ideas of loyalty and devotion to the homeland. "These principles were repeatedly expressed in various forms—in essays, through folk poetry, in accounts of the deeds of national heroes, by simple declarations of individuals, and in proverbs. The student and the new Serbian citizen, after 1878, were told that he should devote his life to his country and that the supreme test of his individual worth was his readiness to sacrifice his life for Serbia."[38] In the case of the poster, families literally placed their sons in the pantheon of Serbian heroes. They had earned the right to sit with the greats in heaven, for they had avenged Kosovo, spilled their "guts" for defense of the fatherland, and had liberated the cities and regions represented on the poster. In addition, the represented images and themes perhaps provided the victims, survivors, and mourners from the "wars of national liberation" with a sense of continuity, sympathy, and identity with others who had suffered the same sacrifice and loss.[39]

Šijački requested similar actions from veterans and the family of soldiers. He wanted to collect individual photographs, personal stories, and remembrances about fallen soldiers, so their experiences and deaths could be bundled together into a common narrative, one that would co-opt the familial or personal remembrance. A lone photograph or a private remembrance of loved ones kept the individual beyond the reach of Serbia's political and cultural elites. Offering family members a place to deposit their mementos or a place to hang a picture meant a single death could be transformed into a national sacrifice and the soldier into a "hero."

"Pictorial Propaganda" in Interwar Serbia

Dušan Šijački's *Vidovdan* was a short-lived endeavor since few Serbs in the immediate aftermath of the war could afford a subscription. Nonetheless several issues of his illustrated magazines were reprinted later in the 1920s and sold throughout Serbia. Efforts to develop or reissue photographs from the war and distribute them were constantly undertaken by the photographers themselves, by publicists, military officers, and the royal government. Few publications and exhibitions, however, had the prestige of those by Marjanović or the head of the Serbian army's photographic division, Lieutenant-Colonel Andra Popović. Their efforts, in the 1920s, to depict Serbia's wartime experiences produced two of the decade's most important photographic narratives. Both gathered and then popularized images that helped to create an iconography of the war and augment in the mind of the Serbian public its heroic sacrifices and contributions to the new state. These images were reproduced and widely distributed using lower-cost media such as postcards, posters, and calendars; and they were often published or supported by veterans associations, the military, and the royal court.[40] Soon the narrative arc of Serbia's wartime experience created by these albums found its way into the Kingdom's interwar textbooks and histories.[41]

After the war, Marjanović moved to publish his war photographs. Asking for a subvention from the Kingdom's Ministry of Education, he wished to compile the photographs into an inexpensive album and stressed its potential significance. Based on his expertise, he argued that there was no more powerful medium for conveying a point of view than illustrations and photographs and that their publication would commemorate "the horrible suffering and sacrifices of the Serbian people ... whose torment during the war and the retreat through Albania is now remembered only as a horrible dream. A free people must not forget the sacrifices made for this freedom." After this appeal against forgetting, Marjanović asked the Ministry that his photographs, as well as war documents, be copied and made available in the form of an inexpensive album "to the people, to schools, to the barracks, to cafes."[42] The commemorative significance of such an album was clear: "This work represents a historical moment which the [Serbian] people will guard, love, and cherish."[43]

Marjanović proposed dividing the album into four chapters, each representing the four main periods of the Serbian people's struggle for liberation and unification: "The Balkan Wars, 1912–1913," "The War Years, 1914–1915," "The Exodus [through Albania]," and "Unification and Liberation." Marjanović however never published this album. Instead, in 1926 he participated in a photographic exhibition at the officers' hostel in Belgrade. His photographs focused on 1912–15 with a special emphasis on the retreat of the "Serbian people and army through Albania."[44] The last photograph in the exhibition depicted the crossing of the Serbian army into Albania in December 1915. Thus only the first sixteen months of the war and the two Balkan wars were on display.

Marjanović narrated both an epic and intimate story of war. Individuals were the focal point demonstrating their determination, their anguish, and common humanity juxtaposed with panoramic scenes of destroyed villages, columns of refugees, and abandoned villages and homes. Later commentary on his photographs, especially those of the refugee columns, noted that he was a master of the mass scene. "He knew how to photograph a military column from a perspective that made it look like a living monster."[45] Yet some of the most evocative of his photographs were shot during Serbia's first months of war. He caught an abandoned toddler on film (figure 5.5), and a circle of mourning women gathered at the graves for loved ones lost to the typhus outbreak of 1915.

In the exhibition in 1926, Marjonović laid out his pictures chronologically and highlighted Serbia's participation in the Balkan Wars. Similar to the narrative presented in his wartime exhibitions, he captioned his photographs but did

Figure 5.5. Rista Marjanović, "Lost Child." Postcard.
Photograph courtesy of the National Library of Serbia (Belgrade).

not always identify the place, the subject, or even the year. He depended on the viewer's own experiences to recognize the sacrifice and heroism of fellow Serbs. He had adopted this strategy during the war when he, his *L'Illustration* editors, and Šijački from *Vidovdan* inserted some of his Balkan Wars photographs into stories and collages about the Great War. Thus, the editors and Marjanović stripped the original context and meaning from the photographs and substituted new meanings, leaving little doubt that the caption and placement as much as the viewer's experience dictated the interpretation. In this manner, Serbia's two Balkan Wars and Great War experience were inextricably woven together in the pictorial narratives (see figures 5.1 and 5.2).

The review of Marjanović's exhibition in *Politika* noted how it recorded the Serbian army's sacrifice for "liberation and unification" of the South Slav peoples. According to the reviewer, Marjanović's photographs allowed the "world" to see the "martyrdom" of Serbs but also the army's heroism as it retreated through Albania. These virtues had been showcased earlier in the layouts in *L'Illustration* and in the photographic exhibitions in Paris and London. At the opening of the Paris exhibition in late 1916, the French President had praised the Serbs for their perseverance and Marjanović for his photographic record of this event. The 1926 reviewer noted how many of the photographs which had been displayed

Figure 5.6. Rista Marjanović, "Through Kosovo: Death and abandonment in the snow," November 1915, first published in *L'Illustration*, 4 January 1913. This was taken in December 1912, not November 1915 as noted in the 1987 edition of *Ratni Album:* Rista Marjanović, Ljiljana Bojanić, Jasmina Alibegović, and Srećko Jovanović, *Ratni album Riste Marjanovića 1912–1915* (Gornji Milanovac, 1987). Photograph courtesy of the Military Museum (Vojni Muzej) Belgrade, Serbia.

during the war were now well-known. Several photographs—"King Petar crossing the bridge at Ljum-Kula" (figure 5.13), "Death and abandonment in the snow" (figure 5.6), and "The carrying of Field Marshal Putnik across the ravines of Albania"—"are not forgotten, but will always remain in our memory."[46]

Especially striking to the reviewer was Marjanović's artistry, his ability to convey the desperation of the retreat, and how the photographs depicting the passage of the wounded through the ravines were "historical documents ... worthy to be in all history textbooks and in the hands of all Yugoslavs." The review also found notable a photograph of infantry retreating under Austro-Hungarian and German fire, as well as one of peasant women pushing artillery guns into place overlooking the Jadar valley as the Serbian army anticipated an attack from Bosnia across the Drina River. Marjanović here had captured the "flight" of Serbian civilians, women, "weak" children, and the elderly, who abandoned their homes, loaded their belongings onto oxcarts, and carried bundles upon their backs, retreating into Serbia's interior. The reviewer concluded by recommending that every citizen of Belgrade should see these historical documents; the public should read one "bloodstained precious book about the sufferings endured by their people to free themselves and their oppressed brothers, for the unification of all Yugoslavs."[47]

Marjanović's artistry and international reputation made his photographs some of the most widely viewed images of Serbia's war. But Samson Černov shared this distinction as well. Černov's talent and entrepreneurial spirit; the Serbian government-in-exile's need to tell its war story; the embrace of "poor Serbia" by a small but influential western elite – all this facilitated the wide circulation of Černov's photographs, not only in postcard collections but also by the Serbian wartime government. In the interwar period his photographs then appeared in numerous published works, but it was the photographic album of Lieutenant-Colonel Andra Popović that provided the most complete compilation.

Popović played an indispensable role in shaping the visual narrative of Serbia's war and it would be his photographic album that became the most widely distributed and viewed album of Serbia's war in the twentieth century.[48] Popović worked independently for several years on a comprehensive war album, one that not only included the Balkan theater but all theaters of the Great War. Simply entitled *The War Album, 1914–1918*, it was a "monumental and voluminous" volume of 448 pages and fifteen hundred pictures, "a photographic collection of the personalities and events of the war in all countries." Here he gathered the work of the best wartime photographers, especially those of Marjanović and Černov, in order to create "a token of gratitude and glory for all the living and dead participants in the Great War, to our own people, as well as to our Allies, the known and the unknown, to all those who, fighting for honor, justice, and Freedom, have with the help of God, contributed toward the realization of the Liberation and the Unity of our nation."[49] The album celebrated a patriotism that tied Serbian history and military defeats, sacrifices, and victories to the foundation of the new kingdom, whether it was the defeat of the Serbs by the Turks at Kosovo field, Serbian victories during the Balkan Wars, the retreat through Albania, or the late wartime victories along the Salonika front.

Following the photographs, Popović included an abridged history of World War I. Printed in Cyrillic and twenty-four pages long, the history began with a declaration of South Slav unity: "We Serbs, Croats, and Slovenes speak one and the same language from time immemorial, are one people with three nations."[50] The abridged history had five sections: "A Short Historical Overview of Events from our Past until Today"; "European Politics and the Slav Question"; "History of the Serbian-Austrian Conflict"; "War in the Balkans"; and "A Short Overview of the Most Important Operations and Events during the First World War." While the early pages of the history summarized the premodern histories of the South Slavs, most of it described Serbia's wartime experience, the text complementing the pictorial narrative that had preceded it. The section on "War in the Balkans" detailed the battles on Serbian soil, the retreat through Albania, and the Salonika front. The only mention of other South Slavs was in a brief section on the "Operations of the 1st Serbian Volunteer Division at Dobrudja" and its transfer to the Salonika front where it was subsequently renamed the Yugoslav division.[51] One reviewer noted:

> On the title page are exaltations to governmental leaders, the armies and victims, and then presented are: the personalities of the ruling Serbian dynasty, members of the government, the officer corps, foreign allies and their military leaders, the wartime operations of the Serbian and Montenegrin armies, the Western front, events in Russia and the murder of the tsarist family, the retreat through Albania, the reorganization of the army on Corfu, the formation of the Yugoslav divisions, the operations on the Macedonian front, the exit and stay in Bizert, Austrian violence, terror and executions, the liberation of cities. The photographs are printed on the best paper and they look perfect. The binding is strong, and the cover is red. On the front cover there is a bronze relief with the figures of King Petar, the Liberator, Regent Aleksandar, the Unifier, and General Mišić standing in a watchtower during the war. At the end there is a short text about the history of the Serbian people and war in the Balkans.[52]

When *The War Album* was first published in 1926, the military journal, *Vojni Vjesnik* (Military Gazette), encouraged its readers to buy it. The editors asserted that "this beautiful edition is for every officer club, every officer, and every non-commissioned officer. The album will help develop a noble spirit in a new generation."[53]

During the war, Černov and Marjanović had narrated an intimate story of war through classic portrait photography and by framing and cropping shots to isolate individuals. Each image froze in time grieving women, abandoned

Framing the Hero in Interwar Yugoslavia | 113

Figure 5.7. Samson Černov, "In Albania." Postcard collection titled *Serbian Warriors* (1918). Research Library, The Getty Research Institute, Los Angeles.

Figure 5.8. Sampson Černov, "Hurry up! The children are cold," 1915. From an album of Černov's photographs sold at the exhibitions. Library of Congress Prints and Photographs Division, Washington, DC.

children, heroic men, and the poignant "exodus" of Serbs from their homeland in November–December 1915. They not only shot the war events but they attempted to capture the individual effort and essence of their subjects. Popović utilized these images in order to stress the courage and determination of the individual Serbian soldier, the selflessness of Serbian women, and the tragedy of Serbia's defeat at the hands of treacherous and barbarous enemies. He often laid out these portraits on a single page instead of grouping them in a collage. While there were no specific references to these portrait photographs in reviews of *The War Album*, the official organ of the Serbian government, *Srpske Novine*, highlighted one of Černov's first publicly displayed images, a colorized photograph of a teenage boy with his arm in a sling, which was the featured image for the 1916 London exhibition:

> In all public places and even in the Underground you could see the large posters, an artist production in several colors. In the middle of the poster is a young boy, Serbian, with a sling on his injured arm, in military dress with a coat thrown over his shoulder. Written in English is "Serbia's Defender: Fourteen-year-old bomb-thrower." And

Figure 5.9. Samson Černov, "A veteran warrior." Postcard collection, *Serbian Warriors* (1918). The first appearance of this photograph was on the cover of *L'Illustration* (16 October 1915) and titled "The Serbian Veteran." Research Library, The Getty Research Institute, Los Angeles.

then below this caption, "Exhibition of Serbian War Pictures by Sampson Tchernoff. Royal Institute Galleries 195, at Piccadilly, London. June–August." [54]

Černov's image for the poster became one of Serbia's iconographic images of the war and was sold in 1918 as part of a postcard collection entitled *Serbian Warriors*.[55]

Yet Popović did not always keep the original caption or meaning of the portraits when he placed them in his own album, thereby redefining what was meant by the "Serbian Warrior." In his wartime displays, Černov had contrasted the youth with an image of a grizzled Serbian veteran who in October 1915 had featured on the cover of *L'Illustration* (figure 5.9). Such a contrast caused one reviewer in 1916 to comment: "One cannot receive a better impression of the heroism of one people when viewing these 260 pictures taken by Mr Tchernoff. You see how a child of fourteen defends his fatherland as well as folks as old as fifty or sixty."[56]

Popović in his album ten years later transformed the young "bomb thrower" of wartime into a "child, injured" and featured it in a layout entitled, "The wounded and their evacuation."[57]

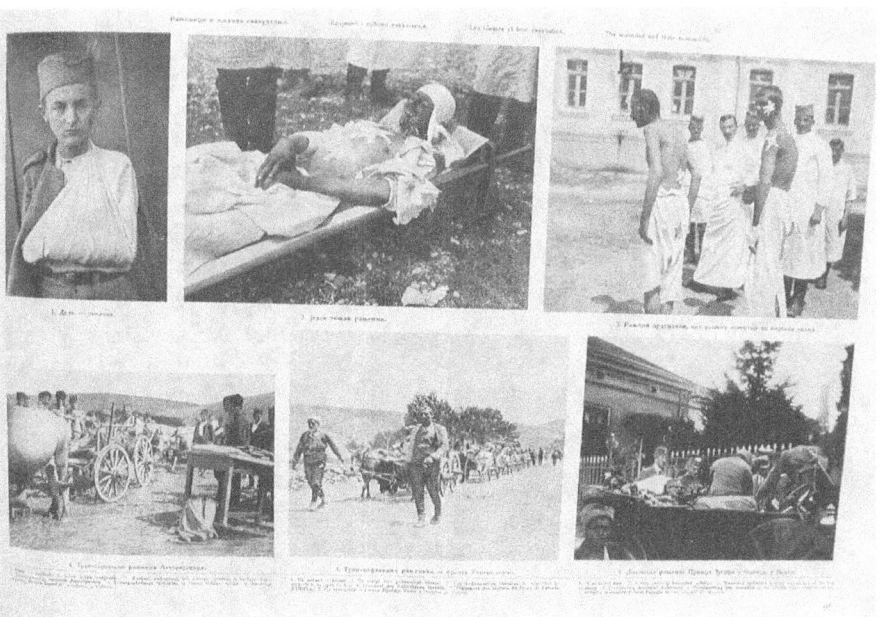

Figure 5.10. Upper left, Samson Černov's "Bombthower" recaptioned by Popović, *The War Album*, as "wounded child." The layout is titled, "The wounded and their evacuation." Photograph courtesy of the Military Museum (*Vojni Muzej*), Belgrade, Serbia.

With the stroke of a pen, the young boy's childhood and innocence had been restored. The grizzled veteran whose image had adorned the cover of *L'Illustration*, who had also featured in Černov's postcard collection, was stripped of his status as "Serbian veteran," and "Veteran warrior" and was placed in a layout titled "Village Life"[58] (figure 5.11). He was now "a pleasant face." Popović also buried, deep in the layouts and pages of *The War Album*, photographs that did not promote a heteronormative and virile martial masculinity.

Relegating the injured young boy and the gap-toothed, wrinkled, and time-ravaged veteran to the status of victim and bystander, Popović redefined the wartime vision of "Serbian warriors" by prominently displaying photographs of able-bodied soldiers and the Karadjordjevićs actively pursuing war. In a layout nestled in a section on the early months of the war, when Serbia had successfully defended its borders from Habsburg forces, Popović featured another one of Černov's photographs: the profile of a handsome, intent infantry soldier gazing out toward the horizon and captioned "Eagle Eye" (see figures 5.12 and 5.3). This image projected "a certain type of body deemed worthy of military investment" and represented the ideal male military body.[59] Unnamed and undated, it became the interwar icon for the heroic, virile Serbian soldier and ideal national

Figure 5.11. Upper right, Samson Černov's "The Serbian Veteran," recaptioned by Popović in *The War Album* as "The pleasant face of one of our peasants from Homolje village." The layout is titled, "Scenes from Serbian village life." Photograph courtesy of the Military Museum (*Vojni Muzej*), Belgrade, Serbia.

Figure 5.12. Samson Černov, "Type of Serbian soldier advancing." Postcard collection *Serbian Warriors* (1918), captioned in *The War Album* as "Eagle Eye." Research Library, The Getty Research Institute, Los Angeles.

citizen. In addition, Popović highlighted it in a part of the album that narrated Serbian victory over the first Habsburg offensives in 1914.

The photographs of the young boy and older veteran, while visually poignant, displayed a vulnerability, physical imperfection, and frailty that served as reminders of the desperate and dire circumstances of Serbs in defeat and retreat. Some images from the wartime exhibitions and postcard collections disappeared entirely from Popović's album. The image of a boy with both arms outstretched, which had been interpreted as a gesture of appeal to wartime allies, was not in the album, nor was that of an abandoned body lying on the ground alongside railway tracks; both photographs had been included in Černov's *Serbian Warrior* collection. Some of Marjanović's photographs from his wartime displays were also ignored by Popović such as that of the abandoned toddler. Poignant and appealing to the sympathies of Serbia's wartime allies, these photographs during the interwar period now served as a reminder of how the Serbian regime could not protect its citizens or care for its dead.

After the war, the royal court and its supporters in Serbia promoted the veneration of the two Kardjordjevićs as liberators and unifiers of the South Slavs. Their portraits, taken by Marjanović, came to symbolize Serbian fortitude and perseverance.[60] As aged and frail as Petar was, Marjanović's photographs portrayed the King as fully in command and never yielding. Even though during Serbia's retreat King Petar had often been carried over the mountains,

Marjanović's 1926 exhibition displayed him walking across a most dangerous bridge at Ljum-Kula (see figure 5.13). After the evacuation of Serbia, the official narrative shifted from his leadership to that of his son. Marjanović's portraits of Aleksandar often framed the prince in such a way as to demonstrate his dignified and resolute military bearing. Such photographs contributed to the royal court's promotion of the dynasty's military prowess mixed with compassion and empathy for its fellow Serbs. Individual heroism, as represented by shots of the two Karadjordjevićs or a soldier on sentry duty, once again became the preserve of the career military and the royal court. The iconographic status awarded to these martial images as examples of ideal heroism and virile, patriotic masculinity meant that military masculinity came to be foregrounded in the Kingdom as a distinct form of masculinity.

Popović also introduced the reader to Serbia's citizen heroes as he narrated the mobilization of Serbian society and the early months of the war when all Serbs had answered the call to defend the borders. None of these citizen heroes however warranted a stand-alone portrait. Popović laid out the citizenry as a national community, not as heroic individuals. One of Marjanović's photographs from the troop mobilization for the First Balkan War was reused in order to demonstrate the enthusiasm of the young for the war against Austria-

Figure 5.13. Rista Marjanović, "King Petar crossing the bridge at Ljum-Kula." Photographic Exhibition, Belgrade, December 1926. Popović's *War Album* captioned it as "A large number of our soldiers and countless refugees have crossed over this fatal bridge." Photograph courtesy of the Military Museum (*Vojni Muzej*), Belgrade, Serbia.

Hungary and captioned "Happily the Serbs are mobilized"[61] (see figure 5.1). On the same page, the purpose of this war was explained with a photograph of a Serbian priest blessing rifles and captioned, "God grant that the rifles herald freedom for our brothers." Popović narrated how the entire nation had mobilized to defend its territory against the enemy with a series of photographs of older men from the second and third reserve units; he even included a page of portrait photographs of Serb *komitadjis* (guerillas), confirming their importance in resisting the Austrian invasion. The album then proceeded to display layouts of Serbia's military preparations—troop training, the positioning of artillery, digging defensive lines, the drafting of women and children to help drag cannons and munition wagons to mountaintops near the Sava and Drina rivers. The album created a sense of foreboding as image after image showed officers and sentries facing forward, waiting for the attack. It was in this part of the album that Popović placed Černov's photograph of the Serbian sentry looking to the horizon.

Photographs of women, children, and the elderly fleeing the initial artillery fire and advances of the Austrians signaled that the war had begun. Popović laid out photographs of troops defending positions along the rivers from where Austria-Hungary invaded. Documenting the battles at Cer and around Mačva and Šabac, he interwove photographs of King Petar, taken by Marjanović, into this narrative arc. In one photograph of the king on horseback, he presented the "great" monarch as "hurrying from one position to another, exposing himself to heavy fire; he passed through the trenches spurring on his troops to fight for the honor and freedom of the fatherland."[62] There followed several pages that showed Serbian troops advancing: all conveyed the determination of the Serbians and their king, but Popović did not hide the costs of this defense of the homeland.

The album further reproduced, reframed, and captioned photographs of dead bodies and death rituals in two separate spreads. Popović presented photographs of the Serbian wounded, corpses, graves, and widows in order to demonstrate "unbearable sacrifices."[63] The first spread of twenty-seven photographs over five pages depicted the wreckage, carnage, and detritus of the battlefield-abandoned wagons, horse carcasses, corpses abandoned along roads and rivers, and the bodies of Serbian civilians executed by the enemy. A series of about ten photographs documented the murder of civilians by Austro-Hungarian and Bulgarian troops. Černov and the Swiss forensic scientist R.A. Reiss had utilized the late autumn light and bare foliage as a backdrop for their shots of the broken, decaying, and abandoned bodies.[64] These corpses silently informed the viewer of the inhumanity of Serbia's enemies. Appearing first in *L'Illustration* and then in the "Exhibition of Serbian War Photographs," Černov's photographs of mutilated Serbian bodies had also been circulated as postcards, while Reiss had used his shots to add photographic evidence to a forensic study of Austrian actions during the first invasion of Serbia.[65]

Taken after the Austro-Hungarian evacuation of Serbia in December 1915, the photographs by Černov and Reiss made Šabac, a river crossing on the Sava, the symbolic center for Serbian wartime suffering. Throughout the interwar period, these images appeared in conjunction with state-sponsored commemorative events like the one planned and executed by the royal court in 1934. At the dedication of a monument in front of Šabac's cathedral church and a mausoleum for the civilian war dead, King Aleksandar pronounced: "There isn't a region, there isn't a village, there isn't a house, which didn't contribute. But no-one, nowhere suffered like Šabac suffered."[66] As explicit and gruesome as some of the photographs were, they could not be left unmediated and thus the photographers, editors and public officials employed a linguistic strategy of binaries, of civilized versus primitive peoples, to inscribe the image with a "truth" of what had happened. In this strategy, the atrocity pictured had to be attributed to a people less civilized, less developed than those who viewed the photograph. Captions, narratives, and commemorative performances informed interwar viewers about the acts behind the photographs.

Members of the Serbian government had collected these photographs immediately after the war and compiled an *Album of Bulgarian Crimes* that was presented as a sequel to a three-volume documentary testament to the Bulgarian occupation. The new interim government of the Kingdom of Serbs, Croats, and Slovenes published this record in order to press its demands for favorable reparations and territorial settlements at the Paris peace conference of 1919. While the documents presented evidence from foreign observers, Serbian victims and Bulgarians, the photographic supplement "authenticated" what was contained in the written record. The preface stated,

> Among the thousands and thousands of authentic documents [and photographs] collected throughout the invaded territories, we have used only a small number. We did not have to make any special selection or choice. It was sufficient to take any one of these documents at random in order to discover that similar horrors were described in each of them. The Bulgarians throughout their reign all over occupied Serbia, no matter where nor who they were, irrespective of rank or office, from the highest to the lowest—in short, all those who represented Bulgaria, in the cities as well as in the village and in the poorest hamlets, from the Morava valley to Macedonia from 1915–1918—showed the same criminal mentality and the same bestial instincts.[67]

The photographs in the supplement grew in significance over the interwar period. While documents and witnesses' words produced a grounded chronicle of the occupations, photographs became instrumental to the broader aim of enlightening the Serbs, their fellow South Slavs, and a new generation about the suffering endured by those under siege and occupation. These photographs leapt off the pages of the supplement as well as albums like *The War Album* in order to bear witness to events. As Barbie Zelizer has noted, "using images to bear witness to atrocity required a different type of representation than did words. Images helped record the horror of memory after its concrete signs had disappeared."[68] Official Serbia and its wartime supporters continued to publish and display atrocity photographs throughout the 1920s as a specific form of collective remembering that interpreted the enemy occupations as deserving of critical attention.

In the first decade after the war, pictures of atrocities committed by Serbia's enemies therefore became standard fare in almanacs, school books, periodicals, anniversary records, and photographic displays. Editors and publishers, like Šijački who reproduced some of these photographs for *Vidovdan* in 1919, had at their disposal numerous photographs from which to choose. This was because cameras had been in the hands of official governmental and military photographers for both sides, but journalists, soldiers, local peoples, foreign nurses, doctors, and observers snapped whatever they saw. Their photographs displayed horrors so wide-ranging and incomprehensible that it enhanced the need to bear witness, forcing the public to remember as their own the suffering and pain so graphically displayed.[69] An early school book written by Professor Atanasije Popović, a reserve officer of the Serbian army, was published in Belgrade in 1922. It reprinted photographs that had been taken by Reiss for his published investigation into Austrian atrocities and its dedication clearly marked this text as a site for remembering those who had died to make liberation possible. The dedication read: "To the enlightened and noble sacrifices of the Serbian people, to the heroic and glorious fallen and dead in all Serbian liberation wars and to the dead Serbs, young and old, men and women, with a warm brotherly heart and with manifest, boundless gratitude this small book is dedicated."[70]

Similarly, a *Jubilation Anthology*, celebrating ten years of Serbs, Croats, and Slovenes together in one state, featured a photographic essay narrating the liberation and then unification of the South Slavs. The essay, as the last volume of three, included among its 170 pages of photographs a dozen images depicting the cruelties of both the Austro-Hungarians and Bulgarians.[71] One layout displayed photographs of a woman hanging between two men, a row of bodies watched over by the enemy, and a firing squad executing civilians on their knees.[72] In the same year through a Belgrade publishing house, R.A. Reiss issued *Pictures* [*Slike*], an album of photographs that visually documented his observations of the Serbian front in 1915 and then his tour along the Salonika front in 1917–18.[73] The photographs, all taken on the front lines, captured everyday life: the soldiers resting; the rocky terrain in the south; the human and material debris of the battlefield; and scenes from the final Serbian offensive of October 1918. Images of the wanton destruction of towns or of discarded corpses had been displayed already in Reiss's 1919 report *Infringements of the Rules and Laws of War* to offer graphic representations that were more difficult to deny than with words. His album *Pictures*, published at the same time as his memoirs in 1928, assumed a role beyond merely illustrating his words. As Zelizer has noted for Holocaust photographs, "The images guided the viewer to the heart of the violence, directing them to the preferred meaning by the fastest route."[74] These photographic essays of the dead focused public attention in order to underscore the "true" meaning of heroism and honor as noble self-sacrifice and to broaden the appeal of those who had made the greatest sacrifice for the nation.

While Andra Popović claimed responsibility for the way he presented the photographs in his *War Album*, he was operating in a discursive space where these images had already been circulating and shaping the understanding of the wars for over a decade. As discussed above, there were other photographic narratives circulating among the public as well. By 1926, Popović's album elaborated "truths" that had been established during the war at home and abroad, and he and others greatly added to the discourse surrounding Serbia's heroic efforts to liberate and unify the South Slav nations. The album, according to one review, was to be seen as "a lively panorama of the world war, as contributing to the patriotic upbringing and sense of purpose for the next generation, and internationally as the most significant record of the superhuman efforts and unbearable sacrifices of our [Serbian] people."[75]

Two separate reviews of *The War Album*, published in *Politika* in late 1926, emphasized the importance of the photographic album to celebrate, commemorate, and thank "all the living and dead of the World War." Both reviewers portrayed the album's value as chronologically detailing the events of World War I and Serbia's place within it, not only as an ally of Russia and the West but also as a South Slav liberator and unifier. The first reviewer, Živko Pavlović, who was a retired division general, noted how accessible the album made Serbia's history of the war since it was available in French and English and would be "fun educational reading for the young." He also enthused that it was an "exceptionally beautiful and everlasting work that depicted the superhuman efforts and innumerable sacrifices which eventually resulted in our courageous people winning freedom and unification and creating our current great and powerful state."[76] A second reviewer, Stanoje Stanojević who was a distinguished historian, echoed these sentiments: "[This album] instructs today's young generation about the torment and fear, the suffering, and sacrifices of those who endured or those who succumbed to the war. The album should be used to show this generation, which didn't live through the horrors and the sacrifices, our pain and our pride at the creation of the state. This album should be in every house, in every school."[77]

The mission of Popović's album was echoed by others, like Marjanović, who believed it vital to remember the Serb sacrifices made in liberating other South Slavs and creating the South Slav kingdom. Černov had grouped together many of these images in his postcard collection, *Serbian Warriors*, in order to narrate to Serbia's allies its heroic struggles. Popović's *War Album*, however, chose to redefine and re-remember who Serbia's warriors were. He constructed a narrative of sacrifice of the self for the collective ideal of liberation and unification as well as the high moral purpose of protecting the new kingdom, and he attached pictures to those sacrifices. What emerged from his photographic album were distinct visual images: the fragile, yet determined liberator-king; the prince regent who was the successful military commander and South Slav unifier; the Serbian military leader who, like his *hajduk* predecessor, was resisting the infidel; the tough and patriotic Serbian peasant soldier; the South Slav volunteer fighting for the unification of all South Slavs; and the selfless, fearless, and compassionate Serbian woman who was often depicted as a mythical figure from Serbia's past or as a national mourner.[78]

Turning Soldiers into Heroes

The ways in which patriotic ideals of heroism, manliness, and maternity were redefined and deployed in photographic displays and albums during and after World War I in Serbia reveal assumptions that informed gender and national identities in the interwar Kingdom of Serbs, Croats, and Slovenes. Soldiers who fight and die on the battlefield do not automatically become heroes, nor do their corpses automatically become sacrificed bodies for the nation. It is only through the acts of the national citizenry and their national "priests" that these dead bodies can be resurrected and turned into martyrs and heroes of the nation. In order to engage in mass warfare, states, politicians, and generals find ways to convince their citizens that the prospect of their own violent death or those of their loved ones will not be in vain, and their acts on the battlefield will not be seen as anything other than heroic and honorable. To turn soldiers into heroes requires a concerted and widespread campaign to reward and remember them, either posthumously or if they survive, upon their return. "The willingness to sacrifice oneself becomes the ultimate sign of devotion to one's nation and is the sign of any patriot, the true member of the nation."[79]

The masculine cast of politics and of national citizenship in the interwar Kingdom was made from the abstract qualities attributed to Serbian soldiers—courage, self-sacrifice, and loyalty to a state that was seen as having been founded upon their heroism and sacrifice against the Habsburg monarchy. The persistence of the traditional image of the hero in the Serb collective imagination proved of considerable benefit to the interwar Serbian elites as they ignored or eliminated the contributions and heroism of other South Slavs from official histories and commemorative activities. The visual commemorative culture of interwar Yugoslavia made it very clear who its heroes were.

Melissa Bokovoy is professor and chair of the Department of History at the University of New Mexico. She is the author of several articles about the politics and memory culture of interwar Yugoslavia and is completing a monograph on this topic. She has recently published "Consecrating Sites: Šabac, Cer and the Mačva Region in Serbia's Commemorative Culture of the First World War," *Centropa: A Journal of Central European Architecture and Related Art* 12/1 (2012); and "Gender and Reframing of World War I in Serbia during the 1980s and 1990s," in *Women and Gender in Postwar Europe*, ed. Bonnie Smith and Joanna Regulska (2012).

Notes

1. Archive of Yugoslavia, Belgrade (Arhiv Jugoslavije: hereafter AJ), fond 66, Fascikle 631, Jedinica 1041, Rista Marjanović to Press Bureau of the Ministry of Foreign Affairs, "Predmet-Piktorijalna Propaganda," 5 November 1920.
2. Marina Zeković, *Ratni slikari, fotografi amateri i dopisnici fotografi u srpskoj vojsci 1914–1918* (Belgrade, 2001), 102. Also Jovan Običan, "Intervju profesora Pavlovića," *Vreme*, 24 May 1939, 5.
3. Dora Apel, "Cultural Battlegrounds: Weimar Photographic Narratives of War," *New German Critique* 76 (Winter 1999): 78.
4. Marjanović to Press Bureau, 5 November 1920.
5. See Aleksandar Ignjatović, "From Constructed Memory to Imagined National Tradition: The Tomb of the Unknown Yugoslav Soldier (1934–38)," *The Slavonic and East European Review* 88/4 (2010): 624–51.
6. A notable exception was the valorization of South Slav volunteers—Serbs from abroad, Croat and Slovene soldiers from the Habsburg army captured and released by Serbia's allies—who were eventually assembled into a separate corps of the Serbian army.
7. Antoinette M. White, "All the Men are Fighting for Freedom, All the Women are Mourning their Men," *Signs* 32/4 (2007): 868.
8. This reflected a background of turbulent infighting between the Serbian dynastic, military, and civilian authorities during the war. See David MacKenzie, *Apis: The Congenial Conspirator: The Life of Colonel Dragutin T. Dimitrijević* (New York, 1989). Postwar photographic displays in magazines and newspapers, especially in western Europe, projected instead an authority and power emanating from King Petar and the prince regent Aleksandar.
9. Some of these men, such as Stjepan Uroić, ended up in the Ustasha. For the Croatian dimension see chapter 9 by John Paul Newman.
10. George Mosse, *Fallen Soldiers: Reshaping the Memory of the World Wars* (Oxford, 1990).
11. See Samuel R. Schwartz, "Art," in *International Encyclopedia of Men and Masculinities*, ed. Michael Flood (London, 2007), 26–29.
12. Similar observations are made by Petra Svoljšak in chapter 10.
13. For women's commemorative activities and how the Serbian state remembered women's roles during the war, see Melissa Bokovoy, "Kosovo Maidens: Serbian Women Commemorating the Wars of National Liberation, 1912–1918," in *Women and War in Twentieth Century Eastern Europe*, ed. Nancy Wingfield and Maria Bucur (West Lafayette, 2006), 157–71; and "Gendering Grief: Lamenting and Photographing the Dead in Serbia," *Aspasia* 5 (2011): 46–69.

14. The phrase "Wars of National Liberation" was immediately used after 1918 in the Kingdom to describe the two Balkan Wars and World War I and took on multiple meanings and usages. Depending on the context, liberation could mean liberating the Serbs from the Ottoman Turks, the dominance of Austria-Hungary, the expulsion of Germans and Bulgarians from ethnically Serb areas, the liberation of all South Slavs from their overlords, or a combination of all of the above. The term's political usage must not be underestimated.
15. Jaša Tomić, *Rat na Kosovu i staroj Srbiji* (Novi Sad, 1913), 51.
16. *Srpske Novine*, 11 December 1912, 5. Notable correspondents who wrote from the Balkans in 1912–13 and were subjected to press censorship include: Jeane Leune and Georges Bourdon of *Figaro*, M.F. de Jessen and Alain de Pennunrun of *L'Illustration*, Bernand Grant of the *Daily Mirror*, Crawford Price of *The Times*, Luigi Barzini of *Corriere della Serra*, and Leon Trotksy of *Kievskaya Mysl*.
17. Zeković, *Ratni slikari*, 14–16.
18. Serbia's press restrictions were similar to those found in Britain and France during World War I. Photographers, artists, and correspondents were subjected to censorship of their dispatches, photographs and drawings; they could not travel to the front lines or take a photograph without permission. Austria-Hungary also believed in strict censorship. For control of journalists, see Mark Cornwall, "Das Ringen um die Moral des Hinterland: Moral, Loyalität und Zensur," in *Die Habsburgermonarchie 1848–1918*, vol XI/I, *Die Habsburgermonarchie und der Erste Weltkrieg*, ed. Anatol Schmied-Kowarzik (Vienna, 2016).
19. There are several different spellings of Tchernoff's name in the American, British, French, and Serbian sources: Sampson Tchernoff, Samson Tchernof, and Samson Černov. In the text, I have chosen Samson Černov but when quoting directly I use the spelling of the source.
20. Atrocity stories circulated, for instance in Belgium during the German invasion, and were exploited by Entente propaganda. Thus the actions of the invading Austro-Hungarian army (the *Balkanstreit Armee*) were reported for their brutality and targeting of civilians. Jonathan Gumz has recently examined the reaction of the Habsburg military to Serbian civilians as potential guerrillas, *komitadijas*, and "opponents" showing the importance of the *komitadji* both to Serbian resistance and to the mentality of the Habsburg High Command. The latter feared that *komitadjis* would encourage a generalized revolt among Serbs and as a result, in the early weeks of hostilities, the Habsburg forces killed up to thirty-five hundred civilians. See Gumz, *The Resurrection and Collapse of Empire in Habsburg Serbia, 1914–1918* (Cambridge, 2009), chapter 5. See also S. Bojković and M. Pršić, *Stradanje srpskog naroda u Srbiji, 1914–1918. Dokumenti* (Belgrade, 2001). For debates about German and Austro-Hungarian treatment of civilians, see John Horne and Alan Kramer, *German Atrocities, 1914: A History of Denial* (New Haven, 2001), and Andrej Mitrović, *Serbia's Great War* (West Lafayette, 2007).
21. The Serbian army's retreat through Albania is often referred to as the "Serbian Golgotha." This reference was used to invoke the idea that just like the biblical Jesus, the Serbian nation was crucified, left for dead, but then resurrected by its own efforts. It was symbolically a victory over the supposed death of the Serbian nation at the hands of its barbaric enemies. To take the symbolism further and tie it to the Kosovo myth, the Serbian nation once again had spilled its blood to defend European interests.
22. "Memories of Three Wars: A Serbian Anniversary," *The Times*, 10 May 1916.
23. There were at least twelve international photographic exhibitions that were either dedicated solely to Serbian war photography or to Allied war photography with Serbian photographs, mostly Marjanović's. They were shown in London, Paris, Rome, New York, Boston, Chicago, and Los Angeles.

24. Serbia's war narrative is structured like a national epic (in particular, Kosovo 1389). In other words, it exists in an absolute past, not negotiable or in dialogue with alternative narratives from, say, Habsburg South Slavs, with which it is difficult to reconcile.
25. See The Carnegie Endowment for International Peace, *Report of the International Commission to Inquire into the Causes and Conduct of the Balkan Wars* (Washington, DC, 1914).
26. Negative images of Serbia as a violent, primitive state lingered at the beginning of the war. An American newspaper, *The Los Angeles Times,* in early 1915 noted that King Petar had ascended the throne under "revolting and hideous circumstances" and Serbia itself "was plunged head first into this last little affray by the murderous inclinations of one of its numerous political societies, which murdered Prince [sic] Ferdinand of Austria and his wife, just to show the world how it really felt about Austria, which had annexed Bosnia-Herzegovina three years before." While the *Los Angeles Times* maintained its disdain for Serbia after the Habsburg invasion, it noted how "newspapers wrote some very touching obsequies for Servia." See "Peter of Servia," *Los Angeles Times*, 16 March 1915, 114.
27. "Serb Prince in London," *The Times*, 16 February 1915.
28. For a discussion of cultural templates from the medieval period, see Allen Frantzen, *Bloody Good: Chivalry, Sacrifice, and the Great War* (Chicago, 2004).
29. Šijački was the first president of the Belgrade section of the Yugoslav press association. Before the war, he had served as a correspondent in the Slovene region and was a member of the Serbian press association.
30. *Vidovdan: Ilustrovana istorija srpskih rata, 1912–1918* (Geneva, 1918).
31. Ibid.
32. Apel, "Cultural Battlegrounds," 51.
33. Frantzen, *Bloody Good*, 149.
34. Ibid., 158.
35. *Srpske Novine*, 10 August 1913.
36. Ibid.
37. Catherine Moriarty, "'Though in a Picture Only': Photography and Commemoration," in *Evidence, History and the Great War: Historians and the Impact of 1914–1918*, ed. Gail Braybon (New York, 2003), 34.
38. Charles Jelavich, *South Slav Nationalisms: Textbooks and Yugoslav Union before 1914* (Columbus, 1990), 75.
39. Mosse, *Fallen Soldiers*, argues that in the aftermath of the war in Germany, efforts such as these were attempts to transform a soldier's death in war into a sacred experience and that the cult of the fallen soldier became a centerpiece of the religion of nationalism.
40. During the interwar period, the Yugoslav royal court gave out subventions for commemorative activities. See AJ, fond 74: Dvor. Kancelarija Kralja. Fascikle 98.
41. See, for example, the illustrated reader, Atanasije M. Popović, *Narodna čitanka*: *Oslobodilačko ratovanje Srbije* (Beograd, 1922). Popović was a reserve officer on the Salonika front and a professor of theology at the University of Belgrade.
42. Rista Marjanović, *Ratni Album, 1912–1915* (Belgrade, 1987).
43. Ibid.
44. "Izložba dokumenata o odstupanju srpskoga naroda i vojske kroz Albaniju 1915.godine," *Politika*, 4 January 1926, 5; 20 January 1926, 4.
45. Zoran Glušević, "A Century and Half of Photography in Serbia," in *A History of Serbian Culture* (Edgware, Middlesex, 1995).
46. *Politika*, 4 January 1926, 5.
47. Ibid.
48. Two thousand copies were published in 1926 and made available to veterans' organizations, schools, and individuals. In 1987, a Belgrade publishing house, BIGZ, reprinted this

album during the revival of Serbian interest in the Great War. In addition, Marjanović's photographs were finally published in a single photographic album by the Archive of Serbia in 1987. More recently, this compilation was made available on the worldwide web by the *Rastko* project that presents "Serbian culture and history to the World Wide Web." For the revival of interest in the Great War see Melissa Bokovoy, "Gender and Reframing of World War I in Serbia during the 1980s and 1990s," in *Women and Gender in Potswar Europe: From Cold War to European Union*, ed. Joanna Regulska and Bonnie Smith (London, 2012), 176–93.

49. Andra Popović, *Ratni Album, 1914–1918* [*The War Album: 1914–1918*] (Belgrade, 1926), 4.
50. Ibid., 401.
51. Volunteers first appeared in the Serbian army in late summer 1914, mostly Serbs and other South Slavs from the Austro-Hungarian monarchy. Over the course of the war, the number of volunteers increased and by 1916 émigré South Slavs and South Slav POWs captured on the Serbian and Russian fronts were grouped together in the 1st Volunteer Division at Odessa. Another division, the 2nd Volunteer Division, was formed later that year. In 1917, the "Volunteer Corps of the Serbs, Croats, and Slovenes" was created out of these two divisions and sent to the Salonika front. The *esprit de corps* was contested between those who believed the ethos should be Serbian and those who believed it should be Yugoslav.
52. "Review of *Ratni Album*," *Vojni Vjesnik* 4/4 (April 1926): 39.
53. Ibid.
54. "Umetnost: Izložba srpskih ratnih slika," *Srpske Novine*, 21 July 1916.
55. In the collection there were fourteen colorized photographs containing the following images: Portraits of King Petar of Serbia, the Prince Regent Aleksandar, Nikola Pašić, the minister of war, and General of the Second Army, Stepa Stepanović, cropped shots of a Serbian artillery colonel, a Serbian soldier on watch captioned "Eagle Eye," a little boy with an outstretched hand captioned "please help my country," a soldier carrying a child in his arms, a young boy whose arm is in a sling captioned "bomb thrower of Belgrade," and a dead soldier lying on the ground captioned "last passenger." See Sampson Tchernoff, "Serbian Warriors," Getty Research Institute, Santa Monica, California, Research Library, Special Collections: Malvina Hoffman papers, Box 31, Folder 3.
56. *Srpske Novine*, 21 July 1916.
57. Popović, *Ratni Album*, 95.
58. Popović, *Ratni Album*, 345.
59. David Harley Serlin, "Crippling Masculinity: Queerness and Disability in U.S. Military Culture, 1800–1945, *GLQ: A Journal of Lesbian and Gay Studies* 9/1–2 (2003): 153. This photograph became ubiquitous in the 1980s as the icon of Serbs during World War I. In 1998, the authors of a textbook chose it for its cover: N. Gaćesa, Lj. Mladenović-Makisimović and D. Živković, *Istorija za 8. razred osnovne škole*, 1st ed. (Belgrade, 1997).
60. Photographs played an important role in the earlier veneration since monuments and public statuary of the two rulers did not begin to appear in any significant numbers until the 1930s.
61. Popović, *Ratni Album*, 51.
62. Ibid., 79.
63. Ibid., 332–38.
64. R.A. Reiss was employed by the Serbian government to document the killing of civilians by Habsburg forces in late 1914, and then in 1917–18 to investigate treatment of Serbian civilians under Austro-Hungarian and Bulgarian occupation. At the time, he was a renowned forensic scientist at the University of Lausanne, Switzerland. He first published *Report upon the Atrocities Committed by the Austro-Hungarian Army during the First Invasion of Serbia* (1916); and then *Infringements of the Rules and Laws of War Committed by the Austro-Bulgaro-Germans: Letters of a Criminologist on the Serbian–Macedonian Front* (1919), which was a

series of letters and photographs he had created for French, Dutch, and Swiss papers. Reiss however always maintained that he was neutral and was simply offering himself as a forensic scientist to document wartime violence, something he clearly abhorred. The Serbian government intended to publish his findings in support of their position and thus Reiss can be seen as a hired expert for the Kingdom of Serbia. During the 1920s, he continued to examine the actions of the occupying forces in wartime Serbia, publishing *The Comitadji Question in Southern Serbia* (1924). His final publications came in 1928 when he published in Serbian both his photographic album, *Slike,* and his memoirs, *Šta sam video i doživeo u velikim danima.*

65. Tchernoff, "Catalogue of the Exhibition of Serbian War Pictures," Getty Research Institute, Malvina Hoffman papers, Box 31, Folder 3.
66. "Velike nacionalne svečanosti u Šapcu, Govor Nj. Vel. Kralja," *Sokolski Glasnik* 5/24, 8 June 1934.
67. *Documents Relating to the Violations of the Hague Conventions and of International Law in General, Committed 1915–1918 by the Bulgarians in Occupied Serbia* (Paris, 1919).
68. Barbie Zelizer, *Remembering to Forget: Holocaust Memory Through the Camera's Eye* (Chicago, 1998), 138.
69. Ibid., 86.
70. Popović, *Narodna čitanka: Oslobodilačko ratovanje Srbije,* inside cover.
71. *Jubilarni zbornik života i rada Srba, Hrvata i Slovenaca 1918–1928* (Belgrade, 1928), III deo.
72. Ibid., 22.
73. R.A. Reiss, *Slike* (Belgrade, 1928).
74. Zelizer, *Remembering to Forget,* 86.
75. Review of *Ratni Album,*" *Vojni Vjesnik* 4/4 (April 1924): 39.
76. Živko Pavlović, review in *Politika,* 1 December 1926, 6.
77. Stanoje Stanojević, review in *Politika,* 4 December 1926, 8.
78. For a discussion of this phenomenon, see Bokovoy, "Kosovo Maidens," 157–71.
79. Carolyn Marvin and David W. Ingle, "Blood Sacrifice and the Nation: Revisiting Civil Religion," *Journal of the American Academy of Religion* 64/4 (Winter, 1996).

Chapter 6

NATIONAL SACRIFICE AND REGENERATION
Commemorations of the Battle of Zborov
in Multinational Czechoslovakia

Nancy M. Wingfield

The Battle of Zborov, one of many on World War I's Eastern front, became a problematic measure of national loyalty in Czechoslovakia after 1918. The anniversary of the battle, 2 July, emerged as one of the main commemorative dates of the nascent Czechoslovak Republic. An important component in the new state's foundational myth, this 1917 engagement came to constitute a major commemorative site of national sacrifice and regeneration in Czechoslovakia's interwar patriotic cult. The themes that the bourgeois-national framers of this holiday stressed, and the symbols they employed, emphasized a particular Czech national history. As a result, the commemoration of Zborov played a centrifugal role, complicating any efforts to expand participation in the newly established multinational state of Czechs, Germans, Jews, Magyars, Poles, Ruthenians, and Slovaks.

The most important theme in the mythographic imagery of the Battle of Zborov was that of Czech wartime heroism and sacrifice on behalf of the new state. Celebrations highlighted the obligations of the living to "national martyrs": heroes from the Czech past as well as Czech and Slovak veterans of the Great War, especially the "legionaries," who had fought alongside the Allies on the French, Italian, and Russian fronts.[1] Other contemporary heroes included Czechoslovakia's "founding fathers," above all the country's first president, Tomáš G. Masaryk, known as the *President-Osvoboditel* or President-Liberator. Together with the Czech Edvard Beneš and the Slovak Milan Rastislav

Štefánik, his cofounders of the wartime Czechoslovak National Council in Paris, Masaryk had helped bring the Czechs and Slovaks to the "promised land" of independence.[2] This trio, whose triple portrait would replace the crucifix of the Habsburgs on classroom walls in the First Republic, was part of the "patriarchy of Czechoslovak state independence."[3] Alongside them in the national pantheon stood the legionary brethren and politicians who were lauded for sacrificing their lives "on foreign battlefields and in domestic prisons for future national independence."[4] The name of Masaryk was explicitly tied to the legionaries, many of whom claimed him as the spiritual leader or commander of all Czechoslovak legionaries, not only in numerous patriotic tomes and illustrations but also in their anthem, "Zdráv buď otče Masaryku!"[5] (figure 6.1).

By the end of the war, popular discourse began mythologizing those Czech soldiers who had deserted from the multinational Habsburg army almost from the beginning of the war. These men, whose numbers are unknown, often surrendered to their fellow Slavs—especially the Russians—and some of them later became legionaries.[6] Above all it was the heroism of the Czech legionaries (including few Slovaks[7]) that was remembered—those forty thousand soldiers who had left the prisoner-of-war camps and formed the Czechoslovak brigade in Russia in order to do battle with the Habsburg army. The emasculating, humili-

Figure 6.1. "To your health, Father Masaryk!": in *Pravda vítězí: Deset československých vlasteneckých zpěvů* (Prague, 1926).

ating experience of captivity that most POWs had experienced was seldom mentioned.[8]

Although legionaries also fought on the Western and Italian fronts during the Great War, their feats at Zborov became a particularly important symbol of the First Republic because that battle was the zenith of the military achievement of the Czechoslovak volunteers and the diplomatic-political efforts of the "founding fathers." The Zborov commemorations established a cult of military heroism and sacrifice that was highly masculine and overwhelmingly Czech. In order to strengthen Czechoslovakia's political iconography, the commemorations also linked World War I with important figures from the past who had themselves been reinterpreted to fit the needs of the young state, especially the medieval Protestant reformer, Jan Hus, and the one-eyed—later blind—Hussite commander, Jan Žižka. The festivities around the 2 July battle offered all members of the Czechoslovak military the opportunity to demonstrate their prowess in the name of the newly created "tradition of Zborov," and the legionaries were given the chance to reassert the importance of their role in the state's creation. Performing a vigorous, military "Czechoslovakism"[9] was especially important in the early postwar years, when in addition to problems with German-speaking recruits, the general staff sought to overcome the latent mistrust, even open tension, between Czechs and Slovaks in some units, which reflected economic, religious, and social differences.[10]

In addition to showcasing the country's military prowess, the commemorations also provided an opportunity to inculcate "Czechoslovak" values into the state's multinational citizenry, particularly for children and adolescents whose sense of national identity was perceived as *tabula rasa*.[11] The annual celebration of Zborov therefore served as a kind of litmus test: participation indicated citizens who possessed an appropriate degree of "Czechoslovakness," while less engaged or appreciative citizens marked themselves as distinct from the Czechoslovak majority (which in turn labeled them as a suspect *other*). The Zborov celebrations permitted little space in commemorative practice for the national minorities, or for those Slovaks who advocated more Slovak autonomy within a Czecho-Slovak state on the basis of the Pittsburgh Agreement, which Czech, Slovak, and Ruthenian émigrés had signed with Masaryk in the United States on 31 May 1918.[12]

From the outset, commemorations of Zborov played an important pedagogic role. The state and its loyal Czechoslovak citizens helped to create a national vocabulary of images that reflected their perception of the First Republic. Zborov's memory took many cultural forms, including books, cinematic and theatrical productions, holiday celebrations, statues and monuments. Much of this imagery collapsed the newly constructed nation ("Czechoslovak") and the newly founded state (Czechoslovakia) into one, denying the multinational element of the country.

The Battle of Zborov and the Birth of the Czechoslovak State

The Battle of Zborov was part of the last large-scale Russian summer offensive of 1917 along the entire Galician front between Lemburg (Lwów/L'viv) and Tarnopol (Ternopil') in what is today Ukraine. Three Czechoslovak regiments occupied a sector of the front on the Russian side near the village of Zborov. Opposite them was a Habsburg infantry division, which was dominated by two regiments with Czech-speaking majorities. In the July offensive, the Czechoslovak brigade attacked the positions of the Habsburg Czechs. It breached the Habsburg line, taking prisoner more than four thousand enlisted men and sixty-two officers, most of them Czech. In contrast, although the Czechoslovak brigade suffered heavy casualties, none were taken prisoner. Whether the victory of the Czechoslovak legionaries was due to heroic military achievement or to the treachery of the Czech regiments would become a subject of intense disagreement between the wars.[13]

Even as Czechoslovakia's existence was being assured, Czech and German nationalists began to draw differing lessons from the Battle of Zborov and its commemorations. As Ivan Šedivý has observed, German nationalist propaganda created the myth of Czech soldiers as traitors and defectors, an image that interwar Czech nationalists built upon to represent every Czech soldier as a "nationally conscious resister."[14]

The legionaries, who fought on the Eastern front as well as elsewhere across revolutionary Russia, brought the Czechs and Slovaks to the attention of the Western Allies. Certainly, despite the legends of heroic valor that grew up around the legionaries, their primary purpose was as propaganda: they were meant to demoralize the overwhelming majority of Czech, Slovak, and other Slav soldiers who continued to fight in the Austro-Hungarian army. Moreover, the victory at Zborov strengthened the arguments made by Masaryk, Beneš, and their National Council that the Czechs and Slovaks were actually on the side of the Entente in the war and that they sought Czechoslovak independence. The Legion in Russia was their most valuable asset—it represented the promise of additional manpower on the Western front—in negotiations with the Entente. As Beneš explained, "In the French general staff they have told us openly: if you want independence, you will have to pay for it with blood like anyone else."[15]

Owing to wartime censorship, the legionaries' feats at Zborov—in fact, their very existence—became known in the Habsburg monarchy only because the Russian General Staff published a report on the battle. Czechs on the home front initially met this news of the battle with curiosity or even skepticism.[16] The report however proved to be accurate, and civilians would soon celebrate the legionaries as conquering heroes when they began arriving in the newly created

Czechoslovakia from the Western, Eastern and Italian fronts at the war's end.[17] The Battle of Zborov soon became legend and its veterans, the "first citizens of the Czechoslovak Republic," were almost immediately honored as pillars of Czechoslovak independence.[18] Throughout the interwar period, the anniversary of the battle as a patriotic-national celebration was second only to 28 October, the foundation day of the First Czechoslovak Republic. Like that date, it was attractive to anticlerical, republican sentiments in the country both because of its association with the struggle against the Habsburg monarchy and because it provided contemporary military heroes to replace previous religious figures (notably the Hussite general Jan Žižka). Some of the Czech patriots who orchestrated commemorations asserted that the celebration of Zborov was not a military occasion, but rather "a celebration of the highest ideals of the Czechoslovak nation, heroism, and courage."[19] Like 28 October, Zborov was a *state* holiday that was often celebrated as a *national* holiday.[20]

The victory at Zborov therefore constituted a historical, political, and psychological milestone in the struggle for Czechoslovak independence. It allegedly represented the first time since the loss at the Battle of White Mountain in November 1620 that the Czechs had taken up arms against the Habsburg monarchy and, this time, they had emerged victorious. Indeed, the Czechs (and less often, the Slovaks) popularly interpreted Zborov as redemption for the defeat of the Protestant Bohemian forces at the hands of the Roman Catholic Habsburgs at White Mountain. During the interwar period, the connection between the two battles took physical form on state holidays when patriotic groups traced a national pilgrimage from White Mountain, on Prague's outskirts, to the tomb of the Unknown Soldier on Old Town Square in the city center.[21]

Since the legionaries formed the backbone of the new state's military, they played an important role in interwar cultural, political and social life. As veterans of an army that was older than its state, they constituted a special interest group with influence far greater than their numbers, and the regiments of the Zborov brigade were among the most highly regarded. legionaries formed veterans' organizations throughout the country to promote their political ends, which more often than not paralleled those of Masaryk, Beneš, and their allies—the "Castle" (*Hrad*).[22] They also founded businesses, the most famous of which was the Legionary Bank (Legiobánka) that, bearing their imprint, proved attractive to patriotic Czechs and Slovaks. Although legionaries held a variety of political views as Katya Kocourek's chapter in this volume shows, many of them were ardent nationalists. Their importance and their loyalty to the state did not go unnoticed by their enemies; their organizations were among the first the Nazis banned in March 1939 following their occupation of the Bohemian Lands and the formation of the Protectorate of Bohemia and Moravia.[23]

Constructing the "Czechoslovak" Nation: Commemorating the Battle of Zborov

Although there were celebrations throughout the new state, the focal point of the annual commemorations of Zborov, like those of 28 October, was the country's capital, Prague. The celebrations on 2 July offered first the Masaryk, and then the Beneš, regime the opportunity to provide its citizens with well-choreographed productions teaching the civics of Czechoslovak nationalism. While the official forms of commemoration were similar throughout the country, their reception was often quite different, especially in the early days of the Republic. These military-civilian patriotic manifestations met with the greatest enthusiasm in predominantly Czech regions, where each town or village enthusiastically performed its own vision of the date's meaning in a variety of ways, including pageants and speeches. This wide popular participation was often organized by the local and national branches of political parties loyal to the Castle, or the state-sponsored Union of Czechoslovak Legionaries (Československá obec Legionářská), the largest and most centrist legionary organization.[24] In Slovakia, politicians loyal to the Castle used the celebrations as an opportunity for "Czechoslovak" nation building; indeed, the commemorations were popular among those Slovaks who supported the "Czechoslovak" ideal.

In contrast, attempts to commemorate Zborov in the predominantly German border regions were often met with hostility or studiously ignored. The commemorative language that Czech officials and the military employed, including many Zborov veterans, celebrated Allied victories over a Habsburg army in which many of Czechoslovakia's German and Magyar citizens had loyally served. It also attacked historic figures and events that the state's Germans particularly respected or revered such as late Habsburg emperors Joseph II and Franz Joseph or the German chancellor Otto von Bismarck. Many of the country's Germans remembered Zborov in terms of the seven-kilometer gap in the front left by deserting Czech troops that Russian troops had poured through, killing "German fathers and sons."[25] Germans also recalled with distaste the earlier desertions of members of the Prague and Mladá Boleslav regiments on the Eastern front. In predominantly German-speaking areas, the patriotic rituals often fomented Czech-German altercations, which began with the trading of national insults or even the caricaturing of President Masaryk. Sometimes the verbal abuse escalated to include fistfights and ended with local Czechs, together with locally stationed legionaries, vandalizing German-owned property or German cultural patrimony.[26]

The decennial anniversaries of the Battle of Zborov in 1927 and 1937 attracted numerous patriotic expressions to celebrate the heroism and sacrifice of the Zborov legionaries. Troop reviews, maneuvers and parades abounded in predominantly Czech regions. Prague and the provincial capitals were major sites of celebrations with members of patriotic civilian organizations, above all the Sokol (the Czechoslovak gymnastic organization), participating enthusiastically in the events. Like the legionaries, Sokol members had supposedly played an important role in the war in providing domestic opposition to the Habsburgs; they considered themselves one of the pillars of the state, regularly recalling the description in German-language newspapers in 1912 of their sixth all-Sokol *slet* (festival) as a "review of the [Czech] national army."[27] Legionary literature duly praised Sokol members for their military discipline and for physically preparing the legionaries.[28] The well-attended civilian celebrations, held primarily in Czech-speaking regions, commemorated the sacrifice of the legionaries with gymnastic performances, museum exhibitions, the unveiling of commemorative plaques, popular festivals, parades, and concerts. Medals were struck and stamps were issued; special children's stories were published; works of art were commissioned; poems and songs were written. Some of the songs were taught in school and became part of the popular patriotic musical canon of the interwar era. World-famous and little-known poets composed verses mourning the heroic soldiers who had died for the state's foundation: "Mother dearest / I write you my last words / here at Zborov," or "Czech and Slovak youth / Sons of the nation / Rejuvenating blood of heroes" (the opening lines of a famous poem on Zborov by battle veteran Rudolf Medek).[29]

The Castle was instrumental in the celebration of Zborov, and by 1927 its version of the Zborov legend was firmly in place. According to the government's English-language newspaper, *Central European Observer*, the heroic behavior of the Czechoslovak Brigade in July 1917 had provided a striking contrast to those Russian troops on either side of it; owing to Bolshevik agitation, they were already an "incapable mass, daily weakened by thousands of deserters." The legionaries, in contrast, had acted decisively, and thus Czechoslovak troops had "cheerfully marched into the trenches with music and song, and flowers in their tunics." Indeed, they entered into the battle with such enthusiasm that for a fleeting moment they inspired the Russian troops with "new spirit."[30]

Speakers at the tenth anniversary celebrations in Prague also praised the work of the Czech domestic resistance and the Czechoslovak National Council abroad within the framework of the battle. They employed Zborov as a representation of wartime national sacrifice, supposedly exemplifying the totality of the Czechoslovak wartime experience. This depiction of Zborov overtly ignored wartime tensions between the Czechoslovak National Council abroad and the Czech anti-Habsburg opposition at home. Moreover, since speeches rhetorically tied Zborov to the loss of the last independent Bohemian army at the Battle of White Mountain, the Prague celebrations took Zborov to White Mountain with a military parade there of the entire Prague garrison. As usual, Masaryk, who habitually wore a military-cut suit and highly polished boots, reviewed the troops on horseback. Onlookers included government ministers, members of the diplomatic corps, and deputies from the National Assembly. Czechoslovak soldiers paraded while military aircraft circled overhead in this masculine-centered commemoration of heroism and sacrifice.[31]

Slovaks usually commemorated Zborov differently from their Czech brethren. They often added a religious component and occasionally Slovak national heroes, while eliminating the national-religious (Protestant) emphasis on White Mountain. In Bratislava in 1927, however, Slovak politicians who supported the coalition government in Prague used the three-day decennial celebrations from 1 July as an opportunity for "Czechoslovak" nation building. That evening, members of local corporate and military organizations marched through the main streets of the formerly predominantly German-Magyar city. They converged at the Slovak National Theater on Ondrejská ulice where a military band played music including the Hussite battle hymn, "Kdož jste boží bojovníci" ("Ye who are God's Warriors"), long part of Czech but not Slovak national celebrations. Afterwards, both a Zborov veteran and a Czechoslovak Agrarian party senator (Vavro Šrobár, a reliable Castle ally) spoke from the theater balcony about the day's significance. As in Prague, the celebrations contained a significant military component. In addition to the standard military review of local garrisons before officers and city and provincial officials, on the morning of 2 July a naval parade was added: a flotilla of seven ships sailed down the Danube before the regional commander. In contrast to the events in Prague, the more religiously observant Slovaks also attended a solemn funeral Mass in the city's cathedral in honor of those who had sacrificed their lives at Zborov.[32]

Elsewhere in Slovakia, towns and cities honored the Zborov heroes with military parades, military band concerts, and numerous other special events similar to those in the Bohemian Lands. In Košice in eastern Slovakia, a large Sokol meeting was held that included 430 participants from Moravia and Silesia, and city officials planned a large celebration to honor both the Sokol and the heroic fallen of Zborov. At the celebratory gathering, the district prefect Juraj Slávik reminded his audience that before this battle "the world knew little of the people called Czechoslovak." It was the bloodshed at Zborov, he asserted, that had won the "hearts and minds" of diplomats (to support the formation of the Czechoslovak state). Slávik situated Zborov in the "glorious tradition" of the troops of Jan Žižka but also of Jan Jiskra, a Hussite-era soldier-of-fortune who for more than twenty years in the fifteenth century had controlled most of "Slovakia." Slávik further linked it to belief in the legacy of the (nineteenth-century national) "Awakeners," of Sokol arms, of the struggle for truth and justice. "Zborov," he continued, "is our slogan, our example, our ideal."[33] It was a speech exemplifying the Czechoslovakist/Castle practice of attempting, however fleetingly, to incorporate Slovak experiences into the predominantly Czech national mythology of the First Republic.

Despite these government-sponsored festivities, not all Slovak newspapers in early 1927 were filled with tributes to Zborov. Indeed, *Slovenská pravda* and *Trenčan*, weeklies associated with Andrej Hlinka's Slovak People's Party, which increasingly sought Slovak autonomy in Czechoslovakia,[34] chose instead to focus on the 5 July commemorations of Cyril and Methodius, the saints credited with bringing Christianity to the Slavs in the ninth century. These same newspapers also ignored celebrations of 28 October in order to focus on the St Martin Declaration, a manifesto Slovak patriots had issued declaring Slovak independence on 30 October 1918.[35]

Also resisting the state-sponsored interpretation of Zborov was the Czechoslovak Communist party (KSČ), the First Republic's only multinational political organization. It was the largest party to reject the Zborov mythology. Although some KSČ members were former legionaries who had become politicized in revolutionary Russia (many of them later joining the Association of Communist Legionaries: Svaz komunistických Legionářů), the Czechoslovak Communists did not participate in the state-sponsored Zborov commemorations after the party was founded in 1921. Rather, contemporary Communist ideology interpreted the formation of the Czechoslovak Brigade and its participation at the front as part of an imperialist war; the summer offensive of 1917, the KSČ claimed, had been undertaken in the interests of counterrevolution and imperialism. Moreover, further legionary struggles in the Siberian "anabasis"—the legionaries' legendary trek across Siberia during the Russian Civil War—constituted counterrevolutionary intervention and crimes against the "Russian working people." The party press denied heroic status not only to Zborov but also to the state Zborov supposedly legitimized. In early July 1927, when most other Czech-language newspapers were filled with news of the festivities and reminiscences of heroic Zborov veterans, such laudatory articles were absent from the Communist party daily, *Rudé právo*.[36]

During the late 1920s, increasing attacks on the central government reflected the growing radicalization, indeed Stalinization, of the Czechoslovak Communist party. Communist leaders seized the opportunity provided by Zborov to argue that life under Czechoslovakia's bourgeois government was not so different from "Old Austria," the liberation from which was being commemorated. The Communists claimed that the Zborov anniversary celebrated an exaggerated form of [Austrian minister Alexander von] Bach's *Prügelpatent*, a reference to the Habsburg neoabsolutist policies of the 1850s. Attempting to appropriate the memory of the Battle of Zborov for their own political ends, the Communists then proposed an alternative narrative to that of the bourgeois nation-state. While they too believed that it "atoned" for the Battle of White Mountain, they stressed the class component of the Zborov legionaries, arguing that the majority of those who had given their lives for an independent Czechoslovakia that day were workers, dreaming of a state with social equality.[37] The Communists sought to undermine the First Republic by using Zborov to signal parallels between "democratic" Czechoslovakia and the repressive, retrograde Habsburg monarchy it had replaced.

In July 1937, the decennial celebration of Zborov occurred in a far tenser international atmosphere, thereby shifting the focus of its representational content. In the context of Nazi rule in neighboring Germany and fascist dictatorship elsewhere in Europe, the Zborov ritual served to claim at home and abroad the strength of democratic Czechoslovakism and of Czechoslovak military might. The honorary executive committee of the event, whose patron was President Beneš, included the Czechoslovak Agrarian Prime Minister Milan Hodža (a Slovak), the mayors of provincial capitals, and the governor of Ruthenia. Every town and village throughout the country was encouraged to commemorate Zborov on 1–2 July at the same time as in Prague.[38]

On 1 July, the evening before the twentieth anniversary, Prague's Old Town Square was filled with formations of infantry and dragoons, as well as the colorful uniforms and folk costumes of the Sokol and defense organizations, to render homage to the Unknown Soldier. František Machník, the Minister of National Defense, made a speech reminding his audience that the celebrations taking place throughout the Republic demonstrated that Zborov and the memory of this glorious victory united the entire Czechoslovak nation and military officers. Indeed, he found in those participating in the commemorations examples of "national unity," as well as self-assurance, determination, and readiness for sacrifice.[39] Later in the evening's program, two seventeen-year-olds, one from Znojmo (Zniam) in southern Moravia and the other from Prešov in eastern Slovakia, swore fealty to the Republic. The two young men assured the crowd that the youth of the country's provinces of Bohemia, Moravia, Slovakia, and Ruthenia were loyal to the high ideals of the Czechoslovak state and, if necessary, would follow in the footsteps of the heroes of Zborov.[40] The 1937 festivities also stressed Czechoslovakia's military strength. President Beneš and his octogenarian predecessor, Masaryk, attended a review of the Prague garrison at the Strahov stadium and were joined there by members of the government, of the diplomatic corps and military attachés accredited to Prague. The Strahov celebration included military formations, displays of military hardware, and athletic competitions as well as scenes from a play, "Obrana státu (Zborov)" ("Defense of the state (Zborov)"), specially written for the anniversary by Colonel A.V. Bičiště. This play featured "magnificent scenes" showcasing the legionary attack on the troops of Austria-Hungary against the background of music like the Hussite battle hymn, which connected Zborov to older Czech national-military traditions. It also, of course, incorporated the patriotic trinity of Czechoslovakia: Masaryk, Beneš and Štefánik.[41]

Meanwhile, in Brno, Bratislava, and Užhorod—the provincial capitals of Moravia-Silesia, Slovakia, and Ruthenia respectively—four main groups participated in the 1937 commemorations: locally stationed military units, Zborov veterans, and provincial and/or national officials. In Bratislava as in Prague, there was a celebratory review of the local garrison in one of that city's main commemorative spaces—Námestí slobodie (Freedom Square)—before local military officials and invited guests. Aircraft flew overhead as the military filed past. Similar mixed military-civilian celebrations occurred elsewhere in Slovakia as people throughout the province "promised to preserve the tradition of the Zborov heroes." According to a local Castle-loyal daily, the *Slovenský deník*, "everyone"—soldiers and citizens alike—would respond to enemy aggression not with words, but with fire and iron, against anyone trying to violate the sanctity of Czechoslovakia's borders. Indeed, they would behave just as Czechoslovak legionaries had acted against German General von Lissingen twenty years earlier at Zborov.[42] As in July 1927, some Slovak newspapers ignored the proceedings altogether. The opposition Czechoslovak National Democrats' *Nitrianske noviny*, for example, focused typically on the 5 July commemorations of Saints Cyril and Methodius.[43]

This time, however, the Czechoslovak Communists were more active participants in the week-long Zborov celebration than they had been a decade earlier, although they still condemned the predominant bourgeois interpretation of the battle. Writing in *Rudé právo*, Communist parliamentary deputy and Zborov veteran Jan Vodička warned that the international situation was again dangerous as in 1917: now increased "Fascist-warmonger" agitation and provocation was aiming to drag the world into yet another war. As a small state, independent Czechoslovakia was threatened and a new serfdom beckoned for its inhabitants. (Although the Communists were still drawing parallels with the Habsburg monarchy, in 1937 Fascism was the key threat.) Vodička duly warned of the danger posed by "bloody Fascist rule," when all democratic, political, and economic rights would be subjugated. In this context he claimed that most of the six thousand people who had recently marched through Prague with Rudolf Medek's "Fascist" Independent Union of Czechoslovak Legionaries (Nezávislé jednoty československých Legionářů) under the slogan "*Národ a vlast*" (nation and homeland) were not legionaries. According to the Communists, the progressive and democratic legionaries, together with other progressive people of Prague, very clearly rejected this "Fascist demagoguery."[44] Vodička urged the legionaries to work with and for the people, and include them in this fighting front for "the old ideals of free and happy lives for all." Indeed, he asserted that only in cooperation with the working people could these goals, which the legionaries had carried with them to the Battle of Zborov, be reawakened.[45]

Nationalizing the Unknown Soldier

Alongside the regular ritual of Zborov, the young republic joined the rest of Europe in commemorating the sacrifice of its war dead by the entombing of an unknown soldier representing those whose bodies had become separated from their names.[46] On Armistice Day, 11 November 1920, the disinterred remains of unknown soldiers from the Great War were ceremoniously carried through the streets of London and Paris to be reburied in a sacred place in the center of each capital. Over the course of the decade, similar ceremonies would be held in virtually all of the former belligerent states except the Soviet Union.

But because the men of what would become Czechoslovakia—as in Italy, reconstructed Poland, and the nascent Yugoslavia—had fought on both sides in the war, the cult of the heroic war dead was complicated. The citizens of this multinational nation-state, with its uncomfortable construction of "Czechoslovak" nationality, needed "a center for the cult of their fallen which would unite the living and remind them not just of death but of their postwar national mission."[47] Yet the Unknown Soldier's tomb in Prague, intended to symbolize the sacrifice of all the "Czechoslovak" war dead, resonated only for the Czechs and some Slovaks, leaving the Germans and Magyars completely outside the triumphalist narrative.[48] Even the date on which Czechoslovakia's Unknown Soldier was reburied marked this memorial as Czech-national: not 11 November, Armistice Day, but rather 1 July, as part of the ceremony commemorating the fifth anniversary of Zborov in 1922.

In late June 1922, the remains of an unknown Czechoslovak soldier were taken from a mass grave near the Zborov battlefield. They were placed in a casket, escorted by rail to the Czechoslovak-Polish border, and turned over to Czechoslovak soldiers. En route to Prague the train stopped regularly, so the representatives of local military garrisons, the Sokol, and other patriotic organizations could honor the Unknown Soldier. Upon arrival in Prague, the remains lay in state in the Pantheon of the National Museum on Wenceslas Square. On 1 July, an honor guard comprising members of infantry, the legionaries, and the Sokol moved the flag-draped casket to the Old Town Square, where the coffin was buried in the chapel of the old city hall. The locating of this tomb on Old Town Square, long a site for gathering to reaffirm Czech national myths, further confirmed the Unknown Soldier buried there as *Czechoslovak*, although the commemoration was in fact entirely Czech. Moreover, as Jan Galandauer has observed, in contrast to the ritual of the Unknown Soldier in other countries, in Czechoslovakia it was not mass death but the result of a particular battle that formed the basis for the state's leading commemorative tradition.[49]

Constructions of Zborov in the Czechoslovak Landscape

The tomb of the Unknown Soldier in Prague was only one of many Zborov memorials constructed after 1918 in an attempt to mark the soil of the Bohemian Lands as Czech. In Czechoslovakia as throughout Europe, a great period of memorial construction followed in the wake of the Great War due to its unprecedented scope and appalling death statistics. This "democratization of death" tried to honor all war dead, irrespective of rank and including the unknown dead.[50] Those monuments to the fallen linked to national independence contained multiple, broad symbolic and, sometimes, contradictory meanings: sacred or nonsacred, fallen or victorious, victims of war or heroic legionaries. And in Czechoslovakia, this symbolism unsurprisingly spoke only to the state's majority people: the "Czechoslovaks."[51]

An important legionary element in Prague's built landscape is the Památník odboje, the museum and archive of the legionaries, renamed Památník osvobození in 1929. The mausoleum-ceremonial hall stands high atop the Vítkov hill, where it can be seen for miles, on the site of Žižka's victory over Habsburg emperor Zikmund in July 1420 (after which Zikmund abandoned Bohemia to the Hussites). This site represented the physical connection of modern Czech military victories to an older Czech military tradition, and as with other Zborov commemorative sites, the historical symbolism here was exclusively Czech. The memorial, intended to house artifacts and documents from the Czech wartime struggle for freedom, was opened with great ceremony in 1932 on the fifteenth anniversary of Zborov.

Many Zborov monuments were erected in connection with the tenth anniversary of the battle in 1927 and the tenth anniversary of the state the following year; others were unveiled in 1937 and 1947. While Czech-speaking communities often constructed local memorials honoring those who had fallen at Zborov or in other legionary exploits, local legionary societies also sponsored memorial plaques to commemorate individual Zborov heroes.[52] Some monuments were simple obelisks inscribed with the names of local fallen Czechs, irrespective of their allegiance. Others included groups or bas-reliefs of legionaries, or historic figures from the state's foundation myth including Hus, Masaryk, and American President Woodrow Wilson. In the multinational state, this iconography was insufficiently universal to include either the national minorities or those who rejected the "Czechoslovakist" propaganda of the Prague government. It repudiated German and Magyar historical icons and war sacrifice, but also ignored specifically the Slovak nationalist agenda as laid out in the Pittsburgh Agreement.

Only rarely, as in the large, ethnically mixed industrial metropolis of Moravská Ostrava (Mährische Ostrau) near the Polish border, was a "nationally inclusive" war memorial unveiled in the Czech lands—one that recognized the sacrifice of all Czechoslovak soldiers. This obelisk, engraved only with the dates, "1914–1918" and the names of the parish war dead (complete with Czech, German, and Polish diacritics), still stands in a churchyard near the city center archive.

Those monuments commemorating Zborov encouraged the conclusion that, regardless of the side on which the soldiers had fought, they had all participated in a battle for national independence. Indeed, in Prague's Olšanské Cemetery, the gravestones of Czech soldiers who died fighting in the Habsburg army stand beside those of fallen legionaries.[53] In a country where the rhetoric of military valor and wartime sacrifice played an important role in the creation of a usable past, the German and Magyar mourning of their war dead was limited to local war memorials in the borderlands—many of them in cemeteries and some of them contested by local Czechs or Slovaks. Only a few of these memorials still survive, reminding the observant passerby that *"Unser Blut und Unser Leben haben wir für Euch gegeben."* (We have sacrificed our blood and our lives for you).

Another significant development in patterns of national memorials was their construction on foreign soil.[54] Most notably, there was a Czechoslovak memorial at Zborov, in what was then Poland (today Zboriv, Ukraine). On the tenth anniversary of the battle, the Union of Czechoslovak Legionaries, the Památník osvobození, and other state institutions sponsored a national pilgrimage to the site. An official delegation of loyal Czechoslovak citizens boarded a special express train festooned in national colors to visit the simple burial-mound shrine of the legionary hero-martyrs at a mass grave near the battlefield. The bilingual Czech and Polish inscription on the commemorative plaque, unveiled in connection with this anniversary, honored the "sons of Czechoslovakia" who slept in old Slav soil having sacrificed their lives "in the holy battle for the liberation of their fatherland."[55] The groups of patriotic citizens and soldiers who travelled there in 1927 from Prague and Košice (Slovakia) were joined by a delegation of Czech-speakers from Volhynia in Galician Poland. Participants noted the warm reception they received from the Polish, Ukrainian, and Jewish residents of the village and the festive air.

During the ceremony at the burial mound, a Czech member of parliament addressed a large crowd that included local Polish officials. He then placed soil from White Mountain on the mound where the soldier-heroes were buried, reflecting the sacral quality of earth related to death and sacrifice.[56] As an example of this Czech variant of *Blut und Boden*, some pilgrims placed soil from their home regions on the mound, while others returned home with a fistful of soil that they incorporated into local commemorative sites alongside earth from other legionary battlefields such as Bachmač and Dosso Alto. Soil from these points on the Eastern and Italian fronts would also be added to the memorial to Czechoslovakia's Unknown Soldier in Prague.[57] It was a ritual that would continue after 1989, when soil from these same sites as well as from Nazi and Communist prisons would be placed in memorials to Czech victims of Fascism and Communism, reflecting the age-old sacrifice made for the Czechoslovak state.

Zborov on the Big Screen: Entertainment and Propaganda

In addition to these monuments dotting the Czech landscape, there was a relatively new commemorative medium available: film. Besides providing a window into the popular political culture of the First Republic, the films about Zborov demonstrate the convergence of pedagogy, propaganda, and entertainment. These cultural products played an active role in representing, but also reinforcing and sometimes constituting, visions of history.[58] Between the wars, the Battle of Zborov was the subject of a number of silent and sound films, both documentary and feature. They often premiered in connection with the commemorations in July or celebration of state independence in October.[59] Documentary films especially were meant to inculcate national values into citizens of all ages, holding up the legionaries as an exemplar.

One individual, Rudolf Medek, was instrumental in both leading and limiting the popular-cultural production of the memory of Zborov.[60] The controversial Medek had, as a Habsburg officer, deserted to the Russians in December 1915 and subsequently became a legionary, poet, novelist, and playwright. He not only helped create the Czechoslovak army, rising to the rank of general, but also helped found the Památník odboje on Vítkov. Fiercely anti-German, anti-Bolshevik, anti-semitic, and closely associated with the Czechoslovak National Democratic party of the 1920s, he came to personify a kind of integral Czech nationalism, which he widely propagated in numerous newspaper articles written for the annual Zborov commemorations.[61]

Conversant in a variety of cultural forms, Medek authored numerous second-rate heroic and adventure novels in which he himself often featured.[62] He was also active in the production of silent and sound films on topics related didactically to Zborov.[63] His drama, *Plukovník Švec* (Colonel Švec), about one heroic Zborov veteran who later committed suicide in the Siberian anabasis, was performed at Prague's National Theater more than a hundred times between 1928 and 1934 and was a critical success when it appeared as a silent film in 1930.[64] Medek also participated in several documentaries and feature films, including *Za Československý stát* (For the Czechoslovak State), which premiered on the tenth anniversary of the state. The film's plot was simple: three friends from a small Czech village join the Habsburg army at the outbreak of war and end up as French, Italian, and Russian legionaries. The film focused on symbolic episodes connected to Czechoslovak independence: how in 1914 the 28th Infantry Regiment was called up on Wenceslas Square (the beloved *Pražské děti* whose unit would be dissolved when they allegedly surrendered en masse on the Eastern front);[65] how the Czechs behaved in Russia including their role at Zborov; and how the declaration of independence occurred in October 1918. The scenes about Zborov promised an "exact replica" of the battle, including a forest "shot to pieces" and a village set on fire.[66]

The links of entertainment, pedagogy, and propaganda were rendered explicit in the timing of these films' release (on national holidays like 2 July or 28 October), as well as through Medek's and the Defense Ministry's role in their production. Their political content was both a source of pedagogy (teaching the nation about its past and creating loyal citizens) and of propaganda (teaching the nation a particular, standardized representation of a history contested by many of its citizens). At the same time, some of the films were commercial, aiming both to entertain and earn a profit, as in the film *Zborov* made at the Barrandov studios in 1938.

An Exclusive Discourse

Festivals and holidays in the Habsburg monarchy had generally been connected to the liturgical calendar or imperial events; voluntary organizations had also organized a variety of local and provincial celebrations. These had provided many, if not most, citizens of Austria with commemorative space. Yet the Habsburg celebrations stood in stark contrast to postwar Czechoslovakia's state holidays. Commemorations of Zborov, intended to be both national and "nationalizing," failed to include all citizens. Zborov's anniversary, also celebrated as "army day," provided all of the legionaries, indeed the entire military, with the opportunity both to commemorate the wartime sacrifice of the "Czechoslovaks" and to celebrate their heroic role in the creation of the Czechoslovak nation-state. In fact, both sacrifice and state were, in Zborov rituals, overwhelmingly Czech. The national rhetoric associated with this holiday, like that of 28 October, resounded negatively for many Sudeten Germans and Magyars because it excluded them. The official Zborov celebrations also closed off participation by those Czechs and Slovaks who were uneasy about the "Czechoslovakist" politics advocated by Masaryk and his supporters, or who had fought loyally on the Habsburg side. Rather than create a unified community, the language of Czechoslovak sacrifice and commemoration around Zborov did the opposite: it deepened divisions within the state.

Indeed, the Zborov narrative—with its focus squarely on Jan Hus, Jan Žižka, and other heroic figures vital to Czech national self-construction—was so predominantly Czech that in the end, it resonated primarily with those Slovaks who were the most enthusiastic advocates of "Czechoslovakism." Zborov commemorations therefore did not contribute to the creation of that common civic

Figures 6.2 and 6.3. Stills from Czech film *Zborov*, 1938. The premiere of *Zborov*, based on an idea of Rudolf Medek, was originally planned for 28 October 1938, the twentieth anniversary of Czechoslovakia, but it was delayed due to the events of Munich. An abridged and adapted version was enthusiastically received when it finally appeared in cinemas in January 1939. Images courtesy of the Národní filmový archiv, Prague.

identity necessary for building a new democratic state. Rather, the privileged state language of Czech sacrifice, commemoration and regeneration greatly complicated efforts to expand membership in the First Czechoslovak Republic.

Nancy M. Wingfield is Presidential Research Professor at Northern Illinois University, specializing in the cultural and gender history of Habsburg Central Europe. Her publications include *Flag Wars and Stone Saints: How the Bohemian Lands Became Czech* (2007) and, as editor with Maria Bucur, *Gender and War in Twentieth-Century Eastern Europe* (2006). She is completing a book-length study on the world of prostitution in late Cisleithanian Austria.

Notes

Themes and ideas presented here were first developed in my book for Harvard University Press, *Flag Wars and Stone Saints: How the Bohemian Lands Became Czech* (Cambridge, MA, 2007). I would like to thank Dagmara Hájková, Katya Kocourek, Lisa Kirschenbaum, and Andrea Orzoff for their comments on earlier versions of this chapter, and Lucie Česálková of Prague's Národní filmový archiv for providing the film images.

1. As Robert Pynsent points out, the soldiers in Russia were originally referred to as the "Czechoslovak Brigade"; they did not use the term "legionary," but rather the Czechoslovak government imposed it on them. See Pynsent, "The Literary Representation of the Czechoslovak 'Legions' in Russia," in *Czechoslovakia in a Nationalist and Fascist Europe 1918–1948*, ed. Mark Cornwall and R.J.W. Evans (Oxford, 2007), 66.
2. On popular perceptions of Masaryk's role in gaining Czechoslovak independence, see for example Andrea Orzoff, *Battle for the Castle: The Myth of Czechoslovakia in Europe, 1914–1948* (Oxford, 2009), 119–32.
3. "Patriarchové československé státní nezávislosti," *Nedělní čtení*, the insert to *Československá republika*, 28 October 1928, 1. On the triple portrait, see Mary Heimann, *Czechoslovakia: The State that Failed* (New Haven, 2009), 31.
4. On the "Manifesto of the Czechoslovak People," read by the Protestant theologian Dr Ferdinand Hrejša at the 1925 Hus festival in Prague, see "Husovy oslavy v Praze" in *Odpolední národní politika*, 7 July 1925. See Národní archiv, Prague, Sbírka blahopřání k výročí republiky, karton 1, sig. 1/49 (Okresní úřad v Mělníku), "manifestation of devotion to the Czechoslovak state" on its eighteenth anniversary from the teaching staff in Mělník "to the great liberating work of Masaryk, Beneš, Štefánik, and the Legionary brethren." A useful study of the legionaries is Karl Pichlík et al, *Českoslovenští Legionáři, 1914–1920* (Prague, 1996).
5. For example, *Pravda vítězí: Deset československých vlasteneckých zpěvů* (Prague, 1928) [no page numbers].
6. Ivan Šedivý, *Češi, české země a velká válka* (Prague, 2001), 83–84.
7. Martin Zückert, *Zwischen Nationsidee und staatlicher Realität: Die tschechoslowakische Armee und ihre Nationalitätenpolitik 1918–1938* (Munich, 2006), 93.
8. The majority of the Czech and Slovak soldiers remained in POW camps. See Alon Rachamimov, "Imperial Loyalties and Private Concerns: Nation, Class, and State in the Correspondence of Austro-Hungarian POWs in Russia, 1916–1918," *Austrian History Yearbook* 31

(2000): 89–90; Z.A.B. Zeman, *The Break-up of the Habsburg Empire 1914–1918: A Study in National and Social Revolution* (New York, 1961), 132; and Zückert, *Zwischen Nationsidee und staatlicher Realität*, 82.
9. "Czechoslovakism," the official ideology of the First Czechoslovak Republic, meant that the Czechs and Slovaks constituted one nation comprising two peoples, the Czechs and Slovaks, and that "the Slovaks were actually Czechs, only less developed," according to Elisabeth Bakke, "The Making of Czechoslovakism in the First Czechoslovak Republic," in *Loyalitäten in der Tschechoslowakischen Republik 1918–1938: Politische, nationale und kulturelle Zugehörigkeiten*, ed. Martin Schulze Wessel (Munich, 2004), 23.
10. Zückert, *Zwischen Nationsidee und staatlicher Realität*, 56–57.
11. On the pedagogical holiday: Alon Confino, *The Nation as a Local Metaphor: Württemberg, Imperial Germany, and National Memory, 1871–1918* (Chapel Hill, 1997), 46.
12. On the Pittsburgh Agreement, see Heimann, *Czechoslovakia*, 33–34; 61–62; Victor S. Mamatey, "The Czecho-Slovak Agreement of Pittsburgh (May 30, 1918) Revisited," *Kosmas* 2/2 (Winter 1983): 41–48; and Mark Stolarik, "The Role of Slovak Émigrés in North America in the Emancipation of the Slovak Nation," *Društevna istraživanja* 7/1–2 (1998): 77–78.
13. Especially the Sudeten Germans made this argument; see Rudolf Frantz, "Der sogenannte Sieg vom Zborov: Der Anfang des Zusammenbruchs der russischen Front," *Bohemia*, 19 June 1927, 5 and "Beim Abschnitt Zloczow im Sommer 1917," *Der 92er* 4 (July/August 1927): 6; as well as *Prager Presse*, 1 July 1937. Richard Lein has argued that the surrender of predominantly Czech units at Zborov was due to strategic errors made by the Habsburg military rather than disloyalty: "Die Schlacht von Zborów," in *České křižovatky evropských dějin. 1918: Model komplexního transformačního procesu?*, ed. Lucie Kostrbová and Jana Malínská (Prague, 2010).
14. Šedivý, *Češi, české země a velká válka*, 147. See also Richard Lein, *Pflichterfüllung oder Hochverrat?: Die tschechischen Soldaten Österreich-Ungarns im Ersten Weltkrieg* (Vienna, 2011), 420, quoting Václav Klaus on myths of the First Republic and how "'strangely' we [many Czechs] interpret the First World War."
15. Todd Wayne Huebner, "The Multinational 'Nation-State': The Origins and the Paradox of Czechoslovakia, 1914–1920," PhD diss., New York 1993, 55, fn145. See also *Central European Observer* 15 (9 July 1937): 223.
16. See for example the articles in the Czech Agrarian newspaper *Venkov* on 6 July 1917, 5; and 7 July 1917, 5 ("Co se stalo u Zborova?").
17. *Nová doba*, 31 October 1918, 3; 2 November 1918, 3; and *Prager Presse*, 2 July 1933, 1. See also Šedivý, *Češi*, 311–12; and for Zborov in Czech national mythology: Jan Galandauer, *2.7.1917 Bitva u Zborova: česká legenda* (Prague, 2002).
18. For example, Miloš Marvan's poem, "Československým Legionářům," dated 30 October 1918, in *Nová doba* (Plzeň), 2 November 2 1918, 3; and [unattributed], "Hymna československých legií v boj za právo!" *České slovo* (evening edition), 30 October 1918, 1. Also, the line "i pod prapory Legionářů," in Stanislav K. Neumann's poem, "28. říjen 1918," *České slovo*, 1 November 1918, 1.
19. *Nová doba*, 3 July 1922, 2.
20. Czechoslovak independence on 28 October was also often celebrated as a national holiday rather than a state one. Even President Masaryk often used the term "national holiday," although he was aware of the need for the country's citizens to recognize 28 October as a "state holiday." See Dagmar Hájková and Nancy M. Wingfield, "Czech(-oslovak) National Commemorations during the Interwar Period: Tomáš G. Masaryk and the Battle of White Mountain Avenged," *Acta Histriae* (September 2010): 426.
21. See, for example, "Vzdejte čest Neznámenu vojínu," in *Večerní české slovo*, 27 October 1928, 1.

22. The literature on the Castle is extensive. See, for example, Karl Bosl, ed. *Die Burg: Einflußreiche politische Kräfte um Masaryk und Beneš*, 2 vols. (Munich, 1973–74); Antonín Klimek, *Boj o hrad*, vol. 1: *Hrad a pětka, 1918–1926* (Prague, 1996); and vol. 2: *Kdo po Masarykovi?: 1926–1935* (Prague, 1998); and Orzoff, *Battle for the Castle*.
23. Legionaries, especially those employed in sensitive positions, like the police, came under Nazi scrutiny: Moravian Provincial Archive, Brno (MZA: Moravský zemský archiv), B26, karton 2353. See also Rudolf Ruhsam, "Es war einmal," *Zeitschrift für die Protektorats-Polizei* 13 (1 July 1942): 297: "There was in these police still another large group, who came before all of the rest, who did not need the help of a party or a parliamentary deputy … They were called the Legionaries."
24. The Československá obec Legionářská—banned under the Nazis, reformed after 1945, banned again after 1948, again reformed after 1989—exists today.
25. Speech of the German National party MP Franz Matzner: *Příloha k těsnopisecké zprávě, 150. schůze poslanecké sněmovny Národního shromáždění Republiky československé*, 28 June 1928, www.psp.cz (accessed January 1, 2006).
26. On legionary "provocations" in the German border regions, see State District Archive Cheb (Státní okresní archiv), fond 38, karton 10, inv. č. 126: Bürgermeisterstellvertreter to Polizei-Kommissariat Eger, 26 June 1926.
27. *Lidové noviny* (morning edition), 2 July 1927, 3.
28. Pynsent, "The Literary Representation," 78.
29. The first is from Josef Pelíšek's "Dopis neznámého vojína," *Lidové noviny* (morning edition), 2 July 1927, 1; the second can be found in Rudolf Medek, *Lví srdce, básně 1914–1918* (Prague, 1919), 28.
30. *Central European Observer*, 8 July 1927, 443.
31. On the festivities in Prague, see for example: *Bohemia*, 3 July 1927, 1; *Československá republika*, 3 July 1927, 3; *Lidové noviny*, 2 July 1927, 4; and *Prager Presse*, 2 July 1927, 4.
32. On the events in Bratislava, see *Slovenský denník*, 1 July 1927, 5; and 3 July 1927, 4. The spelling of *Slovenský denník* was changed to *Slovenský deník* during the interwar period. I have retained the double "n" throughout for consistency.
33. *Slovenský denník*, 1 July 1927, 3; for Slávik's speech, *Slovenský denník*, 8 July 1927, 3.
34. See James Felak, *"At the Price of the Republic": Hlinka's Slovak People's Party, 1929–1938* (Pittsburgh, 1995).
35. See *Slovenská pravda* and *Trenčan*, early July and late October 1927.
36. *Rudé právo*, 3 July 1927, 1–2.
37. Ibid., 3 July 1937, 2.
38. *1917-1937 Zborov*, II. *Zborovský závod branné zdatnosti mládeže 1938 v Brně* (Prague, n.d. [1937]), 6–7.
39. Zückert, *Zwischen Nationsidee und staatlicher Realität*, 217.
40. *Lidové noviny*, 2 July 1937, 4; and *Slovenský denník*, 3 July 1937, 2.
41. See report on the play in Prague's Czech-language newspapers, as well as in Bratislava's *Slovenský denník*, 3 July 1937, 3.
42. *Slovenský denník*, 3 July 1937, 2.
43. See *Nitrianske noviny* from early July 1937.
44. *Rudé právo*, 4 July 1937, 6.
45. Ibid.
46. Thomas W. Laqueur, "Memory and Naming in the Great War," in *Commemorations: The Politics of National Identity*, ed. John Gillis (Princeton, 1994), 153.
47. George L. Mosse, *Fallen Soldiers: Reshaping the Memory of the World Wars* (New York, 1990), 93.

48. There are no reliable data on the number of Czech and Slovak soldiers who died during the war. Šedivý, *Češi, české země a velká válka* (148–49), and others have based their estimates of war dead primarily on Wilhelm Winkler, *Die Totalverluste der öst.-ung. Monarchie nach Nationalitäten* (Vienna, 1919), which contains numbers only through to the end of 1917. Moreover, Winkler does not mention nationality, but rather the districts from which the dead hailed: in other words, Czech, mostly Czech, German, mostly German, etc. For example, 138,128 dead soldiers from solely Czech districts, but 189,015 from all Bohemian districts, 80,248 from Moravian districts, and 19,018 from Austrian Silesia. There were 5,405 Czech and Slovak legionaries who died during the war.
49. See the discussion in Zückert, *Zwischen Nationsidee und staatlicher Realität*, 219–20.
50. Laqueur, "Memory and Naming in the Great War," 150–51.
51. On the meanings of memorials, see James M. Mayo, "War Memorials as Political Memory," *Geographical Review* 78 (1988): 62.
52. MZA: Policejní ředitelství v Brně, karton 495, č .j. 1527/2, 24 July 1927.
53. See Mark Cornwall, "Mémoires de la Grande Guerre dans les pays Tchèques 1918–1928," *14–18 Aujourd'hui. Today. Heute* 5 (June 2002): 89–101.
54. James M. Mayo, *War Memorials as Political Landscape: The American Experience and Beyond* (Westport, CT, 1988), 95.
55. *Lidové noviny*, 2 July 1927, 4; *Pražské noviny*, 7 July 1937, 4; and *Úřední list města Plzně* 5/15 (1 August 1927): 182.
56. *Slovenský denník*, 5 July 1927, 5.
57. "Městské zastupitelstvo," *Úřední list města Plzně* 15/5 (1 August 1927): 182; and *Lidové noviny*, 2 July 1927, 4. On the collection of stones from sites of historic importance in Bohemia and the National Theater, see Hugh LeCaine Agnew, "Demonstrating the Nation: Symbol, Ritual, and Political Protest in Bohemia, 1867–1875," in *The Street as Stage: Protest Marches and Public Rallies since the Nineteenth Century*, ed. Matthias Reiss (Oxford, 2007), 96–97. A 1939 diary entry of Zborov veteran Ludvík Svoboda, head of the Czechoslovak Army in the Soviet Union, as he passed close to the Zborov battlefield reflected the feelings of many patriotic Czechs: Svoboda referred to that soil as "sanctified" by the "blood of Czechoslovak heroes:" Ludvík Svoboda, *Deník z doby válečné: červen 1939-leden 1943* (Prague, 2008), diary entry for 13 September 1939, 53. For other European variants, see also the discussion of Romanian Iron Guard rites concerning sacred soil by Rebecca Haynes in this volume.
58. Scott Spector, "Was the Third Reich Movie-Made? Interdisciplinarity and the Reframing of 'Ideology,'" *American Historical Review* 106 (2001): 460.
59. State Regional Archive Plzeň (Státní oblastní archiv), Měský úřad v Plzni, 19 October 1936: Invitation to the celebratory premiere of the legionary film, "Jízdní hlídka," written by Russian legionary František Langer. This was part of the festivities of that year's 28 October holiday and the 1937 Zborov celebrations.
60. For more on Rudolf Medek, see Chapter 7. See also Katya A.M. Kocourek, "The Czechoslovak Legionary Tradition and the Battle against the "Beneš Doctrine" in Czech Historiography: The Case of General Rudolf Medek (1890–1940)," in *The Past in the Making: Historical Revisionism in Central Europe after 1989*, ed. Michel Kopeček (Budapest, 2007), 97–127; Jitka Zabloudilová and Petr Hofman, "Rudolf Medek," *Historie a vojenství* 6 (1994): 133–57.
61. Medek's work was placed on the Nazi index on 15 March 1939, while the Communists banned it after 1948 because it celebrated the struggle of the Czechoslovak Legions against the Bolsheviks. See Rudolf Medek, *Mohutný sen, Legionářská epopej* (Zurich, 1980). For an example of his newspaper articles, see, Rudolf Medek, "Zborov bol pre nás velkým a slávnym činom," *Slovenský denník*, 21 July 1927, 1.

62. On Medek's lack of literary talent, see Pynsent, "The Literary Representation," 63–88.
63. Rudolf Medek's novels and stories, some of them for children and young people, include: *Legenda o Barabášovi aneb podivuhodná dobrodružství kapitána Mojmíra Ivánoviče Barabáše a Jozefa Jelítka, sluhy jeho* (Prague, 1932); *O našich legiích, dětech a zvířátkách v Sibiři* (Prague, 1921); *O našich legiích: pohádky a povídky* (Prague, 1928); *Kolja Mikulka: Dětská historie z velké války* (Prague, 1927); and František Langer, Josef Kopta, and Rudolf Medek, *Legionářské povídky* (Brno, 1928).
64. Rudolf Medek, *Plukovník Švec*, 3rd ed. (Prague, 1929). On critical acclaim for the film, see *Mein Film: Illustrierte Film- und Kinorundschau* 225 (1930): 10; *Filmové listy* 2 (28 February 1930): 41.
65. For recent Czech-language evaluations of the wartime actions of the 28th, see Josef Fučík, *Osmadvacátníci - Spor o českého vojáka Velké války 1914–1918* (Prague, 2006); and Šedivý, *Češi, české země a velká válka*, 82–83. See also Lein's recent analysis, *Pflichterfüllung oder Hochverrat?* On dramatization of the 28th Infantry Regiment's wartime experiences, see Friedrich Porges, *Mein Film-Buch: vom Film, vom Tonfilm, von Filmstars und von Kinematographie* (Vienna, 1930), 344–45.
66. *Bohemia*, 6 September 1928, 6.

Chapter 7

"IN THE SPIRIT OF BROTHERHOOD, UNITED WE REMAIN!"
Czechoslovak Legionaries and the Militarist State

Katya Kocourek

The experience of the Great War produced a wide range of political views and national allegiances among war veterans. In Czechoslovakia's case these included the volunteer legionary soldiers who had fought on two fronts and under the command of foreign armies in Russia, Italy and France. War was a great transformer but its interpretation in peacetime, in terms of the sacrifice made during the conflict, was also a divisive force in interwar politics.[1] Czech and Slovak legionary veterans, particularly those from the Eastern front, had a wealth of wartime nationalist traditions to draw on when explaining the origins of the new nation-state and the meaning of national independence. The most important of these related to the cult of military sacrifice and martyrdom dating from 1917 to 1918, the time between the Battle of Zborov and the "anabasis" when the Czechoslovak Legion, during its evacuation eastwards to Vladivostok, seized control of key points of the Trans-Siberian Railway from Red Army units. Despite Czechoslovakia's victor status, it still experienced the same kind of conservative backlash as some of the vanquished states due to persisting notions of wartime sacrifice, particularly its depiction as a legitimizing principle for the emergent nation. By the early 1920s, the ideological conflict unleashed by the war made way for homegrown, proto-Fascist movements, inspired by a cult of heroism and anti-Bolshevism. Concomitant with this trend was the appearance of military societies and veteran associations whose primary concern was the preservation of a militarist outlook and distinct wartime mentality. It was expressed through various narratives of sacrifice and heroism.

This chapter analyzes the nationalist ideology championed by the second largest veteran association in interwar Czechoslovakia, the Independent Union of Czechoslovak Legionaries (NJČsL: Nezávislá jednota československých Legionářů), which was largely composed of right-wing legionary veterans. Its creation in December 1925 signified an irrevocable ideological split in the legionary movement after two years of increasing political tensions. Although its membership never crept much above twenty thousand in Czechoslovakia, it was regarded by its leadership and members as an independent movement and styled itself as a military enterprise with a suitably militant nationalist vision.

The NJČsL was led by the nationalist poet and professional soldier Rudolf Medek.[2] During the war Medek, a leading propagandist of the legionary cause on the Eastern front, had helped transform the reputation of the rank-and-file "soldier" from a simple volunteer into a heroic defender of national rights. In the context of the 1920s, a boom-time for war literature, he achieved cult-like status as a legionary author. War for him was a source of political regeneration, and he defended the importance of legionary veteran views for the evolution of the new state in this context. His nationalist verse might be heralded as the intellectual inspiration for the development of Czechoslovak Fascism, but the NJČsL would still attempt to forge a middle ground between the Czechoslovak political center and the Fascist right at a time in the early 1920s when militarism was on the rise.[3] In the following we will explore this proposition with reference to how the movement emerged, analyzing the components that made up its nationalist ideology in the formative years of its existence.

Much recent Czech scholarship has focused on the largest legionary veteran's association in the First Republic, the state sponsored Union of Czechoslovak Legionaries (ČsOL: Československá obec Legionářská). Created in mid-January 1921, it convened its first proper congress on 22 May. Existing scholarship has largely ignored the activities of smaller or marginal groups and their associated ideas.[4] Furthermore, the ideological characteristics that distinguished the ČsOL and NJČsL, particularly their founding principles, including the idealization of warfare and nationalism, have never been properly acknowledged.[5] The NJČsL was not simply the military arm of the conservative-nationalist National Democratic Party, nor was it straightforwardly paramilitary.[6] The fact that legionaries, who belonged to both the National Socialist and Social Democratic parties, were welcome in the NJČsL challenges what has been written about the movement since the changes of 1989: it was not simply a veterans' association primarily for Czech Fascists.[7] Indeed, although it is generally accepted that the NJČsL was a right-wing alliance, little is known about its ideology, the nature of its opposition politics or indeed the manner in which it evolved.[8] Historiography since 2006 has done much to rectify shortcomings about the complexities of veteran transition from wartime to peacetime, particularly in terms of the potential for nationalist violence, ideological instability and paramilitarism, all of which were rooted in the traditions of the Czechoslovak Legions.[9] However, it remains unclear how fringe veteran movements like the NJČsL contested the existing notions of political legitimacy based on national sacrifice; or how their own nationalist myth-making from the wartime experience affected existing political conflicts inside the "victorious" successor states of the Habsburg empire.

War Veterans and Czechoslovak Politics

Veterans' transition to peacetime in the Czechoslovak case was by no means straightforward. The homecoming of the "real" soldiers to emerge from the conflict—legionary veterans engaged in active conflict on the Western and Eastern fronts—was staggered over several years, with the last units reaching Czechoslovakia from Siberia in the summer of 1921. The memorialization of that conflict was further tempered by various political forces, including revolution and civil war in Bolshevik Russia and social unrest at home. In this fluid context, the notion of legionary values and the need to maintain them became a bone of contention between those veterans who had been politicized by their experience and those who had left the trenches with little more than a sense of despair and disregard for politics. For some, particularly those on the right, preserving legionary values translated into a fierce and militant defense of their importance as an energizing force underpinning the political legitimacy of the new post-Habsburg establishment.[10] For others, pacifists and those on the left, the only traditions worth preserving from the horrors of war were those of comradeship and social understanding. Although a majority of Czech veterans returned to their prewar professions upon reaching Czechoslovakia, some—most of them former legionaries from Russia—were employed in state institutions and especially the Ministry of Defense.[11] The Resistance Memorial/Liberation Institute—created in June 1920 as an official memorial to Czech and Slovak legionaries who had fought for the Czechoslovak cause—was also an important employer of former legionaries, including professional soldiers like Rudolf Medek and legionary authors like Josef Kopta. The majority of Czechoslovak legionaries during the war had been left-leaning: many had belonged to the Czech Social Democratic party or been close to Austrian social democracy pre-1914. Therefore most, if not all, of these, including those radicalized by Bolshevik ideas in the east, were members of the ČsOL. The ČsOL remained the largest organization for legionary veterans throughout the First Republic, representing the legionary-veteran left wing (Social Democrat, but also some Communist members).[12] The purpose behind the ČsOL's creation had been to unify the deeply divided legionary movement and represent all legionary interests, left and right. However, by 1923 the movement was becoming overtly politicized and its original purpose transformed into supporting the politics of the "Castle" led by President Masaryk.

The ČsOL had several influential ideologues, all of whom were loyal to the Castle and Foreign Minister Edvard Beneš, most notably the chairman, Josef Patejdl, and legionary journalists Lev Sychrava and Václav Cháb. Beneš patronized the ČsOL informally from its founding in 1921, and as a result the society gradually became part of the political framework of the center-left National Socialist party. The ČsOL was, therefore, very much part of the Czechoslovak political establishment, whereas the NJČsL occupied a unique position on the fringes of politics and received a different type of patronage from the Czechoslovak military establishment, particularly the Chief of the General Staff. The core ideas of both groups were developed in a variety of polemical debates conducted on the front pages of newspapers, specialist journals, and pamphlets.

Lev Sychrava, one of the founding members of the ČsOL and a leading spokesman of left-wing legionaries throughout the interwar period, defined the purpose of the ČsOL in several pamphlets published in the early 1920s. Here military sacrifice was rarely mentioned. Sychrava stressed the social significance of the Great War and how this informed the missionary work of Czechoslovak veterans in peacetime. In *Legionářský socialismus*, published in 1923, he explained that the ČsOL was established primarily to support the social reforms adopted by successive governments from 1921 to 1923 to help stabilize the Republic at a time of social flux.[13] In *Naše národní tradice* (Our National Traditions, 1924), he argued that the Great War was an event of social importance for it heralded an era of "progressive democracy": even the socially down-trodden became important to the development of nationhood, something especially true for small nations like the Czechoslovaks.[14] In pseudo-Marxist terms he went on to explain that the conflict had emancipated the weak from the clutches of socially exploitative regimes (monarchies), and that the ČsOL's purpose was to protect members of the lower social classes against the harmful excesses of private capital, while helping the weak become upwardly mobile in a new social democratic environment.[15] In this respect the legionary mission from the early 1920s was in a state of flux among left-wing veterans who regarded nationalist ideology in Marxist terms as a logical evolution driven by social and economic conflict. The same could not be said of the nationalist right, whose ideology remained largely static and backward-looking, focusing solely on the political significance of wartime sacrifice.

In 1924, Sychrava's pseudo-Marxist platitudes were incorporated by the ČsOL into its official program on social development.[16] This included pedagogic programs for the children of impoverished veterans and benefits for the unemployed. All of these ideas about social justice neatly conformed to Masaryk's idea of "humanity" (*humanita*), itself a socially progressive program that defended a socialism rooted in national and moral precepts. Following Beneš, leading

ČsOL protagonists like Sychrava also believed that socialism, rather than militarism, was the basis of nationalism and legionary patriotism.[17] "Humanity" therefore became the watchword of left-wing legionaries in the early 1920s, and this worried those on the right because of its association with pacifist ideas that undermined the creation of a strong national army capable of properly defending the state.[18] Masaryk's pacifism was of particular concern to those engaged in military life, almost all of whom opposed his idea of creating a popular militia instead of a professional army as the surest means of national defense.[19] The President, inspired by his hatred of excessive militarism and its association with imperialism, had in 1919 frequently referred to this type of institution as a "democratic army" led by a "democratic hero."[20] The first major law on the Czechoslovak army passed in 1920 retained this notion of a popular militia; and in 1922 the idea was adopted by the ČsOL at its founding congress.[21]

The ČsOL in Crisis

The first political cracks in the Czechoslovak legionary movement emerged in the spring of 1923 at the very institute symbolizing legionary military and political unity, the Resistance Memorial Institute (Památník odboje).[22] In March 1923, to mark the fifth anniversary of the creation of Czechoslovakia, the Institute launched a lecture series on behalf of the ČsOL titled "Czechoslovak Revolution" (*Cyklus Československá Revoluce*) about the origins of Czechoslovakia and the role played by legionaries in securing official Allied recognition of the state in 1918. As a ČsOL-themed event, a majority of the lectures were delivered by ČsOL luminaries, such as Josef Patejdl, in addition to leading politicians representing the Social Democrats and National Socialists, like Václav Klofáč. The first lecture in the series was delivered by Beneš on 12 March 1923, titled "The Meaning of [the] Czechoslovak Revolution."[23] Beneš's emphasis on the "socially just" actions of legionaries during the Great War on the Eastern front—reflected most notably in his objection to Czechoslovak military intervention in Bolshevik Russia—heightened tensions between different branches of the ČsOL about the political orientation of the movement, and brought him into direct conflict with right-wing legionaries who regarded the "political struggle" with the Bolsheviks as the Legion's finest hour.[24]

At the annual convention of the ČsOL in Bratislava in late September 1923, the split between the left and right deepened following Radola Gajda's[25] accusation that the ČsOL had failed to properly represent the interests of all Czechoslovak legionaries, in particular the interests of the Slovaks.[26] An official document signed and distributed by the "opposition bloc," which at that time consisted of Gajda, Medek, and Vojtěch Holeček, openly criticized the ČsOL leadership for adopting "Prague's line against the Ľudaks."[27] Even at this point, in the early

1920s, the right-wing breakaway fringe of the ČsOL correctly gauged the importance of Slovak nationalist support for its argument in favor of a strong national state. If it portrayed itself as a better representative of Slovak interests (that is to say, if it recognized the Slovaks as a distinct *ethnie* alongside the Czechs), those like Medek believed that they could drastically increase their chances of creating a separate veteran movement with support from those Slovak legionaries disgruntled with Prague politicians and their rejection of Slovak demands for regional autonomy.[28] The replacement of nationalism with socialism as the main program of the legionary movement (inspired by an apparent creeping "proto-Bolshevism" within the ČsOL) was another right-wing concern.[29] But the overriding issue was Beneš's use of the ČsOL as a political platform. The situation reached boiling point when the congress passed a motion in favor of Beneš's foreign policy views on developing friendlier relations with the Soviet Union.[30] This, coupled with Beneš's views about the Legion's "mistake" in fighting Bolshevik troops in 1918–19, provoked a vitriolic reaction from the rightist opposition who were against any recognition of the Soviet regime. A volatile exchange of polemics and heated debates ensued over 24–25 September 1923; and in the highly charged atmosphere of the closing session of the convention, an agitated Medek was unable to finish his address.[31] The legionary right concluded that the socialist influences within the ČsOL were harmful for both the legionary movement and Czechoslovak nationalist ideology; and it was on this basis that a right-wing opposition crystallized by the end of the congress led by Medek and Holeček with Gajda supporting.[32] After the convention, Medek published a series of articles about the events in the Czechoslovak daily, *Lidové noviny*, in which he vehemently denied that the formation of the opposition bloc within the ČsOL had been a veiled attempt by "Czech Fascists" (led by Gajda) to organize a military putsch against the leadership of the legionary movement.[33]

The Purpose of the Independent Union of Czechoslovak Legionaries (NJČsL)

The rationale behind the creation of the NJČsL was double-edged. It attempted to revive the legionary movement by flushing out left-wing ideas and creating a new association with a distinct Czechoslovak political identity. Those who formed the NJČsL belonged to a distinct interwar elite group made up of former Czech and Slovak legionaries who had fought on the Eastern front. In his memoirs, the first inspector general of the Czechoslovak army Josef Svatopluk Machar referred to this group as "Siberians" (*Sibirjáci*), many of whom took up significant posts at the Ministry of Defense and the General Staff of the Czechoslovak Army.[34] They believed that only those who had experienced the raw daily realities of life on the Eastern front were real legionaries; and only those who had survived the Bolshevik upheavals were legitimate representatives of the legionary cause in peacetime.[35] This group harbored both military and social pretensions about their newfound status in Czechoslovakia as an elite caste of Prague society.[36] However, many had returned to the new Republic with a sense of frustration and disappointment. Some were intensely disgruntled at failing to dismantle the Bolshevik regime in 1918–19, while others were dismayed about the numbers of proto-Bolshevik Communist legionary sympathizers who had returned home from the east.[37] Many felt aggrieved about the way they were treated, and, in some cases, ridiculed, by politicians and citizens in the new Republic.[38] In these circumstances, therefore, right-wing legionaries became protective of the Czechoslovak nationalist heritage of the Great War (notably its core components: brotherhood, leadership, and heroism), something inextricably linked with a concern for their own reputations as veterans representing a distinct military tradition. In the mid-1920s only 28 percent of serving officers in the Czechoslovak army were legionaries, compared to 35 percent who were former Czech officers of the old Habsburg army.[39] This largely unforeseen situation put the legionaries on the defensive and created an additional tension in the military ranks, which, thanks to the resurgence of the right at that time, also manifested itself in the political sphere.

The NJČsL was much smaller than the ČsOL. Its membership rose from 7,492 in 1927 to 13,000 in 1929, but it was still only a third of the size of the ČsOL, whose membership had risen to 50,216 by September 1929. The governing body of the NJČsL—elected on 10 November 1925 at a preliminary committee meeting—was composed almost entirely of former war veterans or current soldiers.[40] The four joint secretaries were professional soldiers and/or employees of the Ministry of Defense: František Turek, Vojtěch Holeček, Josef Vavroch, and the Slovak general Ferdinand Čatloš.[41] Antonín Pastýřík, a civilian, was elected acting-chairman. Although Medek was only elected de facto chairman at a general meeting of the governing committee in July 1926, he had a decisive influence over the mission, particularly its nationalist ideology, throughout the 1920s and early 1930s.[42]

The official founding session of the NJČsL took place on 19 December 1925 at the Hotel Paris in Prague.[43] News of the event caused members of the Castle to suspect that the legionary group had a right-wing political agenda, since its creation coincided with the short-lived resurgence of the political right at the parliamentary elections that autumn. This development precipitated a period of rivalry and political tension between the right and the Castle (Beneš in particular); and it brought the Czechoslovak right closer to Fascist ideas than at any other point during the First Republic.[44] Indeed, Fascist ideas were openly embraced by some quarters of the conservative-nationalist mainstream Czechoslovak National Democratic Party. The NJČsL was established with the full support of Agrarian defense minister František Udržal, who had supported the initiative since September 1923 in response to Beneš's active patronage of the ČsOL.[45] This jostling for political patronage over veteran associations underlined an ongoing conflict among the elite who were well aware of their importance as sources of party political support. Medek personally informed President Masaryk of the creation of the NJČsL at the end of November 1925. Although he had some misgivings, Masaryk had not, Medek proudly reported to fellow legionary Josef Kopta, written it off "as scum."[46] The official establishment view was that the NJČsL was the military arm of the National Democratic Party.[47] Beneš, however, suspected that a more sinister plot was afoot, that the NJČsL was part of a broader "proto-Fascist," anti-Castle bloc in the Republic. These suspicions were seemingly confirmed when in the summer of 1926 Medek was appointed to a governing committee composed of National Democrats and followers of political renegade Jiří Stříbrný in an attempt to create a right-wing opposition bloc to the Castle.[48]

Unlike the ČsOL, which attracted the bulk of formerly rank-and-file legionaries, the NJČsL attracted mainly high-ranking members of the military who in 1918–19 had commanded legionary regiments in Russia at a time when legionaries abroad began identifying with an evolving republican Czechoslovak army at home. At its first session at the Hotel Paris, the first statutes of the movement had been distributed, and a memorandum outlining its aims and scope was issued shortly thereafter. In section II, the founding principles were set out: first, the unification of the Czechoslovak legionary movement on the basis of national solidarity and brotherhood (described as "above-politics" to differentiate itself from the supposedly overly politicized ČsOL); second, the endorsement and propagation of the "idea of national defense," to educate society at large, particularly the young, on the meaning of sacrifice and patriotism, thereby creating Czechoslovak "citizen-soldiers."[49] This emphasis on the political morality and legitimacy derived from an above-politics stance was a defining characteristic of a broader Czech ultra-nationalist movement during this period. It was known as integral nationalism and its designated leader was the right-wing journalist Karel Horký, founder of *Fronta* (The Front) in May 1927.[50] A fringe group of the Czechoslovak National Democratic Party also identified with integral nationalism and its leadership principle.

The overriding mission of the NJČsL was both cultural and political in aiming to preserve a unified and defensible national state of Czechoslovaks; and it was believed that this could not be achieved without a well-ordered and disciplined society whose citizens harbored an unflagging love for their nation and state.[51] This brought it close to the party line of National Democracy, but the military concept in its "national state" distinguished it from the political mainstream. Medek's dominant role in the NJČsL, despite its openness to legionaries of all political persuasions, underlined its reputation as an exclusive club for former legionary commanders of the Czechoslovak Army in Russia.[52] In private, Medek streamlined the membership rules for the NJČsL: the movement was open to all except "Fascists" (who established their own legionary organization as a branch of the National Union of Fascists [NOF: Legionářská obec fašistická]) and "Communists" (meaning radical left-wing members of the ČsOL).[53] In another letter to Kopta in May 1927, Medek explained:

> The idea that NJČsL membership is supposedly incompatible with membership of the ČsOL, that legionaries cannot be members of both at the same time—this is idiotic. According to the ČsOL, the NJČsL is a bourgeois and right-wing association, but this is not the case. It is open to all legionaries who fought abroad for the good of the nation, regardless of their political convictions. We stand for the state and the nation, and those who negate these principles are not welcome; otherwise, all others are welcome. Members of the NJČsL are drawn from the Social Democrats, National Socialists, and clericals [Czech Catholics].[54]

The original governing committee of the NJČsL—as elected in November 1925—represented a cross-section of the political spectrum at that time: Pastyřík was "loyal" to the leader of the National Socialists Václav Klofáč; Turek was a supporter of party radical Jiří Stříbrný; and Holeček was a member of National Democracy and close to the party secretary, František Hlaváček, a key figure from the wartime Czechoslovak Legion in Italy.[55] Although Gajda was a member of the NJČsL, letters exchanged between Medek and Kopta in 1927 reveal that he was not welcome at committee meetings or annual congresses.[56] Following the domestic political crisis of 1925–27, which saw Gajda's discharge from the army on suspicion of Soviet espionage and his complicity in a plot against the Castle, Medek was ever keener to disassociate the NJČsL from Gajda and his Fascist colleagues.[57] This desire is clear from his defense of the movement as one aiming to create an "active and responsible [Czechoslovak] patriot and citizen, one concerned more with order and stability [rather than] a political coup, and with national consciousness rather than corruption."[58] Nevertheless, Medek's earlier association with Gajda meant that he was tainted with the Fascist brush in the eyes of the ČsOL and left-wing figures more generally—and the danger this posed to his reputation was pointed out to him on numerous occasions by ČsOL sympathizer and legionary historian Josef Kudela.

As far as the political right was concerned, although several leading NJČsL figures were supporters of the National Democrats (like Holeček), the party was not particularly interested in the movement. Its general secretary, Hlaváček, although sympathetic to Medek's and Holeček's writings about Czechoslovak nationalism, never attended any NJČsL meetings or annual congresses, and neither did nationalist poet Viktor Dyk.[59] Despite his insistence that he and his movement remained firmly above politics, Medek regarded the NJČsL as a politically centrist movement rather than a "right-wing" association of legionaries, and this represented a political line quite distinct from Masarykian principles.⁶⁰ As he observed, "I place the state and the nation above everything, even above the person and ideology of Professor Masaryk the philosopher … If the interests [of state and nation] were ever threatened, I would be capable of sacrificing anything or anybody, and this includes Masaryk."⁶¹

Affirming a Nationalist Ideology

When the NJČsL held its first official congress in July 1926 in Prague, its insignia illustrated the importance it placed on the concepts of warfare and sacrifice for the political culture of the state. The insignia showed a defiant legionary brandishing a rifle in one hand, while with the other he delivered the "flower of freedom" to the Czechoslovak nation from the fires and chaos of the Great War. Symbolically placed above the "Flower of Freedom" held by the legionary was the transcription of the Hussite battle cry, "*Pravda vítězí*" (Truth will Prevail).⁶² Although this symbolism appealed to a concept of sacrifice that incorporated older nationalist myths (those favored by Masaryk both during and after the Great War), Hussitism and the cult of Jan Hus never featured prominently in NJČsL ideology; this as such remained a legitimating mechanism by which the organization acknowledged Masaryk's political authority in the state.⁶³ The NJČsL clearly styled itself as a carrier of a state tradition older than the state itself, albeit one which only marginally predated the state's creation, specifically from a period of heightened political tension between 1917 and 1919 when the Legion had directly confronted Red Army units. At the core of its ideology, inspired by these experiences, was a militant form of Czechoslovak nationalism geared toward strengthening national solidarity and the defense of a united state of Czechs and Slovaks, according to the following principles: a) legionary brotherhood; b) strong (military) leadership; and c) a cult of military defense taken from examples of individual and collective sacrifice at the Battle of Zborov.⁶⁴ In order to make the new state fully defensible in an increasingly unstable international environment, NJČsL members believed it was necessary to remedy the shortcomings of political culture by emphasizing the significance of wartime nationalist sacrifice, predicated on a masculine culture of soldiering, strength and vitality.

Legionary Brotherhood

Right-wing legionaries believed that the efforts of the Czechoslovak Legion during the Great War had created a state-forming nation, and that they represented the first de facto state of this "Czechoslovak nation."⁶⁵ Accordingly, Czechs and Slovaks were brothers by virtue of their common experiences and, crucially, their joint acts of self-sacrifice on what was portrayed as the most significant battlefield of the Eastern front (Zborov). Medek in particular believed that the military "unity" of Czech and Slovaks during the war, formalized through joint acts of sacrifice, formed the basis of Czech-Slovak unification in one common national state in peacetime.[66] This concept of "Czechoslovak brotherhood"—distinct from the Castle view of stressing the role of the political émigrés—was underlined in the call for its preservation as a defining feature of the legionary experience.[67] Without brotherhood the transformation of Czechoslovak soldier-citizens into fervent Czechoslovak patriots was impossible; and, as such, legionary brotherhood encapsulated a Christian ideal of collective self-sacrifice (the Passion of Christ), specifically for the regeneration of nationhood and the preservation of a strong state in peacetime.[68] The ideal (citizen-)soldiers, moreover, were soldiers in prime moral and physical health who went into battle consciously prepared to give their lives for the national cause.[69] The acceptance of sacrifice as a prerequisite of national regeneration was precisely what made the Czechoslovak soldier an ideal citizen because he put the interests of the nation-state as a whole above those of individual self-interest.

In this respect, the NJČsL followed the established political order of the Czechoslovak state as prescribed by the Versailles Treaty's commitment to national self-determination, placing the interests of the collective nation above those of individual identification with the state.[70] Such a nationalizing program, as supported by the Castle, was reflected in all legionary organizations, left and right; but the NJČsL especially highlighted the sanctity of wartime sacrifice where a greater cause had prevailed over individual desires. Only through this process, driven by individual selflessness, could a nation-state achieve political legitimacy in peacetime. This was not simply messianic blood sacrifice, but sacrifice with the knowledge that the soldier was giving his life for a specific cause: the "regeneration" of (Czechoslovak) nationhood.[71]

Fraternal relations between Czechs and Slovaks were only possible if both engaged in collective acts inspired by their unshakable commitment to the nation-state, something interpreted by the legionary right in the 1920s as a manifestation of political morality.[72] Identification with the state depended on the correct ideological packaging of these military themes and the NJČsL's Czechoslovak agenda was molded accordingly, in part because Medek was keen not to alienate Slovaks from the organization.[73] Following the National Democratic line on Czechs and Slovaks as distinct ethnic groups,[74] the founding manifesto of the NJČsL had clearly distinguished between the two, and decreed that the language of proceedings at meetings and at annual congresses was both Czech and Slovak rather than "Czechoslovak."[75] The recognition of Czechs and Slovaks as "legionary brothers" in all pieces of propaganda during its first year of existence boosted the NJČsL's image and its legitimacy as a fully representative legionary organization for all ethnic and political groups (in contrast to the ČsOL that rarely distinguished between Czechs and Slovaks in its manifestos or newspapers).[76] The Slovak members of the NJČsL constituted the "party faithful" and appear to have been highly regarded: it was in Košice in eastern Slovakia, after all, in September 1923, that Gajda had begun his propaganda campaign against the rival ČsOL.[77] Starting in the early 1930s, in a bid to reflect increasing nationalist demands for Slovak autonomy presented by Andrej Hlinka's Slovak Peoples' Party (SL'S), the NJČsL opened branches in all major towns outside Bratislava, particularly in areas of the Slovak nationalist heartland, such as Ružomberok (Hlinka's home parish), Košice, and Prešov.[78]

Although the NJČsL set the wartime experience as a nationalist-historical benchmark for its ideas in peacetime, it did make use of older Czech national traditions in some of its propaganda in a bid to legitimize its position as a veteran association existing in the political mainstream. The Sokol gymnastics association founded in 1862 inspired much of this thinking about the ideal soldier-citizen.[79] Revered by the NJČsL as a national and apolitical ideal, the Sokol was mentioned in the first official program issued in July 1926 on the front pages of *Legie*, the NJČsL's main newspaper, and again in the official manifesto of the movement published in November 1932.[80] As such, it remained central to the nationalism of the movement until the eve of Munich in 1938 when Medek completed a synopsis for a new documentary film about the Sokol movement and the legionary tradition, revealing an increasing radicalization of his political views.[81] The hero of Medek's film, Jan Horský—a country doctor and Sokol member who joins the Czechoslovak Legion on the Eastern front in 1916—was almost certainly modeled on Gajda.[82] By the time of the May Crisis in 1938, at a time when the military leadership of the NJČsL was beginning to disperse in anticipation of the pending crisis, Medek was viewed by Gajda's National Union of Fascists (NOF) as a natural ally; and, as in the mid-1920s, Medek flirted with Fascism once again (even if he denounced Nazism on the eve of the Munich Agreement). On one occasion in 1937 he had lauded "Imperial Italy and the Duce" in a speech delivered at the unveiling of a Prague monument dedicated to Andrea Graziani, the wartime leader of Czechoslovak legionaries in Italy.

Not only was the Sokol the original liberation army of Czechs and Slovaks, Medek argued, but it also represented a higher Slavonic ideal of national consciousness that bound together Czechs and Slovaks as part of one physically and morally strong unit (the state).[83] Brotherhood was synonymous with the moral and physical health of the nation—it was an expression of physical exercise and exertion under the auspices of a common military history and national spirit during both war and peacetime.[84] The Sokol, in sum, was indispensable for the NJČsL's purified concept of a national state consisting of morally and physically vibrant soldier-citizens able to defend the Republic at times of crisis.[85] This assertion of masculinity, predicated on the concept of a hardened soldier plucked straight from the trenches, also served a political purpose in NJČsL ideology. This type of soldier-citizen was ideally placed to counterbalance any political values emanating from the Castle that were at odds with its militarist outlook and might potentially hamper the NJČsL's mission to educate a new generation of nationalists.[86]

Principle of Strong Leadership

The NJČsL remained outwardly loyal to President Masaryk, respecting his role as the spiritual leader of the Czechoslovak Legion and army. However, this political cult was never propagated as forcefully as that of strong military leadership. It is telling, for instance, that an article celebrating Czechoslovak general Jan Syrový as an anti-Bolshevik hero and commander of the Legion appeared in 1926 in the second issue of *Legie* before any article about Masaryk. In an issue of *Legie* two weeks later, Masaryk's wartime record was featured rather than his political status as President-Liberator.[87]

The NJČsL's concern for discipline and an aversion to "left-wing chaos"— legacies of the Legion's experience from the Bolshevik civil war—became clear in peacetime in response to what it regarded as a messy system of coalition government.[88] Its above-politics stance meant it could distance itself from the fractious nature of mainstream politics, regarded as harmful to its notion of wartime sacrifice and its own survival. The political crisis of the mid-1920s, from which the NJČsL had emerged, seemed to confirm the need for military leadership in public life; and this was accentuated by a sense of disappointment for some legionaries who found it difficult to identify with a Masarykian democracy rooted in humanitarian principles. The latter was perceived as antithetical to the order and discipline to which they had become accustomed, especially during their clash with the Bolsheviks from late 1918. Following the first congress of the NJČsL in July 1926, Medek wrote: "The prevailing atmosphere of conceptual confusion and uncertainty heightens the urgent need for strong leaders to guide the nation and state; the state desperately requires military geniuses, that is, those who represent the spirit of defense and military psyche."[89] This rhetoric signaled the beginning of a wave of militarism in the First Republic, and inspired other conservative and radical nationalists outside the NJČsL to form groups, one of which coalesced around the militantly nationalist journal *Fronta*.[90]

It was the responsibility of leaders, Medek had written in 1924, to instill order in an otherwise disorderly state and inspire moral courage among the rank-and-file so they would sacrifice themselves for the nation-state.[91] The model for these leaders was found in the person of Colonel (*Plukovník*) Josef Švec, a commander of the Czechoslovak Rifle Brigade. In October 1918, he shot himself during the Legion's trek eastwards along the Trans-Siberian Railway when faced with insubordination from his own men.[92] Under the auspices of the NJČsL, the story of Švec's suicide was reinvented and transformed into one of the most powerful nationalist cults of leadership in the interwar period. He could symbolize individual self-sacrifice for the sake of a higher, national ideal and collective good: suicide on behalf of the Czechoslovak nation. Medek's play *Plukovník Švec* premiered at the National Theatre in Prague to mark the tenth anniversary of the state's creation.[93] It sparked one of the most ferocious public debates of the 1920s about the nature of national sacrifice, widening existing political cracks in the legionary movement as a whole. Švec's suitability as a national hero—defended by those on the right on the basis of individual sacrifice driven by moral obligation and love for a sacred nation—was questioned by many, with legionaries from both sides of the political divide becoming embroiled in press polemics. Notably the legionary right attacked the left's rejection of Švec's suicide, calling it a traitorous act inspired by a pacifist Masarykian spirit, according to which Švec should not have committed suicide.[94]

The first secretary of the NJČsL, Vojtěch Holeček, answered Medek's critics with a series of articles published simultaneously in *Legie* and in the right-wing *Národní listy*.[95] Conservative nationalists were also quick to react to the furor surrounding the play, for instance Viktor Dyk, who wrote his response in the form of an amendment to Medek's third act, *Napravený Plukovník Švec* (1929).[96] Dyk's introduction targeted the ČsOL and defended militarism (the underlying theme of Medek's play) and its associated values such as self-discipline, patriotism, and political loyalty as indispensable elements of political society, which only the NJČsL could stimulate:

> The Independent Union of Czechoslovak Legionaries [NJČsL] is the inheritor of great and heroic traditions. It has been forgotten far too quickly that these ideas, which emerged from the stormy weather [of the war], directed our soldiers in performing great deeds. The NJČsL appeals to all legionaries in reminding them of what was sacred [during the war]; to make them aware that they were not only fighting for independence but national independence ... The NJČsL has now established itself as a force in its own right; it is not without influence.... The NJČsL is aware of its obligations and public duties: from those that are now dead springs hope for a celebrated national future. A great tradition equates with a heavy burden [in peacetime]. We must all keep striding forward confidently, growing in strength so that the nation too is strengthened and that, above all else, our republic is properly defended. This is why the NJČsL is so important.[97]

Despite the attempts of the NJČsL to requisition Švec for its own political purposes, the more vocal members of the ČsOL in March 1929 brought temporary closure to this debate. At a special meeting held by the Prague-district ČsOL on the Slavonic Island of the Vltava River, delegates dismissed Medek's historical revisionism as factually inaccurate. At the opening session, the ČsOL leadership publicly rejected Medek's *Švec* as a military-political role model for Czechoslovak citizens: the chairman, Josef Patejdl, announced that a majority of veterans in the Republic were opposed to Medek's concept of the Legion, for his "views were not at all representative of [true] legionary ideas about nationalism."[98] This debate lay dormant until 1937, the twentieth anniversary of the Battle of Zborov. Then, on 14 April, after a special concert organized by the NJČsL at Prague's Municipal House, Medek's use of Švec as a symbol of wartime sacrifice achieved wide popular acclaim in the Czechoslovak broadsheets.[99]

Cult of Defense (Zborov)

After the founding of the NJČsL, the significance of the Battle of Zborov (2 July 1917) was refashioned by the legionary right to suit its own ideological agenda.[100] Legionary writers like Josef Kopta helped perpetuate the Zborov cult after 1918, but it was Medek's version of the events at Zborov, immortalized in his iconic poem written after the battle, that remained the dominant nationalist interwar interpretation. According to those on the right like Medek, the battle was emblematic of national heroism and signified the simultaneous birth of Czechoslovak nationhood and statehood—that is, the will of Czechs and Slovaks to remain together as brothers bound by one common ideal, the state.[101]

The legionary right was particularly interested in the battle's nationalist lessons and how its "moral legacy" might be used to inculcate commitment to the state based on the principles that had created heroes out of ordinary Czechs and Slovaks. On 1 July 1922 in a lecture written to honor the remains of the Unknown Soldier lying in state in the Pantheon of the National Museum on Wenceslas Square, Medek had explained:

> [At Zborov] the Czechoslovak nation stood in direct opposition to the old monarchy. It is significant as a battle that stood for the freedom of our independent state—this manifested itself as a beacon of hope before those who heroically sacrificed their lives for that cause. The national army abroad was the very embodiment of national will, the will for independence of the Czech lands and Slovaks in the great struggle between democracy and German and Prussian aggression ... All of that previously shackled strength was suddenly released [at Zborov], unleashing a torrent of national consciousness and belief in a victorious future. The importance of this episode is that it was a conscious act of Czechs and Slovaks together ... brothers sacrificing themselves for each other in an exalted sense of elation—Zborov, a lasting testament to legionary brotherhood for the sake of a glorious victory; its commemoration is one of the most beautiful of our national and state holidays ... This is the meaning of the moral message of the Zborov spirit. It is, in effect, the source of our courage to defend the state now and in the future.[102]

In 1928, the eleventh anniversary of Zborov provided an opportunity to revisit the battle's political significance. The concept of sacrifice was politicized more aggressively than ever before by the right who insisted that the unleashing of national will at Zborov translated into the need to defend in peacetime the state whose independence had been so hard-won.[103] On this basis the NJČsL argued that defense, and a culture promoting national strength, was far more important than political parties in the life of the state.[104] Its antidemocratic tone was unmistakable, putting the NJČsL on a collision course with the Castle—a conflict personified in the political tensions between Beneš and leading representatives of Czechoslovakia's military establishment by the end of the 1920s.

The Legion and Defense of the National State

The parting of ways between the legionary left and right in the mid-1920s was exacerbated by the level of mutual distrust existing between the military leadership of the legionary right and the Castle, notably the patron of the legionary left, Edvard Beneš. As noted, Beneš used the ČsOL to further his own personal agenda in discrediting the nationalist right and flushing out any possible opposition to the Castle. This became clear at the ČsOL's annual congress held in Prague in September 1926, when he openly discredited the legionary right as Fascist.

Dominance over the national significance of wartime sacrifice was clearly a bone of contention between leading nationalists in Czechoslovakia. As such it was a source of elite conflict and instability at a crucial time when the state was in the process of consolidating the spoils of Versailles. This conflict belied the complex nature of the transition from wartime to peacetime, which presented an obstacle for both politicians and soldiers regardless of their political status during the Great War. The NJČsL negotiated this transition under the guidance of a skilled propagandist. Despite this, it faced the same challenges as those veteran associations who were patronized by the Castle; the biggest challenge was the quest for political legitimacy, which some like Rudolf Medek believed could only be garnered from the Czech and Slovak legionary rank-and-file. As part of this populist surge Medek consciously steered the NJČsL nationalist mission away from the Castle line. The NJČsL's above-politics stance was symptomatic of this integral nationalist trend in favor of a politics that served state nationalism as opposed to a messy system of parliamentary politics.[105]

But another and more important trait was the nationalist ideology of wartime sacrifice propagated by the veterans' association, which combined elements of various nationalist cults: military dead, martyrdom, and heroism. Going against the grain in rejecting broader historical traditions or the Masarykian philosophy of history about the war (as a battle of democracy versus theocracy), the NJČsL regarded the Great War as a new starting point in Czechoslovak national history that could facilitate its nationalizing program for the state. This had an unforeseen consequence in bolstering the NJČsL's image as an isolationist, proto-Fascist group trying to remobilize society. As a result, it was even forced to legitimize its position by appearing outwardly loyal to the Castle out of fear that the political center-ground might ostracize it. Nevertheless, the NJČsL provided a rallying point for veteran nationalists who venerated the state and opposed pacifists and left-wingers.

At the close of the 1930s, Medek stood firm in his belief that the NJČsL had achieved a level of public prestige not achieved by any other right-wing legionary veterans' association in the First Republic.[106] Although founded as a protest movement in negation of the "left" with the help of leading Czech Fascists like Radola Gajda, the NJČsL distinguished itself from Fascism by proposing a program aimed at preserving a state-forming legionary tradition rather than radically altering it for some anarchic political purpose.[107] Even more important for its popular appeal was Medek's directorship of the Liberation Memorial Institute (Památník odboje / Památník osvobození), which became the unofficial headquarters of the NJČsL in the late 1920s, following the relocation of the Institute in 1928 to Vítkov hill in Žižkov.[108] For those belonging to the political right, the Institute symbolized official acknowledgement of the importance of legionary military leadership for the state's creation. Medek's joint directorship of the Institute and his chairmanship of the NJČsL meant that the association was afforded a level of exposure on a par with the ČsOL. Furthermore, on account of its association with the Liberation Memorial, the NJČsL could distance itself from the "morass" of Czechoslovak political parties—a quagmire from which the ČsOL never fully extracted itself due to its association with Beneš—by attaching itself to other institutions of political influence, notably the Ministry of Defense and the Chief of the General Staff. In attempting to create a strong and defensible state, the NJČsL tried to militarize nationalist ideology and Czechoslovak political culture.[109]

Despite its elitist pretensions, the NJČsL also attempted to capture the public mood with populist ideas about military sacrifice and the importance of defending the national state as requisites of Czechoslovak citizenship. Its short-lived success in achieving at least part of this aim only became apparent during the Sudeten crisis of 1938 when Czechoslovak broadsheets made full use of the symbols of wartime heroism previously propagated by the NJČsL during the 1920s. The NJČsL styled its purpose as helping to preserve political belief in heroic acts, educating the public while at the same time fashioning patriotic citizens who could defend the state. Whether intentional or not, this worked in favor of the Czechoslovak government during periods of domestic and international crisis.

Katya Kocourek completed her PhD at University College London, on the concept of interwar Czechoslovakism as espoused by right-wing personalities and political parties. In 2002 she was the founder-editor of the peer-reviewed academic journal, *Central Europe*, which grew out of *The Masaryk Journal*. Her main publication is a biography of the soldier-poet Rudolf Medek: *Čechoslovakista Rudolf Medek: Politický životopis* (2011). She works for a global risk management firm in the city of London.

Notes

The title of this chapter refers to a slogan appealing to all legionaries to join its ranks in the first issue of the newspaper of the Independent Union of Czechoslovak Legionaries (NJČsL): "Bratři Legionáři, vstupte do Nezávislé jednoty!," *Legie. Orgán Nezávislé jednoty československých Legionářů* (hereafter *Legie*), 1/1 (23 December 1925): 1. The author thanks Mark Cornwall, John Paul Newman, Seán Hanley, Tomáš Jakl, Jan Maloušek, Bernard Panuš, Masatake Wasa, and the late Ivan Medek for their comments on this chapter.

1. John Horne, "Introduction," *A Companion to World War I*, ed. John Horne (Oxford, 2010), xvi.
2. On Medek's political biography, see Katya Kocourek, *Čechoslovakista Rudolf Medek: Politický životopis* (Prague, 2011).
3. "My budem se bít / za slávu a svobodu našich zemí / nikoho neživit / nešetřit, nesmlouvat, silami všemi / ku předu letět a vítězit / i slavně mřít / Básník Medek" [nationalist poem accredited to Medek]: *Národní republika*, 3 April 1925, 1.
4. See notably, Zdeněk Kárník, *České země v éře první republiky (1918–1938): Díl druhý. Československo a České země v krizi a ohrožení (1930–1935)* (Prague, 2002), 335–37.
5. Ivan Šedivý, "Vznik Nezávislé jednoty československých Legionářů," *Historie a vojenství* 45/6 (1996): 47–61; and more recently Jan Michl, *Legionáři a Československo* (Prague, 2009), 83–94.
6. Kárník, *České země v éře první republiky (1918–1938)*, 2: 336. A new work on paramilitary organizations in Czechoslovakia mentions Fascist sub-groups, but not the conservative right: Ivo Pejčoch, *Armády českých politiků: České polovojenské jednotky 1918–1945* (Cheb, 2009).
7. Jana Čechurová, *Česká politická pravice: Mezi převratem a krizí* (Prague, 2000), 91.
8. Martin Zückert, *Zwischen Nationsidee und staatlicher Realität: Die tschechoslowakische Armee und ihre Nationalitätenpolitik 1918–1938* (Munich, 2006), 128–29.
9. Martin Zückert, "National Concepts of Freedom and Government Pacification Policies: The Case of Czechoslovakia in the Transitional Period after 1918," *Contemporary European History* 17/3 (2008): 325–44; Robert B. Pynsent, "The Literary Representation of the Czechoslovak 'Legions' in Russia," in *Czechoslovakia in a Nationalist and Fascist Europe 1918–1948*, ed. Mark Cornwall and R. J. W. Evans (Oxford, 2007), 63–88.
10. Rudolf Medek, *Legionářství ve vlasti: Dvacátádruhá přednáška v cyklu o našem národním osvobození, pořádaném jednotami ČSOL. v Praze I.-II.-V. až VII.* (Prague, 1924), 7, 9, 15.
11. "Legionáři českoslovenští," in *Ottův slovník naučný nové doby: Dodatky k velikému ottovu slovníku naučnému*, ed. Bohumil Němec, 1/2 (Prague, 1931), 1116.
12. Martin Kučera, "Významní Legionáři v roce 1938: Příspěvek k výzkumu společenských elit meziválečného Československa," in *Politické elity v Československu 1918–1948. Sborník. Sešity ústavu pro soudobé dějiny AV ČR*, ed. Ivan Koutská and František Svátek, Ústav pro soudobé dějiny, vol. 20 (Prague, 1994), 83.

13. Lev Sychrava, *Legionářský socialismus* (Prague, 1923), 8–9.
14. Lev Sychrava, *Naše národní tradice: Tradice osvobozenská* (Prague, 1928), 43; and Josef Fischer, *Československá obec Legionářská a veřejná činnost* (Brno, 1927), 14.
15. Sychrava, *Naše národní tradice*, 20–21.
16. Lev Sychrava and Ladislav Sýkora, eds., *Památník manifestačního sjezdu Legionářů v Praze 1924* (Prague, 1924).
17. Edvard Beneš, "Náš největší úkol národní," in *Idea Československého státu*, ed. Jan Kapras, František Soukup and Bohumil Němec, 2 vols. (Prague, 1936), 2: 218.
18. Rudolf Medek, *Národní vojsko: První přednáška v cyklu o našem národním osvobození, pořádaném jednotami ČSOL* (Prague, 1924), 10–11.
19. Literary Archive of the National Memorial of Literature, Prague (Literární archiv památník národního písemnictví: hereafter, LA PNP), Rudolf Medek MSS, (2), Rukopisy vlastní, sign. VIII, inv. n. 387, box 4: "Vážení bratři..." [n.d.], 3; VIII, inv. n. 406, box 4: "Vojáci! Dobrý osud..." [n. d.], 1. In order to distinguish between two different collections of archival material relating to Medek in the LA PNP, this chapter adopts "Medek (1)" and "Medek (2)" respectively. Medek (2) relates to that material transferred to the LA PNP from the Military Historical Institute, Prague [Vojenský historický ústav] in the spring of 2005, consisting of Medek's private papers from the First Czechoslovak Republic.
20. T.G. Masaryk, *Cesta demokracie: Soubor projevů za republiky, 1918–1920*, 2 vols. (Prague, 1938), 1: 425; and Emanuel Rádl, *Masarykův ideál moderního hrdiny* (Prague, 1920), 19–20.
21. See Zückert, *Zwischen Nationsidee und staatlicher Realität*, 65–66; Jiří Šolc, "Miliční systém v programu Čs. strany národně socialistické v letech 1919–1938," *Historie a vojenství* 41/5 (1992): 10–16.
22. Renamed the Liberation Memorial Institute in 1928.
23. Jindřich Dejmek, *Edvard Beneš: Politická biografie českého demokrata. Část první. Revolucionář a diplomat (1884–1935)* (Prague, 2006), 214–15.
24. Edvard Beneš, *Smysl Československé Revoluce: První přednáška cyklu "Československá Revoluce" proslovena 12. brežna 1923* (Prague, 1923), 16, 22, 55; and Josef Patejdl, *Sibiřská Anabase: Sedmá přednáška cyklu "Československá Revoluce" proslovena 5. dubna 1923* (Prague, 1923), 58–59.
25. A leading legionary figure of the Czech Fascist movement and former chief of staff, who in 1927 was tried and found guilty by the Czechoslovak government on charges of misconduct.
26. Office of the Czechoslovak President, Military History Archive, Prague (Vojenský historický archiv, Vojenský kancelář presidenta republiky: hereafter VKPR): ČsOL f. 4190/1923, "Věc: Čs. obec Legionářská, sjezd 1923—oposice proti vedení. Tajné!!!," 3.
27. Ibid. The Ľudaks were the Slovak nationalists.
28. Rudolf Medek, "Třásli jsme se o Slovensko," in *Vypád maďarských bolševikov na Slovensko v roku 1919*, ed. Jozef Zimák, Trnava (Bratislava, [n.d.]), 87–88. Before some Slovak veterans joined the NJČsL in December, the Slovaks had their own ČsOL sister organization in Slovakia, but it remained small with only 988 members in 1931. However, an important development came in August 1926 with the founding in Turčiansky Svätý Martin of the Slovak nationalist Sdružene slovenských Legionárov (Union of Slovak Legionaries), to which those belonged who did not join the NJČSL. See Michl, *Legionáři a Československo*, 112.
29. "Věc: Čs. obec Legionářská, sjezd 1923," 2.
30. Václav Kopecký, *ČSR a KSČ: Pamětní výpisy k historii Československé republiky a k boji KSČ za socialistické Československo* (Prague, 1960), 22.
31. Memorandum written by Ricota, head of Masaryk's presidential office, September 1923: VKPR, ČsOL f. 4192/1923, 1.
32. Antonín Klimek and Petr Hofman, *Vítěz, který prohrál. Generál Radola Gajda* (Prague/Litomyšl, 1995), 59–61; and Václav Cháb, *Několik Legionářských co a jak: Poznámky a polemiky* (Prague, 1932), 44–45.

33. Archive of the Academy of Sciences of the Czech Republic/ T.G. Masaryk Institute (Archiv Akademie věd České republiky/Ústav T.G. Masaryka: hereafter, AAVČR), Edvard Beneš MSS I (EB I), sign. 168/3, box 57: "Zrození fašismu" (17 April 1930), 4: report entitled "The birth of Fascism," by Beneš's private secretary. See also, Rudolf Medek, "K Legionářskému sjezdu," *Lidové noviny*, 27 September 1923, 2; "Jak připravovali čeští fašisté převrat. Pokus o získání generálů. Generál Gajda získán.—Vojáci, buďte na stráži!," *Rudé právo*, 26 September 1927.
34. J.S. Machar, *Pět roků v kasárnách: Vzpomínky a dokumenty, 1925–1926* (Prague, 1927), 215–18, 229.
35. Rudolf Medek, "Epilog," in *Legionářská epopeja. Anabase. Román z války*, 9th ed. (Prague, 1929), 566–67.
36. Josef Kopta, *Třetí rota doma: Román* (Prague, 1928), 340–41, 345–47.
37. Rudolf Medek, "Hořký odjezd," *Země* 2/9 (30 June 1921): 241–43; Radola Gajda, *Generál Ruských legií R. Gajda: Moje paměti. Československá anabase. Zpět na Urál proti Bolševikům. Admirál Kolčak* (Prague, 1920), 177–78.
38. Medek, "Epilog," *Anabase*, 572; František Šteidler, *Ideový a vojenský význam československých legií. Přednáška, kterou pronesl Dr. F. Šteidler v Husově škole v Praze dne 24. listopadu 1923 v cyklu přednášek "O vojenství a válce"* (Brno, 1924), 14–17, 19.
39. Zückert, *Zwischen Nationsidee und staatlicher Realität*, 109–10; Ivan Šedivý, "Legionáři a československá armáda 1918–38," in *České země a Československo v Evropě XIX. a XX. století. Sborník prací k 65. narozeninám prof. dr. Roberta Kvačka*, ed. Jindřich Dejmek and Jiří Hanzal (Prague, 1997), 220–21.
40. Medek, *Poslední události a Nezávislá jednota čsl. Legionářů*, 35; Josef Kudela, *Legionáři dnes* (Brno, 1929), 19; "Vznik a dosavadní vývoj Nezávislé jednoty," *Legie* 1/1 (23 December 1925): 2; LA, PNP, Medek (2), f. "Nezávislá jednota československých Legionářů:" František Turek issued the official announcement dated 9 December 1925: *Prohlášení Nezávislá jednota československých Legionářů* (Prague, 19 December 1925).
41. *Kdo jsme a co chceme. (Ideové, hospodářské a sociální snahy Nezávislé jednoty čs. Legionářů a Kruhu jejich přátel s odbory mládeže)*, 2.
42. Prague City Archive (Archiv hlavního města Prahy), AHMP II, sig. XXII, inv. n.1365, box 923: Prohlášení Sekretariatu NJČsL k ministerstvu vnitra, Prague, 25 March 1932.
43. Rudolf Medek, *Poslední události a Nezávislá jednota čsl. Legionářů (Referát, přednesený na schůzi zastupitelstva, konané 7. listopadu 1926 v Praze)* (Prague, 1927), 34.
44. Andrea Orzoff, *Battle for the Castle: The Myth of Czechoslovakia in Europe, 1914–1948* (Oxford, 2009), 97, 99; Andrea Orzoff, "'The Literary Organ of Politics': Tomáš Masaryk and Political Journalism, 1925–1929," *Slavic Review* 63/2 (2004): 277.
45. VKPR, 1937/48 dův.: "Úvodník Rudolfa Medka ve "Venkově"" [Response to article by Medek published in *Venkov* by General Ludvík Krejčí, Chief of Staff], 1 February 1937, 2.
46. LA PNP, Medek (2), inv. n. 243, box 2: Josef Kopta to Rudolf Medek, 18 May 1927.
47. "Legionáři a národní demokracie," *Národní osvobození*, 23 October 1925, 1.
48. AAVČR, Tomáš G. Masaryk MSS, "Republika" (TGM-R), box 440, f. 5: Karel Řežný to T.G. Masaryk, 20 July 1926; Antonín Klimek, *Velké dějiny zemí Koruny České, svazek XIII.1918–1929* (Praha/ Litomyšl, 2000), 553–58, 569.
49. *Stanovy. "Nezávislá jednota československých Legionářů": II. Účel jednoty* ["Purpose of union"], 1; *Kdo jsme a co chceme. (Ideové, hospodářské a sociální snahy Nezávislé jednoty čs. Legionářů a Kruhu jejich přátel s odbory mládeže)*, 8.
50. Rudolf Medek, "K situaci v Legionářstvu," *Fronta*, 6 May 1927, 4–6; Petr Pithart, "'Fronta' proti Hradu (úvahy o pravici a nacionalismu mezi válkami)," *Dějiny a politika: Eseje a úvahy z let 1977–1989* (Prague, 1990), 105–84.

51. Rudolf Medek, *Projev na 4. sjezdu Nezávislé jednoty čs. Legionářů* [n. d.], 14; and *Kdo jsme a co chceme. (Ideové, hospodářské a sociální snahy Nezávislé jednoty čs. Legionářů a Kruhu jejích přátel s odbory mládeže)*, 3.
52. *Stanovy. "Nezávislá jednota československých Legionářů": II. Účel jednoty*, 5.
53. *Kdo jsme a co chceme*, 3–4.
54. LA PNP, Medek (1), 82/88, inv. n. 95, box 2: Medek to Josef Kopta, 20 May 1927.
55. See Mark Cornwall, *The Undermining of Austria-Hungary: The Battle for Hearts and Minds* (New York, 2000), 126, 130–31, 155–59.
56. Medek to Kopta, 20 May 1927.
57. Medek, *Poslední události a Nezávislá jednota čsl. Legionářů*, 10–14; and LA PNP, Medek (2), Typescripts & Unpublished Manuscripts [Personal/authored by Medek], sign. VIII, inv. n. 162, box 2: Medek, "Československý generál o koncentračních táborech" [1934], 5.
58. Ibid., 15.
59. Ibid., 4. See, for instance, Vojtěch Holeček, *Věčnost národa—v jeho hodnotách mravních. (Referát na pracovním sjezdu Nezávislé jednoty čsl. Legionářů a Kruhu jejích přátel dne 24. listopadu 1934)* (Prague, 1934).
60. Rudolf Medek, "K situace v Legionářstvu," *Fronta* (6 May 1927): 4.
61. Medek to Kopta, 20 May 1927.
62. Bernard Panuš, "Nezávislá jednota čs. Legionářů a její odznak," *Drobná plastika: Časopis pro členy České společnosti přátel drobné plastiky* 44/3–4 (January 2008): 34–37.
63. Hussitism as a political theme was restricted to Medek's popular writing (e.g., in the fourth and fifth novels of Medek's pentalogy, *Legionářská epopeja*: *Mohutný sen* and *Anabase*) and did not feature at all in any leading NJČsL propagandist literature published during the interwar period by its leading figures.
64. Medek, *Poslední události a Nezávislá jednota čsl. Legionářů*, 26.
65. See Pynsent, "The Literary Representation," 79.
66. Rudolf Medek, "Legie, národ, stát. (Naše práce a náš směr)" [Předneseno na nedělním zasedání sjezdu dne 27. listopadu 1929], in *Legie, národ, stát. Práce a směr Nezávislé jednoty čs. Legionářů a kruhu jejích přátel. Referáty, projevy a unesení, schválené na společném sjezdu, konaném ve dnech 26. a 27. listopadu 1932 v Praze* (Prague, 1933), 7–8; and František Schwarz, *Kruh přátel Nezávislé jednoty čsl. Legionářů* (Prague, [n. d.]), 8–9.
67. "Bratři Legionáři, vstupte do Nezávislé jednoty!," *Legie* 1/1 (23 December 1925), 1; and Medek, *Poslední události a Nezávislá jednota čsl. Legionářů*, 22, 28.
68. See George L. Mosse, *Fallen Soldiers: Reshaping the Memory of the World Wars* (Oxford, 1990); and *Kdo jsme a co chceme*, 2.
69. Medek, *Poslední události a Nezávislá jednota čsl. Legionářů*, 17.
70. Tara Zahra, *Kidnapped Souls: National Indifference and the Battle for Children in the Bohemian Lands, 1900–1948* (Ithaca and London, 2008), 107.
71. LA PNP, Medek (2), Typescripts & Unpublished Manuscripts, sign. VIII, inv. n. 401, box 4: Medek, "Dámy a pánové…:" transcript of public lecture at Liberation Memorial Institute, Žižkov (November 1929), 2.
72. Medek, *Poslední události a Nezávislá jednota čsl. Legionářů*, 29; Holeček, *Věčnost národa—v jeho hodnotách mravních*, 14–15; and Antonín Pavel, *Pro mravní řád, tvůrčí nacionalismus a silnou demokracii* (Prague, 1934), 3.
73. Medek, *Poslední události*, 22–23.
74. *Řeč dra Kramáře k svědomí národa. Po vstupu Němců do vlády je třeba více nacionalismu! (Stenografický zápis řeči dra Kramáře na manifestační schůzi čsl. národní demokracie ve velké dvoraně "Lucerny" v Praze, proslovené dne 15. listopadu 1926)* (Prague, 1926), 21–22.

75. Stanovy. "Nezávislá jednota československých Legionářů": I. Název, sídlo, obvod působnosti a jednací řeč [Founding statement of NJČsL], 1.
76. Medek, Poslední události, 23 ; and Medek, 28.Říjen, 18–19.
77. Cháb, Několik Legionářských co a jak, 20-22; VKPR, ČsOL f. 4190/1923, "Věc: Čs. obec Legionářská, sjezd 1923—oposice proti vedení. Tajné!!!," 1, 3.
78. The Slovak legionary veteran Otomar Houdek represented Slovak interests on the governing committee of the NJČsL in Prague, and was also a deputy chairman of the movement in the early 1930s.
79. On the Sokol, see Claire E. Nolte, *The Sokol in the Czech Lands to 1914: Training for the Nation* (Basingstoke, 2002), 110–34.
80. *Kdo jsme a co chceme*, 3; "Programové prohlášení. Nezávislé jednoty československých Legionářů," *Legie* 1/14–15 (15 July 1926), 1. See also Medek, "Legie, národ, stat," in *Legie, národ, stát*, 6–34.
81. LA PNP, Medek (2), Typescripts & Unpublished Manuscripts, sign. VIIII, inv. n. 115, box 2: Medek, *Lví silou. Filmová epopej o vítězství veliké myšlenky* [1938], 3–7.
82. Ibid., 2–14.
83. Ibid., 15.
84. LA PNP, Medek (2), Typescripts & Unpublished Manuscripts, sign. VIIII, inv. n. 356, box 4: Medek, "Sokolství a Legionářství" [n. d.], 1.
85. See Melissa Bokovoy's chapter in this volume; and Medek, "Sokolství a Legionářství", 3; Medek, *Národní vojsko*, 9.
86. On masculinity more generally, see John Horne, "Masculinity in Politics and War in the Age of Nation-States and World Wars, 1850–1950," *Masculinities in Politics and War: Gendering Modern History*, ed. Stefan Dudink, Karen Hagemann, and John Tosh (Manchester and New York, 2004), 22–40.
87. Rudolf Medek, "Generál Jan Syrový," *Legie* 1/2 (15 January 1926): 1; Medek, "T.G. Masaryk," *Legie* 1/5 (1 March 1926): 1; Medek, "Vůdce národního odboje," *Legie* 5/24 (10 March 1930): 1.
88. "R" [Rudolf Medek], "Úvaha koaliční," *Demokratický střed*, 1/45 (18 September 1924): 1; "Krize předválečných stran," *Demokratický střed*, 1/31 (15 May 1924): 1–2.
89. Rudolf Medek, "Myšlenky o 28. Říjnu," *Národní listy* (20 July 1926), 5.
90. Lev Borský, "Vůdčí myšlenka," *Fonta*, 1/1 (6 May 1927): 1.
91. Medek, *Národní vojsko*, 14–15.
92. Robert B. Pynsent, *Questions of Identity: Czech and Slovak Ideas of Nationality and Personality* (Budapest, 1994), 205–6; Rudolf Medek, *Legionářská epopeja. Mohutný sen. Román z války*, 6th ed. (Prague, 1929), 262, 540–50.
93. Rudolf Medek, *Plukovník Švec. Drama o třech dějstvích*, 7th ed. (Prague, 1930); Martin C. Putna, *Česká katolická literatura 1918–1945* (Prague, 2010), 776.
94. J.O. Novotný, *O "Plukovníka Ševce." Dokument doby. S doslovem Rudolfa Medka* (Prague, 1929), 8–9, 176–77; Viktor Dyk, "Introduction" in *Napravený Plukovník Švec. Podle rad Československé obce Legionářské III. dějství dramatu Medkova upravuje Viktor Dyk* (Prague, 1929), 10.
95. Vojtěch Holeček, "Politické tažení proti Medkovu 'Plukovníku Šveci'," *Legie* 2/7 (2 November 1928), 1–2.
96. Novotný, *O "Plukovníka Ševce." Dokument doby. S doslovem Rudolfa Medka*, 7–10.
97. Viktor Dyk, "O národní traduce," reprinted in *O národní stát 1930–1931* (Prague, 1938), 7: 367–68; Dyk, *Napravený Plukovník Švec*, 9–10; and Dyk, "Plukovník Švec a národní ideal" [reprinted from *Národní listy*, 2 March 1929], in Viktor Dyk, *O národní stát 1929* (Prague, 1938), 6: 58–60.

98. *Aksaková tragedie. Diskuse. Pořádaná okresním výborem jednot československé obec Legionářské velké Prahy. Konaná dne 25. brežna 1929 na slovanském ostrově*, ed. Viktor Svoboda et al. (Prague, 1929), 5–6.
99. The official title of the gathering was *Hold národního odboje branné moci republiky* (Homage to the national defense of the might of the Republic) and Medek delivered the opening speech.
100. See Nancy Wingfield's chapter on Zborov for a critical overview of the nationalist significance of the battle.
101. *Boj o ducha národního odboje. Pět let práce Nezávislé jednoty československých Legionářů a dvě léta činnosti kruhu jejích přátel. Referáty, projevy a usnesení schválené na třetím sjezdu Nezávislé jednoty čs. Legionářů a na druhém sjezdu Kruhu jejích přátel ve dnech 6. a 7. prosince 1930 v Praze* (Prague, 1931), 13.
102. LA PNP, Medek (2), Typescripts & Unpublished Manuscripts, sign. VIII, inv. n. 324, box 2: Medek, "Poselství od Zborova" [July 1922], 10–11.
103. LA PNP, Medek (2), Typescripts & Unpublished Manuscripts, sign. VIII, inv. n. 288, box 4: Medek, "Myšlenky o Zborovu" [n. d.], 4.
104. Rudolf Medek, "Národní energie a národní víra," *Národní myšlenka. Revue českého nacionalismu* 2/3 (December 1924): 77; Pavel, *Pro mravní řád, tvůrčí nacionalismus a silnou demokracii*, 4.
105. Stanley B. Winters, "Passionate Patriots: Czechoslovak National Democracy in the 1920s," *East Central Europe* 18/1 (1991): 60, 63.
106. LA PNP, Medek (2), Typescripts & Unpublished Manuscripts, sign. VIII, inv. n. 399, box 4: Medek, "Projev ke schůzi předsednictva Nezávislé jednoty čsl. Legionářů," 26 October 1938, 2.
107. Medek, *Poslední události a Nezávislá jednota čsl. Legionářů*, 14–15; Rudolf Gajda, *Ideologie Čsl. fašismu. Cyklus přednášek "O ideologii Českolov. politických stran"* (Prague, 1931), 12–13.
108. LA PNP, Medek (2), Typescripts & Unpublished Manuscripts, sign. VIIII, inv. n. 316, box 4: Medek, "Památník osvobození" [lecture about the Liberation Memorial Institute delivered in 1938], 14.
109. Kárník, *České země v éře první republiky (1918–1938)*, 2: 336–37; and Zückert, *Zwischen Nationsidee und staatlicher Realität*, 129.

Chapter 8

SAVING GREATER ROMANIA
The Romanian Legionary Movement and the "New Man"

Rebecca Haynes

In his introduction to Mussolini's 1917 article "Trenchocracy," Roger Griffin writes that a crucial contribution to the rise of Italian Fascism was "the myth that the trenches had forged a heroic, youthful, and classless elite which after the war would sweep away the sclerotic 'old order,' so out of touch with the minds and aspirations of the war generation."[1] Despite the fact that the majority of active members of the Romanian legionary movement, founded by Corneliu Zelea Codreanu in 1927, were too young to have fought in the Great War, they were nevertheless influenced by the same military ethos as the war generation. Most importantly, the legionaries saw themselves as the youthful guardians of the war veterans' main achievement, namely the creation of Greater Romania, which they believed was threatened by Communist revisionism and the failings of the postwar liberal political establishment and its "Jewish economic allies." The protection of Greater Romania was to be achieved by the legionary movement through the transformation of young Romanians into "tomorrow's Romanian," or the "New Man." Indeed, the very purpose of the Legion was to create and educate this spiritually and morally regenerated individual through whom the Romanian nation as a whole would eventually be renewed. It was, in particular, through the movement's system of work camps that the legionary New Man was to be created. The New Man's virtues to be nurtured in the camps included a sense of national solidarity, military discipline, willingness for self-sacrifice for the Romanian national community, and the creation of a "natural hierarchy" and elite. Such virtues corresponded to those of Mussolini's "trenchocracy" forged in the Great War, which he envisaged as replacing the corrupt liberal democracy of Italy. The presence in the legionary work camps of popular war veterans such as General Gheorghe Cantacuzino served to reinforce the sense of a transmission of Romanian national values between the generations.

At the same time, it should be noted that from its inception the Romanian legionary movement was marked by a strong Christian and spiritual character. Popular Orthodox Christianity had long underpinned the sense of Romanian national identity and, consequently, the Legion's mystical nationalism was virtually inseparable from Orthodoxy.[2] Orthodox Christianity had been, together with Romanian nationalism, a central feature of Codreanu's parental home. Indeed, the infant Codreanu was given the name Corneliu in honor of St Cornelius the Centurion, the first gentile to convert to Christianity, whose Holy Day fell on 13 September, Codreanu's birthday. Furthermore, the involvement of the Orthodox village clergy in the legionary movement is well documented.[3] Many of the legionaries were the sons of village priests, including most notably Ion Moța, effectively Codreanu's deputy, who was himself a further source of religious inspiration to the movement. Thus, as Henry Roberts writes, "[t]he employment of religious symbolism and mysticism was not merely a tactical device of the Legion, but was an integral part of its ideology."[4] This in turn reinforced within the younger generation notions of sacrifice, martyrdom, *Imitatio Christi*, and concepts of regeneration and resurrection, which had also been part of the war generation's military education, enabling them to make sense of their experience of mass death in the trenches.[5]

Participation in the Legion and its activities thus lent the individual a sense of personal rebirth and of "palingenesis."[6] Whereas this term has hitherto been largely applied to the Fascist mission as a whole, it also applied to the individual. By entering into the Legion and endorsing its goals, the individual himself was reborn as a New Man.[7] Given the New Testament origins of the New Man, it is perhaps not surprising that the legionaries perceived him as indistinguishable from Christian man; thus, for Codreanu the New Man was "Christian man projected into public life."[8]

At the same time, the New Man's being was subsumed within the broader collectivity of the legionary movement and the Romanian nation (regarded, in many respects, as interchangeable).[9] Politics and the person thus took second place to the collective idea, and personal renewal was predicated on the prior death not only of the individual will but very often also the life. Only through this act of final sacrifice by the individual might the collective be regenerated and reborn through the Legion's "cult of death."

The Development of Codreanu's Ideology

To understand Corneliu Codreanu's later career and outlook, it is crucial to examine his background and early experiences. He was born in 1899 in Iași in Moldavia, close to the Russian border. His father, Ion, was a committed nationalist who strove for the unification of all the Romanian-speaking regions of the Habsburg and Russian empires with the kingdom of Romania. A teacher by profession, Ion acted as secretary to Nicolae Iorga's and A.C. Cuza's National Democratic Party, which was a nationalist, anti-semitic party aiming to unite all Romanians and reduce Jewish influence in Romanian public life. Cuza became Corneliu's godfather and acted as his mentor when he was a student at Iași University. Cuza was professor of political economy at the university, a post he used to disseminate his anti-semitic views. Codreanu relates in his memoirs that, at a tender age, he had read all the articles written by Iorga and Cuza kept in his father's attic.[10]

Between 1912 and 1916, Codreanu attended the school at Mănăstirea Dealului, north of Bucharest. The school had been established by a conservative politician Nicolae Filipescu to train future military officers. Here Codreanu imbibed a strict military discipline and love of the outdoors through sports, military exercises, Sunday marches in the countryside, and such communal work as tree planting. The importance of Orthodox Christianity, already a central feature of his parental home, was reinforced at the school by a strong clerical presence. Religious services were held eleven times a day, beginning at five o'clock in the morning in the school chapel where on display was the skull of Michael the Brave, the sixteenth-century ruler of Wallachia who had briefly united the principalities of Wallachia, Moldavia, and Transylvania. Confession was also heard several times a day. Filipescu had named the school *Cuibul Șoimilor* (Nest of the Falcons) and this was written above the entrance. The future Legion was to be greatly influenced by Codreanu's school experience. In particular, we can note the use of the word *cuib* (nest) for the smallest unit of legionary organization, as well as the need for prayer, the use of military uniforms, marches and singing, work camps (spring and autumn tree planting), and military discipline.[11]

Codreanu, like the majority of future legionaries, was too young to serve in the Great War, although he followed his father's regiment to the Transylvanian front and was turned down as a volunteer. Nevertheless, he claimed in his memoirs to have taken part in the military advance into and retreat from Transylvania in 1916. Be that as it may, as a result of his military schooling he "learned to love the trench and despise the drawing room." The latter was associated with the idle chatter of intellectuals and politicians, and was the polar opposite of Fascism's "ideology of action."[12] As he later explained, "my military education will be with me all my life. Order, discipline, hierarchy, molded into my blood at an early age, along with the sentiment of soldierly dignity, will constitute a guiding thread for my entire future activity."¹³ In 1917, he spent a year at a military school in Botoșani in Moldavia where he was described as being decisive, energetic, and good material for a commander. Here he remembered, four officers "guided my steps in the ways of battle and sacrifice for my country."¹⁴

With the ending of the Great War, Codreanu felt a responsibility towards the "front generation" to preserve the Greater Romania that had resulted from their sacrifices.¹⁵ He feared that the new country would soon be dismantled by the combined territorial revisionism of Hungary and Bolshevik Russia and by revolutionary forces inside Romania itself. Hungary did not accept the loss of Transylvania nor Russia the loss of Bessarabia; and Romania, with its small but growing working class, was beset by class warfare. Labor strikes reached a peak in 1920, when there were 750, 112 in Bucharest alone.¹⁶ In the same year, Max Goldstein, a Communist from Codreanu's native Iași, blew up the Senate in Bucharest, killing a minister and a bishop. Goldstein's Jewish origins only served to increase the identification in Codreanu's mind of the Jews with Communism. He later wrote, "when I say 'Communists' I mean Jews."¹⁷ In July 1919, with units of the Red Army stationed just beyond Romania's eastern borders, Codreanu, together with some high school students, swore to fight for Romania's defense in the event of a Russian invasion. He and his companions procured weapons and undertook battle exercises in the forest.

The Bolshevik invasion of Romania failed to materialize, however, and so later that same year Codreanu went to Iași University to study law. He and his supporters were particularly incensed by the number of students of Jewish origin at Romanian universities and the implications for the country's future middle class. In 1923, together with the anti-semitic Professor Cuza, he founded the League of National Christian Defense to campaign against the planned constitution under which the country's Jewish population would receive Romanian citizenship. The failure of the campaign led to Codreanu's alienation not only from the older generation of nationalists such as Cuza (still prepared to work entirely within the parliamentary system), but also from liberal democracy as a whole. As Codreanu saw it, not only did the party system divide the newly enfranchised Romanian nation into mutually antagonistic class-based parties, but the democratic system favored the interests of the Jewish minority against those of the Romanian majority. He now wished to create a disciplined, Romanian nationalist youth movement outside the political system.¹⁸

The Creation of the Romanian Legionary Movement

In 1927, Codreanu founded the Legion of the Archangel Michael. Just as it grew out of the student movement of the 1920s, also in the 1930s students would remain its main component.¹⁹ It was, however, infused with the military ideals of the age. As Constantin Iordachi has written, Codreanu's education was characterized by "religious-patriotic militarism", which in turn shaped the nature of the Legion. While the palingenetic nationalism of the pre- and Great War years had been centered on the army's role in national regeneration, the Legion claimed the "young generation's monopoly on the national path to salvation" under the leadership of Codreanu and "redefined militarism as paramilitary *Legionarism*."[20]

Indeed, Codreanu created the Legion based on a disciplined and hierarchical military system where legionary grades corresponded to those in the regular army. He even created decorations such as the *Crucea Verde* (Green Cross) to supplement the paramilitary uniforms of the movement. The legionary New Man was imbued with the qualities of the soldier: discipline, the spirit of sacrifice for his country, camaraderie, and obedience to flag, country, and king. When in 1929 the Legionary Senate was created as the movement's consultative organization composed of veteran members, it included a number of generals and colonels. Indeed, the movement's sense of hierarchy and discipline was a point of attraction for veterans who could integrate easily and rapidly into the movement.[21] Although by September 1940 legionary influence was significant among lower and middle ranking officers and army sympathy had been important in the Legion's coming to power, most of the higher ranks of the army opposed the movement.[22] Clearly, in the context of interwar Romania, military personnel were drawn to nationalist movements since they were called upon to defend the frontiers, but while there were legionary sympathizers in the army, army personnel were also attracted to other more conservative nationalist movements such as the National Christian Party led by Octavian Goga and Codreanu's former mentor, Cuza. It seems that former army officers living on their pensions were particularly targeted and encouraged to join the Legion. In February 1938, Codreanu created the Corps of Former Military Men from former army officers and non-commissioned-officers.[23]

Of all the groups of military men, it was the war veterans who were most attracted to the Legion. In the run up to the election of December 1937 in which the Legion took part, an inquiry titled "Why I believe in the triumph of the legionary movement" appeared in the movement's newspaper *Buna Vestire* (The Annunciation). Here a number of "prominent public figures offered their answers, elaborating on the Legion's ideology and conferring upon it an aura of respectability to an extent it had never enjoyed before." Of the eleven correspondents, four were distinguished war veterans.[24] During Codreanu's trial for treason in 1938, a number of prominent war veterans acted as character witnesses for him, including General Dona who had defended Codreanu in 1934 during his trial for the murder of the prime minister I.C. Duca. Another distinguished war veteran who defended Codreanu in 1938 was General Ion Antonescu who, when asked whether Codreanu was capable of treason, replied that "General Antonescu does not converse with traitors."[25] Dennis Deletant has described how these two key figures met for the first time in 1936, brought together by a mutual mistrust of King Carol II and his "camarilla." The meeting was arranged by another important war veteran, General Gheorghe Cantacuzino.[26]

Cantacuzino had been a Commander of the Frontier Regiment during the Great War and received the order of Michael the Brave for his distinguished war record. Horia Sima, Codreanu's successor as leader of the Legion, describes how Cantacuzino, "a legendary figure in the Romanian army," had returned from the Great War hoping for political and social regeneration, only to be disappointed by the corruption of the political elite. In mid-1933 he had visited the legionary work camp in Bucharest where members of the movement were building the so-called Green House. Here he discovered "a world dear to the heart of a soldier: the spirit of sacrifice, the desire to create, discipline, human worth. Among these young men, who slept in shacks and ate from mess tins, who kneaded clay in suffocating heat and worked while humming patriotic songs, he felt as though he were among his soldiers at the front. It seemed to him to bring back the days of national greatness."[27] Cantacuzino consequently put his money and prestige at the disposal of the Legion; his house became the movement's secret headquarters.

From 1935 to 1937 Cantacuzino was president of the Legion's political wing, All for the Country (Totul pentru Țară). Yet, as Codreanu wrote, the Legion was not so much a political movement as "a great spiritual movement [that] strives to transform and revolutionize the Romanian soul."[28] Thus, despite the movement's ultra-nationalism and anti-semitism, Codreanu originally had no political program. The purpose of the Legion was, rather, to create and educate the New Man: a spiritually and morally regenerated individual through whom the nation as a whole would be renewed. This process would bring an end to the malaise and corruption endemic in Romanian political life. Although Codreanu won a seat as a parliamentary deputy in 1931 and its political wing came third in the 1937 elections, the creation of the New Man remained his "principal objective with regard to our people, because this man, once created, would be able to resolve all the problems of the nation."[29]

This vision was intimately connected to Codreanu's attitude towards the Romanian political establishment and the Jewish minority. The Jews, he believed, were only able to dominate Romanian society thanks to the moral failings of the Romanians and the corruption of their political elite. "A country has only the Jews and the leaders it deserves," he wrote.[30] It followed that political life could not be transformed by party programs unless individuals were first perfected through Christian morality, discipline, and love of nation. "A new state," he wrote, "presupposes in the first place, and as an indispensable element, a new type of man."[31] Since this New Man would be forbidden from entering any political party, the political elite would be starved of young blood and eventually crumble. Excluding a corruptible and anti-national political elite, the "Jewish problem" would be solved.[32]

Codreanu's New Man therefore was to be created out of Romanian youth and educated within a moral medium consisting of the *cuib* as well as a broader system of work camps. Within these structures, the nascent New Man would be "isolated from the rest of the world by the highest possible spiritual fortifications" before being sent out into the world. He would be protected until he was spiritually strong enough to be immune to negative influences.[33] Such was the importance of the work camps as an educational experience for the young legionaries, that Codreanu decreed that no member of the movement should gain a position in the movement's hierarchy unless he had first passed through a work camp.[34] The New Man, with his sense of Romanian nationhood and sacrifice, would be the very antithesis of the materialistic, individualistic democratic politician.[35]

The Role of Work Camps

By 1936 there were seventy-one work camps throughout Romania, as well as thousands of smaller work sites. The work camps were dedicated to a variety of tasks, including agricultural work or building churches, parish halls, schools, bridges, roads, and legionary hostels. But what was the pedagogy that Codreanu believed conducive to the creation of the New Man and that his supporters saw reflected within the work camps? The first principle was that of manual labor, considered "an educational means of the first order" for the camps were believed to have "ennobled the notion of work."[36] Manual labor not only led to physical fitness and good health but also created solidarity between the intellectual middle classes, workers, and peasants. This emphasis was intimately linked to the second principle of the camps, that of communal life. According to the legionary intellectual, Mihail Polihroniade, the camps were "a school of social solidarity and national fraternity" because workers, peasants, and intellectuals worked and lived together.[37]

The third principle was the cultivation of an austere discipline and healthy body. Modern comforts and "frivolities" were eschewed as being conducive to "national decline." Through spartan and disciplined living, a well-balanced, altruistic, and physically healthy nation would be created. In addition, the "natural hierarchy" in the camps would lead to the creation of an ascetic elite with an "athletic spiritual structure" destined one day to challenge the traditional leadership governing Romania.[38] The stress on austerity and discipline was intensified by the stricture that legionaries were forbidden to leave the camp during their stay except in emergencies.[39]

This brings us to the fourth principle, the pedagogic maxim itself. The aim of legionary education was not the acquisition of intellectual knowledge, but that which was conducive to Christian morality, good behavior, and spiritual growth: education of a "spiritual" rather than an academic nature.[40] Codreanu's emphasis on moral improvement and good behavior was clear in one circular written to work camp legionaries in July 1935. He informed them that "this year the camps have the educational aim of creating … the honest man (*omul corect*)"—honest in relation to himself, the movement, his friends, country, and God.[41] Codreanu himself spent time at many of the work camps. He spent the summer of 1936 at Carmen Sylva, the largest of the camps, sharing the legionaries' life and leading their evening discussions.[42] Topics included practical questions, such as their behavior towards other nationalist groups, as well as spiritual issues such as their attitude to the church and legionary mysticism.[43]

This camp on the Black Sea was built by eight hundred legionaries in mid-1935 and was described by a supporter as "an immense monastery in the open air in which the legionaries pray for the whole nation." In view of its austere discipline, dedication to work, prayer, and moral earnestness, this description seems entirely appropriate for how legionaries perceived the overall ethos. The camp was run with military precision by a "service officer" selected every day by Codreanu. Under his direction, legionaries rose at five thirty in the morning for prayers and gymnastics, followed by manual work with brief pauses for singing, bathing, and a frugal breakfast and lunch. Meat was served only twice a week. Following a rest in the afternoon, work continued from four thirty in the afternoon to eight o'clock in the evening, to be followed by time for discussion, singing, prayers, and supper.[44] It was within such an atmosphere that the New Man, part warrior and part monk, was to emerge.

Furthermore, the Carmen Sylva camp was described by George Macrin as "a state in miniature."[45] The legionaries built a number of stone chalets and huts, as well as six kitchens, five fountains and a hen house. Orderly paths were cut between the buildings, and small terraces and flower beds created. The legionaries even laid down a two-hundred-meter road from the camp to the beach, which they named "the Road of Tomorrow's Romanian." The shore line was also consolidated for defensive purposes and deep drainage channels were cut into the banks. Contemporary photographs reveal a series of impressive and orderly constructions. Over five hundred trees were planted, and grain and vegetables grown on land at nearby Tuzla; horses, donkeys and carts were kept in the camp for transportation of provisions.[46] In addition, in 1935–36 the legionaries constructed over a kilometer of main road leading from the camp and running parallel to the sea. This was built using stones extracted from the sea, to show that the Legion could do better than Romania's politicians who had themselves planned such a road using stones from the Carpathian Mountains.[47]

The Legion's claim regarding the cross-class composition of the camps is revealed to have merit when analyzing the membership of Carmen Sylva. Although students made up the largest single group, artisans, workers, and peasants were also well represented, in addition to teachers, lawyers, priests, professors, even pilots, and members of the artistic professions. Women worked there as well as some foreign visitors and older supporters of the movement, including General Cantacuzino.[48] During the summer of 1936, the camp was also home to several dozen children who helped the legionaries.[49] Legionary organizations throughout the country sent children from poor families to stay at the camp for up to twenty days, to benefit from the healthy life by the sea and imbibe legionary propaganda. They received free medical care from the doctors working in the camp's infirmary, while the legionary women acted as nurses.[50] The variety of work being undertaken, as well as the diverse social and regional origins of the camp's members, prompted George Macrin to describe Carmen Sylva as "an archetypal city" (*o cetate ideală*) in which all social classes and age groups worked together allegedly without antagonism.[51]

A Ministry of the Interior report of October 1936 noted that most camps and sites were dedicated to projects "connected to developing religious sentiment and strengthening Christian belief, factors considered to be most beneficial in aiding the propagandistic aims of this organization."[52] Of the six largest and most important work camps operating in 1935–36, two, at Arnota and Susai-Predeal, were directly dedicated to religious purposes. But there were dozens of smaller camps and thousands of work sites in operation throughout the country. Raising crucifixes on mountain tops and building fountains (followed by a religious dedication) were especially popular ideas for smaller projects.

It must be stressed that these works were sometimes directly inspired by memory of the wartime sacrifice. Thus war veterans regularly attended the religious ceremonies attendant upon the completion of work at the camps. Indeed, the camp at Susai-Predeal in the Carpathians had been specifically established to build a mausoleum for bones of Romanian soldiers who had perished there in 1916 defending the border between Romania and Transylvania, then under Habsburg jurisdiction. Codreanu had personally discovered the bones on a walk in the mountains, and was appalled that the soldiers, having sacrificed themselves for Greater Romania, had not received due honor or a Christian burial. It only served to confirm his opinion of the Romanian establishment as an anti-national force. The church hierarchy was directly involved in the Susai-Predeal camp that was inaugurated with a requiem and stone-laying ceremony led by Metropolitan Gurie of Bessarabia. On 5 September 1936, however, local gendarmes destroyed the mausoleum that was nearing completion, discarding crucifixes, icons, and even the bones themselves.[53] General Cantacuzino, who had been present at the camp's inauguration, demanded a government enquiry into this "sacrilege" against "the holy bones."[54]

In October 1936, at a work camp similarly inspired by the sacrifices of the war generation, legionary workers from the Prahova valley erected a spectacular monumental crucifix to commemorate Romanian soldiers who had died during the war on Sorica Mountain near Azuga in the Carpathians. The crucifix was eight meters high and could be seen from distant towns. It had been carved from a massive oak tree by legionary workers in their spare time with materials provided by a local manufacturer; the figure of Christ himself measured five meters and had been painted by a legionary artist. At the blessing of the crucifix, several Orthodox priests officiated in the presence of General Cantacuzino, Gheorge Clime (head of the legionary workers' corps), and a number of legionary commanders; six hundred legionary workers from the Prahova valley were there as well as a delegation of war veterans. It was a very popular event, attracting some four thousand local residents as well as visitors from distant Brașov and Bucharest.[55] This event, together with the camp at Susai-Predeal, reflected the Legion's identification with the sacrifices of the war generation and the government's failure, in the Legion's view, to honor the war dead or live up to that generation's ideals for the Romanian nation.[56]

Spiritual Regeneration: "The Cult of Death" and Resurrection in the Legion

In addition to the work of the Legion's New Men in the work camps, its message of moral and national renewal was transmitted through regular expeditions into Romanian villages, many of which were led by Codreanu himself. Since the Legion ultimately aimed spiritually to regenerate the nation and its peasantry, and peasant values were more or less synonymous with popular Orthodoxy, it was through religious liturgy that the legionaries sought to disseminate their message.

A number of historians have pointed out that modern revolutionary movements, even those of a secular nature, have inevitably drawn upon time-honored religious symbols and rituals, especially those of *The Revelation of John*.[57] The book includes descriptions of the Apocalypse, the resurrection of the oppressed and their entry into the New Jerusalem, while the "perverts, sorcerers, and fornicators" remain outside. *Revelation* has thus supplied a framework in which revolutionary movements have announced their own brands of apocalypse and regeneration.[58] The Legion, with its appropriation of Christianity, was no exception. Moreover, since the forces of secularization were relatively weak within Romanian rural society, the Legion was able to appeal to religious sentiments and imagery that were still very much alive.

One contemporary described the entry of the Legion into a Transylvanian village, with Codreanu resplendent in white and mounted on a white horse.[59]

This may have been a conscious mimicry of the following passage in *Revelation*: "I saw heaven wide open, and a white horse appeared; its rider's name was Faithful and True …. The armed of heaven followed him, riding on white horses and clothed in fine linen, white and clean."⁶⁰ According to Eugen Weber, "not the least influential of John's prophecies was his vision of Christ's Second Coming as a warrior on a white horse, … sword in his hand to smite Antichrist."⁶¹

Moreover, Codreanu's speeches were shot through with Biblical imagery and allusions to the Resurrection and Christ's Second Coming drawn directly from *Revelation*. Through these, Codreanu sought to put forward his own analogous message of Romania's ultimate regeneration. His speech from the first large-scale legionary expedition to Bessarabia in January 1930 was typical.

> The hour of the redemption and of the resurrection of our people is drawing nigh! … New times are knocking at our doors! A world with a soul which dried up long ago is dying, and a new world is being born—the world of those who are strong and have faith. [The final aim of the nation is] Resurrection in the name of the Savior Jesus Christ.... There will come a time when all the peoples of the earth shall be resurrected, with all their dead and all their kings and emperors, each people having its place before God's throne.⁶²

It was fitting, therefore, that the symbol of the Legion should have been the Archangel Michael, rescuer of the souls of the faithful, and leader of the heavenly army against the forces of hell in *The Revelation of John*. Moreover, it is the Archangel Michael who is responsible for binding down Satan, inaugurating Christ's thousand-year reign. When they traveled into the countryside, the legionaries carried icons of the Archangel, together with Codreanu's portrait in icon form. They thereby exploited the ubiquity of icons in Orthodox churches and homes, and their mystical associations. According to the Orthodox bishop Kallistos Ware, "icons act as a point of meeting between the living members of the Church and those who have gone before. Icons help the Orthodox to look on the saints not as remote and legendary figures from the past, but as contemporaries and personal friends."⁶³

This sense that the dead were still alive among the living was given expression in Codreanu's concept of the collective nation. The nation included not only the living members of the Romanian community, but also Romanians as yet unborn and, as Codreanu put it, "all the souls of our dead and the tombs of our ancestors." The nation, he believed, "is an entity which prolongs her existence even beyond this world. Peoples are realities even in the nether world, not only in this one."⁶⁴ As an extension of this idea, the power of ancestral Romanians could be transmitted to the living through prayer. This was invoked by Codreanu as an essential element in the Legion's struggle and ultimate victory over its enemies: "[w]ars were won by those who knew how to summon the mysterious powers of the unseen world.... These mysterious powers are the souls of the dead, the souls of our ancestors who too were once attached to this land." Prayers invoking the power of the ancestors were thus to take place during "nest" meetings on Saturday evenings, and at church on Sundays.[65] This sense of a community in which the dead interacted with the living was given expression at meetings when the names of fallen comrades were read out and one of their living fellows would call out "present." Following the deaths of the two senior legionaries, Ion Moța and Vasile Marin, in the Spanish Civil War, their names were added to the top of the list of all fallen legionaries to be read out and declared as present. Members were also exhorted to hold services and requiems for deceased legionaries.[66]

The legionary ideology of the nation as an interdependent and, indeed, interactive community of the living and ancestral Romanians drew upon the Orthodox Church's concept of the church as a collectivity of the living and the dead.[67] In Orthodox belief, the church is where all its members, dead or alive, are saved together rather than as individuals. The sense that the dead are still part of the living church is also apparent in Orthodoxy's rejection of the notion of Purgatory. The dead are held to be in a sense neither dead nor alive. Their souls are, rather, "sleeping" until their resurrection on the Day of Judgment. The living have a duty to pray for the souls of the dead to ensure their ultimate entry into Heaven; hence Codreanu's injunction to legionaries to pray to the dead at Saturday evening "nest" meetings.[68]

This belief in the power of the ancestral dead for the Legion's victory had also found expression in the legionaries' first "blood and soil" vow-taking ceremony held on St Michael's Day, 8 November 1927. As the legionary periodical, *The Ancestral Land*, explained: "[t]his solemnity began by mixing the earth brought from the tomb of Michael the Brave from Turda, with that from Moldavia ... where Stefan the Great fought his greatest battles, and from every other place where our ancestors' blood was soaked by the earth in ferocious battles, thus blessing it."[69] As Codreanu continued in his memoirs: "[s]mall leather sacks were then filled with [the soil] and tightly tied with laces. These were to be received by legionaries as they took their vow [to the Legion] and were to be worn close to their hearts." He described the sacks as "a symbol which could be a faithful expression of the character of our movement, of our union with the earth of our ancestors, our dead and the heavens."[70] They were also carried by the "Death Teams" created in the 1930s to protect Codreanu and seek vengeance on politicians and others responsible for the persecution of the Legion; the Death Teams took a vow over the bags of soil to this effect.[71] Thus worn, the bags of "sacred soil" directly linked the legionaries to the heroes and soldiers of the past and their sacrifices for the defense of the Romanian nation.

The Legion's cult of death and creation of the Death Teams inevitably led to a glorification of violence and assassination.[72] This was perhaps unsurprising in a society that had only recently emerged from the slaughter of the Great War and regarded itself as the representative of the war generation. Without denying the Legion's potential for violence we should, however, note the brutality of the Romanian government in its handling of its political opponents in this era. Between 1924 and 1937 the Legion committed a total of eleven known murders, together with a great deal of thuggery, but over five hundred legionaries were condemned to death and the movement was frequently outlawed. Between Codreanu's murder in 1938 and the establishment of the National Legionary State in September 1940, some three thousand legionaries were executed or "disappeared."[73] However, for a movement believing in the Christian concept of resurrection, clearly death was not something to be feared. Moreover, a willingness to die made members of the movement—the Death Teams in particular—feel themselves invulnerable in the face of mounting government persecution. As one legionary maxim put it, "Whoever knows how to die, will never be a slave." Or as Codreanu explained, "Not being able to win while alive, we will win dying."[74]

The death of any legionary in the service of the movement was regarded as the ultimate act of sacrifice for the nation. The Legion was thus strongly influenced by the Christian concepts of martyrdom and the *Imitatio Christi*. Legionary supporters frequently likened Ion Moța, and later Codreanu, to Christ, as sacrificial victims for the good of the Romanian nation. Following Moța's death in the Spanish Civil War, Professor Nae Ionescu, declared that "for the salvation of our nation, God had to accept Moța's sacrifice, as for the salvation of the human race he accepted that of the lamb."[75] Indeed, the creation of a legionary martyrology probably did much to increase the movement's appeal among the Orthodox peasantry, long accustomed to venerating martyrs of the church. Pictures of these new martyrs appeared regularly in legionary publications. For instance, a booklet published to mark Moța's death included a full page photograph of the deceased leader and compared his presence among his living comrades with that of the risen Christ among his disciples.[76]

The Spanish Civil War in which Moța perished was seen by the Legion as a fight between Communism and the Church. A group of eight legionaries, headed by General Cantacuzino, left for Spain in November 1936 to present a gift of Cantacuzino's Toledo sword to General Moscardo who had defended Alcazar. Codreanu had ordered the trip to be symbolic only: the group should not become involved in the fighting. Moța, however, insisted that the legionaries should fight with the Spanish nationalist forces. Before leaving Romania, he left a testament that revealed his belief in impending death for the defense of the church. In January 1937 he was killed along with Vasile Marin. As Valentin Săndulescu has noted, until this point the Legion's discourse on self-sacrifice had been dismissed as mere rhetoric, but now "they had dead bodies to prove their ideological commitment [and they] took advantage of this opportunity in order to gain popular support."[77]

The funeral of Moța and Marin, held in Bucharest on 13 February 1937, was large and ostentatious and attended by vast crowds of ordinary Romanians. The coffins were buried at a mausoleum in the Green House, the movement's city headquarters, and were permanently guarded by legionaries. Reports of miracles quickly began to circulate.[78] This however was only the starting point of the Moța-Marin cult. As we have seen, the names of the two legionaries were incorporated into the roll call of the dead to be read out at legionary meetings. In May 1937, the decision was made to construct a monastery and mausoleum on land near Predeal in the Carpathian Mountains to be dedicated to Moța and Marin, under the authority of the archbishopric of Alba Iulia and Sibiu.[79] In January 1938, Codreanu set up the Moța-Marin Corps, an elite body of around ten thousand legionaries ready to die for the nation in the manner of the two martyrs. This represented the very pinnacle of the New Man's spirit of sacrifice. The corps' members were to be under the age of thirty, to be of high moral character and willing to dedicate themselves to a life of austerity and celibacy. They all swore an oath, based upon Moța's writings, acknowledging their willingness to die.[80]

Yet the legionary cult of sacrifice and martyrdom received its greatest boost with the murder of Codreanu by the royal regime in November 1938. That Codreanu himself had been the model for the New Man seems clear. Ion Banea, legionary commander for Transylvania, wrote that Codreanu created New Men out of the legionaries through the example of his own life.[81] During the government of the National Legionary State in late 1940, Codreanu's followers tried to have their deceased leader canonized and to found a new Romanian capital to be named "Codreni" in his honor. Although they were unsuccessful, the Legionary State did not fail to exploit Codreanu's genuine popularity even beyond the grave. A notable feature of the important legionary demonstration held on 6 October 1940 was the use of enormous pictures of Codreanu on which were daubed the words "Corneliu Zelea Codreanu—Present!" as a reminder that the spirit of the dead captain still presided over legionary affairs.[82] Moreover, a messianic comparison was regularly evoked. As one intellectual noted: "[w]ith the exception of Jesus, no dead man has been more present amidst the living. From now on, the country will be led by a dead man. This dead man has spread the perfume of eternity over our human dregs."[83]

The use of commemorations and requiems for the dead as a focus for national consolidation reached its height during the period of the National Legionary State. Indeed, the regime was dubbed by some the "regime of funeral processions" owing to the frequency and pomp with which the many legionaries who had been murdered between 1938 and 1940 were exhumed and reburied.[84] The most important of these was, of course, Codreanu himself. The funeral was held on 30 November 1940—the second anniversary of his death—and the procession that wound its way from Jilava prison, where Codreanu had been buried, to the legionary Green House was several miles long. As well as being an expression of legionary and, by extension, national solidarity, the event was also an opportunity for the consolidation of international alliances. It was attended by senior representatives of Romania's German ally and, in a gesture of nationalist fraternity, German planes dropped wreaths over the open graves.[85] Such was the national significance accorded to the funeral that public services and factories throughout the country came to a standstill.[86]

A Higher Spiritual Vocation

Despite their more ambivalent attitudes towards Christianity, both Nazism and Italian Fascism were deeply marked by the language of millenarianism, the Christian symbolism of death and resurrection, the cult of martyrdom, the veneration of fallen comrades, and the "worship of the corpse."[87] Among the smaller Fascist movements, the Croatian Ustasha, for example, was pervaded by a cult of death of "chiliastic intensity" that "mimicked the rites and beliefs of Roman Catholicism."[88] The Romanian Legion's cult of death and recourse to Christian symbolism was thus no bizarre aberration, but well within the mainstream of European Fascism. It should be noted, moreover, that the "worship of the corpse" to reinforce national or group solidarity was not by any means unique to the radical right in interwar Europe. Quite apart from the display of Lenin's corpse in Bolshevik Russia, the anarchists of Barcelona in November 1936, who only a few months previously had paraded the corpses of monks and nuns in the streets of Barcelona to the jeers of their anticlerical supporters, had their fallen leader embalmed and placed on display in a glass coffin with all the trappings of a secular saint.[89]

Yet for the Romanian legionary movement, like Fascism as a whole, sacrifice, martyrdom, and life after death indicated a higher spiritual vocation in human existence and lay at the very heart of what it meant to be a New Man. Despite Romania's status as a victor in the Great War and its consequent territorial enlargement, the legionaries believed the country to be prey to hostile materialistic forces both within and without in the form of the anti-national Romanian liberal political elite, its "Jewish" economic allies, and Russian Bolshevism. These they saw as an immediate moral and military threat to the fragile new state. The veterans of the Great War acted as an important role model, and link between the generations, for younger members of the legionary movement who had been unable to fight in the war. Thus, the war generation's national and military ideals, and its spirit of sacrifice, were entrusted to the regenerated New Man of the legionary movement. Just as the war veterans' sense of national community had been forged in the trenches, that of the legionary New Man was crafted in the work camps. This new national elite would in turn, it was presumed, resurrect the Romanian nation and force the decadent politicians from power, thereby inaugurating the "Golden Age" of Greater Romania for which the war generation had fought and died. An epitaph for the legionary movement might thus come from the article by Mussolini with which this chapter began. Although written in 1917, it could have easily been written by Codreanu in the 1930s: "The trenchocracy is the aristocracy of the trenches. It is the aristocracy of tomorrow! ... The old parties, the old men who carry on with the exploitation of the political Italy of tomorrow will be swept aside ... It is this prediction which makes us observe with a certain contempt everything which is said and done by the old windbags who govern us, so full of presumption, sacred formulas, and senile imbecility."[90]

Rebecca Haynes is Senior Lecturer in Romanian History at the School of Slavonic and East European Studies, University College London. Her research is focused on interwar Romania with special reference to the Legion of the Archangel Michael. She has published a number of articles on this topic as well as editing (together with Martyn Rady) *In the Shadow of Hitler: Personalities of the Right in Central and Eastern Europe* (2011).

Notes

1. Roger Griffin, ed., *Fascism* (Oxford, 1995), 28.
2. Nicholas M. Nagy-Talavera, *The Green-Shirts and the Others: A History of Fascism in Hungary and Rumania* (Stanford, CA, 1970), 270.
3. See, for example, ibid., 247, 250–51, 265–68; Armin Heinen, *Die Legion "Erzengel Michael" in Rumänien: Soziale Bewegung und politische Organisation* (Munich, 1986), 317–21; Constantin Iordachi, *Charisma, Politics and Violence: The Legion of the "Archangel Michael" in Inter-war Romania* (Trondheim, 2004), 104–17.
4. Henry Roberts, *Rumania: Political Problems of an Agrarian State* (New Haven, CT, 1951), 229.
5. Silviu Hariton writes that as early as the 1860s, "militarism, nationalism and religion became linked ... to constitute a unified set of ideas which were later disseminated in a uniform way across the army," in order to motivate soldiers on the battlefield. Army chaplains were responsible for investing military rites of passage with religious meaning and by the later nineteenth century the names of fallen soldiers were being inscribed into parish records as "martyrs of the Christian faith and of the patria," to be recalled in the religious liturgy for a period of three years. Increasingly, the clergy encouraged soldiers to sacrifice themselves for the nation in an *imitatio Christi*. See Silviu Hariton, "Religion, Nationalism and Militarism in Nineteenth Century Romania," *Études Balkaniques* 44/4 (2008): 11. See also Constantin Iordachi on the militarization of youth in the pre-Great War era "based on the trinity of Church-School-Army" and its influence on the legionary movement. Constantin Iordachi, "God's Chosen Warriors: Romantic Palingenesis, Militarism and Fascism in Modern Romania," in *Comparative Fascist Studies: New Perspectives*, ed. Iordachi (Oxford, 2010), 336.

6. See Roger Griffin's description of Fascism as "a genus of political ideology whose mythic core in its various permutations is a palingenetic form of populist ultra-nationalism." Roger Griffin, *The Nature of Fascism* (London, 1996), 26.
7. For an exploration of the nature of the legionary "New Man," see Valentin Săndulescu, "Fascism and its Quest for the 'New Man': the Case of the Romanian Legionary Movement," in *Studia Hebraica*, 4 (2004): 349–61. Roger Griffin has described the concept of the "New Man" as a "sub-myth" within Fascism's "palingenetic political myth" of transformation. See Griffin, *The Nature of Fascism*, 35.
8. Interview with Horia Sima in 1984, in Gheorghe Buzatu, Corneliu Ciucanu, and Cristian Sandache, eds., *Radiografia dreptei românești (1927–1941)* (Bucharest 1996), 321. For New Testament origins, see Ephesians 2:15 and 4:17–24; Colossians 3:9–11. For the anthropological and religious origins of the "New Man" and its development in the modern era, see Goffried Küenzlen, *Der Neue Mensch: Zur säkularen Religionsgeschichte der Moderne* (Munich, 1994); Griffin, *The Nature of Fascism*, 54 for further Biblical references.
9. While the New Man of the New Testament undergoes his spiritual purification as an individual, the New Man of the twentieth century underwent a collective regeneration. See Alexandra Gerstner, Barbara Könczöl, and Janina Nentwig, "Auf der Suche nach dem Neuen Menschen: Eine Einleitung," in *Der Neue Mensch: Utopien, Leitbilder und Reformkonzepte zwischen den Weltkriegen*, ed. Alexandra Gerstner et al (Frankfurt am Main, 2006), viii.
10. Corneliu Zelea Codreanu, *For My Legionaries (The Iron Guard)* (Madrid, 1976), 6–7 [first published as *Pentru Legionari* (Sibiu, 1936)].
11. Petre Pandrea, *Garda de Fier: Jurnal de filosofie politică. Memorii penitenciare* (Bucharest, 2001), 31–38.
12. Codreanu, *For My Legionaries*, 4–5.
13. Ibid., 4.
14. Ibid., 6; Pandrea, *Garda de Fier*, 31–38.
15. There were more than half a million Romanian dead, wounded, and missing. Civilian victims were also, per capita of the population, the highest of all participating countries: Francisco Veiga, *Istoria Gărzii de Fier 1919–1941: Mistica ultranaționalismului* (Bucharest, 1993), 19.
16. Lucien Karchmar, "Communism in Romania 1918–1921," in *War and Society in East Central Europe, vol. 13, The Effects of World War One: The Class War after the Great War: The Rise of Communist Parties in East Central Europe, 1918-1921*, ed. Ivo Banac (New York, 1983), 162.
17. Codreanu, *For My Legionaries*, 277.
18. Ibid., 87–117, 302–26. For Codreanu's early career and the nationalist student movement in the 1920s, see Irina Livezeanu, *Cultural Politics in Greater Romania: Regionalism, Nation Building and Ethnic Struggle, 1918–1930* (Ithaca, New York, and London, 1995), 245–96.
19. For an analogous discussion of the postwar student generation in Germany and its belief in its leading role to regenerate the German nation, see Sonja Levsen, "Der 'neue Student' als 'Führer der Nation': Neuentwürfe studentischer Identitäten nach dem Ersten Weltkrieg," in *Der Neue Mensch*, ed. Gerstner et al, 105–23.
20. Iordachi, "God's Chosen Warriors," 316, 321.
21. Dana Beldiman and Corneliu Beldiman, "Dreapta românească: Elemente de organizare militară II," *Arhivele Totalitarismului* 8/28-29 (2000): 8–18.
22. See Rebecca Haynes, "Germany and the Establishment of the Romanian National Legionary State, September 1940," *Slavonic and East European Review* 77/4 (1999): 700–25.
23. Dana Beldiman, "Armata Română și mișcările de dreapta și extrema dreaptă, 1921–1937," *Arhivele Totalitarismului* 9/32-33 (2001): 11–20; Constantin Argetoianu, *Însemnări zilnice*, volume 4: 1 ianuarie—30 iunie 1938, ed. Stelian Neagoe (Bucharest, 2002), 92: entry for 5 February 1938.

24. Raul Cârstocea, "The Role of Anti-Semitism in the Ideology of the Legion of the Archangel Michael," PhD diss., London 2011, 118.
25. Kurt W. Treptow and Gheorghe Buzatu, eds., *Corneliu Zelea Codreanu în fața istoriei: Procesul lui Corneliu Zelea Codreanu (Mai, 1938)* (Iași, 1994): 87–105 for the war veterans who supported Codreanu; 98–100 for Antonescu.
26. Dennis Deletant, *Hitler's Forgotten Ally: Ion Antonescu and His Regime, Romania 1940–1944* (Basingstoke, 2006), 37–44.
27. Horia Sima, *Istoria mișcării legionare* (Timișoara, 1995), 82.
28. Corneliu Codreanu, *Cărticica șefului de cuib* (Munich, 1987), 111 [originally published in Bucharest, 1933).
29. Sima, *Istoria mișcării legionare*, 143.
30. Codreanu, *For My Legionaries*, 132.
31. Codreanu, *Cărticica șefului de cuib*, 65.
32. Codreanu, *For My Legionaries*, 133.
33. Ibid., 222. Codreanu considered the state education system to be "under Jewish influence." See Săndulescu, "Fascism and its Quest," 359.
34. Sima, *Istoria mișcării legionare*, 118.
35. According to Leon Țopa, as a result of the Jewish infiltration of the economy in the nineteenth century, the Romanian political elite represented not the interests of the Romanian nation but only "economic interests and the interests of people who lead the economy," i.e., the Jews. See Leon Țopa, "Taberele de muncă obligatorie," *Însemnări sociologice* 2 (November 1936): 26.
36. George Macrin, "O nouă școală romînească. Taberele de muncă," *Însemnări sociologice* 1 (July 1935): 16; George Macrin, "Taberele de muncă. Tabăra dela Carmen Sylva," *Însemnări sociologice* 2 (October 1936): 15; George Macrin, "Taberele de muncă: Aspectul politic," *Însemnări sociologice* 2 (August 1935): 17–18.
37. *Tabăra de Muncă* with a foreword by Mihail Polihroniade (no place of publication, 1936), 1. This volume, containing numerous photographs of the most significant legionary work camps, was clearly produced to celebrate the legionary "year of the work camp" in 1936.
38. Macrin, "Taberele de muncă: Tabăra dela Carmen Sylva," 14; Macrin, "Taberele de muncă: Aspectul politic," 18; Macrin, "O nouă școală romînească: Taberele de muncă," 20; Codreanu, *Circulări și manifeste, 1927–1938* (Munich 1982) [originally published in Bucharest 1940], 162: Câmpina legionary camp, 6 July 1937; *Porunca Vremii*, 30 July 1935. For the importance of the concept of the elite in legionary ideology, see Horia Sima, *Doctrina legionară* (Bucharest, 1995), 168–80.
39. National Central Historical Archives, Bucharest (Arhivele Naționale Istorice Centrale: hereafter ANIC), Ministerul de Interne, Diverse, 2/1936, f. 249, General Directorate of Police, Note, nr 2324, 3 August 1936.
40. Macrin, "Taberele de muncă: Aspectul politic," 18–19; Sima, *Istoria mișcării legionare*, 143.
41. Codreanu, *Circulări și manifeste*, 47: To the legionaries in Arnota work camp, 20 July 1935.
42. Sima, *Istoria mișcări legionare*, 143–44.
43. Macrin, "Taberele de muncă: Aspectul politic," 22.
44. Macrin, "Taberele de muncă: Tabăra dela Carmen Sylva," 23.
45. Ibid.
46. Ioan Scurtu, ed., *Ideologie și formațiuni de dreapta în România. 1919–1938* (Bucharest, 2003), 4:123–24: document 51, 17 August 1935; *Tabăra de muncă*, 31–44; Codreanu, *Circulări și manifeste*, 73–74: Carmen Sylva, 24 April 1936.
47. Author's interview with Dr Șerban Milcoveanu, 19 April 2006. Dr Milcoveanu was the president of the National Union of Romanian Christian Students and attended Carmen Sylva work camp in 1936.

48. *Tabăra de muncă*, with a foreword by Mihail Polihroniade. On page 21 there is a photograph of General Cantacuzino inspecting the work camp at Storojineț where legionaries were making bricks for a Legionary House; on page 31 we see him at work at Carmen Sylva.
49. Macrin, "Taberele de muncă: Tabăra dela Carmen Sylva," 19–21.
50. ANIC, Ministerul de Interne, Diverse, 2/1936, 274: General Directorate of Police, Note, nr 2374, 10 August 1936 (Focșani legionaries to send 60–70 sick children to Carmen Sylva).
51. Macrin, "Taberele de muncă: Tabăra dela Carmen Sylva," 23. The existence of the "Carmen Sylva law" for settling disputes and ejecting miscreants suggests that relations between members were not always as harmonious as Macrin imagined. See Codreanu, *Circulări și manifeste*, 151–52: 1 July 1937 ("The Carmen Sylva law").
52. ANIC, Ministerul de Interne, Diverse, 3/1936, October 1936, fols. 300–21, f. 315, Police Directorate of the Security Services, Information Service, "All for the Country" party.
53. Sima, *Istoria mișcării legionare*, 152–53.
54. Codreanu, *Circulări și manifeste*, 77–78: Dissolution of Susai camp, Bucharest, 9 September 1936, by General Cantacuzino-Grănicerul.
55. Scurtu, *Ideologie și formațiuni*, 4:220: document 120, 27 October 1936 (Cluj: article in *Porunca Vremii* regarding the blessing of a crucifix on Sorica Mountain).
56. For more context on Romanian memorialization, see Maria Bucur, *Heroes and Victims: Remembering War in Twentieth Century Romania* (Bloomington, IN, 2009).
57. Norman Cohn, *The Pursuit of the Millennium: Revolutionary Millenarians and Mystical Anarchists of the Middle Ages* (New York, 1970); Eugen Weber, *Apocalypse: Prophecies, Cults and Millennial Beliefs through the Ages* (London, 1999).
58. For a discussion of Nazism as a millenarian movement, see James M. Rhodes, *The Hitler Movement: A Modern Millenarian Revolution* (Stanford, 1980).
59. Nagy-Talavera, *The Green Shirts*, 247.
60. *The Revelation of John* 19:11.
61. Weber, *Apocalypse*, 30.
62. Quoted in Nagy-Talavera, *The Green Shirts*, 281; Codreanu, *For My Legionaries*, 315.
63. Venetia Newall, "Icons as Symbols of Power," in *Symbols of Power*, ed. H.R. Ellis Davidson (Cambridge, 1977), 91; Timothy Ware, *The Orthodox Church* (London, 1963), 261.
64. Codreanu, *For My Legionaries*, 313, 315.
65. Codreanu, *Cărticica șefului de cuib*, 55–56.
66. Ion I. Moța, *Prezent!* (Bucharest, 1937), 1, 7.
67. See Ware, *The Orthodox Church*, 258.
68. See Adrian Fortescu, *The Orthodox Eastern Church* (London, 1907), 389, 408–9; and Vasile Răducă, *Ghidul creștinului ortodox de azi* (Bucharest, 1998), 201–3.
69. Codreanu, *For My Legionaries*, 249–50.
70. Ibid. For further evidence of the sacred power of the soil from graves, see the investigation of Emily Gerard in the 1880s into Romanian folk beliefs: Emily Gerard, *The Land Beyond the Forest: Facts, Figures and Fancies from Transylvania* (Edinburgh, 1888), 316.
71. Nagy-Talavera, *The Green Shirts*, 291–92.
72. The most famous murders carried out by the Legion were those of the prime ministers Ion Duca and Armand Călinescu in 1933 and 1939 respectively, and of the historian Nicolae Iorga in 1940.
73. Politisches Archiv des Auswärtigen Amtes, Berlin, Deutsche Gesandschaft, Bukarest, 1A5, Rumänien, Innenpolitisch, Bd. 9, 4. 1939–1. 1940, Bucharest, 24 December 1939, Tgb. Nr. 7819.
74. Codreanu, *For My Legionaries*, 218, 226.
75. Quoted in Eugen Weber, "Romania," in *The European Right: A Historical Profile*, ed. Hans Rogger and Eugen Weber (London, 1965), 525.

76. Moța, *Prezent!* 1.
77. Valentin Săndulescu, "Sacralised Politics in Action: the February 1937 Burial of the Romanian Legionary Leaders Ion Moța and Vasile Marin," *Totalitarian Movements and Political Religions* 8/2 (2007): 262.
78. Francisco Veiga, *Istoria Gărzii de Fier 1919–1941. Mistica ultranaționalismului* (Bucharest, 1993), 231. The Ministry of the Interior reported that on 18 June 1937 a fire had broken out at the Moța and Marin mausoleum at the Green House. Although the canopy had burned, the fact that the wooden cross emerged unscathed was regarded as a miracle by the movement's supporters. See ANIC, Ministerul de Interne, Diverse, dosar nr. 9/1937, Secția I-a, Nr 3, 21 June 1937, 19.
79. ANIC, fond Casa regală, dosar nr. 33/1937, Archbishop and Metropolitan of Alba Iulia and Sibiu to Mayor of municipality of Brașov, nr 4785, 18 May 1937, 57.
80. Ibid., Ministerul de Interne, Diverse, dosar 10/1938, Note, 25 January 1938, 17. Members of the Corps were to be under thirty years of age, have no family constraints, and to declare that they had done nothing "at the memory of which you must lower your eyes and head.... The candidate fighter will pronounce the following oath: 'May we have no other ideal than to be granted by God the blessing of dying maimed and tortured for the spark of Truth that we know we have in ourselves and for whose defence we go into battle with the prevailing powers of darkness in a life and death fight. I stand ready for death. I swear.'" *Buna Vestire*, 23 January 1938. I am grateful to Dr Raul Cârstocea for this reference. According to Constantin Argetoianu, although the Corps was only to consist of 10,033 men, over forty thousand legionaries volunteered on the first day. Argetoianu, *Însemnări zilnice*, vol. 4, 58: entry for 23 January 1938.
81. Ion Banea, *Căpitanul* (Timișoara, 1995), 111.
82. Nagy-Talavera, *The Green Shirts*, 313, 322.
83. Z. Ornea, *The Romanian Extreme Right: The Nineteen Thirties*, trans. Eugenia Maria Popescu (New York, 1999), 179, quoting Mircea Eliade.
84. Nagy-Talavera, *The Green Shirts*, 318.
85. Ibid., 321.
86. ANIC, fond Președinția consiliului de miniștri, dosar nr 310/1940, 24, note, 29 November 1940.
87. See for example, Rhodes, *The Hitler Movement*; and Emilio Gentile, *The Sacralization of Politics in Fascist Italy* (Cambridge, MA, 1996).
88. Rory Yeomans, "Cults of Death and Fantasies of Annihilation: The Croatian Ustasha Movement in Power, 1941–45," *Central Europe* 3/2 (2005): 121.
89. W. Bruce Lincoln, "Revolutionary Exhumations in Spain, July 1936," *Comparative Studies in Society and History* 27/2 (1985): 258.
90. Griffin, *Fascism*, 29.

Part III

SACRIFICE IN SILENCE

Chapter 9

SILENT LIQUIDATION?
Croatian Veterans and the Margins of War Memory in Interwar Yugoslavia

John Paul Newman

The mood among the approximately five hundred Croatian war veterans who had gathered at the Metropol Cinema in Zagreb in March 1920 was predominantly one of indignation and hostility toward the government. The men were assembled there under the auspices of the recently formed "Society of War Invalids for the Territories of Croatia, Slavonia, Dalmatia, Istria, Medjumurje with Prekomurje" (hereafter Society of War Invalids). Almost all had been disabled while fighting for Austria-Hungary in World War I. The disappointingly low turnout was attributed to a lack of interest in what was becoming known as the "Invalid Question." "It is more proof," claimed one attendee, "of how few people are concerned [about invalids] in our country." That disinterest would continue to vex Croatian veterans throughout the 1920s, but worse would follow. A disabled veteran named Franjo Meštrić was given the floor and related his experience of a recent trip to the Ministry of Social Policy that he had made for the purpose of requesting financial assistance. He reported the following exchange with an official at the ministry in Belgrade: "he [the official] asked, 'were you at the front in Salonika?' When we answered honestly that we were not, we received the mocking reply: 'then go to [deposed Habsburg emperor] Karl, maybe he will give you something.'"[1]

Although an anecdote, Meštrić's story was illustrative of a broader attitude toward Croatian veterans in the Kingdom of Serbs, Croats, and Slovenes (hereafter Yugoslavia). As chapters 5 and 10 of this volume show, the foundational narrative of the new state was based upon the Serbian army's victorious wars fought for the "liberation and unification" of all South Slavs.[2] This national epic served to marginalize men such as Meštrić and his fellow veterans since they were South Slavs who had not fought in the Serbian army during the war. They were often victims of postwar prejudices that depicted them as soldiers of a defeated enemy, as veterans who had fought against "liberation and unification."

While there was substance in Serbia's story of defeat, retreat, and eventual triumph, the ministry official's flippant remark did not do justice to the range of wartime experiences among Croatian veterans.[3] The simplified dialectic of Serbian victory and non-Serbian defeat concealed a complex and often ambivalent relationship among South Slav veterans of the Habsburg army with both Austria-Hungary and Yugoslavia. Closer examination of these men reveals a sliding scale of loyalty both to the Habsburg and subsequently to the Karadjordjević dynasties. This differentiation among Croatian veterans means that their case study fits more comfortably into a comparative rather than a national framework, since the former reveals the imprint left by Austria-Hungary in this region. However, while that imprint often extended beyond the boundaries of Yugoslavia, Croatian veterans shared a similar fate within their new state. Their experience was overshadowed by Serbia's wars of "liberation and unification," an almost overwhelming salient that permeated all discourses about World War I.

Needless to say, Croatian veterans did not transform the postwar landscape in the same way as their Serbian counterparts. It is unsurprising that there are far fewer monuments or commemorative plaques in postwar Croatia than in Serbia given what is known about the relative material and human costs in these regions.[4] This shortfall means that the historian is faced with the challenging task of measuring and explaining what appears to be a "Croatian silence" surrounding discourses on the war. But while the Croatian case study is certainly dwarfed in terms of the volume and range of primary sources by its Serbian counterpart, the trail is not completely cold. A number of former Croatian soldiers did form or join veterans' societies; their records are a key source for gauging the impact of the war. Some veterans even used literature and the printed word to interpret and communicate their wartime and postwar experiences, including one ex-soldier who would write a minor masterpiece based on his experiences of barracks life during hostilities. This chapter will focus primarily on these veterans' stories, as well as official documents, to reconstruct the story of Croatia's war as told in Yugoslavia. The impact of the conflict on men in Croatia should be understood as a series of fragments, dissimilar to one another, but linked through a shared sense of hardship, disappointment in and distrust of the government, and set against the overwhelming primacy of Serbia's war narrative in postwar Yugoslav culture.

The Invalid Question

A good place to start is with Franjo Meštrić and his fellow disabled veterans at the Metropol Cinema. They represented a small fraction of the thousands of Croatian men who had returned from the war seriously or permanently injured. Often all that linked these men in Yugoslavia was their shared fate as *ratni invalidi* (war invalids), and so it is here that the complexity and diversity of the impact of the war in Croatia is most evident. Accurate data about the number of disabled veterans in Croatia immediately after the war is difficult to trace. Representatives of their veteran organization offered a figure of approximately forty thousand.[5] The Jubilee Anthology of Serbs, Croats, and Slovenes, published in 1929, gave a figure closer to twenty thousand.[6] The veterans' society, of course, had reason to exaggerate their number in order to gain public sympathy.

Whatever the figure, the men were mostly ill-served by their veterans' organization, whose history in the postwar period is marked by divisive internal squabbling, financial mismanagement, and tricky relations with disabled veterans of the Serbian army. A small group with never more than nine thousand members,[7] the Society of War Invalids was unable to unite even its modest membership behind a coherent plan of action. For example, an initial flirtation with Communism, apparently inspired by disabled veterans who had fought in revolutionary Russia, proved disastrous. The emancipatory rhetoric of the Bolsheviks was attractive to many former soldiers in post-Habsburg Croatia, and we will see that this appeal was not restricted to disabled veterans. The society's raison d'être, however, was to negotiate with the government for a better financial deal for their members, and radical ideology did not sit well with that aim. Nor, for that matter, did their fellow disabled veterans from Serbia take kindly to talk of a revolution that would undermine their wartime efforts for the "liberation and unification" of all South Slavs. By 1922, Communism had been discarded and a new current had surfaced in the society, favoring a more moderate line and better relations with Serbian ex-soldiers. Nevertheless, disagreements between the Serbian and Croatian veterans did not evaporate as soon as the latter dropped their Bolshevik sympathies. Minor disagreements over articles in the draft of a law on disabled veterans led to larger rifts between the two groups, symptomatic of the gulf that often separated Serbian and non-Serbian veterans in Yugoslavia.[8]

That gulf was caused in part by the lack of integration in Yugoslavia's legal and political structure manifested in the absence of a single law pertaining to financial benefits for ex-soldiers. Croatian veterans were still being paid (less generous) Habsburg pensions and benefits, while their Serbian counterparts received money according to Serbian law. This meant that the passing of a unified law for all Yugoslav disabled veterans was of paramount importance for these men.

To this end, and at the initiative of the Croats, the two societies put aside their differences and worked together at the end of 1922 to lobby the government and demonstrate outside the Yugoslav parliament building, the Skupština, in Belgrade. Despite the concern of Croatian veterans that the focus of their action might be obscured by the Serbian contingent's desire to add a celebratory note to the occasion (the fourth anniversary of the creation of the Yugoslav kingdom coincided with the protest), the demonstration went well.[9] Thousands of disabled veterans were joined on the streets of Belgrade by former volunteers and civil servants, two groups who empathized with the plight of the wounded men and who also felt that they had been neglected by the government. The national press also raised the veterans' profile. The Zagreb-based daily *Obzor* (Horizon), for example, reported favorably on the demonstration and chided the government for neglecting its responsibilities to the war wounded.[10] This was encouraging: besides the concrete goal of getting their benefits law passed, the soldiers' protest had a subsidiary aim of raising their profile among the general public in Yugoslavia. This second point reflects the anxiety many Croatian veterans, especially disabled veterans, felt about becoming "invisible" in a postwar society that was reluctant to acknowledge their sacrifice, since it had not been made for "liberation and unification."

The demonstration was successful in raising the profile of the "invalid question," albeit only temporarily. The bureaucracy of government, however, proved far less responsive. Ministers' words of encouragement and their promises to find a solution to the "invalid question" were rendered moot when the cabinet was dissolved at the end of December. The government of Nikola Pašić had failed to weather what would be one of a number of storms to wrack the politics of the interwar kingdom. The frustration of disabled veterans who derided the ministers as "national bloodsuckers" is understandable: they had lobbied a lame duck government entirely without profit.[11] It was a frustration shared by many in the interwar period, further proof of the paralysis that marked political life in the kingdom and something essential for understanding the context of veterans' demands.[12]

In fact, arguably the most decisive action the government took on the "invalid question" in the interwar period was to relieve themselves of the duty of care of a large number of disabled veterans at the end of the 1920s. The severity of the financial crisis in Yugoslavia was reflected in large budgetary cutbacks at the Ministry of Social Policy. New and stricter parameters were set for classifying veterans as disabled. The sightless, for example, were no longer part of the "invalid question" in Yugoslavia, resulting in a number of Croatian veterans being told they must leave a school for the blind in Zagreb.[13] The shift in policy was the nadir of what had become a downward trajectory for many disabled veterans in Croatia. As with disabled veterans in other parts of Europe, initial hopes gave way to disappointment and despair, as optimistic official promises made immediately after the war proved impossible to realize.[14]

A large part of the "invalid question" had always been "who should be considered an invalid?" and as a corollary, "what responsibility does the government have to its invalids?"[15] That last point was of particular sensitivity in the Croatian case. Although efforts were made to put veterans of all nationalities on equal terms, the treatment of Franjo Meštrić was probably not an isolated example.[16] As for the former question, by the end of the decade sophisticated calculations by medical experts about "percentages of invalidity" became less relevant than simple fiscal expediency: the government hoped that these men would be cared for by their families rather than by the state.

For Josip Pavičić, a talented writer and an amputee who had lost a leg fighting in Galicia, that hope was an illusion. His poignant stories about "invalid life" in Croatia, first published together under the title *Memento* (Monument) (1931), gave the reader a sense of the ineluctable fate of postwar disabled veterans. Pavičić's protagonists limped through an indifferent or even hostile terrain when they returned home after the war, ignored by the rest of society and by the competent authorities. Nor did Pavičić find any camaraderie among fellow disabled veterans housed in specially adopted homes and schools. The company of other physically and psychically maimed men merely compounded their misery. The way out of these "invalid catacombs" was most frequently suicide, "with a bullet, a knife, with poison."[17] It was a process that Pavičić called "silent liquidation," a tragedy that was primarily personal, although it was also to a certain extent national. The disabled veteran faced a personal crisis since he confronted the postwar world on his own, with no solace from his fellow veterans or from the rest of society. But this tragedy also had a national component, since the sacrifice of the Croatian disabled veteran was less valid, "invalid" as it were, in a state liberated and united by soldiers of the Serbian army.

The Volunteer Question

The two notions of sacrifice, personal and national, were also aligned very differently for Croatian veterans who had fought as volunteers in the Serbian army during the war, a category of men who often found common cause with disabled veterans. The volunteer movement, however, was more coherent and had a clearer understanding of its new role in Yugoslavia. Unlike disabled veterans, former volunteers were not drawn from such disparate prewar and wartime strands. Soldiers of the wartime volunteer movement had been recruited from the ranks of émigré South Slavs throughout the world and from Habsburg POWs captured by the Allies. The majority were recruited from POW camps in Russia, and most were ethnic or Habsburg Serbs. Nevertheless, volunteering proved attractive too for many Croatian (and Slovenian) reserve officers who had been conscripted into the Habsburg army during the war. As a result, these nationalities, while an overall minority, were overrepresented in the officer corps of the division.[18] A number of these men had sought a radical solution to the South Slav question before the war. For them, the transition from Habsburg to Yugoslav Croatia represented the realization of a cherished utopia. Many of the volunteers had protested with disabled veterans outside the Skupština, and together they formed a "Warriors' party" that contested—and was annihilated—in the national elections of 1923. Thus there existed a level of commonality through which veterans were united in the Yugoslav kingdom, based perhaps on material hardship and a sense that the state should take at least partial responsibility for their wellbeing.

In fact the state was bound to its volunteers in more concrete terms than it was to its disabled veterans. The wartime Serbian government, in conjunction with Habsburg South Slav émigrés on the Yugoslav Committee (JO),[19] had promised those who fought as volunteers during the war a parcel of land (five hectares for combatants) in a putative postwar land reform. The manner in which this redistribution was carried out in Yugoslavia seems to be further evidence (along with the unedifying experience of disabled veterans at the Skupština) of a political bureaucracy that was highly dysfunctional. In order to qualify for the land allowance, volunteers needed an official certificate of verification. By 1926, almost forty thousand such certificates had been issued, despite the Ministry of the Army and Navy's assertion that only just over twenty-six thousand volunteers had stood shoulder to shoulder with the Serbian army at Salonika.[20]

Whether corruption or incompetence, it was shabby politics and anathema to what many volunteers had fought for during the war, for unlike disabled veterans such as Josip Pavičić, these ex-soldiers were proud of their veteran identity and were more certain of the value of their sacrifice in the new state. They had made this point clear in a memorandum issued in 1923 by their society, the Union of Volunteers. The document, addressed publicly to the government, read like a quasi-manifesto, admonishing Yugoslav parliamentary politics for its corruption as well as parliamentarians for their self-serving egoism and neglect of the volunteers (the fear of becoming invisible in the new state was again an important motivating factor). The veterans suggested that they had an important role in the government's land reform and policy of colonization in newly acquired territories (notably Macedonia and Kosovo, but also Vojvodina). According to the memorandum the ex-soldiers sent to these regions were to act as latter day *grenzer* regiments, consolidating Yugoslav territory and providing security to other colonists. As a precedent for this policy, the memorandum cited the ongoing colonization of Slovakia by former Czech legionaries.[21]

The volunteers saw themselves as Yugoslav warriors, committed to fighting for the new state in the postwar period just as they had done during the war, offended by the chicanery of day-to-day parliamentary politics in Yugoslavia. Indeed, the "Yugoslav warrior" proved to be an attractive figure for many. The

Organization of Yugoslav Nationalists (ORJUNA) for example, idolized this militarist image and claimed (not entirely without basis) that many former volunteers could be found in the ranks of their movement.[22] ORJUNA responded to real or perceived threats against Yugoslavia in the 1920s by forming uniformed "shock battalions" that used Fascist-style violence against anyone considered to be opposed to Yugoslav unity (most frequently Communists and followers of Stjepan Radić's Croatian Republican Peasant Party).[23] This was "postwar violence" in the sense that many members of ORJUNA shock battalions had been too young to fight in the war, but now wanted to prove they were just as tough as the battle-hardened volunteers they admired.[24]

Volunteers also inspired more moderate pro-Yugoslav forces in Croatia, such as the literary gazette *Savremenik* (The Contemporary), organ of the Croatian Literary Society, and the journal *Nova Evropa* (The New Europe). The editors of these publications saw in the volunteer movement proof that Croats had opposed Austria-Hungary during the war, and that many of them had desired union with Serbia long before 1918. This was a means of drawing a veil over the complicated question of South Slav loyalty to the Habsburgs. There was no ambiguity about postwar transition in Croatia for these publications (nor for ORJUNA). The path that took South Slavs out of Austria-Hungary and into Yugoslavia might not have been smooth, but its final point had been desired and sought after. Here was a chance for the Croat experience to be reconciled with the Serbian trope of "liberation and unification." In fact, the myth of the Yugoslav volunteer was of even more use to Yugoslavists, since it eschewed the nationally exclusive appeal of Serbia's war narrative for a broader story of South Slav struggle and emancipation.

Volunteers themselves were not entirely passive in the process of their own mythologization. Along with the work of the Union of Volunteers, a number of volunteer veterans published memoirs and fictional accounts of their time in the corps, creating a small cycle of "volunteer literature" in the postwar period.[25] Hardly enough to fill a single book shelf, it was at least more substantial than Josip Pavičić's solitary contribution to the invalid genre. Certain constellations can be traced in the moral universe presented by former volunteers in these accounts. The Bolshevik revolution was typically presented as a tragedy that unleashed violence and heartbreak onto the Russian people. This was perhaps a reflection of the fear and hostility many felt toward the Bolshevik revolution and the danger of it spreading to Yugoslavia. In these soldiers' accounts, however, the élan of the volunteer division in Russia was immune to the Bolshevik infection (though in reality many volunteers fought for the Bolsheviks). Nor had Habsburg spies and other anti-Serbian forces infiltrated the volunteer movement (again part of the myth, since maintaining discipline and morale, especially among non-Serbian volunteers, had been problematic). The predominance of Croatian and Slovenian volunteers in the officer corps was perceived as evidence that the ideology of South Slav unification was deeply entrenched among the non-Serbian soldiers.

This highly teleological vision, culminating in the "liberation and unification" of all South Slavs, was shared by the volunteer movement's outstanding figure in the interwar period, a Croat from Bakar named Lujo Lovrić. As remarkable as this veteran's biography is, there are flashes of typicality in it that help us to understand the postwar trajectory of Croatian ex-volunteers. Lovrić was attracted to the movement for South Slav unification while a student in Rijeka, impressed by the figure of the journalist and politician Frano Supilo, and a correspondent of the Bosnian author (and later Nobel laureate) Ivo Andrić.[26] Due to his involvement in radical student groups Lovrić was imprisoned by Habsburg authorities at the outbreak of the war, before being released and conscripted as a reserve officer into the army. He deserted in Russia and volunteered to fight with the Serbian army, seeing action in Dobruja and receiving an injury that permanently blinded him.

As a Croat who had fought in the Serbian army and as (until the policy shift of 1929) one of Yugoslavia's disabled veterans, Lovrić was active among both these veterans' groups in the postwar period. A period at Saint Dunstan's School for the Blind in London and a friendship with the school's English founder, Sir Arthur Pearson, had convinced Lovrić that a similar institution should be established back home.[27] He was instrumental in founding a School for the Blind in Zemun (1919), which provided care and retraining for disabled veterans.

Lovrić remained concerned with the "invalid question" throughout his life, but significantly it was as a volunteer that he was most celebrated. His responsibilities as leader of the Union of Volunteers took him across Europe to meet with Czechoslovak legionaries and French *ancien combattants*. In the 1930s, his visit to a congress of German veterans led to a meeting with Adolf Hitler. He had a number of audiences with King Alexander, and after the king's assassination in 1934, remained a supporter of the monarch's vision of an integral Yugoslavia (as did most former volunteers). Lovrić was determined after 1918 to devote all his energies to the (Yugoslav) national cause, claiming that "every sacrifice and misfortune that could possibly arrive could not surpass that which has already happened."[28] Like Josip Pavičić this former soldier's disability had marked him with a permanent sense of a veteran identity but, unlike Pavičić, Lovrić as an ex-volunteer and hero of the Battle of Dobruja was not reduced to melancholy and despair. His personal sacrifice was meaningful since it was related to a national sacrifice made for Yugoslavia. There were very few Croatian veterans who could reconcile their sacrifice to the Yugoslav national cause in this way. For the handful of Croatian men who had, like Lovrić, pursued the Yugoslav cause in Austria-Hungary before the war and on the battlefield, a position of privilege and perceived responsibility awaited them in Yugoslavia, and they expected their wartime sacrifice to be repaid by the new state.

Lovrić, then, was a volunteer first and a disabled veteran second, and the same hierarchical relationship existed at a broader level between volunteer veterans and Croatian disabled veterans in Yugoslavia. Both these groups wanted to be acknowledged and (just as importantly) to be compensated in material and financial terms. Their point of departure was the perception of their sacrifice in Yugoslavia. Lovrić drew a positive message from his experience as a volunteer and even from his disability, while Pavičić drew no such message from his. With this distinction in mind, one can start to account for the "Croatian silence" surrounding the commemoration of World War I in Yugoslavia. Disabled veterans in Croatia had no great victories to celebrate and nothing to show for their sacrifice after the war, aside from their injuries. This feeling of emptiness was made more acute by the Serbian and Yugoslav narrative of "liberation and unification." Perhaps disabled veterans like Pavičić simply experienced the transition from war to peace as the evaporation of a system that they had fought for reluctantly, and were therefore disinclined to commemorate after the war.

Former Austro-Hungarian Officers of Croatian Descent

At the 1920 Zagreb meeting of disabled veterans, this disinclination was articulated by the very next speaker to take the floor after Franjo Mestrić. A former Austrian officer named Batalo complained that

> We were soldiers, and we did not ask why, since we were raised as higher-ranking Austrian officers. We fought because we had to … You did not want to fight, but you had to. If you did not you would be shot.[29]

Batalo's presence at the Metropol Cinema that night exposes yet another current within the heterogeneous Society of War Invalids: Croats who had served not as conscripts but as professional soldiers, as officers, in the Habsburg army. It was understandable that members of the Society of War Invalids, faced with official hostility as former soldiers of a defeated enemy, would seek to decrease their own level of agency as Habsburg soldiers. In reality, there had been a number of high-ranking officers of Croatian descent in the Habsburg army. The governor general of Bosnia-Herzegovina, for example, Stjepan Sarkotić, was a Croat from the Lika region. In occupied Poland, the position of governor general was held by Antun Lipoščak, and in Serbia, for a short period, by Johann Salis von Sewis, both Croats.[30] Further down the ranks, many Croatian soldiers had fought with distinction as commissioned officers in the imperial army.

At the end of the war, military and political leaders in Yugoslavia were faced with the delicate task of integrating these former Habsburg officers of Croatian descent into the new Yugoslav army. The success of this policy and the experience of non-Serbian officers in the Yugoslav army are areas that require further research.³¹ Official correspondence suggests that problems existed in relations between Serbian and non-Serbian officers. In March 1920, for example, General Branko Jovanović of the Fourth Armored Division (Zagreb) sent a classified memorandum to the High Command in which he voiced concerns about the integration of ex-Habsburg officers into the new corps. These officers, he noted, had filed a number of complaints regarding their status in the new army, including being passed over for promotion, and being treated "tactlessly" by their Serbian colleagues.³² It seems highly unlikely that Croatian officers escaped any kind of prejudice and hostility from veterans of the Serbian army, given the intensity of fighting between Austria-Hungary and Serbia, and the latter's experience of defeat, occupation, and violence at the hands of the former. Then again, Croatian and Serbian officers hailed from very different military traditions, and there were bound to be misunderstandings and frustrations in amalgamating those traditions. In measuring the success of this policy, it should also be noted that most Croatian officer veterans remained in the officer corps of the Yugoslav army in the 1920s.

Those Habsburg Croatian officers who opted out of the Yugoslav army, or who lost their commissions, flowed through channels similar to those of Croatian disabled veterans. Their particular veterans' organization, the Retired Officers' Society, was set up in Zagreb in 1920 as an association of ex-soldiers formed essentially for charitable purposes. Their activities were restricted to fundraising events such as tea parties, often co-organized with the Society of Croatian Women (Hrvatska žena). The gathering together of so many former high-ranking Habsburg officers in one place, however, was an offense unbearable to some. ORJUNA was alerted to the existence of the society and stormed one of the ex-officers' "family evenings" in 1922, brandishing clubs and pistols. The Yugoslav nationalists were particularly appalled at the presence of Johann Salis von Sewis at the meeting, former governor general of occupied Serbia and now president of the Retired Officers' Society. An ORJUNA leader would later describe the action as "the first counter-strike against the shameful remnants of Hungaro-Austrian butchery."³³ For this movement, ex-officers such as Salis von Sewis were the villains of the South Slav wartime drama as much as volunteers were the heroes. But there was greater significance in the attack for ORJUNA. The culture of "liberation and unification" violently adhered to by the Yugoslav nationalist movement often differentiated Croatian veterans on account of where they had fought. The reason for ORJUNA's targeting of Salis von Sewis was his (brief) tenure in occupied Serbia during the war. Croatian soldiers who had been involved in this occupation were more likely to be identified as enemies of "liberation and unification" than Croats who, for example, had fought against Italians on the Isonzo front.

Besides the ORJUNA attack, the Retired Officers' Society received unwanted attention in official circles. In 1923 Yugoslavia's interior minister, Milorad Vujičić, made aware of the Retired Officers' Society after the fracas with ORJUNA, insisted that the organization be dissolved. In a revealing slip, Vujičić incorrectly identified the society as "The Union of Officers of the Former Austro-Hungarian Army" and stated in a letter to local authorities in Zagreb that "it is an anomaly that they [the ex-officers], under the name of a former state which acted against our liberation, associate to this day." The authorities in Zagreb, who had carried out their own investigation and concluded that the group was harmless, nevertheless complied with the minister's request.[34]

In a certain sense, the ex-officers were the antithesis of former volunteers in Yugoslavia. As much as men like Lovrić were feted as Yugoslav warriors fighting before the creation of Yugoslavia, the veterans in the Retired Officers' Society were seen in some circles as unreconstructed Habsburgs lingering on after the monarchy's demise. The experience of postwar transition for these two groups of veterans was also poles apart. The men who were now national heroes as ex-volunteers in Yugoslavia had been persecuted and imprisoned in Austria-Hungary. Ex-officers, on the other hand, had suffered a severe loss of status as they went from being imperial officers in Austria-Hungary to retirees, distrusted and attacked, after the war. The attitude of Milorad Vujičić toward the Retired Officers' Society had much in common with that of the official who told Meštrić to "go to Karl": both saw these Croatian veterans as former soldiers of a defeated enemy. Ex-officers, however, were less convincing when they tried to remove themselves from their wartime records, or portray their wartime sacrifice for Austria-Hungary as sustained under duress. The records of men such as Antun Lipošćak, who also served as the first president of the Retired Officers' Society, and of Salis von Sewis were proof that some Croats had indeed served willingly for Austria-Hungary.

This was certainly also the case for Stjepan Sarkotić, whose wartime record as governor general in Bosnia-Herzegovina—especially his suppression of Serbian cultural, religious, and political elites in the "Banjaluka Trials" of 1916—excluded him from admission to the Yugoslav army. In any case, professional soldiering on behalf of Yugoslavia was not a path Sarkotić wished to take. Soon after the end of the war he emigrated, eventually settling in Vienna and holding court with a coterie of like-minded ex-officers and émigrés who refused to reside in the new state.[35] In his stubborn refusal to accept the Serbian victory and the creation of Yugoslavia, Sarkotić became a figure of talismanic importance to anti-Serbian and anti-Yugoslav forces in the interwar period, including Ante Pavelić, the future Ustasha *poglavnik* (leader). After 1929, Pavelić used ex-Habsburg officers such as Gustav Perčec, Mirko Puk, and Slavko Kvaternik to train the soldiers of his paramilitary terrorist group, the Ustashe, formed for the purpose of violently wresting Croatia away from Yugoslavia. It is not difficult to see how this movement, in its thorough rejection of Yugoslavism and of union with Serbia, appealed to a number of former ex-Habsburg officers of Croatian descent who resented their loss of status. During the Ustashe's brief reign in the Fascist-backed Independent State of Croatia (NDH) during World War II, cultural and military elites sought to restore the Great War sacrifice of the Croatian soldier to its rightful place (a process comparable to that among the Magyars of Transylvania as Franz Horváth shows).[36] In doing so, they were attempting to erase the interwar legacy of "liberation and unification."

For former officers such as these, 1918 and the creation of Yugoslavia was not a *tabula rasa* where they had to radically rethink their national and political affiliations. Because officers like Sarkotić had a dual loyalty both to Austria and to Croatia, unlike Austrian officers they did not experience the collapse of the Habsburg monarchy as an apocalyptic event. Sarkotić had fought during the war partly on behalf of Croatian national interests. The defeat and demise of Austria-Hungary merely shifted the contours of this struggle; it was previously fought against the Allies, and now it was against Yugoslavia. Again, there is a parallel, albeit an inverted one, with former volunteers. Their loyalty to South Slav unity preceded even the war, was intensified through their experience fighting with the volunteer corps, and was apparent in the work of the Union of Volunteers and of men like Lujo Lovrić in the postwar period.

Miroslav Krleža and *The Croatian God Mars*

By now it could be concluded that upon closer scrutiny, the impact of World War I on Croatian men defies a single meaningful interpretation, or that generalization at a national level is impossible. Meštrić was standing before a mixed crowd at the Metropol Cinema, and there is little that links men such as Lujo Lovrić and Stjepan Sarkotić, aside perhaps from mutual antipathy. The idea of a generic Croatian veteran whose wartime cause was coherent and whose postwar identity was palpable may have only existed in the minds of men such as Milorad Vujičić, the official who insulted Meštrić, or the Serbian officers who were not comfortable serving alongside their Croatian counterparts.

The men cited as examples in this chapter are typical only of certain subcategories of Croatian veteran. Writers such as Pavičić and Lovrić sought to interpret their own wartime experiences, but in doing so they also depicted the story of their fellow disabled veterans or ex-volunteers. Sarkotić wrote in the postwar period with a political agenda; nevertheless, he became a beacon for a small group of ex-officers who refused to accept the legitimacy of Yugoslavia and their own diminished status within it. Each of these men may have been representative of a "type" of veteran, but not all Croatian soldiers returned from the front wounded, and still fewer had served as volunteers in the Serbian army or as high ranking Habsburg officers. In fact, the vast majority of Croatian veterans were peasants who had been conscripted into the Habsburg army during the war. The high level of illiteracy among these men meant that they were badly placed to leave traces of their war experiences in literature or memoirs.

It was partly because of this that Miroslav Krleža, the leading Croatian author of the interwar period, felt compelled to write a series of short stories inspired by his experience as a conscript soldier in the Habsburg army during the war. Krleža's route to conscription had been circuitous, and at various points in his prewar and wartime career he had come close to falling into each of the veteran groups we have examined. He had been an outstanding pupil at a cadet school in Pécs, in southern Hungary, and was awarded a scholarship to study at the Ludoviceum in Budapest. His superiors considered him good officer material, noting that he was "diligent, honest, and serious," even "ambitious."[37] Krleža's loyalties, however, were to shift dramatically in the years preceding the outbreak of war. By 1914 he had made two trips to Belgrade with the intention of volunteering for the Serbian army, the first in May 1912, shortly before the First Balkan War, the second in the summer of 1913. On the first occasion he was merely turned away, on the second he was arrested by the Serbian army and sent back to Austria-Hungary whereupon he was expelled from the Ludoviceum. At the outbreak of the war, Krleža was neither a Habsburg officer nor a South Slav volunteer, but a civilian living in Zagreb. He remained out of the war until conscripted into the army in December 1915, serving in Galicia, before returning home to Zagreb at the beginning of 1917 suffering from influenza and nascent tuberculosis. Although not a disabled veteran himself, he had contact with wounded soldiers working at the Narodna zaštita (National Protection) in Zagreb, where he was employed until the end of the war. Krleža's experiences were in many ways untypical, but he had had brushes with many sides of military life: with the Habsburg officer corps, with the Serbian army, with wounded soldiers, and with peasant conscripts.

Krleža became active in the Croatian capital's literary scene upon his return from the front, and a collection of short stories about barracks life during the war were published together in 1922, under the (ironic) title *Hrvatski Bog Mars* (The Croatian God Mars). Unlike its forerunner *Le Feu* by the French veteran Henri Barbusse, *The Croatian God Mars* was free of visceral descriptions of death and horror, perhaps partly because Krleža had not been under fire himself during the war. Like Barbusse, however, Krleža wrote as a "moral witness" of the war, and his intention was to record its impact on Croatia. He emphasized the reality of the "Croatian veteran" about whom one could write meaningfully. The vast majority of Croatian soldiers who had fought for Austria-Hungary during the war were peasant conscripts who, according to Krleža, had fought and died defending the imperial system that had enslaved them. These peasant protagonists were living in the "thick fog" of feudal times, accepting conscription into the "Habsburg war" with indifference, since "it was not the first nor the last misfortune to befall these people."[38] His fiction shared the same attitude toward the meaninglessness of the war experience as Pavičić's, but the latter restricted his scope to disabled veterans in the postwar period. Krleža's ambition was greater, writing about the war as a national tragedy. Croatian peasants had died for Austria-Hungary and absolutely nothing had been gained; indeed nothing could have been gained whatever the outcome of the war, since Austria-Hungary's cause was alien to that of the Croatian nation.

For Krleža then, Croatian officers such as Sarkotić were deluded if they believed that fighting for Austria-Hungary could advance Croatian national life. In *The Croatian God Mars,* such officers were satirized with particular ferocity. They were men who had been so saturated by regimental history and Habsburg victories long past that they were blind to the futility of the present conflict, of the reality of the doomed monarchy, and of the hatred in which they were held by their soldiers.[39] Nor did Krleža accept the narrative of "liberation and unification" in the 1920s, despite his hostility toward Austria-Hungary and Croatia's role in the "Habsburg war." Despite his earlier admiration for Serbia, he also rejected the "Vidovdan cult of defeat and catastrophe" as a "phantasmagoria" that had been rendered obsolete by the experience of Croatian soldiers during the Great War.[40] Similarly, the postwar culture of South Slav unity espoused by, *inter alia,* former volunteers, was branded as "the new lie."[41] For Krleža, the prewar Habsburg and the postwar Yugoslav elites were both guilty of neglecting or exploiting the peasant masses, the men who had died by the hundreds of thousands for a foreign cause during the Great War. They had been able to do this because the unlettered, unenlightened peasants had no voice of their own, and it was for this reason that Krleža, by writing *The Croatian God Mars,* intended to tell the story of their war.

Unfortunately, Krleža's veteran constituency, the former soldiers on whose behalf he claimed to speak, was both the largest (80 percent of all Croat veterans) and the least historically visible. There was, for example, no veterans' organization for former Croatian peasant conscripts. Croatian peasants were, however, given a voice in the political sphere at the end of the war. The hugely restricted prewar franchise under which Croatian peasants lived in the empire was replaced with universal manhood suffrage at the end of the war. This was also part of the project of "liberation and unification," part of the political and constitutional legacy of the Serbian kingdom that was bequeathed to all South Slavs after 1918. Throughout the 1920s, Croatian peasants voted uniformly for Stjepan Radić and the Croatian Peasant Party. Like Krleža, Radić felt that Croats had been forced during the war to fight for a foreign power. He also shared Krleža's view that those on the lowest rungs of Croatian society had suffered the most, claiming that "this was really a peasant and workers' war, in so far as all of its suffering and horrors were most acutely and most terribly felt by the poor peasants and workers."[42] For Radić, like so many across Europe, the lesson of World War I was that wars should never be fought again. He preached a gospel of anti-militarism and pacifism throughout the Croatian countryside in the 1920s, advising Croatian peasants to ignore conscription into the Yugoslav army since it, just like the Habsburg army, compelled Croats to serve for interests that were alien to their own.[43]

Continued Negotiation with Identity

Fragmented, overshadowed, and often frustratingly oblique, the impact of the war in Croatia should not be dismissed as insignificant. The various fates of Croatian veterans still reveal much about the impact of that conflict and the legacy of the Habsburg monarchy in the successor states. Indeed, the differences between men such as Josip Pavičić, Lujo Lovrić, Stjepan Sarkotić, and Miroslav Krleža serve as an injunction against historians who would view the various nationalities of the Habsburg empire as homogenous units. It seems that in the Croatian case study, social and cultural as well as national affiliations were important. Perhaps one of the most surprising findings of the Croatian case study is the complete lack of commemoration for the defunct empire. Nevertheless, all of the men studied in this chapter had some sense of affiliation to Croatia and some notion of Croatian sacrifice during the war, which went deeper than loyalty to the monarchy. Some, like Sarkotić, felt that Croats should fight to remain within the imperial framework. Others, like Lovrić, felt that it was within a unified South Slav state that Croatian national life would find its fullest expression. Then there were men like Krleža, skeptical of any end to national exploitation and oppression, whether Croatia was Habsburg or Yugoslav. It is best to think of the postwar transition and the impact of the war in Croatia not as a complete re-configuration or as a radical break with the past, but as a continued negotiation over a contested and disintegrated national identity. This negotiation had taken place within the Habsburg monarchy, and would now take place within Yugoslavia. In this sense, there is continuity between the prewar and the postwar periods: in each case Croats were trying to find their place within a larger political and social entity.

The impact of the war was also dynamic in the interwar period. The vicissitudes of Yugoslav and European history allowed for new meanings and interpretations of combat experience to emerge. For example, Radić's assassination in the Skupština in 1928 led to a reconfiguration of his pacifist program and that of the Croatian Peasant Party. Radić's successor, Vlatko Maček, allowed for paramilitary formations known as the "Peasant Guard" (Seljačka zaštita) and the "Civic Guard" (Gradjanska zaštita) to escort him at party meetings. These formations were comprised in large part of former Habsburg officers of Croatian descent, and were a consequence of the alienation and hostility of many Croats toward the Yugoslav state in the wake of Radić's assassination and King Alexander's royal dictatorship. The Ustashe were an extreme (and of course, tiny) manifestation of this rejection. Once again, a number of ex-officers came out of retirement to serve in the ranks of this movement.

At the other end of the political spectrum, there were those Croatian soldiers who gravitated toward Communism in the interwar period, many of whom had fought and been captured in Russia and had been incidental witnesses of or active participants in the Bolshevik revolution. Among these was a noncommissioned officer named Josip Broz, the man who would become Tito. The victory of his supranational Partisan movement at the end of World War II meant that the second Yugoslavia, unlike the first, had a truly Yugoslav foundational narrative. One convert to the movement was the disabled veteran and author Josip Pavičić. His stories, which had been censored by the regime of Prince Paul during the 1930s, were republished at the end of World War II, under the title *In Red Letters*. The new edition included four stories about the Partisans and the anti-Fascist struggle, and a new preface by the author in which he explained how he had found a war worthy of sacrifice. Pavičić noted how disabled veterans in the Yugoslav kingdom "were for the capitalist order too much of an encumbrance, ballast which needed to be cast away so as not to hamper the rise of their balloon. And so the ballast was cast away."[44]

Miroslav Krleža, of course, would go on to become the leading literary figure of his generation and an author with an international reputation. His decision not to join the Partisans and to remain in Zagreb during World War II provoked anger and surprise from many, and remains one of the great mysteries of the writer's life, since Krleža had been a member of the Communist Party of Yugoslavia in the interwar period and a vocal supporter of the movement. The poet Vladimir Nazor, although not a Communist, did join the anti-Fascist resistance. He was reported to have asked Krleža why, as a Communist, he had not fought with the International Brigades in Spain. "'I have a horror of death, corpses, and stench,' replied the veteran. 'I had enough of it in Galicia during World War One.'"[45] In the final analysis there is little doubt that, beneath the war myths, stories, and foundational narratives of whatever ideological dint, there were many Croatian veterans of the Great War who felt exactly the same way.

John Paul Newman is lecturer in twentieth-century European History at Maynooth University, Ireland. He has been a postdoctoral fellow at University College Dublin and a research fellow at the Imre Kertesz Kolleg in Jena. He is the author of *Yugoslavia in the Shadow of War: Veterans and the Limits of State Building, 1903–1945* (2015), and editor (with Julia Eichenberg) of *The Great War and Veterans' Internationalism* (2013).

Notes

1. Croatian State Archives, Zagreb (Hrvatski Državni Arhiv: hereafter HDA), fond Pravila društava, fond 4684: "Udruženje ratnih invalida na području Hrvatske, Slavonije, Istre, Međumurja."
2. See also Danilo Šarenac's excellent monograph *Top, vojnik i sećanje—prvi svetski rat i Srbija 1914-2009* (Belgrade, 2014).
3. On the experience of Habsburg soldiers of Croat descent during and after the war, see John Paul Newman, *Yugoslavia in the Shadow of War: Veterans and the Limits of State Building, 1903-1945* (Cambridge, 2015); and Filip Hameršak, *Tamna strana Marsa: Hrvatska autobiografija I svjetski rat* (Zagreb, 2013). See also the unpublished doctoral dissertation of Richard B. Spence, "Yugoslavs, the Austro-Hungarian Army, and the First World War," PhD diss., Santa Barbara 1981. Constructions of gender and masculinity in relation to the war are addressed by Melissa Bokovoy: see Melissa Bokovoy, "Croatia," in *Women, Gender, and Fascism in Europe 1919–1945*, ed. Kevin Passmore (Manchester, 2003), 111–24. Croatian military history during the period was covered, incompletely, by Slavko Pavičić in *Hrvatska ratna i vojna povijest* (Zagreb, 1943). For political developments during the war, see Bogdan Krizman, *Raspad Austro-Ugarske i stvarnje jugoslovenske države* (Zagreb, 1977) and Bogdan Krizman, *Hrvatska u prvom svjetskom ratu* (Zagreb, 1989).
4. According to the historian Jozo Tomasevich, Serbian and Montenegrin losses for World War I and the two Balkan wars which preceded it amounted to between 750,000 and 800,000. Tomasevich put the figure of Habsburg South Slav losses at about 150,000. See Jozo Tomasevich, *Peasants, Politics, and Economic Change in Yugoslavia* (Stanford, 1955), 222–23.
5. *Ratni Invalid* (Zagreb), 11 November 1922. For a detailed analysis of figures in the light of few reliable statistical records, see Ljubomir Petrović, "Diskriminacija invalida u jugoslovenskom društvu 1918–1941. godine. Oblici socijalne represije nad osobama sa invaliditetom," *Tokovi istorije* 3–4, (2003): 25–27.
6. *Jubilarni zbornik života i rada Kraljevine Srba, Hrvata, i Slovenaca 1918–1928* (Belgrade, 1928), 675–78.
7. *Ratni invalid*, 1 July 1922.
8. See, for example, ibid., 1 March 1922.
9. Ibid., 15 December 1922.
10. *Obzor*, 3 December 1922.
11. HDA, Pravila društava, 4684: "Udruženje ratnih invalida."
12. See Dejan Djokić, *Elusive Compromise: A History of Interwar Yugoslavia* (London, 2007).
13. Archive of Yugoslavia, Belgrade (Arhiv Jugoslavije: hereafter AJ), fond 39, "Ministarstvo za socialnu politiku i narodno zdravlje 1919–1941," box 7.
14. See Robert Weldon Whalen, *Bitter Wounds: German Victims of the Great War 1914–1939* (Ithaca, 1984), Joanna Bourke, *Dismembering the Male: Men's Bodies, Britain, and the Great War* (London, 1996).
15. Those were the kind of questions posed by Yugoslavia's first Minister of Social Policy, Vitomir Korać, in a national conference held on the topic of men disabled during the war, in 1919. See AJ, fond 39/7.
16. For example, an official report into the Moslavina school for disabled veterans documented how the school's director had called a Croatian veteran a "kraut whore" in a derogatory reference to his wartime record. The report found that the insult was characteristic of relations between staff and pupils at the school over the years. See ibid.
17. Josip Pavičić, *Crvenim slovima* (Zagreb, 1946), 6.

18. See Ivo Banac, "South Slav POWs in Revolutionary Russia," in *War and Society in East Central Europe: Volume 5: Essays on World War One: Origins and POWs*, ed. Samuel Williamson and Peter Pastor (New York, 1983).
19. The Yugoslav Committee, or JO (in Serbo-Croat *Jugoslovenski odbor*) was established by émigré South Slavs, mainly from Dalmatia, who had left the Habsburg monarchy at the beginning of the war. Its purpose was to promote the cause of Yugoslav unification in Allied circles. It was based in London from 1915 and its most prominent members included Ante Trumbić (as president), Frano Supilo, and Ivan Meštrović.
20. Stanoje Stanojević, writing in *Vidovdan*, 31 January 1926.
21. *Memorandum Saveza dobrovoljaca Kraljevine Srba, Hrvata, i Slovenaca* (Belgrade, 1923).
22. See Niko Bartulović, *Od revolucionarne omladine do Orjune: istorijat jugoslavenskog omladinskog pokreta* (Split, 1925).
23. A detailed survey of the history of ORJUNA is provided by Branislav Gligorijević, "Organizacija jugoslovenskih nacionalista (ORJUNA)," *Istorija XX veka: zbornik radova*, vol. 5 (Belgrade: 1963), 315–96.
24. See Ivan Bošković, "Splitski orjunaški list i Stjepan Radić," *Časopis za suvremenu povijest* 39/1 (2007): 117–32. On this subject see also John Paul Newman, "Post-imperial and Postwar Violence in the South Slav Lands, 1917–1923," *Contemporary European History* 19 (2010): 249–65.
25. See, for example, Dane Hranilović, *Iz zapiska jugoslovenskog dobrovoljaca* (Zagreb, 1922), Ante Kovač, *Impresije iz jedne epohe* (Zagreb, 1923), Lujo Lovrić, *Suzna jesen* (Zagreb, 1922), Lovrić, *Kroz snijegove i magle* (Zagreb, 1923), Slavko Diklić, *Putničke bilješke jugoslovenskog ratnog dobrovoljca: od Dobruže do Soluna preko dalekog Istoka* (Osijek, 1932), Diklić, *Pred olujom: roman jugoslovenskih ratnih dobrovoljaca u Rusiji* (Osijek, 1932).
26. Biographical details from Boris Grbin, *Portret Luje Lovrića* (Zagreb, 1985).
27. Lovrić, *Kroz snijegove i magle*, 80.
28. Ibid., 225.
29. HDA, Pravila društava, 4684, "Udruženje ratnih invalida."
30. For extra light on Salis von Sewis, see Jonathan Gumz, *The Resurrection and Collapse of Empire in Habsburg Serbia, 1914–1918* (Cambridge, 2009).
31. For a critical account of the attempt to create an integrated corps, see Ivo Banac, *The National Question in Yugoslavia: Origins, History, Politics* (Ithaca and London, 1984), 150–52.
32. Mile Bjelajac, *Vojska kraljevine Srba, Hrvata, Slovenaca 1918–1921* (Belgrade, 1988), 95.
33. Niko Bartulović, *Od revolucionarne omladine do Orjune: istorijat jugoslavenskog omladinskog pokreta* (Split, 1925), 79.
34. HDA, Pravila društava, 4998: "Udruga umirovljenih oficira i vojnih činovinika u Hrvatskoj i Slavoniji."
35. See Richard B. Spence, "General Stephan Freiherr Sarkotić von Lovćen and Croatian Nationalism," *Canadian Review of Studies in Nationalism* 17/1–2 (1990): 147–55.
36. On Ustasha cultural politics in the NDH, see Rory Yeomans, *Visions of Annihilation: The Ustasha Regime and the Cultural Politics of Fascism 1941–1945* (Pittsburgh, 2013).
37. Stanko Lasić, *Krleža: Kronologija života i rada* (Zagreb, 1982), 90.
38. Miroslav Krleža, *Hrvatski Bog Mars* (Sarajevo, 1973), 11.
39. For example, the comically named "Rikard Weiserhemb Ritter von Reichlin-Meldegg und Hochenthurm" in the story *The Battle by Bistrica Lesna,* irritated that his Russian counterpart has had the insolence to move grenadiers close to his lines, moves red markers into Bistrica Lesna "as if he was playing chess." In fact, far from executing a *coup de main* against his enemy, he has sent his soldiers to certain death. See ibid., 26.
40. Miroslav Krleža, *Davni dani: Zapisi 1914–1921* (Zagreb, 1954), 130.
41. Lasić, *Krleža*,134–35.

42. Stjepan Radić, "Seljačka stranka na čelu hrvatskog naroda," in *Stjepan Radić: politički spisi, autobiografija, članci, govori, rasprave*, ed. Zvonimir Kulundžić (Zagreb, 1971), 336.
43. Radić's appeal seems to have been successful. In December 1921, for example, the commander of the Sava Division, located in Zagreb and covering Croatia and Slavonia, reported that 56 percent of recruits who had been issued with documents for conscription into the army had failed to report for duty. Republican agitation and Radićist calls for "no more army" were, he felt, the cause of this poor turnout. See HDA, fond 137, "Pokrajinska za uprava Hrvatske i Slavonija u Zagrebu—Predsjedništvo," box 15.
44. Pavičić, *Crvenim slovima* 6.
45. The exchange is reported by Milovan Djilas in his memoir of World War II, *Wartime* (London, 1980), 303.

Chapter 10

THE SACRIFICED SLOVENIAN MEMORY OF THE GREAT WAR

Petra Svoljšak

World War I was unequivocally an epochal event for Slovenes. The Slovenian writer Ivan Cankar named it "the years of horror": a watershed between two eras, a period that required discussion so that the world could draw the necessary conclusions and prepare itself for a new age.[1] As an active and critical Social Democrat politician, Cankar had already presented a critique of war in a 1913 lecture titled "Slovenes and Yugoslavs," where he defined the Slovenes' fraternity and integration with other South Slav nations. His understanding had sharpened during the Balkan Wars, which he viewed as an inconceivable shedding of "young, luscious blood." But his most scathing criticism was saved for the Habsburg foreign minister Count Berchtold, whose ultimatum to Serbia in July 1914 had driven Austria-Hungary into a "sacred homeland war." Cankar's criticism was shaped at that time by personal experience. Already in the first days of the war, he was charged with spreading anti-state propaganda, arrested, and imprisoned for six weeks at the behest of the military court at Ljubljana Castle. The following year, however, he was drafted in spite of his political unreliability. For a month, in the hinterland in Judenburg, he was able to experience the life of a soldier; he maintained an unrelenting antiwar stance through insubordination, refusing even to touch a bayonet, and allegedly reading Goethe in his room with a cognac in his hand during military training. He later described his impressions of the war in a collection of sketches, "Pictures of Dreams" (*Podobe iz sanj*): how the conflict had produced moral depravity, mass death, unspeakable suffering, but perhaps also hope and redemption.

The war left a deep imprint on Slovenian historical memory. So many Slovenes had participated in the world conflict—as soldiers of the Austro-Hungarian and Italian armies, as prisoners of war, as volunteers in the Serbian army, as rebels, refugees, or internees—and one of the bloodiest battlefields, the Italian front, was located on Slovenian soil. The front cut through fertile terrain, turning the western Slovenian provinces into an epicenter of destruction and creating a battlefield out of that territory. It shook the Slovenian nation to its very core, honeycombing so deeply into its fabric that no one was spared the war's devastating toll. Given the diversity of wartime engagements, the Slovenian experience may justly be described as a key case study for showing how a community responds to war, survives it, and then (re)constructs its memory. The Slovenian population perceived the war both as a military event that had wreaked havoc on civilian life, and as a series of political developments that undermined the very foundations of the many-centuries existence under the "safe" patronage of the Habsburg crown.

Since Slovenian historiography and journalism have essentially concentrated on the political aspects of the war, particularly those related to the creation of the Yugoslav state, it seems appropriate here to focus on the imprint that the military experience left on Slovenian historical memory.[2] After the war there was an apparent lack of interest in commemoration in the Slovenian lands, at least in the public sphere, for the soldiers had served in a defeated army and had been subjects of a state that had collapsed. It took a long time for Slovenes to realize that the defeated have the most to learn from their experience.[3] Slovenes were slow to accept the fall of Troy as the prototype for defeat, according to which defeat is an end but also a beginning, a process in which war, death, and rebirth are cyclically linked.[4] This chapter will analyze the Slovenes' perception of their war experience during the first postwar decades, emphasizing especially the spiritual and moral burden placed on war memory by the external (and political) consequences of the war. Its focus is Slovenian soldiers and their experiences in war, and on the memory of occupation, especially in the Slovene-inhabited lands that were annexed by Italy after the war.

The Slovenian Soldier—The Victim of War

During the war Slovenian newspapers and their illustrated supplements overflowed with heartrending words and images of fallen heroes. Behind each story there was a name, a soldier whose death was mourned. These names were just the tip of the iceberg: for each of the fallen heroes there were countless other nameless figures, found only in the work of statisticians and a few historians. It is impossible to arrive at an exact estimate of losses inflicted in a war, and such an investigation is always a thankless task. The Great War involved the mobilization of seventy million soldiers, and Austria-Hungary, as the world's fifth largest military power, mobilized 7.8 million.[5] At the start, the monarchy had drafted a total of 3.35 million soldiers, sending two million armed men into battle; an initial 102 infantry regiments had increased to 141 by the end of hostilities.[6]

What was the Slovene percentage of Austro-Hungarian troops? An overview of the army's national composition dated May 1918 showed that most Slovenian soldiers served in fifty different Habsburg infantry regiments.[7] The "Slovenian regiments" fell under the III Army Corps based at Graz, but Slovenes were to be found in all parts of the Habsburg armed forces.[8] In terms of linguistic composition, the 1st Feldjäger battalion, the Kaiserjäger regiment and two infantry regiments were regarded as exclusively Slovene-language units.[9] But in the army as a whole it was Germans who had the highest percentage of soldiers (25 percent) while Slovenes were only two percent. The ratio was subject to considerable fluctuation until the end of war. In the officer ranks there were five active and eight reserve Slovenian officers per one thousand men.[10] In August 1914 around a hundred thousand soldiers, including thirty thousand Slovenes, were sent to battle from the III Army Corps area.[11] Austrian official reports stated that, in spite of some Yugoslav aspirations, Slovenian soldiers had readily heeded the emperor's call, hoping that their dynastic loyalty would be rewarded with greater political autonomy.[12] As the newspaper *Slovenec* noted in December 1914, they were "selflessly willing to sacrifice everything, even their last drop of blood. Slovenian men fight everywhere and have shed blood for their beloved homeland. Therefore we firmly believe that our rights at home will not be infringed."[13]

After the war, Wilhelm Winkler made three official statistical reports on the "fallen soldiers" of Austria-Hungary. The aim was not to establish the total number of dead but to analyze their distribution by nationality, age, and vocation, based on figures obtained at the end of 1917. According to his calculations, Carinthia had paid the highest blood toll of the monarchy's provinces, with 36 fallen per 1,000 inhabitants; Carniola (24) and Gorizia-Gradisca (20) ranked in the middle, whereas Istria and Trieste occupied the bottom rung of the scale for Austria's crown lands. The Austrian average numbered 23.3 per 1,000 while the Hungarian average was 25.7 per 1,000. Carinthia could be documented as having, relatively, the highest number of fallen Slovenian soldiers and was followed by Carniola. Slovenian Styria, including the German-speaking cities of Maribor, Celje and Ptuj, numbered 17,514 fallen soldiers, Carinthia 14,833, Carniola 13,583, the Austrian Littoral 1,590, Gorizia-Gradisca 5,430, and Slovenian Istria 1,327. Concerning the language structure of the crown lands, 32,368 fallen soldiers were from districts that were more than 80 percent Slovene, and 3,600 from (two) districts with a predominantly Slovene-speaking population. The total number of fallen soldiers hailing from a district that was exclusively or predominantly Slovene-speaking thus amounted to 35,968. Winkler's statistics on age were derived from a figure of 120,000 fallen soldiers gathered together from several lists. In the Austrian part of the monarchy the highest number of casualties occurred among soldiers born in 1895–96; while in the Hungarian, this "honor" belonged to soldiers born in 1894 and 1897. This important data all highlighted "Slovenia's" significant relative contribution to military casualties. In 1921, in addition, there were documented to be 31,049 war widows, 49,182 dependent family members, and 17,000 war orphans left in the Slovene lands.[14]

The Slovenian Soldier—the Victim of Written Memory

To what extent were these casualties preserved in the Slovenian collective memory during the two decades after the Great War? Oto Luthar has described the process of war remembrance in Yugoslavia as follows:

> In Europe and the USA the collective memory of this particular war is rooted in its monumentality and the watershed events that followed in its wake. In Great Britain, Germany, and the USA, it entails an unspoken apology for the untold casualties—in the German case an apology to the victims of defeat, in Great Britain and the USA an apology for the (excessively) high price of the victory in a war that posed no imminent threat to their citizens and territories. In the territory of the former Yugoslavia, which was formed from previously warring nations, the collective memory of World War I was suppressed. First, because it was impossible to celebrate victory and suffer defeat at the same time: the Serbian victory at Cer, for example, reminded the Slovenian or Croatian participants in this battle of their frantic escape from Serbia. And second, because the memory of World War I was overshadowed by that of World War II. Not only was World War II constitutive for the Socialist Federative Yugoslavia. The triumphant ideology confirmed at every step that Brotherhood and Unity, which had been built by the resistance movement, bridged the gap that had (also) been created among the Yugoslav nations during the previous war.[15]

Indisputable proof of the resulting schizophrenic situation was the memory literature produced in Yugoslavia (until 1929 the Kingdom of Serbs, Croats and Slovenes). The largest number of texts dealt with Yugoslav military volunteers—Slovenes, Croats, and Serbs who were either the subjects of Austria-Hungary or hailed from the South Slav diaspora, but had fought against the monarchy under the command of the Serbian or Allied armies. On this subject, the most notable book was *Volunteers: Forgers of Yugoslavia 1912–1918* (1936), edited by Ernest Turk, Josip Jeras, and Rajko Paulin.[16] This monumental work recounted the memories of Slovenian men who had been volunteers in the Balkan Wars and the Great War (probably no more than two thousand in number). It depicted the Yugoslav volunteer as a Croat, Slovene, or Serb who had bravely renounced his family and material possessions in order to enlist in the Serbian army as the soldier of a common Yugoslav state as yet to be created. Their sacrifice in blood on the Salonika front and other Balkan battlefields was allegedly the first step towards liberating and unifying all Slovenes, Croats, and Serbs. The exact number of Slovenian volunteers who had died for that cause remained unknown and was never discussed in these writings. But in any case, numbers were less important than the propaganda value that these soldiers represented.[17]

Another attempt at evaluating the volunteer movement was made by the Ljubljana branch of the Union of Volunteers of the Kingdom of Serbs, Croats, and Slovenes. In 1938 the organization started publishing a collection entitled *Volunteer Library* in order "in tumultuous times, to kindle in our nation the fire of a constructive, defensive, and volunteer spirit that our youth will unwaveringly carry in their hearts towards our successors' unknown future."[18] The authors wanted to provide their compatriots in popular form with a "true, unadulterated history" of all those Slovenes who had taken up arms and fought "for Slovenian and Yugoslav freedom."[19] Such initiatives were self-financed and undertaken to show the significance of the Slovenian contribution to the "liberation and unification" of the Yugoslav state.[20]

Yet despite these efforts, the Slovenian war contribution in interwar Yugoslavia was considered to be of minimal importance. Instead, as Melissa Bokovoy shows in this volume, the story of the Serbian army's withdrawal to Corfu through Albania in the winter of 1915—undoubtedly a key tragic episode—became the constitutive element of Yugoslav war mythology. Since many Slovenian volunteers had participated in that "Golgotha," the ordeal was vividly portrayed in the memories of Slovenian authors as well.[21] They usually extolled the Serbian nation while at the same time describing the disposition of the wartime Slovenian nation, suggesting that most Slovenes were not ready for freedom as they were so accustomed to life under the Habsburg yoke. By presenting such views, Slovenian volunteer authors contributed to the glorification of the Serbian nation at the expense of their own. A special place in the memory of volunteers was also allotted to those Yugoslavs who had served in the Italian army under Ljudevit Pivko, a Slovene who in September 1917 had deserted the Austro-Hungarian lines in order to fight for the Allies. In Italy, Pivko raised a volunteer squad of captured Czech and South Slav officers and fought with them on various sectors of the Italian front. After the war, however, amid the political turmoil that engulfed the Slovenian provinces, he was seen by some Slovenes as a traitor because he had fought for the benefit of the enemy Italian army.[22]

The 1920s and 1930s also saw the publication of a series of memoirs of war captivity that came to constitute the largest bulk of Slovenian war literature. Many Slovenian soldiers in the Habsburg forces were captured on the Eastern front. Some wrote their memoirs about Russian captivity, about the Russian Revolution and Civil War, and above all about the difficult and turbulent journey home from distant Siberia. Even though they were not seeking literary recognition (their names are largely forgotten), the writings of each of them were an expression of someone whom destiny had plunged into a whirlpool, drowning with thousands of others. Their simple intention was to offer at least a vague picture of what had been endured. Such memoirs constituted an "encyclopedia" of human resourcefulness and were vivid examples of travel writing since the authors traveled almost half way around the world to reach home; cities and landscapes were carefully described, accompanied by striking depictions of peoples and customs. They all shared a roguish style and simple narrative, devoid of boasting or self pity. We should note too that for many Slovenian soldiers, entering the global war arena was their first contact with the wider world.

The interwar period was, at least on Slovenian territory, marked by a notable lack of war monuments or any other public discussion about what had actually happened on the Italian front, much of which had passed through Slovenian territory. Such indifference toward a battlefield, which had destroyed local civilian lives and deeply affected all surviving Slovenes, may stem from the fact that the Italian front was never recognized as a Slovenian battleground. Rather, it was perceived as the scene of contest between disintegrating Austria-Hungary and voracious Italy, where not a drop of "Yugoslav" blood had been spilled and no "struggle" had been fought for the Yugoslav state. Almost all Slovenian memoirs about the Italian front were written from a strict military viewpoint rather than that of a Slovene in Austro-Hungarian uniform. However, they suggested no moral qualms about serving in a "foreign" army, something that became a constant feature in the post-World War II literature, nor did they even seek to justify the "Slovenian" presence in the Habsburg army.[23] Special attention too was given to the "Lion of the Isonzo," Field Marshal Svetozar Boroević von Bojna, an ethnic Serb; the translation of his memoirs, *Reflections on the War Against Italy*, was published in 1923 as part of an effort to prove that Italy had obtained new territory by political machinations rather than in battle. The editor of these memoirs, the Slovenian diplomat Otokar Rybař, tried to unveil the truth about the so-called Italian victory but also to give the Serb commander the recognition he deserved. Thus Slovenian writing about the war was colored by the political postwar milieu, its most prominent themes seen through the prism of political imperatives. "Yugoslav" themes were favored, for obvious reasons, both in the first Yugoslavia and after 1945, yet there was greater variation in the interwar period than after World War II.

The Union of War Fighters—The Struggle for Memory and Veterans' Rights

Information about the experience of Slovenian veterans in the interwar period can be gleaned from their organization, the Union of War Fighters. The Union was an independent and apolitical veteran organization, formally established quite late (1931) though it held its first general meeting in the village of Brezje as early as 1924. Its mission was often misunderstood. Some feared that it was militaristic, handing its members rifles with bayonets or collecting money for explosives; others assumed that its only purpose was the annual visit to Brezje or some other pilgrimage. In fact, its activities were dedicated mainly to honoring the memory of fallen soldiers. The rationale for existence, as defined in its regulations, was to maintain camaraderie among its members and provide them with moral, legal, and material support. The organization spared no effort in building war memorials, overseeing the construction of no less than 150 across Yugoslav territory. In addition, it undertook to maintain military cemeteries and ensured the memory of the dead was kept alive. Throughout its existence it persistently placed great importance on cultivating the wellbeing of the nation and the state—promoting both Slovenian national consciousness and affiliation to Yugoslavia—as well as reciprocity and friendship among the Slav nations.

The Union's structure was simple and effective. Its central committee was subordinate to local groups while simultaneously providing them with adequate conditions for independent work. On Slovenian territory, forty-four branch offices were active under the name "Union of Fighters," while 130 branch offices were registered under the simple name "Fight," an organization affiliated to the Union. Martin Colarič, a retired major, was initially appointed the Union's first president and army chaplain Franc Bonač as its secretary. After Colarič's death in 1930, the presidency was taken over by General Rudolf Maister and then by Stane Vidmar, a former Yugoslav volunteer in Italy.[24] In memory of the first president, the Fighters established the Colarič Fund to support poor comrades as well as their widows and orphans. They were also involved in setting up charitable institutions and funds, and collecting photographs, diaries, and other literature to create a war museum. A periodical, *Bojevnik*, served as the Union's mouthpiece, circulating between 1931 and 1936 to raise awareness among members of the important mission. This occurred too through public gatherings organized by local committees or at the main annual gathering at Brezje.

As a wider task, the Union moved to oppose the suppression of national minorities in Europe. Drawing once again from their personal war experience, they called for international peace, recognizing the potential for a new war in the decisions made at Versailles, which had created new national minorities within the borders of the New Europe. First and foremost, the Union drew attention to the situation of the Slovenian minority in the Littoral and Carinthia (in Fascist Italy and Austria respectively).

Otherwise, in the Yugoslav memorial environment, the Union established its quintessential position by persistently promoting Slovenian national independence on the one hand and the Yugoslav state community on the other. It adamantly opposed any move toward fusion in some new Yugoslav national community. An automatic and sincere shift from the Austro-Hungarian tradition ensured that it was tolerated by the state but not unconditionally supported. Nonetheless, the turbulent second half of the 1930s forced the Union to engage more actively in politics, accelerating its inclusion into the Association of Yugoslav Combatants (Boj). In the spring of 1935, a faction surrounding the paper *Bojevnik* split from the Association of Yugoslav Combatants because it was increasingly identifying with the Fascist Ljotić movement, which ultimately caused the Association's demise. The democratic faction, however, joined the Popular Front movement and thus set off on a new path, while still remaining faithful to its fundamental memorial mission. Its final decline was precipitated by World War II and the occupation of Slovenia.

Annually, the Union gathered its members together at Brezje where, on Assumption Day (15 August) in 1915, ten thousand pilgrims had assembled to pray for peace. When former combatants first gathered there in 1923, around ten thousand veterans vowed to meet every summer at the Chapel of Our Lady of Brezje. The following year a memorial plaque was unveiled in the church near the chapel. In 1937, on the thirtieth anniversary of installing the image of Our Lady of Mercy, a proposal was made to convert the church courtyard into a memorial park and build a tomb to the Unknown Soldier on behalf of all Slovenian soldiers buried in the region. In a typical gesture, every parish in the region would be expected to contribute earth for the tomb from its cemetery in special urns that symbolized the joint sacrifice of all Slovenes. Another proposal envisaged the construction of a fountain with the statue of Our Lady of Mercy in the center of the convent garden to symbolize the font of her love and mercy. This plan was entrusted to the school of the Slovenian architect, Jože Plečnik, with designs drawn up by his student, Janez Valentinčič. The memorial would be a symbol of peace, reconciliation, and friendship, expressing "gratitude to tens of thousands of Slovenian boys and men who bled and died, offering their blood and lives for the liberation of our nation."[25]

Faithful to its principal mission of honoring the memory of the dead, the Union also strove to ensure that the victims of war would obtain a permanent memorial in Ljubljana's central St Cross Cemetery. During the war, soldiers of various nationalities and religions had been buried there, including POWs who had died in Ljubljana's military hospital. Protestant, Jewish, and Muslim soldiers were buried separately in the Protestant cemetery at Saint Christopher. After the Union repeatedly failed to get the competent authorities to act and organize the cemetery grounds at St Cross, the city municipality of Ljubljana finally took the initiative in 1932. The main task was entrusted to Plečnik, who drafted a plan for the military cemetery and thus "in a flight of artistic imagination ... paid a splendid tribute of the greatest reverence to the dead."[26]

In 1923 the remains of the victims of the Judenburg military revolt had been transferred to the Cemetery of St Cross. The Judenburg mutiny of May 1918 had been one of several rebellions (three of them Slovenian) by ex-Habsburg POWs who had returned from Bolshevik Russia and expected peace. Judenburg was the most serious Slovenian military mutiny and had been fiercely suppressed by the authorities with four death sentences.[27] These national martyrs were now solemnly reburied beneath a stone statue of Janez of Carniola, the work of two Slovenian sculptors, Svetoslav Peruzzi and Lojze Dolinar.

On the same site Plečnik envisaged the construction of a memorial comprising three pyramids, and a monument that would not only serve as a prominent landmark of the cemetery but, with the Kamnik Alps in the background, would "stand as a … reminder to humanity to help it sober up, come to its senses, and realize that the bloody settling of scores leads only to doom, despair, and death."[28] The project, however, was never completed. Instead, a military charnel house, designed by Edo Ravnikar, a student of Plečnik, was constructed and consecrated in December 1939.

On an everyday basis, the Union of War Fighters was dedicated to the lives of its members who often lived in poverty, the majority from rural or working class backgrounds. The organization fought against social exploitation and called for justice. A self-help program drew on the spirit of the trenches where the soldiers had allegedly known no differences and helped each other; in times of economic crisis it was the same mutuality that proved a guarantee for effective help. Many groups under the Union established support funds that were raised from voluntary gifts, paid fees, and the net profit of events. The purpose of self-help was also to cover funeral expenses after the deaths of members or their relatives on the basis of mutual assistance. On joining the organization, every member paid fees that secured them the right to insure themselves or their relatives. After the death of the insured person, the organization reimbursed the member or their family the funeral expenses.

Another important task was to improve the situation of disabled veterans, whose most pressing concern was the question of disability allowances and pensions. These veterans were an important legacy of the war: according to the figures from 1922, there were between 72,830 and 85,290 disabled war veterans in Yugoslavia, 66,446 of whom had been wounded at the front.[29] Until 1925 there was no unified law for disabled veterans in the new state, so the Slovene lands continued to abide by prewar Austrian law. According to data supplied by France Kresal, the financial situation of Slovenian disabled veterans was desperate. As many as 67 percent of them had no place of residence and 23 percent of them possessed inadequate means of subsistence.[30] Indeed, the benefits and disability allowances provided to both veterans and civilians disabled during the war amounted to no more than 5 percent of the bare minimum needed to provide for a family of four.

It can thus be concluded that "disability pensions were merely recognition of the current state of affairs rather than crucial assistance necessary to maintain the family of a dead soldier or facilitate a dignified life for the disabled person."[31] Such a situation partly resulted from the fact (as John Paul Newman's chapter shows) that disability pensions were determined politically, that only certain categories of disabled veterans or the families of fallen soldiers were eligible for disability allowance. In this respect, the struggle for the Yugoslav state was clearly recognized as the basic criterion, because any sacrifice for Yugoslav "liberation and unification" was rewarded at twice the amount of the standard disability allowance. Of course, this privileged group included primarily disabled veterans of the former kingdoms of Serbia and Montenegro, as well as the families of dead and missing soldiers from those armies. Concerning people from the "newly-associated provinces,"[32] the privileged group only comprised disabled volunteers and the families of dead and missing volunteers who were eligible for support under the Serbian law of 1914. Eligibility was restricted to former internees, those disabled by the enemy or families of those who had been killed by the enemy, or had died during internment.[33] The remaining war veterans, mostly former soldiers of the Austro-Hungarian army, received disability pensions according to the laws of the defunct monarchy. Personal disability pensions to war veterans from the former Austro-Hungarian provinces were 55–71 percent less than those of war veterans from the territory of Serbia and Montenegro, while family disability allowances were 55–85 percent lower.[34] Lina Mohor, whose husband had been killed fighting in the Habsburg army in 1916, was not among the privileged after 1918. Her grandson, Miha Mohor, wrote of how

> [t]he war had torn him [Lina's husband, in 1916] away from her even before they could begin to live together. She received a miserable war widow's pension, but those few crowns she had soon melted away in the outrageously overvalued dinar of the new state. She felt humiliated, and even half a century later she would still take tremendous pleasure in recounting how she used to fling her little Miha, who was five at the time, on the counter in front of the local clerks saying, let them have him if they can afford to provide for him with that chicken feed. She had to be resourceful.[35]

There was discrimination also in the officer corps of the Yugoslav army and navy. Even in the Yugoslav navy, which could not function without the contribution of Croat and Slovene officers, there were problems. As Ivo Banac has noted, "here also former Austro-Hungarian officers were made to feel second-best."[36] The allegiance of officers of Croat and Slovene nationality was continuously called into question. Since military patriotism stood above all for devotion to Serbian state traditions and symbols, there were always plenty of reasons to doubt the loyalty of non-Serbian commissioned officers. According to Banac, things would go wrong even in the simplest, everyday situations, such as whether to use the Cyrillic or Latin alphabets (the latter was often described as fostering antistate sentiments). These problems led many commissioned officers to leave the army, much to the dissatisfaction of the military authorities, who decided to intern initiators of petitions who complained about inequality. On the eve of World War II there were only thirty-one Croats and twenty-two Slovenes among

191 staff officers.³⁷ The close connection between the army and the crown, as well as the army's deep roots in Serbian political tradition, Serbian national ideology, and Serbian war mythology, were major obstacles to establishing equal relations among the nations of which Yugoslavia was comprised.

The Slovenes and the Memory of the Italian Occupation

World War I offers many opportunities to research the treatment of civilian populations under military occupation. In interwar Yugoslavia, the greatest public attention was given to the experience of Serbs under Austro-Hungarian occupation from 1914 to 1915 and under Austro-Hungarian and German occupation from 1915 to 1918. Conversely, far less was known about the Italian occupation of Slovenian territory.³⁸ The Italian occupation from 1915 to 1917 was, until the end of the 1980s, consigned to historiographical oblivion. This marginalization is understandable within Yugoslavia itself, but what is surprising is the way the occupation was blotted out of the memory and the history of the war in Italy. The aim here is not to offer a detailed description of the Italian occupation regime in Slovenian territory, but to highlight several aspects that determine its (dis)similarity to other occupation systems. One such development was the "espionage psychosis" where Italian soldiers and their commanding officers saw an Austrian spy in every person, especially those wearing a cassock.³⁹ Forty-one Friulian and eighteen Slovenian priests were arrested and interned in the first few days of the occupation in May 1915, identified as key sympathizers of the Habsburg crown and the most rabid opponents of the Italian occupying forces. Similar measures were undertaken against the political and intellectual elites in Friulian and Slovenian areas.

Neither the Friulians nor the Slovenes awaited the Italian occupation forces with enthusiasm—much to the surprise of Italian soldiers, who saw themselves as heroes coming to the rescue of their unredeemed brothers. The psychological state of the population might be characterized as quiet or indifferent. Benito Mussolini described it as resigned, but covertly hostile, lurking behind mysterious faces that loathed the Italians.⁴⁰ The Italian commander in chief tasked his armed forces to discipline the occupied territories and "strike with exemplary severity" if necessary.⁴¹ The newly created code of conduct also provided for the execution of violators of law and order and the demolition of their homes. Such measures were devised to persecute those who had committed hostile acts against the Italian army; they were first implemented on 29 May 1915 in the Friulian county of Vilesse with the execution of six men, including the local secretary, in the town square. Soon afterwards, on 4 June, six farmers from Slovenian villages were executed in retaliation for the military failures of the Italian army and as a warning to anyone who collaborated with the enemy.

Caporetto (Kobarid in Slovenian) became the administrative center of the Italian-occupied Slovenian territory. With the establishment of a "Secretariat-General for Civilian Affairs," the Italian authorities set the foundations for the planned postwar administration of a triumphant Italy enlarged by territories granted to it under the Treaty of London. It is precisely in this respect that the occupation of Slovenian territory appreciably differed from, say, the occupation of Belgium or Serbia. The Italian occupying authorities were completely focused on the future. Most measures and provisions were introduced specifically with a view to laying a base for the future administration, something that was in clear violation of the fundamental rules of war (i.e., that the occupation was temporary). The Italian authorities introduced radical changes in personal and geographical names, made a complete break with the existing Austrian education system and supplanted it with their own Italian curriculum. Italian was introduced as both the state and official language (in contrast, for example, to Belgium, where the Walloon and Flemish parts retained their own languages and traditions), and Italian national holidays were enforced and celebrated. In spite of all this, it should be borne in mind that the occupation authorities also actively undertook broad-based social policy to benefit the occupied population and alleviate the plight of war-stricken civilians. This included providing regular supplies of basic necessities and establishing an active health care network.

Other violations of the international laws of war took place in the spheres of economy, agriculture, and finance, where the Italian occupation authorities initially imposed a series of measures, but soon took to passing legislative acts and enforcing the same tax system as that established on Italian state territory. Such conduct, coupled with a complete absence of appropriate sanctions against those who violated the international laws of war, provides a good reason for questioning the existence of legal norms and regulations. The Italian wartime occupation of Slovenian territory clearly demonstrated that in practice, those states that occupied hostile territory either on their own or through an alliance proved most successful in later territorial disputes—even though military occupation under international law did not automatically lead to territorial gains. On 3 November 1919, the Italian army returned to Slovenian territory and occupied it in compliance with the provisions of the 1915 Treaty of London, relocating the border between Italy and Slovenia further to the east. In the summer of 1919 the military administration was replaced by a civilian one. Following the Treaty of Rapallo on 12 November 1920, which finalized the border between Italy and the Kingdom of Serbs, Croats, and Slovenes, these territories were annexed to Italy.

Researching and interpreting the occupation, and the origins of military violence committed there against civilians, may be understood both within the context of a transnational and cultural history of warfare. First, transnational history constitutes an appropriate conceptual framework: research cannot be confined to the sources of one particular nation (state), since victims and perpetrators of violence are of different national and state origins. Second, cultural history constitutes an important element in historical research, for it primarily concerns collective memory that has been maintained through narratives, family stories, and diaries. Nevertheless the war's historical aftermath had a most decisive impact on the "memory hole" that is encountered when investigating memorial manifestations of the Italian occupation. In the Slovenian case, historical events—reoccupation of Slovenian territory, annexation to Italy, Italianization—prevailed over memory and prevented its open expression. Or, rather, because the historical, material, and factual conditions of everyday existence remained largely unchanged, memory was perpetuated as part of reality.

The situation further deteriorated when Fascists came to power and swept through every aspect of Slovenian national life in Italy, forcing Slovenian culture to retreat into the private sphere. The Italian authorities prohibited any form of public remembrance of fallen soldiers and other casualties of the Great War. For this reason there are—with two exceptions—no memorials to perpetuate the memory of dead Slovenes in the Slovenian ethnic territory allotted to Italy under the Treaty of Rapallo. The new Italian state, which had just incorporated more than two hundred and fifty thousand Slovenes, built magnificent charnel houses at Caporetto, Oslavje, and Redipuglia, to commemorate its own victories on the front.

A somewhat distinctive form of remembrance are family stories, but in the Slovenian case they were seldom documented and collected in written form due to temporal distance and public disinterest. The exception appears to have been the memory of Slovenian refugees on either side of the frontline. On the eve of the Austrian-Italian war (1915) the Habsburg authorities had ordered an evacuation of the local population from the endangered zone into the empire—around eighty thousand Slovenes were sent to refugee camps—while the Italian authorities then moved twelve thousand local Slovenes off the battlefield into Italian cities. Refugee memory was also preserved in the central (Yugoslav) part of Slovenia, due both to the postwar influx of new Slovenian refugees who had fled the Italian-occupied areas of the Littoral and sought refuge in the newly established Yugoslav state, and the presence of the remaining "wartime" refugees. Their ordeals and stories, which were mostly disseminated through newspapers, became an integral part of Slovenian collective memory. But during the first Yugoslavia this memory struggled to survive in the shadow of Serbian mythology, which drew its strength from the experience of occupied Serbia and the traumatic retreat of the Serbian nation through Albania. As we have seen, this non-Slovenian experience was also vividly illustrated in Slovenian memorial literature by a few Slovenian volunteers who had fought in the Serbian army.

From a political perspective, the Slovenian refugee memory must have been neutral enough to endure in the Yugoslav reality, and it represented one pillar of Slovenian memory of the Great War until the 1980s, when research on wartime and military events on the "Slovenian" battlefield reached its zenith, particularly at a journalistic level. Otherwise, the memory of the war erupting in the Slovenian hinterland, the arrival of the Italian army, and the threat that it would remain on Slovenian soil—all these themes had been constantly nurtured by preeminent Slovenian artists like Maksim Gaspari, Hinko Smrekar, and Ivan Vavpotič. Their unforgettable wartime postcards containing war motifs left a lasting impression on the Slovene public. And their artistic narrative was soon joined by poetry. Featuring refugees as principal characters, Slovenian poetry in the twentieth century became the major vehicle for preserving the memory of the immense human tragedy. Even though it might fail to provide the necessary closure, poetry continued to serve as a unique witness to time, intimacy, and the deepest corners of the human soul. The old world crumbled away and a "new order" began to be built, imbued with a firm belief that this war was also the last—leaving an endless memory, but never to be repeated.

Caught between Defeat and Victory

In the interwar period, Slovenian memory of the war oscillated between forgetting and triumph, between nearly denying the war trauma of Slovenian soldiers of the defeated Habsburg army and the triumphant rhetoric of the Serbian (or Yugoslav) volunteer war experience. This therefore emphasized a limited Slovenian participation and an era of minor importance in Slovenian history. In 1918, moreover, the Slovenian provinces had fundamentally changed their historical perspective, not only due to the disintegration of the monarchy and the sudden creation of Yugoslavia, but also thanks to the loss of one third of the national territory in the following two years. From the perspective of historical remembrance, political unification meant replacing an Austrian concept of the past with an ethnocentric Yugoslav interpretation of history. Historical remembrance was a controversial experience in the first Yugoslavia due to the discriminatory relationship between the victors/liberators/unifiers and the vanquished/liberated/united, where it was virtually impossible to celebrate both victory and defeat at the same time. This, however, did not have a decisive impact on the Slovenians' remembrance of the war, but rather on the place of their war experience in the state-building memory of the Great War in Yugoslavia. Based on Yugoslav identity, the state conception and its war mythology only acknowledged the Slovenian volunteer minority. And Slovenian memorial literature, too, adapted to the central political current of creating a common Yugoslav culture and uniform memory.

The Isonzo front provides a telling example of how the Slovenian war was interpreted. Although many disturbing newspaper articles appeared in the interwar period about the battles of the Isonzo, the Isonzo front never received any official or state attention. Thus, it remained in the shadows of interwar Yugoslav remembrance, even though it was the war on the Isonzo that had dramatically affected most Slovenes. One of the fundamental reasons for pushing that memory into the private sphere was because that front was not a war for the Southern Slav community, regardless of some attempts in Italy to raise volunteer units. The crucial role in those developments had been played by the Yugoslav Committee abroad, which officially only supported Yugoslav volunteers in the Serbian Army, refusing to compromise the relationship between Serbia and Italy. After the war, the territories defined in the London Pact as border areas were annexed to Italy, and this unfavorable legacy only further burdened the memory of warfare on the Isonzo. There is still however no explanation for why Slovenian veterans were so passive in remembering the Isonzo front.

Indeed, the only public bearers of interwar Slovenian memory were the war veterans. They had to persuade their Serbian and Montenegrin compatriots, whose war had been crowned with victory, that the Slovenian experience of war should not be neglected. As John Paul Newman has noted, a victorious memory culture was prioritized in the postwar first Yugoslavia, despite the fact that individual veteran groups realized the gap between the victors and the vanquished, and despite efforts to incorporate all of them into their ranks.[42] In this regard, there were often complaints from Italian veteran organizations within the international veteran movement who criticized Croatian veterans in particular for having fought on the Habsburg side against Italy. Any reconciliation between the former military protagonists was therefore an endless process, both for the international veteran movement and for individual successor states like Yugoslavia, where at least two parallel narratives existed: one Yugoslav/Serbian and one ex-Habsburg. It was this that prevented any uniform Yugoslav historical discourse about the experience of the Great War.

Petra Svoljšak is head of the Milko Kos Historical Institute at the Research Centre of the Slovenian Academy of Sciences and Arts (Ljubljana) and associate professor in the department of Cultural History of the University of Nova Gorica where she teaches the history of warfare in the twentieth century. She is the author of *Soča, sveta reka: Italijanska zasedba slovenskega ozemlja 1915–1917* (Soča, the Sacred River: The Italian Occupation of Slovene Territory) (2003), and many articles on the Slovenes during World War I, refugee problems, the demographic impact of the Great War and its memory.

Notes

1. Ivan Cankar, *Podobe iz sanj* (Ljubljana, 1917), introduction.
2. For political developments, see Janko Pleterski, *Prva odločitev Slovencev za Jugoslavijo: Politika na domačih tleh med vojno 1914–1918* (Ljubljana, 1971); Fran Erjavec, *Iz bojev za slovensko avtonomijo* (London, 1958); Lojze Ude, *Slovenci in jugoslovanska skupnost* (Maribor, 1971); Ivan Lah, *V borbi za Jugoslavijo* (Ljubljana, 1928); Silvo Kranjec, *Slovenci na poti v Jugoslavijo: Spominski zbornik Slovenije* (Ljubljana, 1939); Albin Prepeluh, *Pripombe k naši prevratni dobi* (Ljubljana, 1938). Dragovan Šepić, *Italija, saveznici i jugoslovansko pitanje 1914–1918* (Zagreb, 1970); Bogumil Vošnjak, *U borbi za ujedinjnjenu narodu državu* (Ljubljana, 1928).
3. Wolfgang Schivelbusch, *The Culture of Defeat: On National Trauma, Mourning, and Recovery* (New York, 2001), 1. The author quotes Heinrich Mann.
4. Ibid., 2.
5. "Trenches on the Web. Timeline. 1914–1918 Casualty Figures." http://www.worldwar1.com/tlcrates.htm:
6. Edmund Glaise von Horstenau et al, eds, *Österreich-Ungarns letzter Krieg: 1914–1918* (hereafter OULK), 7 vols. (Vienna, 1930–38), II: *Das Kriegsjahr 1915* (Vienna, 1931), Tabelle 4; see also Janez Švajncer, *Svetovna vojna 1914–1918* (Maribor, 1988), 31–32.
7. Richard Georg Plaschka, Horst Haselsteiner, Arnold Suppan, *Innere Front: Militärassistenz, Widerstand und Umsturz in der Donaumonarchie 1918*, 2 vols. (Vienna, 1974), II: 335–57. The units included the 17th infantry "Kranjski Janezi" regiment, the 47th Lower Styrian infantry regiment, the 87th Celje infantry regiment, the 97th Trieste infantry regiment, the 27th Ljubljana Home Guard infantry regiment (2nd mountain rifle regiment), the 26th Maribor-Celje home guard infantry regiment (26th rifle regiment), the 7th Kaiserjäger regiment, and the 26th and 27th Black Army regiment.
8. For a detailed description of Slovenian regiments, see Švajncer, *Svetovna vojna*.
9. OULK, II, Tabelle 4.
10. Švajncer, *Svetovna vojna 1914–1918*, 13.
11. Jurij Mušić, "Ognjeni Krst slovenskih fantov 1914 (ob petdesetletnici)," *Kronika* XIII/2 (1965), 84.
12. OULK, I: *Das Kriegsjahr 1914* (Vienna, 1930), 42.
13. *Slovenec*, 5 December 1914, 1
14. France Kresal, "Invalidi in vojne vdove kot trajne posledice prve svetovne vojne, njihov status, število in struktura," in *Množične smrti na Slovenskem*, ed. Stane Granda and Barbara Šatej (Ljubljana, 1999), 307.
15. Oto Luthar, *O žalosti niti beside: Uvod v kulturno zgodovino Velike vojne* (Ljubljana, 2000), 97–98.
16. Ernest Turk, Josip Jeras, Rajko Paulin eds., *Dobrovoljci, kladivarji Jugoslavije 1912–1918* (Ljubljana, 1936).
17. For example, in October 1916 there were only 1,727 Slovene volunteers among 30,242 soldiers in the volunteer corps in Odessa. Due to extreme violence in the corps, 13,000 soldiers left the corps and returned to the POW camp, only 234 Slovenes remaining. See also Ivo Banac, *The National Question and Yugoslavia: Origins, History, Politics* (Ithaca and London, 1984), 121.
18. Introduction to volume 1 of "Dobrovoljska knjižnica," 4.
19. Ibid., 3.
20. Ernest Turk, *Dobrovoljci proti Avstro-Ogrski* (Ljubljana, 1978), 152–93.

21. For example, Vitomir Feodor Jelenc, *1914–1918: Spomini jugoslovanskega dobrovoljca* (Ljubljana, 1922); Josip Jeras, *Planina smrti: Dobrovoljčevi spomini na srbski umik čez Albanijo leta 1915* lst ed. (Ljubljana, 1929). See also Frana Radešček, *Preko Albanije*, a feuilleton that appeared in the *Slovenec* newspaper from January to July 1921.
22. Ljudevit Pivko, *Proti Avstriji* (Maribor, 1923). For Pivko's significant propaganda work on the Italian front, see Mark Cornwall, *The Undermining of Austria-Hungary: The Battle for Hearts and Minds* (New York, 2000), 131–49, 231–40.
23. Ivan Matičič, *Na krvavih poljanah* lst ed. (Ljubljana, 1923); A. Vitalis. *Doberdob, slovenskih fantov grob* lst ed. (Celje, 1936); Rado Pavlič, *Ljubezen in sovraštvo: Moja pot preko cvetočih in krvavih poljan. Slike iz svetovne vojne* (Ljubljana, 1924); Vinko Gaberc–Gaberski, *Brez slave: Spomini na svetovno vojno* (Celje, 1935).
24. On Vidmar's work as a Yugoslav volunteer, see Cornwall, *The Undermining of Austria-Hungary*, 143, 237–38, 380.
25. *Brezje: Slovenskem žrtvam svetovne vojne* (Ljubljana, 1937), 20.
26. "Spominsko pokopališče bojevnikov na pokopališču pri Sv. Križu," *Bojevnik* II/3 (25 June 1932): 2.
27. Plaschka, Haselsteiner, Suppan, *Innere Front*, I: 324–40.
28. *Bojevnik* II/3 (25 June 1932): 2.
29. The data on the number of war invalids in the Kingdom of Serbs, Croats, and Slovenes vary and are indicative only. As Ljubomir Petrović has noted, this is due to the fact that Yugoslavia failed to found a single organization responsible for the centralized processing of statistics until the 1930s, while institutions charged with collecting the data on (war) invalids continued to perform their task with utter negligence and incompetence. See Ljubomir Petrović, *Nevidljivi geto: Invalidi u Kraljevini Jugoslaviji 1918–1941* (Belgrade, 2007), 118–19.
30. Kresal, "Invalidi in vojne vdove," 310.
31. Ibid., 311.
32. The term used for the former Austro-Hungarian provinces in the 1921 "Act on Temporary Support to Disabled Persons and the Families of Dead and Missing Soldiers, and Other Civil Casualties of War."
33. France Kresal, *Zgodovina socialne in gospodarske politike v Sloveniji od liberalizma do druge svetovne vojne* (Ljubljana, 1998), 233.
34. Ibid., 239.
35. *Miško Piše*, ed. Miha Mohor (Kranj, 1992): letters of Mihael Mohor, an artilleryman on the Isonzo front who published the *Gorenjec* weekly during 1915–16.
36. Banac, *The National Question*, 151.
37. Ibid.
38. The subject is treated in depth in Petra Svoljšak, *Soča, sveta reka: Italijanska zasedba slovenskega ozemlja 1915–1917* (Ljubljana, 2003).
39. See John Horne and Alan Kramer, *German Atrocities, 1914: A History of Denial* (New Haven, CT, 2001).
40. Benito Mussolini, *Dall' intervento al fascismo (15 novembre 1914–23 marzo 1919)* (S. Christina Gela, 1992), 141.
41. Branko Marušič, "Italijanska okupacija Posočja (1915–1917)," *Zgodovinski časopis* 43/2 (1989): 232.
42. John Paul Newman, "Allied Yugoslavia: Serbian Great War Veterans and their International Ties," in *The Great War and Veterans' Internationalism*, ed. Julia Eichenberger and John Paul Newman (Basingstoke, 2013), 97–117.

Chapter 11

THE DEAD AND THE LIVING
War Veterans and Memorial Culture in Interwar Polish Galicia

Christoph Mick

On 4 April 1925, a strange ceremony took place in the Great Hall of the Polish War Council in Warsaw. The eyes of generals, ministers, and bishops rested on a corporal, the youngest bearer of the *Virtuti Militari*, the highest military order of the Second Polish Republic. The young corporal was standing beside an urn containing fifteen folded paper slips. The corporal removed one slip and passed it on to Prime Minister Władysław Sikorski. He unfolded the paper and read aloud: *Bojowisko Lwowskie* (The Battle of Lwów). The suspense abruptly dissolved into loud applause. The decision had been made: the Polish Unknown Soldier had died in the Polish-Ukrainian War 1918–19. His remains would be transferred from Lwów (today Lviv) to the empty tomb of the Unknown Soldier in the arcades of the Saxon Palace, the seat of the War Ministry in Warsaw, only a few meters away from the place where the ceremony was being held.[1]

Poland was emulating a European trend that had started in 1920. Following the French and British examples, many countries built a central tomb in which to bury the remains of an unidentified soldier. These tombs became national shrines, with the Unknown Soldier standing at the heart of a political cult of the dead, representing all those who had died for the nation not merely in this war but also the dead of previous and future wars. The Unknown Soldier was a powerful symbol, which in Britain or France appeared to unite the majority of the nation behind it.[2]

In Poland, as in most other Eastern European countries, things were different. More than three million Polish soldiers had fought in the Great War, but only a few of them in national Polish units; the overwhelming majority had been soldiers fighting in one of the three imperial armies. About eight hundred thousand Poles had fallen in Habsburg, Russian, or German uniforms. Could one of those soldiers become the Polish Unknown Soldier? The answer was clearly no. Only the names of battles or uprisings occurring after November 1918 were written on the slips of paper. The authorities wanted to ensure that their Unknown Soldier had fought and died for Poland and no unidentified soldier of the Great War could guarantee this. More importantly, was it possible to give death in World War I national meaning? Could it be excluded that the Unknown Soldier had been killed by a bullet from another Polish soldier wearing the uniform of another nation or empire? Such considerations were much too complex and potentially divisive for a symbol intended to unite the postwar nation.

What does this story tell us? First, it is an example of the marginalization of the Great War in interwar Poland. The focus of official remembrance was on the subsequent state-building wars, uprisings, and the war against Soviet Russia. The Polish national meaning of these events was undisputed. It was much easier to accept the "highest sacrifice" that had been demanded of soldiers and their families if the soldier had died clearly wearing a Polish uniform.

Second, it indicates that in interwar Poland, as in interwar Yugoslavia, there were many different types of war veterans. Their "symbolic capital," based on their military record, could have widely different value, depending on the units they had belonged to, on which side and in which war they had fought, and in the specific national context that their "symbolic capital" had been invested. Soldiers who fought for the Habsburg monarchy had lost their "investment." The only way of saving their "symbolic capital" from complete devaluation was to give their war experience national meaning. Veterans unable to do so, either because they still had residual Habsburg loyalties or because they were unable to reinterpret their participation in the war, were ignored or fell silent. This question was especially important for the war invalids who depended on the recognition of and material compensation for their suffering. The state, on the other hand, had to decide whether it would care for all those whose health had suffered in the six years of hostilities. Was the new Polish state also responsible for those who had died or were injured fighting for imperial causes?

Third, any analysis of how the Great War and subsequent wars were dealt with offers insights into the social, ethnic, and political conflicts of the Second Polish Republic. In Galicia after 1918, the Polish-Ukrainian war and antisemitic pogroms and violence had poisoned ethnic relations. The new Polish state inherited these conflicts, which permeated the veterans' organizations and were reflected in memorial culture.

This chapter will determine the place of dead and living soldiers in interwar Poland. A considerable part addresses questions that were relevant for the Second Polish Republic in general, but a special focus is on the former Austrian crown land of Galicia and Lodomeria, where the Polish state faced the difficult task of integrating more than three million Ukrainians and eight hundred thousand Jews. To understand the challenges facing the Polish government in 1918, we need to take a closer look at this former Austrian crown land and how it was affected by the Great War and the subsequent state-building wars.

Galicia During the War

The Habsburg crown land of Galicia and Lodomeria was an artificial creation, uniting two heterogeneous provinces of the old Kingdom of Poland: Red Ruthenia with its urban center Lemberg (Lwów/Lviv), and Little Poland with the old Polish capital Cracow. Overall, those identifying as Poles were slightly in the majority (about 46 percent according to the 1910 census); but in Eastern Galicia they were in the minority, about 25 percent as opposed to 62 percent who were Ruthenian (as the Ukrainian-speaking population was usually termed) and 12 percent who were Jewish.[3] Most Poles could not imagine the crown land or a future Polish state without Eastern Galicia, while for the Ukrainians the region was ancient Ukrainian territory; their immediate aim was its partition into Ukrainian and Polish sectors. In turn most Jews were neutral and clung to the continued existence of the Habsburg monarchy.

This was the ethno-political situation when the Great War began and Galicia became one of the major battlefields of the Eastern front. It was also one of the very few regions where the population of the Central Powers was given firsthand experience of foreign occupation. The Austro-Russian front swept across the eastern part of Galicia several times, devastating the landscape. Writing in August 1917, the German general consul in Lviv could not imagine how Austria would be able to fund the reconstruction in the wake of the Russian occupation.[4] Yet the initial suffering in the crown land had been at Austrian hands. After their defeat in the first battles of 1914, the Austrian military authorities had looked for scapegoats among the Ruthenian peasantry and Russophile priests who were accused of supporting Russian troops. The military authorities executed an unknown number of people and arrested more than twenty thousand Ruthenians, interning them in camps in Austria. In November 1917, fifty-seven hundred Ruthenians were imprisoned in appalling living conditions in the Thalerhof camp near Linz alone; many perished or became invalids.[5] Ukrainian sources have estimated that some twenty-five thousand Ukrainian civilians were executed or died in Austrian camps, although this may be an exaggeration.[6] While traditional Ruthenian loyalty to the Habsburgs was thus severely tested, Galicia's Jewish population had the Russian troops to fear. As Russian occupation became imminent, more than a hundred thousand Galician Jews fled west to the Austrian heartlands. The Russian military authorities discriminated against those left behind, deporting thousands and generally failing to stop antisemitic violence. Innumerable reports of atrocities, often committed by Cossack troops, demonstrate the suffering of Galician Jewry.[7]

Like the Jewish population, the Ukrainophile part of the Ruthenian population still had good reasons to support Austria. The Russian government flatly denied the existence of a separate Ukrainian nation, the military governor closing all national Ukrainian institutions or handing them over to local Russophile Ruthenians. For the Russian authorities and Russian nationalists alike, Ruthenians/Ukrainians were nothing more than a branch of the Russian nation, and it was expected that with time they would return to the faith of their ancestors, and embrace the Russian Orthodox church.[8] In turn, the Russian occupiers told the Poles that Eastern Galicia would not form part of a reconstituted Kingdom of Poland but become an ordinary province of the Russian empire. Thus, not surprisingly, most of the Galician population was overjoyed when the Habsburg army returned in mid-1915. Vienna appointed a German-Austrian general to the position of *Statthalter* (governor) and placed Galicia under military rule.[9] This however was followed by a wave of prosecutions aimed at collaborators. Relationships between Jews, Ukrainians, and Poles deteriorated as there was mutual denunciation, each accusing the other of collaboration or of profiting from the war.[10]

In the months after the return of Austrian rule a wave of trials against collaborators and plunderers swept through the countryside. The German consul reported that by the end of 1915 32,498 people had been investigated.[11] This weakened Polish and Ukrainian loyalty to the Habsburgs, deepening anti-semitism as the availability of food and material supplies diminished. Indeed, after the Russian February Revolution, loyalty to Austria weakened further, partly because of the deteriorating material conditions, partly because of the new political options open to Poles and Ukrainians alike.[12] The Austrian government made a series of errors of judgment: alienating Poles by (secretly) promising Ukrainians to divide Galicia into Ukrainian and Polish sections and to give the Cholm region to a new Ukrainian People's Republic, but then alienating the Ukrainian elites by revoking those promises. By the summer of 1918 even Polish civil servants were disillusioned with Austria. While Polish politicians now tried to create an independent state, the majority of Ukrainian politicians still entertained hopes of an Austro-Ukrainian solution. In October 1918 only the loyalty of the Jewish population to Austria was unquestioned.

Finally Austria-Hungary imploded. While a few key nationalities such as the Poles and Czechs moved to create their own states, the Western Allies were not interested in keeping the empire alive. It was clear that Western Galicia would become part of a new Polish state, but Eastern Galicia remained contested. The Ukrainian National Council in Lviv proclaimed a Western Ukrainian state without formally severing the connection to the Habsburg monarchy, and on 1 November 1918 Ukrainian troops (recruited from Ukrainian former Habsburg soldiers) took control of Lviv and Eastern Galicia. Secret Polish military organizations there resisted and were supported by the Polish population of Lviv. The Jewish *kehilla* (community) however declared its neutrality and a quickly assembled Jewish militia defended the Jewish sector against plunderers. This fighting in Lviv between Ukrainians and Poles lasted for three weeks whereupon, after fresh Polish troops arrived, the Ukrainian army withdrew. On the same day, some Polish soldiers, accompanied by local civilians, started a pogrom against the Jewish population: they accused the Jewish militia of having sided with the Ukrainians, but for the marauders it was merely a pretext for murder, blackmail, and robbery.[13] It took the Polish military authorities three days to reestablish order. Seventy-three Jews were killed and hundreds of shops and houses were plundered. Dozens of houses were burned down as Jews were forced to surrender their valuables.[14]

After the Polish victory, Lviv was besieged by Ukrainian troops who controlled most of Eastern Galicia. What began as a civil war between former subjects of the Habsburg monarchy evolved into a war between the newly proclaimed Second Polish Republic and the Western Ukrainian People's Republic. The fighting ended in the summer of 1919 with a Polish victory, but it was not the last war in the region. In the spring of 1920 Eastern Galicia became a battlefield of the Polish-Soviet war, a conflict that ended on 18 March 1921 with the peace treaty of Riga.[15]

After the collapse of all three partitioning powers it was Poland that finally filled the power vacuum. The strength of the quickly improvised Polish army, the support of the Western Allies, and the fear of Bolshevik Russia allowed the new state to incorporate territory with a minority Polish population. This Second Polish Republic was predominantly Polish-speaking (69 percent in 1931), but in the eastern borderlands the majority was Belorussian or Ukrainian. The latter was the most numerous minority (14–16 percent of the population), followed by the Jews (9–10 percent), Belorussians (3–6 percent), and Germans (2–4 percent).[16] There was broad consensus across Polish society that Ruthenians were too "immature" to have their own nation state and would be better off under Polish tutelage. After the fall of the independent Ukrainian People's Republic in Eastern Ukraine, so the argument ran, any independent Ukrainian state in Western Ukraine would inevitably be swallowed up by Bolshevik Russia. Thus according to the Polish *raison d'état*, these lands had to be protected—if necessary against the will of the population.[17]

Nor did Ukrainian suffering stop with the end of hostilities. In the early 1920s discrimination against the Ukrainian population was widespread. In 1920 several thousand still languished in Polish prisons and thousands of soldiers of the Ukrainian Galician Army were held in internment camps. The tactics of Ukrainian politicians and of the Western Ukrainian government-in-exile in

Vienna made it easy to justify such discrimination as they refused to accept Polish rule in Eastern Galicia (still to be confirmed by the Allies), referring to it as a Polish occupation of Ukrainian lands. While most Ukrainian state employees from the Habsburg era refused to swear an oath of allegiance to the Polish state and were dismissed, Ukrainian politicians called for a boycott of the 1921 census and the 1922 parliamentary elections. Veterans of the Ukrainian Galician Army played a prominent role in terrorist attacks carried out by the Ukrainian Military Organization (UVO: Ukrains'ka Vijs'kova Orhanizatsiia), and after 1929 many junior officers from this army went on to join the Organization of Ukrainian Nationalists (OUN: Orhanizatsiia Ukrains'kykh Natsionalistiv), conducting a merciless campaign against the Polish presence in the region.[18]

Already in 1923 it was clear that all Ukrainian attempts to weaken the Polish grip on Eastern Galicia had failed. Since the Allies needed Poland as a bulwark against German revisionism and revolutionary Russia, the Conference of Ambassadors in Paris confirmed that Eastern Galicia was indeed part of the Polish state, which in turn had to promise to give the province autonomy and minority rights. These promises were never kept. The crown land was divided into four voivodeships, with Eastern Galicia officially becoming Małopolska Wschodnia (Eastern Little Poland).

Dead Soldiers: War Cemeteries and the Political Cult of the Dead

Apart from the ethnic conflicts confronting the new Polish state, the mass deaths created logistical, material and ideological problems. The state was forced to deal with the physical remains of the dead soldiers, exhuming bodies from provisional graves, collecting body parts from the battlefields, identifying them where possible and building war cemeteries to rebury them. But the state also had to explain to returning soldiers and the bereaved why their comrades, husbands, fathers, or sons had died. Failure to give a deeper meaning to the suffering and mass death in the wars threatened the legitimacy and stability of the political order.[19]

Amid the practical problems connected to the war was the fact that Galicia had been a major battlefield. Many towns and villages had been destroyed, the landscape was scarred and full of war debris. The subsequent wars of the Polish Republic produced more battlefields to be cleared and more casualties to be buried. The Polish authorities not only had to manage the remains of Polish soldiers but, according to international agreements laid down in the peace treaties, provide burial grounds for hundreds of thousands of fallen soldiers of the imperial armies, the Red Army, and the armies of the two Ukrainian states. In Galicia, however, the Polish state could build on work started by the wartime Austrian authorities. After the Central Powers had reconquered Galicia in 1915 they had tried to clear the battlefields as quickly as possible to prepare them for spring sowing. During the battles the soldiers of both sides had often been provisionally buried where they fell. In November 1915 the Austro-Hungarian War Ministry set up a Department for War Graves (Kriegsgräberabteilung), responsible for battlefields behind the front lines. This decision was not made merely for pragmatic reasons but was guided by a "natural feeling of reverence" and the wish to build "graves of honor" (*Ehrengräber*) for the heroes who had fallen "for the glory and honor" of Austria-Hungary.[20]

In Western Galicia in the spring of 1915 the Cracow military command had duly established its own War Graves Department under Major Rudolf Broch and started to clear the 10,000 square kilometer area where a vast number of widely dispersed graves were left behind. The exhumation teams in ten "cemetery regions" faced many obstacles. Graves were not registered or contained more corpses than expected. The teams also found Russian mass graves that had not been marked at all. Initially, the commission planned to concentrate the fallen soldiers in 150 grave sites, but they soon found that even 350 sites would not suffice.[21] About three thousand people, including Italian and Russian POWs, worked for the Department and finally more than four hundred cemeteries and grave sites were planned. Most of them (95 percent) could be completed before the end of the war. Some 60,829 dead soldiers (42,749 of them previously exhumed from existing burial sites) of the three imperial armies were buried in 378 military cemeteries along with civilians killed during hostilities. Fifteen burial sites were located at Jewish cemeteries.[22]

One of the reasons the Austrian military authorities published a book about these military cemeteries was to comfort the bereaved. They should see "with proud satisfaction" the efforts that had been made to preserve "the memory of the dead on the West Galician battlefields for ever more." This was additionally intended to help reconcile families to the fact that they could not recover the bodies of their loved ones for their local cemetery where, the authors argued, after a few decades the graves would be neglected or even removed.[23] The military cemeteries were meant to express the fatherland's gratitude for the "sacrificial death" (*Opfertod*) of its soldiers. The cemeteries should clearly demonstrate to the whole world that all nations within the Habsburg monarchy lamented the "many thousands of warriors" as "beloved and revered brothers":

> These cemeteries will also be sites of purification and elevation for us and our descendants for a long time to come. They will emanate a force that will give heart to those who are wavering, guide back those who have erred, and in the hour of new trials reignite the holy flame of love for our fatherland and of enthusiasm for our superb cultural treasures, fanning it into a burning fire.[24]

To achieve such aims, gravesites had to be given an appropriate form. It was decided to keep most cemeteries simple, to present an image of "severe, simple, and calmly massive monumentality." The location of existing sites and agricultural demands also had to be considered. The gravesites had to "fit organically into the respective landscape," expressing "the deepest connection to nature." The architects therefore often designed the cemeteries as forest cemeteries (*Waldfriedhöfe*), with plain crosses and simple walls or fences; their integration into nature helped save money but was also meant to impress visitors.[25]

The work of the Austrian War Graves Department in Cracow, however, was not universally praised. Polish artists and architects criticized the design of the cemeteries and the lack of consultation. The design, they argued, was not compatible with Polish cultural traditions and on Polish soil Poles should be responsible. The design was also considered too monumental, too "Teutonic." The organization of Polish architects duly held their own design competition but the Austrian military authorities chose to ignore the results. If the Polish criticism was based on aesthetic and nationalist arguments, we should not forget that involvement in building these cemeteries also offered material advantages. Polish architects participating in the work of the Department were later often accused of having worked for an "alien" project.[26]

After the Great War the Austrian authorities were no longer responsible for dealing with Galician cemeteries. The task was first taken on by the Polish army command, particularly by the Department for Military Building (Zarząd Budownictwa Wojskowego) in Cracow while the Ministry of Military Affairs (Ministerstwo Spraw Wojskowych) was responsible for the military cemeteries. Other organizations dealing with military cemeteries were the Society for the Protection of the Graves of the Heroes (Towarzystwo Opieki nad Grobami Bohaterów) and the Polish Society of the Mourning Cross (Towarzystwo Polski Żałobny Krzyż). Poland formally complied with its obligations to preserve the Great War cemeteries, but many were soon neglected and fell into disrepair. This applied especially to imperial Russian military cemeteries in Galicia that neither Poland nor the Soviet Union were interested in maintaining. In 1937 the Lviv local authority decided to consolidate the military cemeteries on its territory, exhume the remains of Russian soldiers from the Hill of Glory (*Kholm Slavy*) and transfer them to the eastern part of the Austrian military cemetery. As in most Galician cemeteries, more than ten thousand soldiers of the imperial armies were now buried in close proximity.[27]

Yet if preserving imperial military cemeteries was seen as an inconvenient obligation, the gravesites of Polish soldiers, particularly those who had fallen fighting in the Legions or the Polish army, had a deeper emotional significance. Already in July 1919 a Society for the Protection of the Graves of Polish Heroes (Straż Mogił Polskich Bohaterów) was established in Lviv. One of its first projects was to build a cemetery for Poles who had fallen defending the city against Ukrainian troops in November 1918. A field of graves near the Lyczaków (Lychakiv) Cemetery came to be known as the "Cemetery for the Defenders of

Lwów." In the subsequent months and years, the remains of Polish fighters killed in battle were transferred to this final resting place. Indeed, the Cemetery of the Defenders was such a popular burial place that by February 1922 the municipal council had to refuse any further requests for burials.[28] Thereafter, only commanders or highly decorated soldiers were permitted burial there, making it an extremely prestigious site. In Polish memoirs of the period, much is made of pilgrimages undertaken there on All Souls and All Saints Day.[29]

For Polish Lwów, the cemetery of their dead comrades became a key symbol: Polish sacrifice, so the argument went, had made this soil eternally Polish.[30] Cemeteries for fallen soldiers of the Polish legions had already been built during the war in Łowczówek, Cracow, Jastków, Nowy Sącz, and other places, but monuments and chapels were only added after the war, making them true sites of national memory. This was not the case with the other Great War cemeteries. Although more Polish soldiers were buried in such cemeteries and they were places where the bereaved could mourn, they did not become national sites of memory. As large numbers of Galician soldiers had fought on the Russian front, most cemeteries for the dead of the Great War were in Galicia or in the Lublin region and could easily be visited by the bereaved. It was different with cemeteries located on the former Italian front or in central Ukraine. The remains of Ukrainian, Jewish, and Polish soldiers from Galicia could be found in German and Austrian war cemeteries all over Europe, but we do not know how far relatives traveled outside Poland to visit these graves.

Polish memorial culture culminated in the cult of the Unknown Soldier where religious metaphors were very prominent, the Unknown Soldier implicitly compared to Christ. In giving his life the Unknown Soldier had redeemed the nation and his sacrifice was celebrated as "life-giving." One author had the Unknown Soldier saying: "My silent death was the birth of a new life for my nation."[31] Another newspaper perceived in the cult of the Unknown Soldier an expression of gratitude for his sacrifice but also proof of the "spiritual rebirth" of the nation.[32] Yet some critical voices were also raised after the war against a continued focus on the dead and a cult of the past. The National Democratic daily *Słowo Polskie* criticized the Polish "cult of mourning" in the last prewar decades: "Our poetry gave us tears for breakfast, desperation and revenge for lunch, and grey ghosts for dinner." The article, however, celebrated the rejuvenating power of the war and the new freedom.[33]

Motives of Christian sacrifice and rebirth also permeated Ukrainian commemorations. The Ukrainian elites emulated the Polish cult of martyrs, offering a powerful example of how to strengthen a nation through commemoration. The intention was to plant the national idea in people's hearts but, according to the Ukrainian newspaper *Dilo*, freely honoring those who had fallen for the national cause was impossible until Ukrainians had their own state. Nor could soldiers who had fallen in Habsburg uniform be honored, except for the *Sich* riflemen who were seen as the nucleus of the Ukrainian Galician Army, the army of the short-lived Western Ukrainian People's Republic.³⁴

In 1921, having founded a Regional Commission for the Preservation of War Graves in Lviv, some Ukrainian intellectuals published a booklet with writings by the poet Vasyl' Shchurat about the "fallen heroes." Ukrainians, it suggested, had died by the thousands in places that through this sacrifice had become "the eternal property [of Ukraine] for which they paid with their heart's blood":

> We will create thousands of legends of heroism, we will create thousands of miraculous places of heroism, to which people will flock every year in their thousands … for the purification of their soul, for the reinvigoration of their hearts … We will bring the children to them—for prayer. We will develop a cult of the fallen for those who have remained!³⁵

According to Shchurat, no stranger would have any doubt as to whom the land belonged. Educating the young Ukrainian generation, mobilizing them for future battles, and showing the outside world that this was genuine Ukrainian territory—all were essential elements of the campaign to construct military cemeteries and monuments.

Six years later, the Ukrainian Society for the Preservation of War Graves was officially registered. At the founding meeting, the chairman Ivan Nimchuk again emphasized the need to cover the country with Ukrainian emblems of remembrance. The Ukrainians' claim to the land was supported by their military sacrifice. The existence of Ukrainian graves in Eastern Galicia had therefore more national meaning than Ukrainian graves in Western Galicia or Italy.³⁶ The Ukrainian military cemeteries were part of the nation-building efforts and presented the Ukrainians as a cultured nation.³⁷ Nimchuk complained that in recent years thousands of Ukrainian graves, "our most precious treasure, our biggest moral capital" from the wars of liberation, were threatened with annihilation. He recommended emulating the Polish example and intensifying the "cult of our tradition" through the honoring of fallen soldiers as a "cult of meritorious ancestors, a cult of heroes." Plaques in "honor of the fighters for Ukrainian freedom" should be mounted everywhere and crosses erected.³⁸ The Ukrainian War Graves Society followed this program. Burial sites of *Sich* riflemen and soldiers of the Ukrainian Galician army were transformed into sites of memory. These were more modest than their Polish counterparts, not least because the Polish authorities imposed restrictive conditions on the erection of monuments in Ukrainian cemeteries.³⁹

Polish observers in turn were concerned that in areas with a strong Ukrainian majority, military cemeteries of the Great War were being neglected or even profaned. The Polish historian Józef Białynia-Chołodecki complained that tombstones were used as building material, wooden tablets as fuel; cattle grazed in the cemeteries and boys played football there. Białynia-Chołodecki did not believe that a low level of Ukrainian culture was responsible for this sacrilege but assumed that this behavior was aimed against the Polish state. Such a neglect of military cemeteries would give the German government the opportunity to accuse Poland of not complying with its international obligations. And while the Great War cemeteries were falling into disrepair, Ukrainians were honoring their own graves from the Polish-Ukrainian war of 1918–19. Such national military cemeteries were staking a claim on Eastern Galicia. Białynia-Chołodecki therefore believed it essential to preserve the cemeteries of Polish soldiers and heroes in the eastern borderlands.[40]

The early Polish governments, which included National Democrats, not only tried to de-Ukrainize the public space but to denationalize the Ukrainian population. Here they continued to differentiate between Ruthenians and Ukrainians. Ukrainians—as these Polish nationalists saw it—lived in Little Russia (Russian Ukraine) and differed from the East Galician Ruthenians. According to this interpretation, a handful of Ukrainian agitators, supported by the Austrian and German governments, had talked the Ruthenians into perceiving themselves as Ukrainians and were ultimately responsible for the trouble. *The Invalid* (*Inwalid*), the journal published by the Union of War Invalids of the Polish Republic (Związek Inwalidów Wojennych Rzeczypospolitej Polskiej), noted in 1919, full of condescending good will towards the Ruthenian "brother nation":

> It is not right to apply the name "Ukrainians" to all Red Ruthenians who, while under the thumb of the *hajdamak* [Ukrainian-speaking insurgents who opposed their Polish overlords in the eighteenth century], fought against the Poles. We know that the *hajdamaks* even forced Poles to join their troops. We know that the majority of Red Ruthenians opposed being called "Ukrainians." Poland therefore should regard as a Ukrainian only someone who refers to himself as such; all others should be treated like the Poles who were forced into the service of the *hajdamak* gangs. If we treat Red Ruthenians equal to Poles, then we will bind them even more strongly to Poland.[41]

In Eastern Galicia however such a position was not compatible with reality and underestimated the strength of the Ukrainian idea among the Greek Catholic peasantry. The Polish government needed other measures to fight the Ukrainian idea and strengthen the "Polish element" in the region.

As a result of educational reforms passed in 1924, many monolingual Ukrainian schools in towns became bilingual (Polish/Ukrainian) and the government actively supported Polish settlement in the Eastern voivodeships. The Polish parliament (*Sejm*) passed a law creating a credit facility amounting to 50 billion złoty to support the settlement of veterans of the Polish army. Until 1938 between a hundred thousand (Polish computations) and two hundred thousand (Ukrainian calculations) settlers arrived in Volhynia and Eastern Galicia. As in other successor states, these veterans and their families profited from the interwar land reform and preference was given to them when positions in the local administration became available. They were intended as a bulwark against the Ukrainians to ensure that the region would stay Polish and were naturally viewed with derision by the local Ukrainian inhabitants.[42]

While the Polish authorities prohibited public demonstrations by Ukrainian organizations, particularly if such demonstrations commemorated the Western Ukrainian People's Republic and the Polish-Ukrainian War, they did not dare forbid church services or religious processions. The founding of the Western Ukrainian People's Republic was therefore commemorated in special Greek Catholic services. There veterans of the Ukrainian Galician army were given places of honor and fallen Ukrainians were remembered. A procession was regularly held after divine service on All Souls' Day, with participants solemnly marching to the cemeteries where the fallen had been buried. The celebrations sometimes ended in violent clashes. Thus in autumn 1928 in Lviv, Ukrainian nationalists attacked symbols of the Polish victory, damaging one monument and defacing another while placing the Ukrainian flag at strategic vantage points across the city. The police intervened and dispersed the Ukrainian demonstration held that evening, while Polish nationalist students attacked various Ukrainian official buildings in an attempted reenactment of November 1918.[43] On 29 May 1939, three thousand Ukrainians marched from eight Uniate (Greek Catholic) churches in Lviv to the graves of Ukrainian riflemen in Lychakiv Cemetery. A commemorative service was celebrated by a Uniate prelate and twenty priests, one of whom declared: "The graves of the fallen Ukrainian heroes are proof of the continued fight of Ukrainians for their independence."[44]

As for the third major ethnic and religious group in Galicia, the Jews, there was no positive meaning they could draw from their wartime suffering. There was no political cult of fallen Galician Jewish soldiers comparable to the Polish and Ukrainian acts of remembrance. During the war this had been different. The Austrian authorities had attempted to honor fallen Jewish soldiers and glorify their sacrifice for the Habsburg fatherland. In November 1916 the Jewish cemetery in Lviv had been given a new area in which fallen Jewish soldiers were buried. An obelisk was erected and on the opening day representatives of the Habsburgs, the city council, the German consulate and the Jewish community honored the "heroic fallen soldiers."[45]

Yet after November 1918, only a connection to the Polish nation could give meaning to the Jewish war dead. This was attempted by some members of the Jewish progressive community, some Jewish Poles, and organizations such as the Union of Jewish Participants in the Fight for Polish Independence (Związek Żydów-Uczęstników Walk o Niepodległości Polski). The Związek was formed in 1929 in order to unite all Jews who had participated in the struggle for Polish independence, and in 1932 it founded a branch for the three south-eastern voivodeships in Lviv. Yet the marginalization of Great War veterans was also visible here: there was no Jewish organization that represented soldiers of the Habsburg or other imperial armies. The Związek's main aims were to instill a sense of civic responsibility in the Jewish population, to look after the graves of Jewish fighters, to help Jewish-Polish rapprochement, and to propagate the Jewish contribution to Polish independence.[46] In 1937 the Związek had more than twenty-five hundred members in the four Galician voivodeships,[47] but it was caught up in the increasing anti-semitism of interwar Poland when some Polish veteran organizations wanted to exclude it from the umbrella organization of Polish veteran associations.[48]

In Lviv, Jewish public mourning for pogrom victims was marginalized anyway by the dominant Polish cult of the dead. It remained confined to synagogues and the Jewish cemetery where the pogrom victims could be commemorated. In December 1919 and early 1920 thousands of representatives from almost all Jewish organizations participated in commemorative events there. Whether this tradition continued thereafter is not clear, but Polish celebrations and Polish newspapers generally ignored the pogrom.[49]

In the end Poles, Ukrainians, and most Jews formed separate, vertically integrated communities, with their own forms of remembrance and commemoration. The dead of World War I were eclipsed and played no role in public remembrance. They had died for the wrong cause, and their deaths could not be integrated into the two main national narratives. The war experiences of the Galician population had therefore not united but further divided Poles, Ukrainians, and Jews. In the next section we will see what consequences this division in Galician society had for ethnic relations and how veterans of the imperial armies reacted to the marginalization of their war experience.

The Living: War Veterans and War Invalids

After the Great War the new political leaders struggled to find words exalted enough to express their nation's gratitude for the "ultimate sacrifice." Yet many veterans were unable to cope and found it very difficult to reintegrate into society. While they based their claims for more influence and privileges on the contribution they had made on behalf of the nation, the new regime's cult of the "glorious dead" produced a growing sense of entitlement. For war invalids this "symbolic capital" was even more important; the loss of their health or even of body parts was presented as a sacrifice for the nation. For Polish, Ukrainian, and Jewish soldiers from the former imperial armies there was inevitable disappointment. What they had fought for had completely disappeared, the empires no longer existed, and the new nation states or national movements were not interested in their sacrifice.

Indeed, satisfying veterans was easier if the nation had won the war, more difficult if the war had been lost, and very complicated if the veterans had fought on both sides, in imperial armies, in state-building or revolutionary wars. The Polish war veterans were also deeply divided. Very bitter were the animosities between political and former military leaders of the different camps, especially between supporters of Józef Piłsudski and of Roman Dmowski's National Democrats. For the most part the veterans organized themselves according to the units they had served in or according to their political orientation, but this only covered those who had fought in Polish national units or participated in one of the uprisings in Silesia or Greater Poland. In contrast, only a minority of the soldiers who had fought in one of the imperial armies were organized. Most soldiers from the Great War ignored the veterans' movement that was dominated by former legionaries and combatants of the Polish national army. Polish memorial culture in turn was dominated by the rebirth of the Polish state. It was extremely difficult for suffering to be recognized that did not comfortably fit into that national narrative. This may explain the reluctance of veterans of the Habsburg and other imperial armies to join the veterans' movement. Approximately 3.39 million Polish soldiers had fought in the Great War and around eight hundred thousand of them had fallen. Some 2.58 million soldiers returned home. According to official data 23.6 percent (only 15.6 percent according to Marek Jabłonowski) became members of veterans' organizations. Most of them had either served in one of the wartime Polish national units, participated in one of the subsequent uprisings, or had later joined the Polish national army.[50]

There was a close connection between public glorification or forgetting of fallen soldiers and the social prestige of the survivors. Veterans of the imperial armies played no role in commemorative events in contrast to the war veterans, invalids, widows, and orphans of Polish national units. This was again the case when the body of the Unknown Soldier was brought to Warsaw. Invalids from Polish national units or the Polish army were accorded places of honor in the processions, marching directly behind the sarcophagus. During the commemorative events, organizations of the Polish Legions and the "defenders of Lwów" were omnipresent, while Great War veterans formed part of the audience but were not officially included in the ceremonies.[51]

Piłsudski understood that the support of organized veterans was crucial for his success. After his coup d'état in May 1926 the new government hoped to profit from his popularity among war veterans and unite them behind the *Sanacja* regime. In 1927 the Federation of Polish Unions of the Defenders of the Fatherland (FPZOO: Federacja Polskich Związków Obróncow Ojczyzny,) was founded. It competed with the Legion of the Polish Republic (LRP: Legion Rzeczypospolitej Polskiej), which was close to the National Democrats and united those veteran groups opposed to the May coup. Attempts in 1928 to merge the Legion and the Federacja failed, and during the following three years the two organizations fought each other for preeminence. In 1931 the Federacja, receiving financial and political support from the government, was finally successful and the Legion lost most of its influence.[52]

The marginalization of Great War soldiers within the veterans' movement did not however affect the war invalids. Already in spring 1919, when it became clear that their common interests made a strong unified organization mandatory, the Związek Inwalidów Wojennych Rzeczypospolitej Polskiej (ZIW: Union of the War Invalids of the Polish Republic) was founded, uniting all war invalids including those of the former imperial armies. The ZIW was founded on the principle of national, religious, and political neutrality. For the next decade it remained the biggest and most influential veteran organization in Poland, with 33,581 members in the four Galician voivodeships alone in 1937.[53]

Yet the material conditions of war invalids, as we have seen for Croatia, were unenviable. There were insufficient houses and sanatoriums and most invalids had to wait a long time for prosthetic limbs as only a few factories manufactured them and their quality was usually poor. Without specific legal regulations they were dependent on the goodwill of the authorities. An important aim therefore was to secure the passing of a law that would define their status and their rights; this was one of the demands voiced in invalid demonstrations held in June 1920 in Warsaw, Łódz, Lviv, and other cities. The invalids asked for aid, for special shops, more houses for invalids, and better prostheses.[54] After these demonstrations they did receive some money, depending on their disability.[55]

In 1921 the Law on Invalids, Orphans, and Widows was passed. As the ZIW had advocated, it did not differentiate between invalids who had suffered in the service of imperial armies or of the specifically Polish national units. A war invalid was defined as a person whose health had been damaged due to military service in the Polish army after November 1918, in Polish military units, or in the armies of the partitioning powers between August 1914 and 1 November 1918, as long as they were now Polish citizens.[56] Those invalids who had fought for Polish independence before and after 1914 and the invalids of the army of the (Eastern) Ukrainian People's Republic that had sided with Poland in the Polish-Bolshevik War were also entitled to benefits—as long as they now lived in Poland.[57] Conflicts between different ministries and several changes of government however delayed the implementation of the law. New protests and demonstrations of war invalids followed.[58] The conflict between ZIW and the government culminated in the confiscation of several editions of the organization's newspaper *Głos Inwalidów*. Finally, in January 1923 the minister of finance Bolesław Markowski signed a decree making it possible to enact the law, but the conflict continued.[59] The ZIW felt that state support was insufficient. The ZIW-owned coffee factory in Grodno, for example, went bankrupt after the army refused to order its coffee from this factory.[60] However, the war invalids now at least had access to free prostheses and free healthcare, as long as their health problems were related to a war injury.

Indeed, the ZIW was the most comprehensive of all veterans' organizations and the only organization where the majority of its members were former soldiers of the imperial armies. No wonder it battled during the interwar years for equal treatment for all war invalids. The disabled fought for their interests together and came into conflict with a state that—not untypical for postwar Europe—faced budget constraints and was trying to minimize the expenditure in dealing with thousands of invalids. In 1934 the state recognized there to be 172,000 of them. More than a hundred and thirty thousand had suffered injuries while serving in imperial armies. Poles were slightly overrepresented (76.5 percent), while Jews were dramatically underrepresented (2.9 percent), partly perhaps because some Jews chose to describe themselves as Polish. It is worth noting too that the number of Ukrainians recognized as war invalids (21,197 or 12.3 percent) was slightly lower than the Ukrainian proportion of the population (15.8 percent).[61]

Unsurprisingly, conflicts arose in the ZIW between different types of Polish war invalid. Those from the Polish Legions and the postwar Polish army felt they should be granted more privileges than veterans from the Great War. This in turn was criticized by the latter. Lazar Kornblüth from Tarnów in Galicia, a Jewish soldier who had served in the Habsburg forces, stated that he had fought for the liberation of Poland. In fact, he had sometimes even fought under the same command as the Polish Legions: "We are therefore not second class war invalids."[62] But it was hard for former soldiers of the Habsburg monarchy to get public recognition and invalid disunity was clear. Early attempts by veterans of Polish units to secede from the ZIW failed, but in 1926 several thousand from the Polish army left the ZIW and set up the League of Invalids of the Polish Army named after General Sowiński (Legia Inwalidów Wojsk Polskich imeni gen. Sowińskiego).[63] Initially, this brought them no advantages and in 1930 they complained that life had become very difficult for their families. Many provisions of the law passed in 1921 had not been implemented. Nor had they profited much from the land reform in Galicia and other regions, and Polish army invalids had no access to cooperative shops. Many lived inadequately, in cheap, dark lodgings for which they had to pay rent out of their small pensions; medication was only free if it related directly to a war injury and families gained no help.[64] Nevertheless, the new organization continued to hope that, having left the ZIW it would win recognition and additional benefits for its members. A new law to protect invalids and their families was vital for those "who had done their duty for the fatherland, risked their lives, and sacrificed their health."[65] In 1931 as a result of these protests the Ministry of Army Affairs permitted former legionaries and those who had rendered outstanding services to the fatherland to be treated in military hospitals.[66]

During the first half of the 1920s Jewish war invalids had also been members of the ZIW. But in 1926 they too founded a separate Union of Jewish War Invalids, Widows, and Orphans (Związek Żydowskich Inwalidów, Wdów Sierot Wojennych), which had a strong base in Galicia. Their argument was that Jewish invalids were not treated as equal to Poles but as second class members. In the ZIW they had faced anti-semitism causing many to think it illusory to expect support from a Polish organization.[67] In contrast to Polish invalids, for example, they had no privileged access to civil service positions:

> This proves that the Jewish war invalid is unfortunately a third class war invalid. If he is born a Jew he is already an invalid; as a consequence of the disability he received in the war he becomes an invalid for the second time. And now with the moral pain done to him because of his origins he is handicapped for the third time.[68]

When the global economic crisis hit Poland and mass unemployment became a major problem, the state did intervene in favor of war invalids. From 1932, companies with a workforce of more than fifty were obliged to employ at least one invalid, while bigger companies had to take on three invalids for every hundred employees.[69] Not all invalids however continued to receive benefits. Those with jobs were seen as no longer in need of state support. In 1933, out of 168,737 registered war invalids only 132,857 received state pensions; in 1930 an invalid with a 15 percent incapacitation received 18.75 złoty per month, while the highest benefits went to those who were totally disabled who were granted 208.23 złoty per month.[70] In total the government spent 40 million złoty on pensions and rents for war invalids from an overall annual budget of two billion. This was seen as too high a burden and therefore in 1933 a new Law on Invalids was passed to cut costs. From April 1934 invalids could no longer demand a change in their invalidity classification if their health deteriorated.[71]

A further step toward the discrimination of certain types of war veterans was to end the pensions of those invalids from the imperial or non-Polish armies who were less than 25 percent incapacitated. Thus, payments were stopped to those Ukrainian invalids who had fought in 1920 against the Bolsheviks alongside the Polish army but were less than 25 percent disabled, and the rents and pensions of all war invalids were summarily reduced by 10 percent. Some forty thousand invalids and seven to eight thousand widows lost their state pensions. The 1933 law violated the principle of equal treatment for all war invalids, and many from the former imperial armies were now disadvantaged. The ZIW did not organize mass protests—the influence of the government was too strong—but almost every regional or local ZIW branch protested against the changes.[72] The Legia Polskich Inwalidów followed suit and was at last (partially) successful. The President of the Polish Republic granted veterans holding the Cross of Independence monthly subsidies of 60–90 złoty. Soon impoverished veterans with other decorations also began receiving financial support, and from January 1938 were given priority when applying for state positions. This was a major step towards privileging specific groups of war veterans.[73]

Yet the protests of the ZIW also had some impact. The organization was involved in writing a new version of the Law on Invalids passed on 1 July 1937, as a result of which the discrimination between invalids from Polish forces and imperial regiments was partially revoked. Veterans who had lost their pensions in 1934 because their incapacitation was classified as less than 25 percent were given a pension when they turned 55, and once again invalids could ask to be reclassified if their health deteriorated.[74]

Indeed, by 1935, 166,733 war invalids were still registered by the state (52,447 of whom had fought in the Habsburg forces), and in 1937, 80,690 war invalids from the imperial armies were recorded as receiving pensions. The dominance of imperial veterans is demonstrated by another figure: only 6,804 of those receiving pensions had been soldiers fighting in "Polish units." An additional 61,619 widows, 26,808 orphans, and 24,358 parents received pensions; overall, 200,279 people were given special pensions.[75]

It seems clear that during most of the interwar period the Polish state formally treated all war invalids equally, with one exception. Those who had fought against Polish troops after the collapse of the Habsburg monarchy, especially soldiers of the Western Ukrainian People's Republic, were excluded from receiving benefits. This had a major impact in Eastern Galicia where about a hundred thousand "Western Ukrainians" had fought against Polish troops as soldiers of the Ukrainian Galician Army. In 1921 the Ukrainian Civic Committee in Lviv calculated that there were about twenty-five thousand Ukrainian war invalids from the Great War and about ten thousand from the Polish-Ukrainian war. While the first group received state pensions, the Polish state did not recognize the latter as war invalids and their care fell to the Ukrainian community. Most invalid veterans of the Ukrainian Galician army had no prostheses and were living in poverty. The Civic Committee complained that the state failed to meet its obligations as laid down in international law. It should not matter in which army a soldier had fought: "Their only crime was their struggle against Polish troops for the liberty and independence of their own country."[76]

Foreign help, the Ukrainian Civic Committee complained, went almost exclusively to Polish invalids. Many soldiers of the Ukrainian Galician Army had become invalids during their internment in Polish camps where they had lived under appalling conditions, spending the winter in unheated barracks without medical help; some had lost their legs from blood poisoning. The Civic Committee therefore founded a section for invalids and set up a home for twenty-five invalids. The house was provided by the Ukrainian insurance company *Dnister*, while beds and some of the medications were supplied by the American Red

Cross. As long as the future of Eastern Galicia had not been decided, international organizations ought to help:[77]

> The Polish Occupation Authorities neglected the care of disabled soldiers even of Polish origin.... The care of disabled soldiers of Ukrainian origin is out of the question, because it must be emphatically stated that the Polish authorities make a principle distinction between soldiers of Polish origin disabled during the World War and those of Ukrainian origin.[78]

Polish war invalids received help from Polish and international humanitarian organizations. Most Polish war invalids lived in towns, were members of cooperative societies and had access to state-sponsored shops. Ukrainian war invalids lived mainly in villages and were thus automatically disadvantaged. Disabled Polish soldiers also had the possibility of obtaining a job in the public sector, which was denied to Ukrainians.

> But the main damage done to Ukrainian disabled soldiers consists in disabled Polish soldiers receiving plots of land under very advantageous conditions while Ukrainian disabled soldiers are completely excluded from this.[79]

Campaigns by the Ukrainian émigré community did little to improve the situation. The American Ukrainian newspaper *Svoboda* appealed to its readers to give money to the invalids of the Ukrainian Galician Army.[80] In April 1922 Ukrainian veterans and politicians, including Evhen Konovalets (later leader of the Organization of Ukrainian Nationalists) founded the Union of Ukrainian Invalids (Sojuz Ukraiins'kykh invalidiv) in Lviv. The Union planned to organize workshops, producing prostheses, where invalids could be trained. The line of argument was always the same, that Ukrainians were obliged to help their heroes:

> The care for our invalids, for those who are the living proof of our aspirations for freedom, our right of an independent existence, has become a question of national honor.[81]

The Union urged as many Ukrainians as possible to join the new Union so that their fees could cover the costs of the projects. However, it does not appear that these efforts were successful as the complaints about material conditions continued.

Thus, supporting invalids of the Ukrainian Galician army was very difficult. A Ukrainian Society for the Help of Invalids appealed to local communities to reward their invalids' heroism and sacrifice and declared 1 November (the anniversary of the attempted Ukrainian takeover of Lviv in 1918) the day of Ukrainian Invalids. It was argued that the Ukrainians had given their blood "for us" and we should repay them. In 1934, two thousand invalids were registered with the Ukrainian Civic Committee, five hundred of whom were severely disabled. However, voluntary contributions declined over the years, and in 1933 alone the Committee was three times obliged to lower the pensions it paid out. Ukrainian war invalids thus only received the equivalent of 10 percent of the state pension.[82] By 1934 the situation was unchanged. The Committee complained that as time passed the Ukrainian community was increasingly less inclined to donate money. The health of the two thousand invalids was deteriorating and they faced a daily struggle in providing for their families. The Committee insisted that the community ought to be saving its invalids from starvation and averting further fatalities arising from insufficient medical treatment. The "honor of the nation" depended upon it.[83]

Restricted Memorial Cultures

The late Habsburg empire with its balancing of ethnic conflicts and its considerable degree of political participation had created conditions where the Polish-Ukrainian conflict could be contained. Six years of war, however, disrupted Galician society, destroying the comradeship between Galician Jews, Poles, and Ukrainians of the old Habsburg army. In the new Poland the Great War was marginalized. Loyalty to the Habsburg monarchy had become an embarrassment, since for Poles or Ukrainians it undermined the claim of their political elites that both nations had always fought for their own nation states and never accepted foreign domination. For Jews, nostalgic feelings for the vanished empire may have been strong among the general population, but their political elites—whether Zionist, Polish patriotic, or Orthodox—made it clear that the political reality had to be accepted. As long as Palestine was out of reach, the future of Galician Jewry lay in the Polish state, to which the Jews now owed their allegiance.

Poland took over the obligation to care for the war cemeteries in Galicia and to pay pensions to invalids of the Habsburg army, but the Polish political cult of the fallen soldier emphasized that Polish rebirth was due to the sacrifice of soldiers who had died for an independent Poland. Although more Poles had died as soldiers of the former imperial armies, their commemoration was of little interest for the Polish state and was largely left to the bereaved. This was accompanied by the marginalization of veterans who had fought in one of the imperial armies. Some Great War veterans tried to reinvent themselves as fighters for Polish independence and participated in official commemorations, but their specific war experiences held no real public interest.

The integrative power of the cult of the fallen soldier was certainly impressive. Bitter fighting between different political camps and military organizations stopped during commemorations and the imagined unity of November

1918 was usually evoked and relived.[84] However, Polish memorial culture was limited, integrating only ethnic Poles. A considerable number of the Republic's minorities had not intended to become Polish citizens in the first place and had fought—often against Polish troops—for their own nation state. Polish memorial culture did not appeal to most Ukrainians who refused to abandon their national aspirations, developing their own memorial culture in direct opposition to Polish interpretations of the past. The cult of the Polish Unknown Soldier illustrates well the integrative strength and the limitations of Polish memorial culture. He had fallen in a war that had denied the Ukrainians their right of self determination, while Jews could not be sure whether prior to his death the Unknown Soldier had not participated in the Lviv pogrom.[85] In the end, only progressive Jewish communities participated in the annual commemoration, with the cult becoming an integrative symbol mostly for Roman Catholic Poles.[86]

Nevertheless, Polish and Ukrainian memorial culture showed many structural similarities in focusing on post-1918 hostilities. The sacrifices of Ukrainian soldiers from the Great War had no part in the Ukrainian national narrative and played no role in Ukrainian memorial culture. Of the Ukrainian soldiers who served in the Habsburg forces, only the *Sich* riflemen were honored, while the West Ukrainian cult of its fallen soldiers concentrated on veterans of the Ukrainian Galician army.

The peculiarities of the cult of the fallen soldier in Poland were reflected at the political level too. The ethnic and political conflicts in the Second Polish Republic deeply influenced the organizations of war veterans and invalids. Piłsudski and his opponents tried to unite the war veterans behind their respective parties. In these maneuvers, veterans of the former imperial armies were marginalized, while veterans of Polish national units or the Polish army played an important role in Polish politics. The war invalids, on the other hand, were initially united by common interests in forming a special organization, the ZIW. For the 1920s all invalids were treated equally, but subsequently those of the imperial armies were disadvantaged. The unity of war invalids was further broken when in 1926 some Jewish invalids and those from the Polish Legions left the ZIW because they no longer felt themselves properly represented. The fact that the Ukrainian community received no help from the state to support invalids of the Polish-Ukrainian war strengthened Ukrainian beliefs that they would always face discrimination in a Polish state and that a better future was only possible in an independent Ukrainian state.

Christoph Mick is Professor of Russian and Eastern European History at the University of Warwick, specializing in war remembrance in interwar Europe. His major publications include *Forschen für Stalin: Deutsche Fachleute in der sowjetischen Rüstungsindustrie 1945–1958* (2001), *Kriegserfahrungen in einer multiethnischen Stadt: Lemberg 1914–1947* (2010) and "Endgame: 1918," in *The Cambridge History of World War I: vol. 1: Combats*, ed. Jay Winter (2014).

Notes

1. Christoph Mick, "Der Kult um den Unbekannten Soldaten im Polen der Zwischenkriegszeit," in *Nationalisierung der Nation und Sakralisierung der Religion im östlichen Europa*, ed. Martin Schulze-Wessel (Stuttgart, 2006), 181–200; Joanna Hübner-Wojciechowska, *Grób Nieznanego Żółnierza* (Warsaw, 1991), 84–89; Wanda Mazanowska, "Geneza Symbolu Nieznanego Żółnierza," in *7599 dni Drugiej Rzeczypospolitej*, ed. E. Sabelenko and F. Koziniewski (Warsaw, 1983), 112–43.
2. Ken S. Inglis, "Entombing Unknown Soldiers: From London and Paris to Baghdad," *History and Memory* 5 (1993): 7–31; George L. Mosse, *Fallen Soldiers: Reshaping the Memory of the World Wars* (New York and Oxford, 1990), 94 ff.
3. A. Podraza, "Problem pograniczy w Europie środkowo-wschodniej (na przykładzie pogranicza polsko-ukraińskiego)," *Prace Komisji Środkowoeuropejskiej*, vol. 4 (Cracow, 1996), 106; Rudolf A. Mark, *Galizien unter österreichischer Herrschaft: Verwaltung—Kirche—Bevölkerung* (Marburg, 1998), 17.
4. Political Archives of the Foreign Ministry, Berlin (Politisches Archiv des Auswärtigen Amtes: hereafter PA-AA), R-8977, Heinze (German general consul in Lviv) to Reichskanzler Michaelis, 31 August 1917,
5. K.u.k. Kriegsüberwachungsamt to Statthalterei in Graz, 9 November 1914, in *Talerhofskij Al'manach. Propamjatnaja Kniga*, vol. 4, part 2 (Lviv, 1932), 134 ff.
6. Central State Historical Archive of Ukraine, Lviv (Tsentral'nyj Derzhavnyj Istorychnyj Arkhiv Ukrainy, m. Lviv: hereafter TsDIAL), f. 462, op. 1, spr. 90, ark. 1–4: Aide mémoire of the Ukrainian Civil Committee in Lviv, 4 December 1920.
7. Jakób Schall, *Żydostwo Galicyjskie w czasie inwazji rosyjskiej w latach 1914–1916* (Lviv, 1936), 8–20; Alexander Victor Prusin, *Nationalizing a Borderland: War, Ethnicity, and Anti-Jewish Violence in East Galicia, 1914–1920* (Tuscaloosa, 2005), 24–28.
8. Christoph Mick, "Kriegsalltag und nationale Mobilisierung: Lemberg im Ersten Weltkrieg," *Nordost-Archiv* 17 (2008): 58–82.
9. Christoph Führ, *Das k.u.k. Armeeoberkommando und die Innenpolitik in Österreich 1914–1917* (Graz, 1968), 65–71.
10. Christoph Mick, *Kriegserfahrungen in einer multiethnischen Stadt: Lemberg 1914–1947* (Wiesbaden, 2010), 138ff.
11. PA-AA, R-8975, German consul in Lviv to the German ambassador in Vienna, 21 February 1916.
12. Mick, *Kriegserfahrungen*, 181ff.
13. William H. Hagen, "The Moral Economy of Ethnic Violence: The Pogrom in Lwow, November 1918," *Geschichte und Gesellschaft* 31 (2005): 203–26.
14. Mick, *Kriegserfahrungen*, 232ff; Josef Bendow, *Der Lemberger Judenpogrom* (Vienna, 1919).
15. On the Polish-Soviet war, see Norman Davies, *White Eagle—Red Star: The Polish-Soviet War, 1919–20* (London, 2003); Adam Zamoyski, *Warsaw 1920: Lenin's Failed Conquest of Europe* (London, 2008).

16. Łucja Kapralska, *Pluralizm kulturowy i etniczny a odrębność regionalna Kresów południowo-wschodnich w latach 1918–1939* (Cracow, 2000), 98; Z. Landau and J. Tomaszewski, *Robotnicy przemysłowi w Polsce 1918–1939* (Warsaw, 1971), 35; J. Tomaszewski, *Rzeczpospolita wielu narodów* (Warsaw, 1985), 35.
17. For example the article "Lwowski Listopad," *Słowo Polskie*, 1 November 1920; *Słowo Polskie*, 24 November 1923.
18. On UVO and OUN see Franziska Bruder, *"Den ukrainischen Staat erkämpfen oder sterben!" Die Organisation Ukrainischer Nationalisten (OUN) 1929–1948* (Berlin, 2007); Grzegorz Motyka, *Ukraińska partyzantka 1942–1960* (Warsaw, 2006); Alexander J. Motyl, *The Turn to the Right: The Ideological Origins and Development of Ukrainian Nationalism 1919–1929* (Boulder, CO, 1980); John A. Armstrong, *Ukrainian Nationalism*, 2nd ed. (Littleton, CO, 1980).
19. Reinhart Koselleck, "Einleitung," in *Der politische Totenkult. Kriegerdenkmäler in der Moderne*, ed. Reinhart Koselleck and Michael Jeismann (Munich, 1993), 9.
20. Rudolf Broch and Hans Hauptmann, *Die westgalizischen Heldengräber: Aus den Jahren des Weltkrieges 1914–1915* (Vienna, 1918), 1.
21. Ibid., 2ff.
22. Adam Bartosz, "Jewish War Cemeteries in Western Galicia," http://www.museum.tarnow.pl/judaica/jewish.html (accessed 27 March 2011).
23. Bruch and Hauptmann, *Die westgalizischen Heldengräber*, 8ff.
24. Ibid.
25. Ibid., 6ff. Similar to the *Heldenhaine* in East Prussia: see Robert Traba, "Der Friedhof im Kulturwandel: Ostpreußische Kriegsgräber aus dem Ersten Weltkrieg von 1915 bis 1995," *Nordost-Archiv* 6 (1997): 109–29.
26. Jan Szubert, *Austriackie cmentarze wojenne w Galicji z lat 1914–1918* (Cracow, 1992), 30 ff.
27. Pavlo Hrankin, "Z istorii vijs'kovykh zvyntariv L'vova (1914–1918 r.)," *Halyts'ka Brama* 5–6 (traven'-cherven' 1998), 14–15; O. V., "Cholm Slavy 1914–1915 rr.," *Halyts'ka Brama*, 16ff; Khrystyna Kharchuk, "Avstrijs'kyj vijs'kovyj tsvintar," *Halyts'ka Brama*, 18–20.
28. State Archive of the Lviv Region (Derzhavnyj Arkhiv L'vivskoi Oblasti: hereafter DALO), f. 257, op. 2, spr. 183, ark. 17–18: Magistrate of Lviv to the Society for the Protection of the Graves of Polish Heroes, 27 February 1922.
29. For example Kazimierz Żygulski, *Jestem z lwowskiego etapu* (Warsaw, 1994), 21; Archive of the East of the Centre Karta, Warsaw (Archiwum Wschodni Ośrodku Karta: hereafter AW), II/1773: Alma Heczko, "Dziennik-pamiętnik," diary entry for 1–2 November 1938.
30. "W obronie wschodniej Małopolski," *Słowo Polskie*, 23 November 1919.
31. *Słowo Polskie*, 1 October 1925.
32. *Kurier Lwowski*, 1 November 1925.
33. *Słowo Polskie*, 5 November 1920.
34. *Diło*, 1 November 1922.
35. Vasyl' Shchurat, "Dlja tych, shcho vstanut' …," *Vichny pamjat' herojam* (Lviv, 1921), 9.
36. Ivan Nimchuk, "Kul't poliahlykh heroiiv," *Diło*, 17 May 1927, 13–15.
37. "Zhyvi svidky nedavn'ominuloi slavy," *Novyj Chas*, 1 November 1934.
38. *Diło*, 14 May 1927.
39. Orest Dzjuban, "Strilec'ki nekropoli L'vova," *Halyts'ka Brama* 5–6 (traven'-cherven' 1998), 3–6.
40. Józef Białynia-Chołodecki, *Wojenny posiew Anioła Śmierci i kult pamięci poległych* (Lviv, 1926), 12ff.
41. *Inwalida* 8 (1919).
42. Mirosława Papierzyńska-Turek, *Sprawa Ukraińska w Drugiej Rzeczypospolitej 1922–1926* (Cracow, 1979), 167.

43. Mick, *Kriegserfahrungen*, 362 ff.
44. TsDIAL, f. 205, op. 1, spr. 500, ark. 140–43: Daily report of the police in Lviv, 30 May 1939.
45. TsDIAL, f. 701, op. 3, spr. 388, ark. 13: Protocol of the Jewish religious community (excerpt), 15 November 1916.
46. Wacław Wierzbieniec, "Związek Żydów Uczestników Walk o Niepodległość Polski we Lwowie (1932–1939)," in *Lwów. Miasto—społeczeństwo—kultura*, ed. Henryk W. Żaliński and Kazimierz Karolczak (Cracow, 1998), 283.
47. Marek Jabłonowski, *Sen o potędze Polski: Z dziejów ruchu byłych wojskowych w II Rzeczypospolitej, 1918–1939* (Olsztyn, 1998), 104.
48. Ibid., 213; Wierzbieniec, "Związek," 299.
49. "Ofiary," *Chwila*, 16 December 1919; "Uczczenie pamięci ofiar rozruchów listopadowych," *Chwila*, 7 December 1920.
50. Jabłonowski, *Sen o potędze Polski,* 103.
51. Mick, "Der Kult um den Unbekannten Soldaten."
52. Jabłonowski, *Sen o potędze Polski*, 56 ff, 87ff.
53. Ibid., 29, 104.
54. TsDIAL, f. 146, op. 8, spr. 3807, s. 49–51. Director of the Police in Lwów, Reinlender, to the Präsidium der Statthalterei, 19 June 1920.
55. Jabłonowski, *Sen o potędze Polski*, 253.
56. This applied to soldiers of the German army from August 1914 until 27 December 1918, to soldiers of the Russian army until 1 March 1918, and to soldiers of the Habsburg army until 1 November 1918.
57. "Ustawa 18 March 1921 on war invalids etc," *Inwalida* 14, 3 April 1921.
58. *Inwalida* 3 (1921), 1ff.
59. Jabłonowski, *Sen o potędze Polski*, 254ff.
60. Ibid., 34.
61. 3,508 Belorussians, 3,587 Germans, 15 Russians, and 88 others were also recognized as war invalids: *Inwalida Zydowski* 11 (1934).
62. *Inwalida Zydowski* 7 (1934).
63. Jabłonowski, *Sen o potędze Polski*, 104 ff.
64. *Reduta Ilustrowana* [published by the Legia Inwalidów Wojsk Polskich], 1 (February 1930), 20.
65. Ibid.
66. Jabłonowski, *Sen o potędze Polski*, 267.
67. *Inwalida Zydowski* 12 (1926).
68. *Inwalida Zydowski* 6, 7, 8, 9 (1930).
69. Jabłonowski, *Sen o potędze Polski*, 258.
70. *Inwalida Zydowski* 11 (1934).
71. Jabłonowski, *Sen o potędze Polski*, 259.
72. The journal *Inwalida* shows this trend well.
73. Jabłonowski, *Sen o potędze Polski*, 232ff.
74. Ibid., 260.
75. Out of 166,733 war invalids, 127,649 were Poles, 25,661 Ukrainians, 3,883 Belorussians, 3,595 Germans, 656 Russians, 5,236 Jews, and 52 of other nationalities. The three south eastern voivodeships were home to 38,199 invalids. Grouped according to their degree of disability, more than 85,000 were in one of the first three categories, almost 40,000 were in categories 4–8 and only 2,082 were in category 9–10 with a disability of 90–100 percent: *Inwalida* 20/1 (10 January 1938), 9–10.

76. TsDIAL, f. 462, op. 1, spr. 180. Report of the *Invalidenreferat* of the Ukrainian Civic Committee, 1921; TsDIAL, f. 462, op. 1, spr. 180, ark. 15–21. Note on Ukrainian disabled soldiers, July 1921.
77. After the Polish victory in the Polish-Ukrainian war, the Supreme Allied Council approved Polish control of the territory of the Western Ukrainian People's Republic (more or less identical with Eastern Galicia), but the Conference of Ambassadors in Paris only formally recognized the eastern borders of the Second Polish Republic on 15 March 1923.
78. TsDIAL, f. 462, op. 1, spr. 180: report of the *Invalidenreferat* of the Ukrainian Civic Committee, 1921; TsDIAL, f. 462, op. 1, spr. 180, ark. 15–21: Note on Ukrainian disabled soldiers, July 1921.
79. Ibid.
80. "Sprava Ukrains'kykch Invalidiv," *Svoboda*, 12 June 1921.
81. "Communiqué of the Union of Ukrainian Invalids in Galicia, Sojuz Ukrajins'kykh Invalidiv v Halychyni," *Svoboda*, 18 May 1922.
82. *Novyj Chas*, 1 November 1934.
83. "Lystopad—misjats' ukraiins'kych invalidiv!," *Dilo*, 1 November 1935.
84. For Lviv, see Christoph Mick, "War and Conflicting Memories—Poles, Ukrainians and Jews in Lvov 1914–1939," *Simon Dubnow Institute Yearbook* 4 (2005): 257–78.
85. Polish authors did not cease to accuse the Jewish population of collaboration with the Ukrainian troops. See Ludwik Baar, "Milicja wojskowa w obronie Lwowa," in *Obrona Lwowa*, 2 (Lwów, 1936; reprint Warsaw, 1993), 47–64. Similar views were held by the Polish commander of the Obrona Lwowa: Czesław Mączynski, "O stanowisku Żydów w czasie listopadowej obrony Lwowa w 1918 r.," in *Obrona Lwowa*, 2, 830–41. See also criticism of the Polish position in a letter by the Jewish lawyer Izaak Bürger, autumn 1933: DALO, f. 257, op. 2, spr. 1753, ark. 95–99.
86. Mick, "Der Kult um den Unbekannten Soldaten," 199ff.

Chapter 12

DIVIDED LAND, DIVERGING NARRATIVES
Memory Cultures of the Great War
in the Successor Regions of Tyrol

Laurence Cole

For a country so directly responsible for its outbreak, Austria-Hungary has been strangely absent from much historical discussion on World War I. As Oswald Überegger has argued, Austrian scholarship itself has generally failed to engage with a series of debates relating to the conflict: its origins and unfolding; the social, economic, and cultural history of the home front; the experiences of soldiers and POWs; the experiences of refugees and internees; the propaganda war; the defeat; and, just as importantly, its memorialization and aftermath.[1] In particular, there have been no transnational comparisons of memory cultures in what may be termed the "successor regions" to the Habsburg monarchy's Alpine provinces, despite the fact that territorial partition post-1918 was a widespread phenomenon.[2]

Of those Alpine lands, the province of Tyrol was the most bitterly fought over. After Italy's entry into the war in May 1915, the front ran through the south of this region, where in 1910 German-speakers had been in a slight majority (around 55 percent) over Italian-speakers (around 44 percent), with a small minority of Ladin-speakers (1 percent). With the collapse of the Habsburg state, the territory south of the Brenner pass was awarded to Italy in line with the secret Treaty of London of 1915. Taking the area covered by the old borders of Tyrol, this chapter analyzes the memory cultures in its three successor regions, each undergoing a different kind of postwar experience: 1) Tyrol or "Austrian Tyrol," those areas that formed part of the Austrian Republic, thus being "a losing region in a losing state"; 2) South Tyrol, annexed by Italy in 1919 and hence "a losing region in a winning state"; 3) Trentino, the former Italian-Tyrol, long coveted by the irredentist movement and likewise gained by Italy after the war, thereby constituting—ostensibly, at least—"a winning region in a winning state."

In comparing the aftermath of wars, John Horne has identified five kinds of "defeat cultures": temporary defeat (in a longer, ultimately successful war); definitive defeat (a clear verdict in battle, which is reflected in the subsequent peace); total defeat (where the enemy loses sovereignty); internal defeat in civil war; and partial defeat (a military loss, but without necessarily incurring political or territorial consequences).[3] Austrian Tyrol and South Tyrol represented different forms of "defeat culture": the former experienced a "definitive defeat," encompassing military collapse, political revolution (regime change from the Habsburg monarchy to the First Austrian Republic), and territorial loss; South Tyrol suffered a "total defeat," where military defeat was followed by occupation and loss of political sovereignty to a foreign regime. Much more than the victors, the defeated are placed in a position where explanations of the outcome are urgently necessary, making issues of reaction, reform, or regeneration imperative. In such cases, there is also the question as to when the war fully ended in the sense that those defeated accept and come to terms with their changed position.[4] For Trentino, the situation was more complex, and here one could augment Horne's typology by adding the category of "hidden defeat," a phenomenon that is arguably typical of many former border regions of the Habsburg monarchy where territory changed hands after 1918. While formally part of a "victory culture," there was in fact a strong element of "suppressed defeat," because the actual experience of many Trentines in fighting on the losing side was more or less excluded from public commemorations of the war.

In addressing these issues, this chapter concentrates on social memories of war, understood as a "process (or processes) through which a knowledge or awareness of past events or conditions is developed and sustained within human societies," but without "excluding the workings of the memory that is individual."[5] A comparative structure to the analysis is provided by an examination of official attempts at shaping and sustaining memories of the Great War. Acts of "collective remembrance" and the use of monuments as "memory material" will be analyzed with regard to their reception in society at large, their effectiveness compared to other *modi memoranda*, and their relationship to alternative memory narratives.[6]

The Shadow of Defeat: Austrian Tyrol

Even before the terms of the peace settlement had been announced, a general disillusionment was widespread in Tyrol after 1918, due to the hard years of war, the collapse of the Habsburg monarchy, and the chaos and disorder of the immediate postwar period.[7] The popular mood in the immediate aftermath of 1918 developed the critical views toward the conflict that had begun to emerge during the course of the war.[8] In 1919 when a priest, Anton Müller, popularly known as Brother Willram and well-known for his patriotic poems and fiery rhetoric, tried to invoke the mood of wartime government propaganda in a commemorative ceremony on the Berg Isel outside Innsbruck, he was roundly booed by ex-soldiers before being pelted with snowballs and forced to abandon his speech.[9]

Despite this overt rejection of the war, it was nevertheless difficult to establish a clear break between the end of the conflict and "normal" peacetime conditions. While Austrian Tyrol was initially occupied by Italian troops, the presence of the latter actually proved less destabilizing than the immediate social, economic, and political circumstances of 1919 (the Italians did not interfere in the political administration of the region and helped distribute scarce food supplies). As in other parts of central Europe, the end of the war and troop demobilization were accompanied by unrest and political polarization, which encouraged paramilitary mobilization. Civil guards were established in Tyrol's main cities, while a number of volunteers joined in the fighting between neighboring Carinthia and the emerging state of Yugoslavia.[10] With rumors in June 1919 about the impending loss of South Tyrol to Italy, the sense—especially among political elites—that the struggle was not over intensified still further.[11] This development meant first, that the outcome of the war assumed as great a significance in public memory as the war itself, and second, that World War I was seen as another round in a long-standing conflict, so that Italy's entry into the war in May 1915—the moment of "Italian treachery"—became equally as important a date for Tyrol as August 1914, if not more so. In one contribution to a veterans' journal published in the mid-1920s, the fateful events of 1915 were placed in a direct line with the invasions from the south experienced in the Napoleonic period and the wars of Italian independence, such that French and Italians merged into one hereditary enemy: "as in the famous years 1797, 1805, 1809, 1848, and 1866 the men girded themselves full of enthusiasm for the fight against the 'foreign' (*welsch*) hereditary enemy who threatened the borders of the beautiful, beloved homeland."[12]

Italy completed the formal annexation of South Tyrol in October 1920, and in November the provincial Diet (Landtag) in Innsbruck responded with an official pronouncement of grief (*Trauerkundgebung*). Joseph Schraffl, provincial chief minister from the Christian Social party, set the tone for how Tyrolean public memory of the war would be framed, comparing the outcome to the Napoleonic Wars, when the land had also been torn apart after defeat in an 1809 uprising against the Bavarians and French, led by the innkeeper Andreas

Hofer. Schraffl stated that the divided land had eventually been reunited (in 1814) thanks to the prayers of their forefathers, before linking that history to the recent sacrifice in the Great War:

> Never shall we forget, that the first man from Tyrol, who fought for its freedom and that of the German people and for which he spilt his blood, Andreas Hofer, was a South Tyrolean … Finally, I thank also in the name of the whole country the most noble of its sons, who sacrificed their health and their lives out of ardent love for the Fatherland. They are many thousands; they were always the bravest on all of Austria's battlefields and won the admiration of the whole world. Should all this heroism, all this patriotism be a vain sacrifice?[13]

Contained here are two of the key elements in how Tyrol would publicly remember the war: sacrifice and reunification. Linked to the religious, deeply rooted idea of martyrdom, which was also an essential component of the cult around national hero Andreas Hofer,[14] there is the idea that no province in Austria had produced a greater sacrifice. And yet the hope remained that—as in 1809—defeat would be followed by reunification. From 1921 onward (until 1937) an official "day of mourning" (*Trauertag*) was held in Innsbruck on 10 October 1920 to commemorate Italy's formal annexation of South Tyrol, meaning that the loss of territory—rather than the end of the war—became the "density point" in official memory of the conflict.[15] This formed a key theme of contemporary publications and regional journals, such as *Tiroler Heimat*, which laid out other elements in the understanding of the war: despite the loss of the war by Austria-Hungary, Tyrol's soldiers had been unbeaten on the field of battle; Austria-Hungary had been betrayed by Italy in 1915; the military had been stabbed in the back by the monarchy's non-German nationalities, Jews, and socialists; and the defense of the province's borders by the local militia was stylized into the heroic actions of mountain warriors, fighting side-by-side in a brotherhood-of-arms with Imperial German soldiers, for Germanness (*Deutschtum*) and the German people (*deutsches Volkstum*).[16]

The binding elements in the Tyrolean discourse on World War I found their symbolic center on the Berg Isel outside Innsbruck, which had been the scene of several battles during the 1809 uprising and had become the primary Tyrolean *lieu de mémoire* before 1914. It was here that a statue to Andreas Hofer had been unveiled in 1893; the area was also a home for the tradition of the Kaiserjäger (the Tyrolean "house regiment"), which had a shooting range and officers' pavilion on the site. In June 1919 when it became clear that Tyrol was in danger of losing its southern territory, the Berg Isel was the automatic choice for a major demonstration. During the 1920s, the area's symbolic importance was strengthened by the addition of new markers commemorating the Great War. In 1923, a grave of honor to the "unknown" Kaiserjäger was erected on the south side of a memorial chapel, as the symbolic resting place of the nearly twenty thousand Kaiserjäger dead, many of whom had been buried on the Eastern front, where cemeteries were difficult to access for next of kin.[17] A monumental bronze relief shows a Kaiserjäger holding high the regimental flag, proclaiming "Honor above Death." Nearby stood another bronze relief of a book page, with the last verse of the Kaiserjäger song:

> Fought like heroes
> Bled man upon man.
> Only songs will tell
> Of the great deeds you have done. And should one find graves
> In the sand, which no one knows:
> Those were Kaiserjäger
> from the great regiment.[18]

First opened in 1880, the adjoining Kaiserjäger museum was reopened in the 1920s, with a series of rooms dedicated to the fallen warriors of World War I, seamlessly integrated into the narrative of Tyrolean heroism. In 1927, a Heroes' Book of Honor inscribing the names of all Tyrol's war dead from 1796 onward would be placed there too. In the museum catalog from 1937, the notions of a "stab-in-the-back" and invincibility—and thus the rejection of the idea of defeat—were explicitly stated: "In October 1918, the Austro-Hungarian monarchy broke up from the inside; the brave Tyrolean Kaiserjäger regiments remained, however, undefeated until the end."[19]

What is interesting about the Berg Isel site is the fact that no major war memorial was erected there, and this proves symptomatic of the social tensions and divergent experiences produced by the war. The lack of a national war memorial in Austrian Tyrol was partly influenced by the fact that a large monument to soldiers of the 2nd Kaiserjäger regiment had been planned during the war itself, with work already having commenced in Bozen, the main town in southern Tyrol. Yet, after the latter's annexation and the abandonment of that monument, proposals for a large monument to the ordinary Tyrolean soldiers who had served in the reserve regiments and militia—the so-called Standschützen (as opposed to the regular troops in the Kaiserjäger)—were never realized. Plans were drawn up in 1923 to remember those "who had sacrificed their blood for the fatherland, but also those, who for three long years placed their lives on the line for the homeland, in a word, for 'Tyrol's last line' that is embodied by the Standschützen."[20] With the backing of the provincial executive and Innsbruck town council, the initiative was taken by a committee headed by Baron Gotthard von An der Lan, who had commanded a militia battalion during the war.[21] In seeking to mark the tenth anniversary of May 1915, the public appeal for financial donations subscribed to the official war narrative, whereby duty was triumphantly fulfilled in the spirit of the 1809 uprising:

Thousands and thousands of young boys, mature and elderly men stood on the borders of our holy land. And then came the struggle, the victory [*sic*] and the end.... On the icy peaks, on the rugged prongs of the Dolomites ... they fought and bled, and many, many rest under lonely crosses on the distant mountains. The 'last line' did its duty! ... It shall be a monument, which should preserve the memory of our second *Anno Nine* for future generations.[22]

Despite a declaration by the provincial chief minister that the erection of such a monument was a patriotic duty, the organizing committee failed to raise sufficient funds for work on the monument to be started—let alone completed—before the tenth anniversary. A design competition was held, but May 1925 was marked only by a commemoration day on the Berg Isel. In the presence of Austrian General Viktor Dankl, former military commander of the region, Baron An Der Lan thanked the German comrades who had stood "shoulder-to-shoulder" with the Tyrolean reserves, before claiming that the troops had "fought for the one, whole Tyrol, and we are all inspired by the warmest desire, that our old Tyrol might be resurrected again."[23] Reversal of the war's outcome and the achievement of "a reunited, happy land of Tyrol" thus provided the main focus for this event, which was reasonably well attended by sharp-shooter companies (comprising around twelve hundred men in total) from Innsbruck and the surrounding area.

Ultimately, however, the project ran out of steam. This was indicative of the limited resonance achieved by a commemoration of the war based chiefly on heroic rhetoric.[24] In the first place, newspaper reports make clear that it was only sharp-shooter companies from Innsbruck and the surrounding district who were involved. An Der Lan got few responses to his request for definite replies on numbers participating, and the committee seems to have bowed to the inevitable by accepting that the Innsbruck event would be mainly a local one, with equivalent commemorations held in other districts.[25] Second, parts of the armed forces had already constructed their own memorials. For example, one for Tyrolean artillerymen had already been consecrated in July 1921; similarly, the renamed successor regiments to the Kaiserjäger each held their own annual day of remembrance, commemorating different battles from the war (usually the first major battle the regiment had been involved in).[26] Third, priority was given to the erection of local war memorials rather than to a more grandiose provincial monument, meaning that financial resources were too stretched to donate to more than one project.[27] An Der Lan was told by a colleague from Kufstein that the company of sharpshooters there could not take part in the project because of the acute need to erect their own war memorial, but also because the town was obliged to complete an Andreas Hofer monument that had been planned before the war.[28] The lack of interest emerges too from a letter sent by the former head of the shooting range and militia company in Tux in the Ziller valley. While personally enthusiastic, he lamented the lack of support for militia activities from the village council, which had sold the shooting range ground and continually pressed for the dissolution of the company and the removal of all weapons.[29]

This revealed a great decline in sharpshooting activities after 1918, in contrast to the pre-1914 period, when militia companies had boomed.[30] Among the ordinary population, there was a rejection of militaristic activities and a reluctance to engage in heroic commemorations of the war.[31] Particularly noteworthy about one commemoration in Landeck in 1925, for example, was the speech by a former field chaplain, in which he described the event "not as warmongering, but as a reunion for the preservation of mutual loyalty and maintenance of the old ideals, of love and loyalty to God, to the Fatherland, and to one's fellow human beings."[32] Rather than stressing the "blood sacrifice," this anti-heroic emphasis on comradeship appears to be one that reflected more accurately how many chose to remember the war. What counted for the ordinary soldier was the remembrance of fallen comrades, as reflected in the photographs of lost companions added into the war chronicle produced by Oswald Kaufmann of his time in a militia battalion on the South Tyrolean front.[33] While Kaufmann was from neighboring Vorarlberg, his simple remembrance of comrades seems suggestive of the popular mood in Tyrol, which was wary of glorifying the slaughter.

Pragmatic considerations reinforced this distance from heroicized forms of commemoration. In the straightened economic circumstances of postwar Austria, which was even harder hit in the 1920s than Germany, the choice between a comparatively costly form of public commemoration or welfare assistance for surviving soldiers, widows, and orphans, fell to the latter.[34] Organizations involved in caring for the victims of the war, chiefly the Provincial Union of War Invalids, Widows, and Orphans, subscribed to a less militaristic image of the war. A publication to mark the association's tenth anniversary, for instance, brought in poems and contributions that portrayed the sufferings of war without embellishment, including an extract from the famous "Declaration of War against War" by Jean Paul. However, it also contained work from patriotic propagandists such as Anton Müller (Brother Willram), who reminded readers of the "victorious keeping of the watch on the border," and expressed the desire for a "free and united Tyrol."[35]

Where, for the ordinary soldier, the remembrance of fallen comrades took place in the locality, there were also corporate manifestations of "commemorative comradeship," especially at the officer level. A good example is the erection of a marble memorial tablet in the church of St John provided by former members of the infantry officer school in Innsbruck. Led by one Colonel Zempirek, who laboriously pieced together a detailed list of the 147 fallen alumni, the project reached completion at the end of September 1927, when a "day of honor" was held in Innsbruck and the tablet was unveiled. In contrast to the simple commemoration of fallen comrades among the rank-and-file, this project showed a greater willingness to use heroic rhetoric, as well as displaying an undiluted harking after the "the good old days."[36] For one former officer, the guard-of-honor at the unveiling ceremony gave the impression "that they were just as upright and disciplined as the old imperial army."[37] The old officer corps had, of course, felt the loss of the monarchy most keenly and was anxious to preserve the honor of the Habsburg army, but also the sense of personal status, attachment and belonging they had felt as part of an elite cadre serving the emperor.[38] Former officers decisively shaped what Gergely Romsics has termed the "old Austrian" interpretation of the end of the monarchy, with the war being positively remembered because the soldiers had done their duty before the final collapse.[39]

Indeed, the actions of Zempirek and his colleagues were symptomatic of a wider trend with regard to how influential members of the old officer corps increasingly monopolized public commemoration of the war.[40] As part of the fundraising activities to pay for the memorial tablet, for example, Zempirek organized low-priced cinema evenings showing *The Kaiserjäger Film*.[41] Produced by the Kaiserjäger Museum, it followed the uncritical, heroic narrative adopted by former officers in Austria, who wrote the history of the war as a kind of "club history."[42] Former Kaiserjäger officers such as Hans Bator and Viktor Schemfil played a leading role in this process of "historical engineering," producing a number of publications glorifying the battles on the Alpine front and the common struggle alongside German troops.[43] Due to his involvement in the leading provincial association for helping war victims, Bator was certainly not blind to the sufferings it had caused, but as a former officer he was also concerned about preserving the reputation of the army and its commanders. From around 1921 onward, Bator was among those conservative-patriotic former officers who sought to provide a more positively weighted memory of the war to counter social-democratic criticism (particularly evident in Landtag debates after 1918). In this vein, in July 1921 he helped organize a first Kaiserjäger reunion on the Berg Isel.[44] Publications produced at this time revealed the potential difficulties involved, and acknowledged that many ordinary veterans might not want to look back on the years of slaughter. Yet, for Bator, the impulse to counter allegedly derogatory portrayals of the army and to provide a patriotic history for "our Austrian fatherland" overrode these painful memories.[45] These aims were backed by declarations of support from Austrian Chancellor Ignaz Seipel and former Chief of the General Staff Franz Conrad von Hötzendorf, both of whom praised the organization's upholding of the Tyrolean regiments' "heroic traditions." In the veterans' yearbook, mystical accounts of the war were accompanied by uncritical, reverential portraits of former commanding officers. Thus, Viktor Dankl, former commander on the Southwest front, was described in the 1925 yearbook as "a genuine Austrian soldier-type, a leader in the fullest sense of the word," who remained "a General still worshipped by his soldiers."[46] Similar sentiments to these were reflected in war novels by Tyroleans from north and south of the Brenner border, such as Luis Trenker and Anton Bossi Fedrigotti.[47] With time, this heroicization overlapped with a more radical German-national view, as in Bossi Fedrigotti's novel *Standschütze Bruggler*, published in Germany in 1934 (and filmed two years later, as one of the first films produced by the National Socialist Propaganda office).[48]

Overall, social memory of the war in Austrian Tyrol came to be dominated by a discourse of martyrdom and injustice, deriving on the one hand from the war's outcome and the loss of South Tyrol, and on the other from the notions of heroic sacrifice, fulfillment of duty and brotherhood-in-arms propagated by former army elites and conservative-national writers. The mapping out of the Berg Isel site, where the influence of the Kaiserjäger was so strong, is indicative of this. In the case of the abortive Standschützen memorial on the Berg Isel, the fact that the association of former Kaiserjäger officers (Alt-Kaiserjägerclub) owned the ground gave it a decisive influence in deciding if and where a memorial should be erected. In practice, this group never enthusiastically embraced the idea of a memorial to the common soldiers fighting in reservist formations, expressing concerns about whether the monument could be accommodated where a number of commemorative objects and buildings were already in place.[49] The situation was not helped by a polemic between An Der Lan and others as to whether the sharpshooter companies should form part of the Kaiserschützenbund, the veterans' organization run by former members of the Kaiserjäger officer corps. An Der Lan tried to maintain the independence of reservist formations from military control (much as civilian politicians had tried—in vain—to do during the war itself), while the former officers sought to exert their influence over this association, which did in fact become an umbrella organization for army veterans and reservists.[50]

In Tyrol, therefore, 1918 was seen as a "temporary defeat"—an outcome that needed to be revised, and not the "definitive defeat" implied by the peace treaty. As the Kaiserjäger-Yearbook from 1924 stated:

> We want to preserve the memory of the heroic battles of the Kaiserjäger … so that the fire of enthusiasm and love of the homeland will always be nourished by them and by the memory of our dead; so that thoughts of a 'German land from Kufstein to Salurn' always remain alive in us Kaiserjäger and in all Tyroleans, until the day comes when the sacred justice of the German people victoriously brings misery to its enemies and our Tyrolean eagle powerfully stretches its wings into flight over our free fatherland.[51]

The Shadow of the *Fasces:* South Tyrol

If collective remembrance of the war dead in Austrian Tyrol was always linked to the notion of Tyrolean territorial unity, the emotionally laden narrative of heroic sacrifice followed by unjust treatment was a fundamental feature of the group psychology of the German minority in the Italian Kingdom after 1918.[52] Here too, protests about the outcome of the war and against the new regime were placed within the historical master narrative of the 1809 uprising. As in Innsbruck in 1919, a major protest in favor of autonomy was held in front of the Andreas Hofer statue in Merano (Meran) on 9 May 1920.[53] Yet, the changed circumstances of the post-1918 era meant that there was perhaps a greater uniformity to interpretations of the war among South Tyroleans. Even if dissent from elite interpretations of the war was evident, such as in the criticism of "saloon officers" in individual memories of the war experience,[54] the fundamental reality of being placed under Italian sovereignty meant that the wartime rhetoric of "defending the land" against the "treacherous enemy" formed an essential defensive mechanism after 1918.

Under an Italian government that viewed the war as a struggle for national freedom against the Austrian and German oppressor, there was a self evident clash in South Tyrol over the meaning of the war. At the end of 1919, Julius Perathoner, the long-serving mayor of Bozen (or Bolzano, as it was now officially renamed), articulated the problem of organizing an appropriate public reception for those returning home from captivity, voicing "in the council's name his thanks for the fact that they had put their life and health on the line over many years, fighting on the borders to defend the fatherland," while deeply regretting that, "under the present political circumstances, it is not possible to organize a large celebration in their honor."[55] This situation, together with general economic difficulties, reinforced the initial concern for survivors and those left in need by the war. Hence, the municipality did its best to provide financial support to the War Invalids Association by granting it the use of a room in the town hall for administrative purposes, helping to fund secretarial work, and giving assistance in renovating a home for military veterans.[56]

While it remains unclear how far South Tyroleans were able to commemorate their war dead before the fall of the Italian liberal government in 1922, there is evidence to suggest that collective remembrance occurred within certain limits. Public celebrations for returning soldiers were unwelcome, but a confidential survey conducted by the Fascist authorities in the late 1930s indicates that at least 49 war memorials were erected to the war dead in South Tyrol in the early 1920s.[57] Most of these were erected in the period before the end of 1922: at Lana, for example, a monument had been inaugurated in late 1919, although at Cermes (Tscherms) a memorial bearing the inscription, "Pray for the Heroes 1914–1918," was consecrated as late as 1925.[58]

During the transitional years from 1918 to 1922, acts of collective remembrance could take place in smaller localities where Italian administrative control had yet to penetrate fully, while the authorities adopted a firmer line in the regional capital of Bolzano. There was no question, for example, of work continuing on the major public memorial in the town, which was to commemorate the dead from the 2nd Kaiserjäger regiment, although the regimental officer corps sought to keep open the possibility of its completion. It asked the municipality to assume ownership of the site, while stipulating that at no point should the monument be surrendered to, or completed by, the Italians (not even for the purposes of erecting a common monument to the dead of both countries).[59] In doing so, the Austria-based officers recognized the need to divest themselves of property in what was now a foreign state, as well as the fact that the partially built foundations were falling into disrepair and being raided for building materials. In acceding to the request in mid-1920, the town council reaffirmed its intention to see the monument eventually completed, but recognized that there was no immediate prospect of finishing the project, given the lack of sufficient funds; it was not optimistic that the work would ever be finished.[60]

While before 1922 the Italian authorities sought to restrict overt displays of collective remembrance, the subsequent seizure of power by the Fascists dramatically increased tensions in the region. Conflict over the war's meaning became an integral part of the practical and symbolic struggle between the state and the German-speaking minority. One of the most notorious incidents of Fascist violence occurred on 14 April 1921, when a folkloristic procession in Bolzano was attacked by a black shirt squad led by Achille Starace, the future party secretary. Many were wounded and a teacher, Franz Innerhofer, was killed, reportedly while trying to protect two youngsters from the marauding thugs.[61] In a highly emotive speech at Innerhofer's funeral procession, prominent local politician Eduard Reut-Nicolussi praised the "most recent martyr" for the Tyrolean homeland, equating his death with the sacrifice of those fallen in the war and imploring youth to take inspiration from his courage.[62] Yet, such public protests would become increasingly difficult with the tightening of political restrictions, press censorship and a program of Italianization of public offices and schools imposed from the start of 1923.[63]

The figure of Reut-Nicolussi, who was from a bourgeois family in the German language island of Lusern in Trentino's Fersina valley and fought in the 4th Kaiserjäger regiment during the war, came to personify the initial struggle against Italian rule and for international recognition of the South Tyrolean question.[64] Politically, Reut-Nicolussi bridged the gap between German nationalism and Catholic conservatism, albeit leaning increasingly toward the former (when later in exile in Austrian Tyrol he worked for nationalist organisations). He was a tireless campaigner whose speeches and publications became widely known thanks to the numerous personal links between activists in Austria and South Tyrol, many of whom belonged to the pressure group for the South Tyrolean cause, the Andreas-Hofer-Bund, founded in 1919. A standard programmatic statement by Reut-Nicolussi from the end of 1927 focused, as always, on the outcome of the war but also on South Tyrol's "German" past. As had Landeshauptmann Schraffl in 1920, Reut-Nicolussi saw 1809 as the highpoint of Tyrolean history, not least for the hope it held out of eventual territorial division. In turning to World War I, he looked back on Italy's "betrayal" in 1915, before asserting that Tyrol's heroic defense of its freedom had cost four times as many lives as on the Italian side, underlining the ongoing injustice.[65]

Inevitably, given the nature of the Fascist movement and its triumphalist attitude toward the acquisition of South Tyrol, Bolzano became the major site for the display of Fascist power. The symbolic expression of this was a Victory Monument unveiled in July 1928. Although the most active proponents of Italianization on the ground in South Tyrol were the radical nationalist Ettore Tolomei (from nearby Rovereto) and the Legione Trentina (composed of volunteers who during the war had crossed over from Trentino to fight on the Italian side),[66] the initiative for this monument came from Mussolini himself. Having advocated the acquisition of the Brenner border and having spent time in Trentino in the company of fellow socialist and journalist Cesare Battisti before 1914, Mussolini had a special interest in the newly annexed provinces. He envisaged the monument as a commemoration of the tenth anniversary of Battisti's execution by the Austrian regime in 1916. At the same time, his decision was an immediate response to a speech by the Bavarian Minister-President Heinrich Held on 5 February 1926, protesting against the "brutal rape of Germandom" in South Tyrol. Mussolini countered with an aggressive speech in parliament, in which he described the Tyrolese minority as an "ethnic relict" and proclaimed the right to Italianize the population. A month later, he entrusted officials with the job of finding a way to "give shape to the united and unflinching will of the nation" to celebrate the victorious war.[67]

Highly significant was the choice of location for the new monument because it was erected on the site where the Austrians had, since 1916, been planning the war monument to the Kaiserjäger, only the foundations and base of which were completed before war's end. The selection of this site meant that the monument acted as a gateway to the Italian new town (*città nuova*) in Bolzano, on the opposite side of the Talfer River to the old town center. Marcello Piacentini, the regime's star architect, was responsible not just for designing the victory monument, but also some imposing new barracks and the layout of the new town, where Italian migrants, especially administrative officials, came to live.[68] The arch thus celebrated victory at a national level, affirming a positive narrative and laying to rest the shadow of Caporetto and the notion of a "mutilated victory" that had dominated early discourse on the war in post-1918 Italy.[69]

While impressive financial backing enabled the monument to be completed in a relatively short time, the regime's objectives had to be modified when it became clear that members of Battisti's family were opposed to a memorial to him in Bolzano, considering Trento, where he had lived, worked, and been executed as the more appropriate location. Hence, the monument became a more general commemoration of the Italian victory, with lower key depictions on the inside of the arch of Battisti and his fellow martyrs, Fabio Filzi and Damiano Chiesa.[70] Unveiled at a lavish ceremony in July 1928 attended by the king, the monument became a focal point for Fascist displays and a much detested symbol for the South Tyrolean population (regular "victory ceremonies" were subsequently held there on an annual basis).[71] Displaying the intrinsic self-image of Fascism as a bellicose force, the Associazione Nazionale Volontari di Guerra (comprising those, who like Battisti, Filzi, and Chiesa had left Austria-Hungary to serve in the Italian army) sent a message to Italians on the eve of the unveiling ceremony. Decrying the "German arrogance" of the planned Kaiserjäger monument to "the victory of the Austro-Teutonic hordes," the association asserted that the God of arms, freedom, and justice had ensured that the spot was now marked by a monument to "the Italian victory, the true victory," while also hoping for future victories and proclaiming that "the Italy of Benito Mussolini is on the march. And no human force can stop it."[72]

The Victory Arch in Bolzano was a highpoint in a wider campaign to implant the Italian nationalist-Fascist memory of the war across the border region, as a series of ossuaries were erected during the 1920s and 1930s.[73] In the nine new provinces acquired by Italy after the war, the ossuaries were meant to act as a chain of silent, monumental sentries, protecting the "sacred borders" of the state.[74] While some were erected in the 1920s, the real drive came after the regime decreed in 1931 the closure of many military cemeteries, which could no longer be properly maintained, some of them having been erected on a provisional basis near battlegrounds. In their stead, a specially constituted "Commissariat for the Honoring of the Fallen" was given the task of building new charnel houses, which drew on a monumental style and symbolic language borrowed from Roman antiquity in a way typical of many buildings under the Fascist regime. From the mid-1920s, the ossuaries became both places of pilgrimage for relatives of the fallen and also national tourist sites attracting thousands of visitors.[75]

As implied by the Victory Monument, the corollary of Fascist memory strategy was to erase or diminish South Tyrolean commemorations of their war dead. Thus, the remains of South Tyrolean soldiers were often included in these ossuaries, reburied as "Italians" with Italianized first names. A case in point is that of Montepiano [Nasswand], near the old border between Italy and Austria-Hungary, which was the site of an extensive military cemetery, having been a transit point for war wounded. While there were practical reasons for disbanding the numerous, often not easily accessible cemeteries like Montepiano, the overriding ideological purpose is evident from the fact that, at the start of the 1930s, the remains of 446 soldiers were exhumed and reburied in the ossuary at Pocul, near Cortina d'Ampezzo (in the neighboring province of Belluno, formerly part of Tyrol).[76] In South Tyrol, an area that had scarcely been affected by the actual fighting, ossuaries were constructed near the three most important crossing points on the border: at Burguisio (Burgeis–Reschen) in the west (1939), at Colle Isarco (Gossensaß) to the north (1937), and at S. Candido (Innichen) in the east (1939). These physical expressions of the Fascist attempt to take possession of the Alpine landscape were also reinforced by national "pilgrimages" made by Fascists and members of the Legione Trentina to the new border at the Brenner pass, and by the organization of national veterans meetings in the region, such as that held by the Associazione Nazionale Combattenti in Bolzano in September 1924.[77]

Where the ossuaries constituted prestige projects, the Fascist authorities sought to combine Italianization policies with control of war remembrance by enacting legislation affecting inscriptions on gravestones. In 1923, a decree had made Italian the sole language of public use throughout the region, including all official signs and other notices, inscriptions or signs that were openly visible (e.g., on shops). By extension, the Fascist authorities sought to prevent war graves and cemeteries in South Tyrol from bearing anything other than religious inscriptions. These moves were accompanied by random acts of violence by Fascist groups against war memorials throughout the 1920s. Reut-Nicolussi wrote in outrage after one serious incident at Brunico (Bruneck): "The language of the oppressor is such that it even proclaims, over the fallen bones of the dead Tyroleans, that the world war was fought for the liberation of peoples—namely for their liberation from respect for God and what is worthy of respect, liberation from pious modesty before the majesty of death."[78]

The situation became more acute when in the autumn of 1927 the provincial prefect, Umberto Ricci, sought to extend the 1923 language provisions by specifically including gravestones in a supplementary decree on the public use of Italian. Reports sent clandestinely out of South Tyrol to the Viennese and German press claimed that Fascist policy was leading to the erasure of inscriptions on war graves, thus highlighting an emotive issue that attracted international attention. As one British expert on minority problems in interwar Europe, John Stephens, wrote in 1929: "After 27th September 1927, a decree of the Prefect of Bolzano required even the inscriptions on gravestones to be written in Italian. Few outrages against minorities have done as much as this to arouse public feeling in Europe and America."[79]

Despite repeated efforts by prefects, the government adopted a cautious approach, meaning that numerous exceptions were allowed, above all when it came to inscriptions relating to the fallen from the war or the burial of former soldiers.⁸⁰ When in 1933 a marble plaque honoring the dead of 1914–18 was placed in the civic cemetery at Merano, the prefect confirmed that it was not necessary for names to be transcribed into Italian; German was permissible, so long as it was in Latin script (rather than Gothic).⁸¹ Ultimately, therefore, the sphere of collective remembrance testifies to the "incomplete Italianization" of the region, as Andrea Di Michele has indicated.⁸² For example, the military cemetery of St Jakob in Bolzano had been established in the nineteenth century and was then extended in the course of the Great War, with numerous soldiers being buried without distinction of nationality. The Italian authorities took over part of the cemetery after 1918 in order to bury victims of the Spanish influenza epidemic, and this section was then sold to the Italian military in 1921. However, the remaining cemetery continued to be cared for by the head of the local veterans' association, who pledged to the authorities in 1924 to continue to maintain it as before. As well as making some minor improvements, the association even managed—thanks to skillful negotiation and the understanding of the clergyman responsible—to prevent the transfer of the remains of twelve South Tyroleans from St Jakob to the new ossuary at Burguisio.⁸³ The situation was then helped by the fallout from the controversy over inscriptions on war graves. The *podestà* of Bolzano recognized in 1934 that there were non-Italian inscriptions there, but stressed that his administration had no authority in the matter, and no one seemed keen to stir up further trouble.⁸⁴

Out of the Habsburg Shadow: Trentino

In line with the official policy evident in South Tyrol, a similar drive toward the nationalization—and later "Fascisticization"—of war memory was evident in neighboring Trentino, which together with Alto Adige formed part of the administrative region of Venezia Tridentina after 1918 (from 1927 onward, Trento and Bolzano were administered as separate provinces). While Trentino differed from South Tyrol in the fundamental respect that Italy saw this "redeemed" province as naturally part of the nation and the local population was "liberated" rather than defeated, in practice the situation was more complex, for the experiences of the majority of ordinary soldiers fighting on the Austro-Hungarian side were publicly forgotten.⁸⁵

In contrast to South Tyrol, Trentino had been a real battleground during the war, while the local population suffered tremendous upheaval. Out of a population of about 384,000 in Trentino, some 60,000 had been enrolled in the Austro-Hungarian army, with 11,000 killed; 150,000 were evacuated by the Habsburg authorities from the southernmost part of the territory after it was declared a war zone in 1915; a further 30,000 either fled south or were evacuated by the Italians from stretches of territory that they captured.⁸⁶ While the war experience decisively turned the mainly peasant population against the Habsburg regime, enthusiasm for the new government and incorporation into the centralist Italian state was less evident among the masses and their main political representative, the Popular Party. These political and social contrasts were underlined by a fundamental contradiction with regard to collective remembrance of the war, as the reality of Trentine participation in the Austro-Hungarian war effort and eventual defeat contrasted with the Risorgimento-inspired and then Fascist-influenced narrative of victory.

In shaping the discourse of collective remembrance, many members of the local bourgeoisie who had been prominent in the Italian national movement before 1914 played an important role immediately after 1918 in celebrating the region's "liberation," and seeking to lay down a heroic interpretation of the war. For these people, the victory derived from the heroic qualities of the Italian Alpine soldier, with the landscape itself forming part of the pictorial tapestry of commemoration.[87] Above all, the "fallen legionaries"—volunteers who had deserted to Italy after May 1915, or in some cases, before—formed the center of attention, with pride of place being given to Battisti, Filzi, and Chiesa, all of whom had been captured in action and executed as traitors. During the early 1920s a series of memorial stones commemorating legionaries were placed on mountain-tops around the region, constituting a small-scale, second-line counterpart to the massive ossuaries erected along the new national borders. At Mori, for example, in 1925 a marker stone to the legionary Federico Guella was placed on nearby Mount Albano, while a commemorative plaque for four other legionaries was installed at the cemetery in 1930.[88] In terms of visibility and their prominence in public discourse (and subsequently, in terms of regional historiography), the forty-one dead legionaries (out of approximately eight hundred volunteers) thus assumed a prominence far out of proportion to their number, as streets, squares, hospitals, schools, parks, and alpine hostels throughout the region were renamed in their honor.[89]

With regard to long-term impact, however, perhaps more important than these monuments was the institutionalization of collective memory in the form of two museums founded in the 1920s, the *Museo Trentino del Risorgimento* in Trento (1923), and the *Museo Storico Italiano della Guerra* in Rovereto (1921).[90] As the name of the former implies, the museum and its accompanying journal sought to document the oppression of Italians under Habsburg rule and to place the events of the war within the tradition of the Italian Risorgimento, with a prominent role being played by Battisti's widow, Ernesta Bittanti, along with her close friend, Bice Rizzi.[91] Located in the castle at Trento, where Battisti had been hanged and subsequently photographed in perhaps the most notorious piece of Austrian wartime propaganda, the museum's first exhibition was dedicated to the Trentine volunteers, reflecting the fact that the Legione Trentina had played a key role in founding the museum, alongside prominent local nationalists. In a similar way, but with a greater emphasis on the battlefield events and the physical destruction of the Trentine countryside, the museum in Rovereto acted as a national as well as regional *lieu de mémoire*. Where Battisti's death was explicitly commemorated at the Trento museum, a form of shrine to Filzi and Chiesa was placed in its Rovereto counterpart, thereby confirming the Risorgimento-derived interpretation of war, while sharing similarities with the Fascist interpretation of the war as a source of national rebirth.[92]

Although these initiatives by nationalists in Trentino accorded with the message propagated by the Italian state, the narrative of national redemption was nevertheless much questioned in Italy as a whole in the immediate postwar years.[93] In Trentino however, Socialist criticism of monuments glorifying the war was partly diminished by internal disputes and the problematic, ambivalent legacy left by the nationally minded Battisti. Hence, political Catholicism proved far more influential in challenging the liberation narrative, thanks to its electoral and organizational strength which made it the largest political force in the region. Political Catholics, such as the Popular Party regional leader Alcide De Gasperi, felt obliged to recognize Battisti's heroic sacrifice, yet clearly distanced themselves from the latter's Marxist "propaganda." In a newspaper commentary written in July 1921, De Gasperi instead emphasized the role of Damiano Chiesa, the Catholic irredentist.[94] The Catholic Church likewise placed a different emphasis on remembrance of the war, stressing the need for peace and reconciliation within an Italian-patriotic framework. Outside Rovereto, for example, there was placed an enormous "bell for the fallen" (*Campana dei Caduti*), dedicated to *Maria Dolens*, on the initiative of the local priest, Don Antonio Rossaro, a man whose identification with Italy did not preclude an appreciation of the sacrifice made by those local soldiers fallen in Austro-Hungarian colors. The bell stood as a symbol condemning war and encouraging peace; cast in bronze from cannons obtained from all the belligerent nations of the world conflict, it rang out its first tones on 4 October 1925 in the presence of King Victor Emmanuel III, after a moving procession through the streets of Rovereto.[95]

While the Popular Party accepted the transfer from Austrian to Italian sovereignty, it voiced the concerns among many of the Trentine population that their war memories were being ignored. As the party newspaper, *Il Nuovo Trentino*, argued in 1920: "Two years have passed since our redemption, patriotic festivals are organized, but our humble heroes are never thought of by the erection of a stone or monument to their eternal memory.... It is our holy and sacred duty and obligation to remember those who died for the fatherland."[96] Partly encouraged by such calls, and with the support of the clergy, numerous communities did then erect monuments or place memorial stones in cemeteries or town squares. Some state officials even displayed some tolerance towards these actions. For example, Luigi Credaro, the General Civil Commissar for Venezia Tridentina, did not refrain from participating in the inauguration of monuments to those fallen on the Habsburg side. Moreover, he intervened against—and eventually removed—the Civil Commissar in Cortina d'Ampezzo: the latter had disbanded a local committee set up to build a memorial chapel commemorating those who had died in the Austro-Hungarian ranks on the basis that this was an "anti-Italian" act.[97]

In short, many communities in Trentino were able to erect monuments to their dead in the first postwar years, but there were nevertheless residual difficulties with regard to their location and the form of commemoration. The case of Arco, as investigated by Aldo Miorelli, is instructive. In late September 1919, Cesare Moser, director of the local technical school, requested a plot of land from the council for a war memorial, but the council only responded six months later, after the Popular Party newspaper had taken up the cause of commemorating the "many martyrs." Moser had proposed a mausoleum to all the fallen (including those on the Italian side), but the council was not keen and—partly for reasons of cost—approved instead a memorial stone tablet for the Austro-Hungarian dead in the shape of a cross, placed on a simple stone pyramid. However, even this more modest version failed to find sufficient funding; the eventual solution was a simple tablet placed against one of the cemetery walls, inscribed with the words: "Arco—To its loved ones killed in the world war." Thus, a memorial was erected, but it was comparatively modest and inaugurated without the fanfare that accompanied monuments to the Trentine legionaries. It contrasted starkly also with a more extensive, free-standing monument erected in the same cemetery to the Czechoslovak legionaries who had died on the Italian side of the front, fighting against Austria-Hungary. In other words, the relative marginalization of the Arco monument showed how the national-liberal bourgeois elites, as represented by the town mayor, sought to subordinate the process of collective remembrance to the logic imposed by the prevailing "liberationist" national discourse, which only grudgingly acknowledged the need to commemorate the fallen from the other side. As the leading national-liberal paper, *La Libertà*, stated bluntly in June 1919: "Our fellow citizens killed in the uniform of the Austrian soldier are not and do not want to be the object of our gratitude and cannot in any way be proposed for veneration and imitation by future generations."[98]

Hence, the memorials to Trentino's war dead were in certain respects "non-monuments," as Miorelli terms them, because they were not openly commemorating the Austro-Hungarian fallen and because they remained marginal to the official narrative of the war. Nils Arne Sørensen has suggested a three-fold typology to the wording on these monuments, within which a non-heroic memorialization of "Austro-Trentine" soldiers was possible. First, a number of communities made their dedications in a spare, neutral language. Such was the case at Grauno, where the memorial was consecrated simply "To its fallen," or at

Brione, where the monument was erected "To its sons / fallen in the war 1914–1918."⁹⁹ Second, many communities sought to subsume the fact that their dead had died for "the enemy" through simple religious inscriptions. For example, at Caldes, the memorial read: "Caldes / to pious Jesus / to remember the strain endured by its beloved / perished in the ferocious conflict during the World War 1914–1918."¹⁰⁰ Third, some included a national element in remembrance of those killed fighting for Austria-Hungary. Good examples here are monuments at Sarche and Calceranica, which spoke respectively of the dead being "innocent victims" and dying "far from all they held dear."¹⁰¹ Significantly, most of these types of monuments were modest and contemplative in tone. They were usually placed in local cemeteries, embedding the memory in a traditional religious context. Moreover, they were to be found in the smaller villages and valleys. In towns such as Trento, Rovereto, Borgo, Cles, Riva, and Primiero, where liberal-national influence was stronger, such monuments were absent.

The restricted nature of memorial inscriptions was partly a result of nationalist pressure before 1922 (as at Arco), and partly a response to restrictions imposed by the Fascist authorities thereafter. In this sense, local nationalists anticipated much of what would become the official culture of commemoration under the Fascist regime. Although it would be a mistake to assume a direct overlap between the two, some 80 percent of the Legione Trentina did go on to become Fascist party members, with key figure Giuseppe Cristofolini constantly invoking the "Italy of the war combatants."¹⁰² Right after the Fascist assumption of power, local Fascists and the Legione Trentina pushed for the dismissal of Civil Commissar Credaro, with his tolerance of commemorations for the Austro-Trentine dead being a major cause of contention. Credaro was removed from his post in October 1922, and the Legione stepped up pressure on the administration by protesting in 1923 about "the worthless fashion in our country to erect monuments in the squares to those fallen in Austrian ranks. Those killed under the insignia of the oppressor merit respect and sorrow, but not an exaltation that could give rise to interpretations offensive to the patriotic sentiment of the Trentine population and in particular to those who sacrificed themselves voluntarily for the Fatherland."¹⁰³ In response, the prefect issued a decree informing local authorities that memorial inscriptions should embrace the notion of national redemption and seek to avoid the term "fallen" (*caduti*) because this concept was connected to death for the fatherland (*patria*); other words such as "perished," "killed," or "died" were to be used.

After this decree, some communities still sought to adopt religious inscriptions or neutral, minimalist wordings, but increasingly there was a trend toward "redemptive" rhetoric. At Cognola, nearby Trento, for example, the memorial inscription read: "Redeemed Cognola, which witnessed the Passion of Trento during centuries of oppression, and with Trento exulted on the radiant day of its hoped for redemption, remembers faithfully its sons deceased in war, constrained to fight for the foreigner."[104] Miorelli has calculated that, of 280 monuments subjected to historical analysis and erected in Trentino between 1919 and 1940, 240 still contain the original inscriptions. Only fifty of these were dedicated to the fallen *(caduti)*, thereby carrying an acknowledgement of their having died in Austria-Hungary's name, and most of these were erected before 1923.[105]

From the mid-1920s, at the latest, the Fascist imprint on collective remembrance in Trentino became ever more prominent. Here too, this was manifested in the building of ossuaries on the fringes of the province. On the border with the province of Vicenza, for instance, a major ossuary was consecrated at Pasubio in 1926, containing five thousand Italian soldiers and about sixty unidentified Austro-Hungarian soldiers. It explicitly reinforced the link between commemoration and the claim to the new borders: "The first army, attacked twice, threw back the proud enemy from Pasubio to the Brenner, assuring to Italy its sacred boundaries."[106] Further ossuaries were erected at Pocol near Cortina d'Ampezzo in 1935 and, above all, at Castel Dante (near Rovereto) inaugurated on 4 November 1936, where the remains of Chiesa and Filzi were ceremonially interred.[107]

Most prominent of all the Trentine war memorials was the mausoleum to Cesare Battisti, completed in 1935 after a comparatively lengthy gestation period that reveals some of the tensions between regional and national interests. Just a couple of weeks after Battisti's execution in July 1916, the Italian Prime Minister Paolo Bosselli had decreed the intention to erect a national monument to him in (as yet, uncaptured) Trento. The project took several years to develop, partly due to indecision as to the most appropriate location—in a town square, in the castle where he had been executed, or elsewhere—before it was agreed to build the monument on the Doss Trento, a rocky outcrop overlooking the town. Here, the mystical link between Battisti's national martyrdom and the quest for the Alpine borders could best be demonstrated, argued Italo Lunelli, a former legionary and Fascist deputy: "We see it as the monument for the valley and all the land of Trentino …, which one sees from afar, with its lofty lines profiled against the sky.... The great base awaits the monument, so as to raise it from the circle of mountains so dear to the Saint's heart and consecrated to his heroism."[108] The delay had, however, also resulted from the tensions inherent in the Fascists commemorating a democratic socialist.[109] When the Italian King and local Fascist leaders were laying the foundation stone for the Victory Arch in 1926, Battisti's son Camillo and former socialist companions decided instead to mark the tenth anniversary of his execution in simple fashion at his grave in Trento. The priority given to the Victory Arch in Bolzano and continuing reservations on the part of Battisti's family meant that it was not until 1935 that the mausoleum on the Doss Trento was inaugurated with full Fascist pomp. Battisti's family only participated in the ceremony reluctantly.[110]

Despite the tensions evident in the Battisti mausoleum project, its completion demonstrated how nationalists in Trentino and the Fascist regime pursued largely overlapping agendas. The monuments to Battisti and other legionaries, together with the ossuaries, represented a definite nationalization of regional remembrance of the war. Yet, it is doubtful that this hegemonic discourse reflected the sentiments of the wider population.[111] As recent scholarship suggests, the problems of the immediate postwar period and widespread support for political Catholicism meant that much of the population was skeptical about the benefits of Italian rule, above all under the Fascist regime.[112] Moreover, as Sørensen argues, the numerous memorials to those who had died wearing the Habsburg colors indicated that a different social memory of the war experience was articulated, even if only indirectly. At the same time, work by Quinto Antonelli on individual memories of the war—whether on the battlefield or in internment camps—indicates that popular recollections of the war were frequently at variance with the official paradigm of "national redemption."[113]

The Legacy of the Great War from a Transregional Perspective

After 1918, memory cultures of World War I in the successor regions of Tyrol reflected clear national oppositions established before 1914, as the fierce battles on the mountain-sides reinforced for both German and Italian-speakers the notion of the Alps as a natural border and "fortress" in the landscape of national memory.[114] In both South Tyrol and Austrian Tyrol, collective remembrance practices rejected the outcome of the war, without normalization or acceptance of the new situation. The "total defeat" experienced by South Tyrol amounted to a form of role reversal, whereby the formerly dominant German ethnic group became a minority, whose collective remembrance of the war was oppressed—albeit not suppressed entirely—by the Italian state. By contrast, "victory" was officially embraced in Trentino, but the traumatic experience of the war led to simple expressions of bereavement among the ordinary population, something at odds with the liberationist rhetoric of the political elites. Overall, the Fascist regime's efforts at instrumentalizing commemorations of the Great War were undermined by the limited success of nationalization policies in South Tyrol and by the contradictions between war experiences and public discourse in Trentino.

Yet, while official narratives achieved differing degrees of resonance, in none of the regions did counter-memories emerge with sufficient institutional, political, or social power to displace the official discourse.[115] As Wulf Kansteiner has argued, "those people who experienced traumas such as war will only see their narratives enter the public realm if their vision meets with compatible social or political objectives and inclinations among other important social groups."[116] This was because key social groups, in conjunction with provincial and national authorities, decisively shaped collective remembrance of the war, with prominent roles played in Tyrol by former officers and in Trentino and South Tyrol by war veterans in the Legione Trentina.

In Austrian Tyrol, a heroic depiction of the war was in harmony with—and helped to reinforce—the shift towards authoritarianism from the late 1920s.[117] Under the corporatist dictatorship, the trend would culminate in the pseudo-monarchism of the 1930s, where invocation of the Habsburg army (including the Austrian army's re-adoption of the old imperial uniforms), commemoration of the last Emperor Karl, and glorification of the events on the Alpine front were fused in the "Austrianist ideology" of the *Ständestaat*.[118] Former officer Hans Bator, for example, ended up leading the Ostmärkische Sturmscharen, the Catholic-patriotic youth organization within the dictatorship's Fatherland Front movement.[119] During the 1930s, 240 Tyrolean communities named the pretender Otto von Habsburg an honorary citizen and the links between legitimism and war commemoration were symbolized in June 1936 by the consecration of an Emperor Karl memorial chapel at the military cemetery in Lienz, in the presence of ex-Archduke Eugen, a former commander on the Southwest front.[120]

At the same time, regional memory practices shed light on the question of national identity in the Austrian First Republic. While Ernst Hanisch and Robert Kriechbaumer have implied that Austria's political polarization led to a failure to create a unified memory culture of the war and, by extension, a strong national identity, the strength of regionalized memory cultures was as much a factor as ideological conflict.[121] As in other partitioned Alpine provinces, such as Styria and Carinthia, the rhetoric of heroic sacrifice and unjust victimhood became a defining feature of national discourse at the regional level, through its focus on the protection of "German" land.[122] Moreover, if the fusion of Christian iconography with the language of national defense helped create a degree of common ground between Christian Social and German National groupings,[123] it did not prevent nationalist resentment being taken in a more radical—National Socialist—direction by a younger generation who had not served in the war.[124] On the other side of the border, resentment at Italianization, together with disappointment at the Austrian Republic's seeming inability to deal with the South Tyrolean agenda and its foreign political reliance on Mussolini, increased sympathies for National Socialism among the young bourgeoisie. The rhetoric of an "undefeated" defense of the land in World War I provided a binding thread to national discourse among the German minority in the region, many of whom came to look to Germany (rather than Austria) to defend their interests.[125]

In Trentino, the Fascist regime sought to create a sense of direct continuity between the experience of war and Fascism, to turn the fallen soldiers of World War I into precursors of—and martyrs for—Fascist ideals, and to "educate the people for war" by heroicizing those soldiers who had died for the Italian fatherland. Yet, whatever the medium-term success of the nationalists and Fascists in shaping collective remembrance, this discourse appears to have penetrated popular mentalities only superficially. Indeed, the problem of matching ideology to practice was evident from a typical diatribe by the arch-priest of Italianization in Trentino and South Tyrol, Ettore Tolomei, who was enraged in the 1930s by the war memorial in Cavalese, Val di Fiemme, which had been placed in the town's main square and remembered those fallen for Austria: "For Cavalese, there is an order, not executed, from the Prefect, that the inappropriate monstrosity be removed. It is still in its place."[126] From a later perspective, Jaro Stacul's anthropological study of the village of Caoria, in the Vanoi valley, during the 1990s is also suggestive of the dissonance between official and popular memories of the war. Local historical memory of the arrival of the Italians after 1918 described them as "foreigners," while many villagers had positive views of Austria due to its schooling system (influenced, too, by the fact that several who had fought in the Habsburg army were deported for two months to central Italy in the war's aftermath). As Stacul comments, "it is no accident that several households in the valley keep a collection of photographs of ancestors wearing the Austro-Hungarian uniform during the Great War," while the villagers also kept their distance from the "nationalized" monumental landscape of war cemeteries and museums glorifying the liberation.[127] The lasting remembrance of the war among the wider population remained one of victimhood and suffering—a narrative that could only be openly reclaimed and come to terms with from the 1980s.

Laurence Cole is Professor of Austrian History at the University of Salzburg. He is the author of *Für Gott, Kaiser und Vaterland: Nationale Identität der deutschsprachigen Bevölkerung Tirols 1860–1914* (2000) and *Military Culture and Popular Patriotism in Late Imperial Austria* (2014). He has edited (with Daniel Unowsky) *The Limits of Loyalty: Imperial Symbolism, Popular Allegiances, and State Patriotism in the Late Habsburg Monarchy* (2007), and (with Christa Hämmerle and Martin Scheutz), *Glanz—Gewalt—Gehorsam: Militär und Gesellschaft in der Habsburgermonarchie (1800–1918)* (2011).

Notes

1. Oswald Überegger, "Vom militärischen Paradigma zur 'Kulturgeschichte des Krieges?' Entwicklungslinien der österreichischen Weltkriegsgeschichtsschreibung im Spannungsfeld militärisch-politischer Instrumentalisierung und universitärer Verwissenschaftlichung," in *Zwischen Nation und Region: Weltkriegsforschung im interregionalen Vergleich. Ergebnisse und Perspektiven*, ed. Oswald Überegger (Innsbruck, 2005), 63–122.

2. Compare Martin Moll, "Die deutschsprachige und slowenische Historiographie zur Steiermark," in Überegger, *Zwischen Nation und Region*, 179–96.
3. John Horne, "Defeat and Memory in Modern History," in *Defeat and Memory: Cultural Histories of Military Defeat in the Modern Era*, ed. Jenny Macleod (Basingstoke, 2008), 11–29.
4. Horst Carl et al., "Krieg und Kriegsniederlage—historische Erfahrung und Erinnerung," in *Kriegsniederlagen. Erfahrungen und Erinnerungen*, ed. Horst Carl et al. (Berlin, 2004), 1–11.
5. Geoffrey Cubitt, *History and Memory* (Manchester, 2007), 14–15.
6. Jay Winter and Emmanuel Sivan, "Setting the Framework," in *War and Remembrance in the Twentieth Century*, ed. Winter and Sivan (Cambridge, 1999), 6–39; Astrid Erll, *Kollektives Gedächtnis und Erinnerungskulturen* (Stuttgar and Weimar, 2005), 101–42.
7. Egon Pinzer, "Tirol von innen am Ende des Ersten Weltkrieges," in *Handbuch zur neueren Geschichte Tirols. Bd. 2 Zeitgeschichte, 1. Teil Politische Geschichte*, ed. Anton Pelinka and Andreas Maislinger (Innsbruck, 1993), 39–94.
8. Hans Heiss, "Andere Fronten: Volksstimmung und Volkserfahrung in Tirol während des Ersten Weltkrieges," in *Tirol und der Erste Weltkrieg*, ed. Klaus Eisterer and Rolf Steininger (Innsbruck and Vienna, 1995), 139–77; Bernhard Mertelseder and Sigrid Wisthaler, "Soldat und Offizier in ihren Erinnerungen: Methodische Überlegungen zu österreichischen Kriegstagebücher," in *Ein Krieg—zwei Schützengräbern. Österreich—Italien und der Erste Weltkrieg in den Dolomiten 1915—1918*, ed. Brigitte Mazohl-Wallnig et al. (Bozen, 2005), 63–85.
9. *Volkszeitung*, 25 November 1919.
10. Richard Schober, "Die paramilitärischen Verbände in Tirol (1918–1927)," in *Tirol und der Anschluß. Voraussetzungen, Entwicklungen, Rahmenbedingungen 1918–1938*, ed. Thomas Albrich, Klaus Eisterer, and Rolf Steininger (Innsbruck, 1998), 113–41; Wolfgang Rebitsch, *Tirol—Land in Waffen. Soldaten und bewaffnete Wehrverbände 1918 bis 1938* (Innsbruck, 2009), 117–54.
11. Richard Schober, "Die Friedenskonferenz von St. Germain und die Teilung Tirols," in *Die Option: Südtirol zischen Faschismus und Nationalsozialismus*, ed. Klaus Eisterer and Rolf Steininger (Innsbruck, 1989), 33–50; Hans Haas, "Südtirol 1919," in Pelinka and Maislinger, *Handbuch zur neueren Geschichte Tirols*, 95–130.
12. *Jahrbuch 1925 der Kaiserschützen, Tiroler Landesschützen und Tiroler Landstürmer*, ed. Bundesleitung des Kaiserschützenbundes (Innsbruck, 1924), 144.
13. "Trauerkundgebung des Tiroler Landtages über den Verlust Südtirols," 16 November 1920. Cited by Rolf Steininger, *Südtirol im 20. Jahrhundert. Dokumente* (Innsbruck, 1999), 21.
14. Laurence Cole, *Für Gott, Kaiser und Vaterland: Nationale Identität der deutschsprachigen Bevölkerung Tirols 1860–1914* (Frankfurt and New York, 2000), 225–321.
15. Josef Riedmann, "Der Tiroler 'Landestrauertag' am 10. Oktober im jährlichen Gedenken an die Annexion Südtirols durch Italien," in *Tirol im 20. Jahrhundert. Festschrift für Viktoria Stadlmayer zur Vollendung des 70. Lebensjahres in Würdigung ihres Wirkens für das ganze Tirol*, ed. Franz Riedl et al. (Bolzano, 1989), 191–202.
16. Laurence Cole, "'Fern von Europa'? The Peculiarities of Tirolian Historiography," *Zeitgeschichte* 23 (1996): 181–204; Oswald Überegger, *Erinnerungskriege: Der Erste Weltkrieg, Österreich und die Tiroler Kriegserinnerung in der Zwischenkriegszeit* (Innsbruck, 2011), 15–48.
17. Paweł Pencakowski, "Monumenti dimenticati agli 'eroi di nessuno'. I cimiteri austriaci di guerra nella Galizia occidentale," in *Sui campi di Galizia 1914–1917. Gli italiani d'Austria e il fronte orientale: uomini, popoli, culture nella guerra europea*, ed. Gianluigi Fait (Rovereto, 1997), 461–79.
18. *Katalog zum Museum der Tiroler Kaiserjäger und der Andreas-Hofer-Galerie* (Innsbruck, 1937), 13.
19. Ibid., 23.

20. Tiroler Landesarchiv, Innsbruck, Vereinsakten (hereafter TLA-V): Tiroler Standschützen Denkmalausschuß 1923–1925 (hereafter TSD), Mappe: Schriftensammlung 1923–1925, An Der Lan to Ferdinand Andri, 22 March 1924.
21. TLA-V, TSD, Mappe: Schriftensammlung 1923–1925, Verzeichnis des Zentralkomités.
22. TLA-V, TSD, Mappe: Sammlung bei den Großen und Behörden, Denkmal für die Tiroler Standschützen—Aufruf! (April 1924).
23. *Tiroler Anzeiger*, 25 May 1925.
24. Oswald Überegger, "'Erinnerungsorte' oder nichtssagende Artefakte? Österreichische Kriegerdenkmäler und locale Kriegserinnerung in der Zwischenkriegszeit," in *Glanz—Gewalt—Gehorsam. Militär und Gesellschaft in der Habsburgermonarchie (1800–1918)*, ed. Laurence Cole, Christa Hämmerle, and Martin Scheutz (Bochum, 2011), 293–310.
25. TLA-V, TSD, Mappe: Tiroler Standschützen Erinnerungstag 1924/25, Protokoll über die vorbereitende Besprechung über die Erinnerungsfeier anlässlich des Ausmarsches der Standschützen vor 10 Jahren am 22. März 1925; (Sitzungsbericht) Erinnerungstag anlässlich der 10-jährigen Wiederkehr des Ausmarschstages der Standschützen, 22 March 1924.
26. Rebitsch, *Tirol—Land in Waffen*, 111–13.
27. On local memorials, see Überegger, *Erinnerungskriege*, 127–44.
28. TLA-V, TSD, Mappe: Schriftensammlung 1923–1925, Schützengilde Kufstein to An Der Lan, 12 March 1924.
29. TLA-V, TSD, Mappe: Schriftensammlung 1923–1925, Georg Tankhauser to Tiroler Standschützen Denkmalausschuß, 25 February 1924.
30. Cole, *Für Gott, Kaiser und Vaterland*, 413–501.
31. Überegger, *Erinnerungskriege*, 114–26.
32. *Tiroler Anzeiger*, 25 May 1925.
33. Oswald Kaufmann, *Meine Kriegs-Chronik: Mit dem Standschützen Bataillon Bezau in Südtirol und Albanien* (s.l, 1997), 274–80. On the importance of solace from family and friends, rather than the state, see Jay Winter, *Sites of Memory, Sites of Mourning: The Great War in European Cultural History* (Cambridge, 1995), 34.
34. There is no study of war veterans and invalids for interwar Austria, but some information on Tyrol can be gleaned from Christian Fornwagner, *Leid lindern: Die Kriegsopferversorgung und -fürsorge im Bundesland Tirol seit dem Ersten Weltkrieg (1914–1993)* (Innsbruck, 1993), 51–59, 84–97, 142–48. On legislative aspects, see Edith Leisch-Prost and Verena Pawlowsky, "Kriegsinvalide und ihre Versorgung in Österreich nach dem Ersten Weltkrieg," in *Der Erste Weltkrieg im Alpenraum. Erfahrung, Deutung, Erinnerung / La Grande Guerra nell'arco alpino. Esperienza e memoria*, ed. Hermann Kuprian and Oswald Überegger (Innsbruck, 2006), 366–80.
35. *Tiroler Kriegsopfer: Gedenkschrift. Anläßlich des zehnjährigen Bestandes des Landesverbandes der Kriegsinvaliden,—Witwen und Waisen Tirols von diesem herausgegeben*, ed. Hans Bator (Innsbruck, 1928), 18.
36. TLA, Depot Oberst Zempirek, Akten betr. Gefallenengedenktafel der ehem. Infanterie Kadettenschule in Innsbruck in der Kirche am Innrain Denkmalausschuß, Kn. 824/1 (hereafter DOZ), Pos. Nr.264 Andrian to Zempirek, 27 April 1927.
37. TLA, DOZ, Pos. Nr.105 Maly—Zeitungsauschnitt (*Innviertler Zeitung*, 5 October 1927).
38. Peter Melichar, "'Die Kämpfe merkwürdiger Untoter'. K.u.k. Offiziere in der Ersten Republik," *Österreichische Zeitschrift für Geschichtswissenschaften* 9 (1998): 51–84.
39. Gergely Romsics, *Myth and Remembrance: The Dissolution of the Habsburg Empire in the Memoir Literature of the Austro-Hungarian Political Elite* (New York, 2006), 13–49.
40. Klaus Eisterer, "'Der Heldentod muss würdig geschildert werden': Der Umgang mit der Vergangenheit am Beispiel Kaiserjäger und Kaiserjägertradition," in Eisterer and Steininger, *Tirol und der Erste Weltkrieg*, 105–33.

41. TLA, DOZ, Pos. Nr.111 Zempirek an den hochlöbl. Stadtmagistrat der Landeshauptstadt Innsbruck, 27 November 1926.
42. Oswald Überegger, "Tabuisierung—Instrumentalisierung—verspätete Historisierung: Die Tiroler Historiographie und der Erste Weltrkrieg," *Geschichte und Region / Storia e Regione* 11/1 (2002): 127–47.
43. Among Schemfil's publications, see *Das k.u.k. 3. Regiment der Tiroler Kaiserjäger im Weltkriege 1914–1918* (Bregenz, 1926); *Die Pasubio-Kämpfe 1916–1918* (Bregenz, 1937).
44. Rebitsch, *Tirol—Land in Waffen*, 111. These seem to have become regular annual events; for an extensive description of one such gathering, see *Jahrbuch 1924 der Kaiserschützen, Tiroler Landesschützen und Tiroler Landstürmer*, ed. Bundesleitung des Kaiserschützenbundes (Innsbruck, 1923), 161–78.
45. *Jahrbuch 1924 der Kaiserschützen*, 19–20.
46. *Jahrbuch 1925 der Kaiserschützen, Tiroler Landesschützen und Tiroler Landstürmer*, ed. Bundesleitung des Kaiserschützenbundes (Innsbruck, 1924), 24–26.
47. Überegger, "Tabuisierung."
48. Christoph von Hartungen, "Die Tiroler und Vorarlberger Standschützen—Mythos und Realiät," in Eisterer and Steininger, *Tirol und der Erste Weltkrieg*, 92–93.
49. TLA-V, TSD, Mappe: Standschützendenkmal Schriftensammlung 1923–1925, Altkaiserjäger-Klub to An Der Lan, 26 March 1924.
50. For further discussion, see Überegger, *Erinnerungskriege*, 91–109.
51. *Tiroler Kaiserjäger: Ein Gedenkbuch zur Erinnerung an die 10jährige Wiederkehr der Feuertaufe 1914–1924, herausgegeben vom Tiroler Kaiserjägerbund* (Innsbruck, 1924), 5–6.
52. Leopold Steurer, *Südtirol zwischen Rom und Berlin 1919–1939* (Vienna, Munich, and Zurich, 1980), 28–51.
53. Gottfried Solderer, ed., *Das 20. Jahrhundert in Südtirol. Bd. 2 1920–1939, Faschistenbeil und Hakenkreuz* (Bolzano, 2000), 32–33.
54. Thus the memoirs of "Herr E.," recounted in Martha Verdorfer, *Zweierlei Faschismus: Alltagserfahrungen in Südtirol 1918–1945* (Vienna, 1990), 26.
55. City Archive Bolzano (Stadtarchiv Bozen / Archivio Municipale Bolzano: hereafter SB/AMB), Gemeinderatsprotokolle 1919, Protokoll über die ordentliche, öffentliche Gemeinderatssitzung, 4 December 1919.
56. SB/AMB, Magistratsprotokolle 1919, Protokoll über die Magistratssitzung vom 19.12.1919; Magistratsprotokolle 1920, Protokolle über die ordentlichen Magistratssitzungen vom 2.1.1920, 27.1.1920, 7.5.1920, 21.5.1920, 10.9.1920; Magistratsprotokolle 1921, Protokolle über die Magistratssitzung vom 19.8.1921.
57. State Archive Bolzano (Archivio di Stato di Bolzano / Staatsarchiv Bozen: hereafter ASB/StB), Commissariato del Governo per la Provincia di Bolzano (ex Prefettura) Busta 224, Cartella: Iscriziono funerararie in lingua straniera—Iscrizioni sui nastri di corone funebri (hereafter Comm./B.224): Pr. No. 522, Prefetto di Bolzano to Ministero dell'Interno, 26 February 1937.
58. ASB/StB, Comm./B.224: Pr. No. 3528, Capitano comandante del Legione Territoriale dei Carabinieri reali di Bolzano to Prefetto, 29 September 1938; Segratario PNF di Bolzano to Prefetto.
59. SB/AMB, Magistratsprotokolle 1920, Protokoll über die Magistratssitzung vom 22.10.1920; SB/AMB, XV Monumenti D-112, Aktenkonvolut Denkmalbau in kais. Talfergasse 1920, Stadtmagistrat Bozen Zl.04171/9.7.1920, Offizierkorps 2. Reg. Tiroler Kaiserjäger to Stadtmagistratsrat in Bozen, 15 June 1920.
60. SB/AMB, XV Monumenti D-112, Aktenkonvolut Denkmalbau in kais. Talfergasse 1920, SMB Zl.4171-2, Städt. Bauamt to Stadtmagistrat, 25 October 1920.
61. Stefan Lechner, *Die Eroberung der Fremdstämmigen: Provinzfaschismus in Südtirol* (Innsbruck, 2005), 120–60.

62. Michael Gehler, ed., *Eduard Reut-Nicolussi und die Südtirolfrage 1918–1958. Streiter für die Freiheit und Einheit Tirols. Teil 2: Dokumentedition, vorwiegend aus dem Nachlass* (Innsbruck, 2007), 50–51.
63. Andrea Di Michele, *Die unvollkommene Italianisierung: Politik und Verwaltung in Südtirol 1918–1943* (Innsbruck, 2008), 145–228.
64. Michael Gehler, *Eduard Reut-Nicolussi und die Südtirolfrage 1918–1958. Streiter für die Freiheit und Einheit Tirols. Teil 1: Biographie und Darstellung* (Innsbruck, 2007).
65. Gehler, *Eduard Reut-Nicolussi. Teil 2*, 99–106.
66. Josef Fontana, "Die Legione Trentina und Südtirol," in Riedl, *Tirol im 20. Jahrhundert*, 83–123.
67. Cited by Oswald Zoeggeler and Lamberto Ippolito, *Die Architektur für ein italienisches Bozen 1922–1942* (Lana, 1992), 111.
68. Harald Dunajtschik and Gerald Steinacher, "Die Architektur für ein italienisches Südtirol 1922–1943," *Geschichte und Region/Storia e Regione* 17/1 (2008): 101–37; Zoeggeler and Ippolito, *Architektur*, 110–26.
69. Vanda Wilcox, "From Heroic Defeat to Mutilated Victory: the Myth of Caporetto in Fascist Italy," in Macleod, *Defeat and Memory*, 46–61.
70. Ugo Soragni, *Il Monumento alla Vittoria di Bolzano. Architettura e scultura per la città italiana (1926–1938)* (Vicenza, 1993), 1–81.
71. Thomas Pardatscher, *Das Siegesdenkmal in Bozen. Entstehung—Symbolik—Rezeption* (Bozen, 2002), 37.
72. Josef Fontana, ed., *Südtirol und der italienische Nationalismus: Entstehung und Entwicklung einer europäischen Minderheitenfrage. Teil 2: Dokumente* (Innsbruck, 1990), 316–17 (Proklamation der "Associazione Nazionale Volontari di Guerra," 12 July 1928).
73. Thomas Kahler, "'Kriegerdenkmäler im Felde und Daheim.' Materialien zur Gestaltung von Kriegerdenkmälern für die Gefallenen des Ersten Weltkriegs in Österreich und Italien." PhD diss., Salzburg 1990, 172–94.
74. Massimo Martignoni, "Il progetto monumentale in Italia tra le due guerre," *Geschichte und Region/Storia e Regione* 17/1 (2008): 80–100; John Foot, *Fratture d'Italia* (Milan, 2009), 83–89.
75. Marco Armiero, "Nationalizing the Mountains: National and Political Landscapes in World War I," in *Nature and History in Modern Italy*, ed. Marco Amiero and Marcus Hall (Athens, OH, 2009), 231–50.
76. Birgit Strauß, "'Große Geschichte' am kleinen Friedhof: Der österreichische Soldatenfriedhof Nasswand bei Toblach," *Der Schlern* 78 (2004): 40–49.
77. *Das 20. Jahrhundert in Südtirol. Bd. 2 1920–1939, Faschistenbeil und Hakenkreuz* (Bolzano, 2000), 46.
78. Gehler, *Eduard Reut-Nicolussi. Teil 2*, 108–110.
79. John S. Stephens, *Danger Zones of Europe* (London, 1929), 47. See further Hannes Obermair, "Danger Zones—der englische Historiker John Sturge Stephens (1891–1954), der italienische Faschismus und Südtirol," in *Italienischer Faschismus und deutschsprachiger Katholizismus*, ed. Richard Faber and Elmar Locher (Würzburg, 2013), 137–61.
80. Oswald Überegger, *Freienfeld unterm Liktorenbündel* (Innsbruck, 1996), 116–17.
81. ASB/StB, Comm./B.224: Pr. No. 2199, Podestà di Merano to Prefetto di Bolzano, 2 November 1933; Prefetto to Podestà di Merano.
82. Di Michele, *Die unvollkommene Italianisierung*, 145–228.
83. Viktor Malfèr, "Der Soldatenfriedhof in St. Jakob bei Bozen," *Der Schlern* 39 (1965): 317–21; Viktor Malfèr, "Zwei Ehrenmäler am Bozner Soldatenfriedhof," *Der Schlern* 39 (1965): 433–35.
84. ASB/StB, Comm./B.224: ad Pr. No. 2422, Podestà Bolzano to Prefetto di Bolzano, 2 August 1934.

85. Quinto Antonelli, *I dimenticati della Grande Guerra: la memoria dei combattenti trentini (1914–1920)* (Trento, 2008).
86. Franco de Battaglia, "Da una cultura di popolo a una cultura popolare," in *Storia del Trentino. Vol VI: L'età contemporanea*, ed. Andrea Leonardi and Paolo Pombeni (Trento, 2005), 691–724.
87. Marco Cuaz, *Le Alpi* (Turin, 2005), 87–105; Lisa Bregantin, "Culto dei caduti e luoghi di riposo nell'arco alpino," in Kuprian and Überegger, *Der Erste Weltkrieg*, 383–96.
88. Aldo Miorelli, "'Ai martiri dell'ubbidienza.' I monumenti ai caduti in Trentino ed in particolare nell'Alto Garda-Ledro e nella Vallagarina," *Museo Storico Italiano della Guerra Annali* 1–2 (1992–93): 80–85.
89. Nils A. Sørensen, "Zwischen regionaler und nationaler Erinnerung: Erster Weltkrieg und Erinnerungskultur im Trentino der Zwischenkriegszeit," in Kuprian and Überegger, *Der Erste Weltkrieg*, 397–411.
90. Nicola Fontana, "Das Trentino und der Erste Weltkrieg: Regionale Quellenbestände in Trentiner Archiven," in Überegger, *Zwischen Nation und Region*, 219–32.
91. On Rizzi, see Paola Antolini, *Vivere per la patria: Bice Rizzi (1894–1982)* (Trento, 2006).
92. Giovanna Procacci, "Die italienische Forschung über den Ersten Weltkrieg: Die 'patriotische Deutung' des Krieges und die Kontroversen über die Legitimations- und Delegitimationsprozesse," in Überegger, *Zwischen Nation und Region*, 33–62.
93. Foot, *Fratture d'Italia*, 59–80.
94. Mariapia Bigaran and Maurizio Cau, eds., *Alcide De Gasperi. Scritti e discorsi politici. Vol. II Alcide De Gasperi dal Partito Popolare Italiano all'esilio interno 1919–1942. Tomo I* (Bologna, 2007), 683–85.
95. Renato Trinco and Maurizio Scudiero, *La Campana dei Caduti: Maria Dolens: Cento rintocchi per la pace* (Mori, 1998).
96. Cited by Miorelli, "Ai martiri dell'ubbidienza," 43.
97. Aldo Miorelli, "Il non-monumento ai caduti in Trentino," in *Monumenti della grande guerra: progetti e realizzazioni in Trentino 1916–1935*, ed. Patrizia Marchesoni and Massimo Martignoni (Trento, 1998), 93–104.
98. Ibid.
99. Sørensen, "Zwischen regionaler und nationaler Erinnerung"; Miorelli, "Il non-monumento."
100. Miorelli, "Il non-monumento," 98.
101. Sørensen, "Zwischen regionaler und nationaler Erinnerung," 401.
102. Fontana, "Die Legione trentina"; Fabrizio Rasera, "Dal regime provisorio al regime fascista (1919–1937)," in Leonardi and Pombeni, eds., *Storia del Trentino. Vol. VI*, 7–130.
103. Cited in Miorelli, "Il non-monumento," 98.
104. Ibid., 99.
105. Ibid.
106. Kahler, "*Kriegerdenkmäler,*" 156–64.
107. Ibid.,174–76, 190–94. On Castel Dante, see the brief history in Isabella Bolognesi, Nicola Fontana, and Sabina Tovazzi, "Fonti per la storia del combattentismo in Trentino nell'archivio del Museo della Guerra," *Museo Storico Italiano della Guerra Annali* 14–16 (2006–08): 141–77.
108. Cited by Martignoni, "Il territorio e la memoria dei caduti," 37.
109. Massimo Tiezzi, *L'eroe conteso: la costruzione del mito di Cesare Battisti negli anni 1916–1935* (Trento, 2007).
110. Vicenzo Calì, "Battisti simbolo della nazione? Strumentalizzazioni, usi e riusi di un mito," in Calì, *Patrioti senza patria: I democratici trentini fra Otto e Novecento* (Trento, 2003), 113–41.
111. For discussion, see Roberta Pergher, "Staging the Nation in Fascist Italy's 'New Provinces'," *Austrian History Yearbook* 43 (2012): 98–115.

112. Rasera, "Dal regime provisorio"; Mauro Scroccaro, *Dall'aquila bicipite alla croce uncinata. L'Italia e le opzioni nelle nuove province Trentino, Sudtirolo, Val Canale (1919–1939)* (Trento, 2000), 74–78.
113. Antonelli, *I dimenticati*.
114. Cuaz, *Le Alpi*, 47–86; Fabio Todero, "Geburt eines Mythos: Der Gebirgskrieg und die Alpini in der Literatur," in Mazohl-Wallnig, *Ein Krieg—zwei Schützengräbern*, 109–24; Marco Mondini, *Alpini: Parole e immagini di un mito guerriero* (Rome-Bari, 2008).
115. Cubitt, *History and Memory*, 226–32.
116. Cited in Joanna Bourke, "Introduction: Remembering War," *Journal of Contemporary History* 39 (2004): 473–85.
117. Überegger, "Vom militärischen Paradigma."
118. Werner Suppanz, "'Die Großtat will große Erben.' Der Erste Weltkrieg im Alpenraum in den Gedächtniskonstruktionen des autoritären Ständestaates," in Kuprian and Überegger, *Der Erste Weltkrieg*, 427–40.
119. Robert Kriechbaumer, *Ein vaterländisches Bilderbuch: Propaganda, Selbstinszsenierung und Ästhetik der vaterländischen Front 1933–38* (Vienna, 2002), 36.
120. Martin Kofler, *Osttirol: Vom Ersten Weltkrieg bis zur Gegenwart* (Innsbruck, 2005), 68.
121. Ernst Hanisch, "Politische Systeme und Gedächtnisorte," in *Handbuch des politischen Systems Österreichs: Erste Republik 1918–1938*, ed. Emmerich Tálos et al. (Vienna, 1995), 421–30; Robert Kriechbaumer, *Die großen Erzählungen der Politik: politische Kultur und Parteien in Österreich von der Jahrhundertwende bis 1945* (Vienna, 2001), 130–35.
122. Steurer, *Südtirol*, 35.
123. Kriechbaumer, *Die großen Erzählungen*, 147.
124. Sabine Falch, "Ein Volk, kein Reich, kein Führer: die Tiroler NSDAP vor 1938," in *Tirol und Vorarlberg in der NS-Zeit*, ed. Rolf Steininger and Sabine Pitscheider (Innsbruck, 2002), 11–30.
125. Steurer, *Südtirol*, 189–234, 256–71.
126. Cited in Miorelli, "Il non-monumento," 100–1.
127. Jaro Stacul, *The Bounded Field: Localism and Local Identity in an Italian Alpine Valley* (Oxford and New York, 2003), 128, 134–40.

Select Bibliography

Bobič, Pavlina. *War and Faith: The Catholic Church in Slovenia 1914–1918.* Leiden, 2012.
Bodo, Bela. *Pál Prónay: Paramilitary Violence and Anti-Semitism in Hungary.* Pittsburgh, PA, 2011.
Bokovoy, Melissa. "Gendering Grief: Lamenting and Photographing the Dead in Serbia." *Aspasia* 5 (2011): 46–69.
Böttcher, Bernhard. *Gefallen für Volk und Heimat: Kriegerdenkmäler deutscher Minderheiten in Ostmitteleuropa während der Zwischenkriegszeit.* Cologne, Weimar, and Vienna, 2009.
Botz, Gerhard. *Gewalt in der Politik: Attentate, Zusammenstöße, Putschversuche, Unruhen in Österreich 1918 bis 1938.* 2nd ed. Munich, 1983.
Bucur, Maria. *Heroes and Victims: Remembering War in Twentieth Century Romania.* Bloomington, IN, 2009.
Cole, Laurence. *Military Culture and Popular Patriotism in Late Imperial Austria.* Oxford, 2014.
Cole, Laurence, Christa Hämmerle, and Martin Scheutz, eds. *Glanz—Gewalt—Gehorsam. Militär und Gesellschaft in der Habsburgermonarchie (1800–1918).* Bochum, 2011.
Cornwall, Mark. *The Undermining of Austria-Hungary: The Battle for Hearts and Minds.* New York, 2000.
———. *The Devil's Wall: The Nationalist Youth Mission of Heinz Rutha.* Cambridge, MA, 2012.
Doppelbauer, Wolfgang. *Zum Elend noch die Schande: Das altösterreichische Offizierskorps an Beginn der Republik.* Vienna, 1988.
Eichenberg, Julia, and John Paul Newman, eds. *The Great War and Veterans' Internationalism.* Basingstoke, 2013.
Galandauer, Jan. *2.7.1917 Bitva u Zborova: česká legenda.* Prague, 2002.
Gerstner, Alexandra et al, eds. *Der Neue Mensch: Utopien, Leitbilder und Reformkonzepte zwischen den Weltkriegen.* Frankfurt am Main, 2006.
Gerwarth, Robert. "The Central European Counter-Revolution: Paramilitary Violence in Germany, Austria and Hungary after the Great War." *Past & Present* 200 (2008): 175–209.
Gerwarth, Robert and John Horne, eds. *War in Peace: Paramilitary Violence in Europe after the Great War.* Oxford, 2012.
Hájková, Dagmar and Nancy M. Wingfield. "Czech (-oslovak) National Commemorations during the Interwar Period: Tomáš G. Masaryk and the Battle of White Mountain Avenged." *Acta Histriae* 18/3 (2010): 425–52.
Hameršak, Filip. *Tamna strana Marsa: Hrvatska autobiografija i svjetski rat.* Zagreb, 2013.

Hämmerle, Christa. "'Vor vierzig Monaten waren wir Soldaten, vor einem halben Jahr noch Männer . . .' Zum historischen Kontext einer 'Krise der Männlichkeit' in Österreich nach dem Ersten Weltkrieg." *L'Homme. Europäische Zeitschrift für feministische Geschichtswissenschaft*, 19/2 (2008): 51–73.

Healy, Maureen. *Vienna and the Fall of the Habsburg Empire: Total War and Everyday Life in World War I*. Cambridge, 2004.

———. "Civilizing the Soldier in Postwar Austria," in *Gender and War in Twentieth-Century Eastern Europe*, ed. Nancy M. Wingfield and Maria Bucur. Bloomington, IN, 2006.

Horváth, Franz Sz. *Zwischen Ablehnung und Anpassung: Politische Strategien der ungarischen Minderheitselite in Rumänien 1931–1940*. Munich, 2007.

Hübner-Wojciechowska, Joanna, *Grób Nieznanego Żołnierza*. Warsaw, 1991.

Ignjatović, Aleksandar. "From Constructed Memory to Imagined National Tradition: The Tomb of the Unknown Yugoslav Soldier (1934–38)." *The Slavonic and East European Review* 88/4 (2010): 624–51.

Iordachi, Constantin, *Charisma, Politics and Violence: The Legion of the "Archangel Michael" in Inter-war Romania*. Trondheim, 2004.

———, ed. *Comparative Fascist Studies: New Perspectives*. Oxford, 2010.

Kocourek, Katya, *Čechoslovakista Rudolf Medek: Politický životopis*. Prague, 2011.

Koselleck, Reinhart, and Michael Jeismann, eds. *Der politische Totenkult: Kriegerdenkmäler in der Moderne*. Munich, 1993.

Kovács, Ákos, ed. *Monumentumok az első háborúból*. Budapest, 1990.

Kresal, France. *Zgodovina socialne in gospodarske politike v Sloveniji od liberalizma do druge svetovne vojne*. Ljubljana, 1998.

Kuprian, Hermann, and Oswald Überegger, eds. *Der Erste Weltkrieg im Alpenraum. Erfahrung, Deutung, Erinnerung / La Grande Guerra nell'arco alpino. Esperienza e memoria*. Innsbruck, 2006.

Lasić, Stanko. *Krleža: Kronologija života i rada*. Zagreb, 1982.

Lein, Richard. *Pflichterfüllung oder Hochverrat?: Die tschechischen Soldaten Österreich-Ungarns im Ersten Weltkrieg*. Vienna, 2011.

Livezeanu, Irina. *Cultural Politics in Greater Romania: Regionalism, Nation Building and Ethnic Struggle, 1918–1930*. Ithaca, NY, and London, 1995.

Luh, Andreas. *Der deutsche Turnverband in der ersten Tschechoslowakischen Republik*. Munich, 1988.

Luthar, Oto. *O žalosti niti besede. Uvod v kulturno zgodovino Velike vojne*. Ljubljana, 2000.

Macleod, Jenny, ed. *Defeat and Memory: Cultural Histories of a Military Defeat in the Modern Era*. Basingstoke, 2008.

Marchesoni, Patrizia, and Massimo Martignoni, eds. *Monumenti della grande guerra: progetti e realizzazioni in Trentino 1916–1935*. Trento, 1998.

Markovits, Rodion. *Siberian Garrison*. trans. George Halász. London, 1929.

Michl, Jan. *Legionáři a Československo*. Prague, 2009.

Mick, Christoph. "War and Conflicting Memories—Poles, Ukrainians and Jews in Lvov 1914–1939." *Simon Dubnow Institute Yearbook* 4 (2005): 257–78.

———. *Kriegserfahrungen in einer multiethnischen Stadt: Lemberg 1914–1947*. Wiesbaden, 2010.

Mócsy, István I. *The Uprooted: Hungarian Refugees and their Impact on Hungarian Domestic Politics 1918–1921*. New York, 1983.

Mosse, George. *Nationalism and Sexuality: Middle-Class Morality and Sexual Norm in Modern Europe*. Madison, 1985.

———. *Fallen Soldiers: Reshaping the Memory of the World Wars*. Oxford, 1990.

Nagy-Talavera, Nicholas M. *The Green-Shirts and the Others: A History of Fascism in Hungary and Rumania*. Stanford, 1970.

Newman, John Paul. "Post-imperial and Post-war Violence in the South Slav Lands, 1917–1923." *Contemporary European History* 19 (2010): 249–65.

———. *Yugoslavia in the Shadow of War: Veterans and the Limits of State Building, 1903-1945*. Cambridge, 2015.

Orzoff, Andrea. *Battle for the Castle: The Myth of Czechoslovakia in Europe, 1914–1948*. Oxford, 2009.

Petrone, Karen. *The Great War in Russian Memory*. Bloomington and Indianapolis, IN, 2011.

Petrović, Ljubomir. *Nevidljivi geto. Invalidi u Kraljevini Jugoslaviji 1918–1941*. Belgrade, 2007.

Prusin, Alexander. *Nationalizing a Borderland: War, Ethnicity, and Anti-Jewish Violence in East Galicia, 1914–1920*. Tuscaloosa, 2005.

Pynsent, Robert. "The Literary Representation of the Czechoslovak 'Legions' in Russia," in *Czechoslovakia in a Nationalist and Fascist Europe 1918–1948*, eds. Mark Cornwall and R.J.W. Evans. Oxford, 2007.

Rebitsch, Wolfgang. *Tirol—Land in Waffen: Soldaten und bewaffnete Wehrverbände 1918 bis 1938*. Innsbruck, 2009.

Reulecke, Jürgen. *"Ich möchte einer werden so wie die ...": Männerbünde im 20. Jahrhundert*. Frankfurt am Main, 2001.

Riesenfellner, Stefan, ed. *Steinernes Bewusstsein: Die öffentliche Repräsentation staatlicher und nationaler Identität Österreichs in seinen Denkmälern*, vol. 1. Vienna, 1998.

Romsics, Gergely. *Myth and Remembrance: The Dissolution of the Habsburg Empire in the Memoir Literature of the Austro-Hungarian Political Elite*. New York, 2006.

Săndulescu, Valentin. "Fascism and its Quest for the 'New Man': the Case of the Romanian Legionary Movement." *Studia Hebraica* 4 (2004): 349–61.

Scurtu, Ioan, ed. *Ideologie și formațiuni de dreapta în România, 1919–1938*. Bucharest, 2003.

Stauda, Johannes. *Der Wandervogel in Böhmen 1911–1920*. 2 vols. Reutlingen, 1975–78.

Svoljšak, Petra. *Soča, sveta reka. Italijanska zasedba slovenskega ozemlja 1915–1917*. Ljubljana, 2003.

Treptow, Kurt W. and Gheorghe Buzatu, eds. *Corneliu Zelea Codreanu în fața istoriei: Procesul lui Corneliu Zelea Codreanu (Mai, 1938)*. Iași, 1994.

Überegger, Oswald, ed. *Zwischen Nation und Region: Weltkriegsforschung im interregionalen Vergleich. Ergebnisse und Perspektiven*. Innsbruck, 2005.

———. *Erinnerungskriege: Der Erste Weltkrieg, Österreich und die Tiroler Kriegserinnerung in der Zwischenkriegszeit*. Innsbruck, 2011.

Wingfield, Nancy, M. *Flag Wars and Stone Saints: How the Bohemian Lands became Czech*. Cambridge, MA, 2007.

Zeidler, Miklós. *Ideas on Territorial Revision in Hungary 1920-1945*. Boulder CO, 2007.

Zückert, Martin. *Zwischen Nationsidee und staatlicher Realität: Die tschechoslowakische Armee und ihre Nationalitätenpolitik 1918–1938*. Munich, 2006.

INDEX

Adler, Viktor, 45
Alba Iulia, 80
Aleksandar/Alexander Karadjordjević
    Audience with Lujo Lovrić (Yugoslav
        volunteer), 204
    Dedicates monument in Šabac, 120
    Travels to England, 105
    All Souls' Day, 20–21, 24
Anti-Semitism, 44, 63
    In Austria, 45, 46
    In Hungary, 44–46
Antonescu, Ion, 179–180
Apis (Dragutin Dimitrijević), 103
Aussig (Ústí nad Labem), 60
Austria
    conflicting perspectives on war sacrifice
        in, 3
    fear of communist violence in, 41
Austria-Hungary, 1, 257
    fails to win decisive military victory in
        First World War, 1–2
    successor states, 2
    war casualties, 2

Baarenfels, Eduard Barr von, 37, 38
Banac, Ivo, 225
Battisti, Mausoleum to Cesari, 277–278
Bauer, Otto, 45
Beneš, Edvard, 154
    As founder of Czechoslovakia, 129–130
    Claims that Czechs and Slovaks fought
        on the side of the Entente, 132
    Shares political aims with Czechoslovak
        Legionaries, 133
    Commemorates Battle of Zborov, 138
Bialynia-Chołodecki, Józef, 242–243
Bismarck, Otto von, 134

Blüher, Hans, 56–57, 60
Bokovoy, Melissa, 220
Boroević von Bojna, Svetozar, 221
Böttcher, Bernhard, 80
Bohemian Lands Movement, 60–61
Böhmisch Leipa (Česka Lípa), 59
Bozen, 265–267
Bratislava, 139
Brno, 139
Brubaker, Rogers, 5
Bucharest, 3
Budapest, 38
Buna Vestire, 178
Burgenland, 40
Burgtor, 15, 27

Cankar, Ivan, 216
Cantacuzino, Gheorghe, 179, 182
Caporetto (Kobarid), 227
Carinthia, 40
    Plebiscite, 20
    Paramilitary violence in, 39
Carnegie Endowment for International
    Peace, 104
Čatlos, Ferdinand, 157
Central European Observer, 135
Černov, Samson, 103–104, 111, 114–115
Codreanu, Corneliu Zelea, 174
    His Anti-Semitism, 179–180
    Biography 176–177
    His murder, 187
    Use of biblical imagery in speeches, 184
Conrad von Hötzendorf, Franz, 1, 265
    Celebrates fiftieth anniversary as officer,
        23
Corfu, 104
Croatia, 7

Veterans, 8–9
Cserny, Jósef, 41
Csíkmadaras, 81
'Culture of defeat', 4
Cuza, Alexandru Ioan, 177, 178
Czechoslovak army, 2
Czechoslovakia, 5
    Dominant Czech war narrative in, 5–6
    German minority in, 4
    German war memorials in, 2
Czechoslovak Communist Party, 137
Czechoslovak Legionaries, 6, 8, 151, 273
    Commemorate Battle of Zborov in 1937, 138
    Crisis of 1923, 155–156
    Formation of, 130–131
    Mausoleum in Vitkov, 141
    As wartime propaganda tool, 132

Dankl, Viktor, 23, 261
Darvas, János, 83
Deletant, Denis, 179
Deutsch, Julius, 23
Deutsche Turnverbund, 54
Dimitrijević, Dragutin, 103. See also Apis
Dmowski. Roman. 246
'Duchy of Bohemia' (Herzogtum Böhmen), 60

Eger (Cheb), 69

Fatherland Front, 15
Filipescu, Nicolae, 176
Frantzen, Allen, 106
Franz Ferdinand, 82, 83
Franz Joseph, 22, 134
Freikorps, 37, 40, 47
Freischaren, 59
Fronta, 163

Gajda, Radola, 155–156, 159
Galicia, 8–9, 234
    During the War, 235–238
Gaspari, Maksim, 229
Gasperi, Alcide De, 274
George, Stefan, 53, 56, 63, 65
Goga, Octavian, 178
Gömbös, Gyula, 37, 86
    Explains Hungary's defeat in First World War, 46

Graz, 24, 38
Griffin, Roger, 174
Grossglöckner, 18
Gyáfás, Elemér, 86
Hanisch, Ernst, 16
Hašek, Jaroslav, 82
Haynes, Rebecca, 68
Hejjas, István, 37
Heldendenkmal (in Vienna), 25
    Unveiled in 1934, 15, 18, 26–28
Heimwehr, 37, 41
Heinrich, Walter, 65
Henlein, Konrad, 55, 62
    Transforms German gymnastics organizations in Bohemia, 66–67
    Unveils fresco in Eger memorial hall, 69
Herceg, Ferenc, 76
Hergl, Walter, 61, 63
Hildebrandt, Kurt, 65
Hlinka, Andrej, 137
Hodža, Milan, 138
Holeček, Vojtěch, 157, 164
Horký, Karel, 158
Horne, John, 258
Horthy, Miklós, 47, 79
Hungary, 3
    Post-war violence in, 4, 41–42
    Territorial losses after the First World War, 39
Hus, Jan, 131, 145, 160

Innsbruck, 19
Innsbrucker Nachrichten, 35
Invalid Question in Yugoslavia, 199–201, 224–225
Ionescu, Nae, 186
Iordachi, Constantin, 178
'Iron Guard'. See Legion of Archangel Michael
Isonzo Front, 230–231
Italy, 226–229
    Annexes South Tyrol, 260–261

Jakabffy, Elemér, 86
Jansen, Wilhelm, 56
Jaschke, Carl, 25
Jiskra, Jan, 136
Joseph II, 134

Kansteiner, Wolf, 276

Karl, Habsburg Emperor, 22, 43
Karácsony, Benő, 83
Károlyi, Mihály, 79
Keleti Újság, 82
Kingdom of Serbs, Croats, and Slovenes, 5.
    See also Yugoslavia
Kletzl, Otto, 58–59, 60
Kocourek, Katya, 133
Kolozsvár (Klausenburg, Cluj), 75, 78, 86
Kopta, Josef, 153, 157
Kratochvill, Károly, 78–79
Kraus, Alfred, 43–44
Krems, 17
Krleža, Miroslav, 208–211, 212
    Croatian God Mars, the, 209–210
    Military service in First World War, 209
Krummau (Český Krumlov), 59
Kun, Béla, 42, 45
Kuncz, Aladár, 83
Kvaternik, Slavko, 207

Le Bon, Gustav, 39
Legion of Archangel Michael (Iron Guard), 6–7
    Creation of, 178–179
    Cult of the Dead, 184–186
    And Orthodox Christianity, 175
Leitmeritz (Litoměřice), 57
Leitsung, Ertl, 25
'Lenin Boys', 41
L'Illustration, 103, 110, 115–116
Linzer Tagblatt, 23
Lipoščak, Antun, 205
Lovrić, Lujo, 204–205
Lukács, Győgy, 77
Luthar, Oto, 219
L'viv (Lwow, Lemberg), 239–241

Maček, Vlatko, 211–212
Machar, Josef Svatopluk, 156–157
Machník, František, 138
Maister, Rudolf, 222
Marjanović, Rista, 114
    Asks for money from the Minister of Foreign Affairs, 97
    Moves to publish war photographs, 108–111
    Photographic portraits of Petar and Aleksandar Karadjordjević, 117–118
    Uses photographs, 102

Markovits, Rodion, 81–82, 84
Markowski, Bolesław, 248
Männerbund, 4
Masaryk, Tomáš G., 130, 163
    Argues that Czechs and Slovaks fought for the Entente during First World War, 132
    Reviews his troops, 135
Medek, Rudolf, 6, 139, 143, 161, 166–167
    As leader of the Independent Union of Czechoslovak Legionaries, 152
    Informs Masaryk of the formation of the Independent Union of Czechoslovak Legionaries, 158
    His play *Plukovník Švec,* 163–164
    Outlines rules of Union, 159
    Speaks at Tomb of Unknown Soldier in Prague, 165–166
Metzner, Karl, 57, 59, 60
Mick, Christoph, 102
Mikes, Imre, 83–84
Mosse, George, 28
Moța, Ion, 186–187
MOVE (Magyar Országos Véderő Egylet: Hungarian National Defense Union), 37
Müller, Anton (Brother Willram), 260, 264
Mussolini, Benito, 174, 189, 226

Napoleon, 1
Nazor, Vladimir, 212
Neue Freie Presse, 28
Newman, John Paul, 224, 230
Nova Evropa, 203
Novoe Vremya, 103

Obzor, 200
Opfertage, 26
Organization of Yugoslav Nationalists (ORJUNA), the, 203, 206–207
Osztenburg, Gyula, 37

Pavelić, Ante, 207
Pavičić, Josip, 201, 202, 204, 212
Pavlović, Dragoljub, 98–99
Pavlović, Živko, 122
Pašić, Nikola, 200
Pastýřík, Antonín, 157, 159
Perčec, Gustav, 207
Petar Karadjordjević, 118–119
Pfitzner, Josef, 61

Piłsudski, Józef. 246–247, 253
Pivko, Ljudevit, 220
Plečnik, Jože, 223–224
Polihrondiade, Mihail, 180
Politika, 110, 122
Poland
    Jewish population in, 244–245
    National composition of, 237
    War losses, 234
Popović, Andra, 108, 111–112, 122
    And 'The War Album', 111–112
Popović, Antanasije, 121
Prónay, Pál, 37, 42, 46
Puk, Mirko, 207
Putnik, Radomir, 103

Radić, Stjepan, 99, 210–211
Rauter, Hanns Albin, 37, 38, 46
Reiss, Rudolf Archibald, 119–120, 121
Reulecke, Jürgen, 54
Risorgimento, 273–274
Romania, 6–7
Romsics, Gergely, 263
Rothziegel, Leo, 45
Rudé právo, 139
Rutha, Heinz, 61–63, 64
    And the Comrades Union, 66
Ruthenians, 236
Rybař, Otokar, 221

Salis von Sewis, Johann, 205
Sarkotić, Stjepan, 205, 207–208
Savremenik, 203
Sassmann, Hans, 22
Schreckenstein (Střekov), 60
Schurtz, Heinrich, 56
Schuschnigg, Kurt von, 15
Schutzbund, 22, 37
Šedivý, Ivan, 132
Serbia, 1
    Hegemonic war discourse in Yugoslavia, 5, 98
    Medieval Kingdom of, 105
    War exhibition in London 1916, 104–105
Siberian Garrison, 82
Siegfriedskopf, 20
Siepel, Ignaz, 263
Šijački, Dušan, 105–108
    And Vidovdan, 108–109

Sikorski, Władysław, 233
Slávik, Juraj, 136
Slovakia, 136
Slovenia, 8
    Wartime losses, 218–219
Smrekar, Hinko, 229
Sokol (in Czechoslovakia), 135
    Revered by Legionary movement, 162–163
Sombart, Nicholas, 60
Spann, Othmar, 64–65
Srpske Novine, 114
St Germain, Treaty, 39
Stanojević, Stanoje, 122
Starhemberg, Ernst Rüdiger Fürst von, 28, 37, 38, 47
    On militarism of 'war youth generation', 40
    Fantasizes about fighting communism, 41
Stauda, Johannes, 59, 61
Štefánik, Milan Rastislav, 129–130
Steidle, Richard, 45
Styria, 24, 40
Sudeten Germans, 53
    their front experience in the First World War, 55–56
    their national mission, 53–54
    Sudeten German Party, 68–69
Sulyok, István, 86
Supilo, Frano, 204
Sychrava, Lev, 154–155
Szálasi, Ferenc, 46
Szamuely, Tibor, 45
Szeged, 38
Székely Division, 78–79

Tomić, Jaša, 103
Transylvania, 3, 6, 38
    German war memorials in, 2
    Transylvanian veterans, 78
    Union with Romania, 84
Trentino, 9, 272–278
Trianon, Treaty, 3, 87
    Anger in Hungary due to, 77
    As synonym for Hungary's defeat, 83
    Hungary's losses due to, 39
Turek, František, 157, 159
Turnverband, 66
Tyrol, 9, 259–260

'Austrian Tyrol', 261–266
Kaiserjäger regiments, 263
South Tyrol, 267–272
   Language decrees in, 271
   Strength of Volkswehr and Heimwehr in, 37
Tyrolean Germans, 3

Überegger, Oswald, 258
Ukraine, 237–238
   Commemorations of war, 242–243
   Polish attitudes towards, 243–244
Ukrainian Military Organization, 238
Ukrainian National Council, 237–238
Unknown Solidier, 223
   In Czechoslovakia, 133, 138, 140
   In Poland, 9, 233–234, 241
Upper Silesia, 40
Urmánczy, Nándor, 87
Ustashe (Croat fascists), 8, 188, 207–208
Užhorod, 139

Vaugoin, Carl, 18–19
Vavpotič, Ivan, 229
Vidmar, Stane, 222
Vienna, 1, 15, 22, 24
Vienna Award 1940, 87
Vodička, Jan, 139
Vojni Vjesnik, 112

Volkswehr, 18, 23, 37
Volkszeitung, 23
Vorarlberg, 1
Vreme, 98–99

Wagner, Richard, 60
Wandervogel, 56–57
Wartenberg, 68
'War youth generation', 39–40
Watzlik, Hans, 53
Willer, József, 80
Wingfield, Nancy, 102
Winkler, Wilhelm, 218

Yugoslav Committee (JO), 202, 230
Yugoslavia, 5
Yugoslav volunteers, 8, 201–205, 219–220

Zborov
   Battle of, 132
   Commemorated in interwar period, 134–140
   Myth in Czechoslovakia, 6, 129–130
   Refashioned by Czech right, 165–166
   Slovaks and, 136
Zehner, Wilhelm, 28
Zelizer, Barbie, 120–121, 122
Ziemann, Benjamin, 36
Žižka, Jan, 131, 133, 136, 145

www.ingramcontent.com/pod-product-compliance
Lightning Source LLC
Chambersburg PA
CBHW072145100526
44589CB00015B/2105